INTERNATIONAL LAW IN DOMESTIC LEGAL ORDERS

Series Editors

ANDRÉ NOLLKAEMPER

Professor of Public International Law at the University of Amsterdam

AUGUST REINISCH

Professor of International and European Law at the University of Vienna

The Role of National Courts in Applying International Humanitarian Law

INTERNATIONAL LAW IN DOMESTIC LEGAL ORDERS

The topic of international law in domestic legal orders has risen in prominence since the end of the Cold War. The last decades have witnessed a tremendous increase in international agreements on various subjects, impacting on domestic law and proving to be relevant to domestic litigation. These changes mean that domestic courts have the potential to make a greater contribution to the application and development of international law. This series analyses and examines these trends, looking at questions of international law in domestic legal orders from a variety of perspectives.

The Role of National Courts in Applying International Humanitarian Law

SHARON WEILL

OXFORD
UNIVERSITY PRESS

OXFORD
UNIVERSITY PRESS

Great Clarendon Street, Oxford, OX2 6DP,
United Kingdom

Oxford University Press is a department of the University of Oxford.
It furthers the University's objective of excellence in research, scholarship,
and education by publishing worldwide. Oxford is a registered trade mark of
Oxford University Press in the UK and in certain other countries

First Edition published in 2014
Impression: 1

Published in the United States of America by Oxford University Press
198 Madison Avenue, New York, NY 10016, United States of America

British Library Cataloguing in Publication Data
Data available

Library of Congress Control Number: 2013956209

ISBN 978–0–19–968542–4

Printed in Great Britain by
CPI Group (UK) Ltd, Croydon, CR0 4YY

Acknowledgements

This book is based on the doctoral thesis I defended at the University of Geneva. I wish to thank Professor Marco Sassoli for his supervision, support, and dedication. Any critical legal reading requires not only a critical spirit but also a founded legal knowledge. Through his supervision and lectures Professor Sassoli equipped me with an excellent knowledge of positive IHL, as well as a studying method based on case studies. My way of deconstructing IHL case law is largely influenced by his teaching methodology. I am also grateful for the support I received from Eyal Benvenisti and Aeyal Gross at Tel Aviv University and from the Suisse National Fund for Scientific Research (FNS). Andrew Clapham, Stuart Casey-Maslen, and Annyssa Bellal, of the Geneva Academy have been dear colleagues and friends throughout these years, and I am grateful to them for their encouragement and support.

During my field research I had the chance to meet and work with outstanding human rights lawyers and practitioners, who inspired me then and keep inspiring me now. To a large extent my understanding has been shaped by the fascinating discussions and meetings with Michael Sfard, Nery Ramati, Lea Tsemel, Hassan Jabareen, Rina Rosenberg, Limor Shlomo, Daniel Machover, Katherine Kallinger, Dimi Reider, Carmi Leker, Ishai Menuchin, Bana Shoughry-Badarne, Mahmoud Zeidan, Raji Sourani, and many others. I owe many thanks to all of them, and I look forward to reading their next cases. I am grateful for Michael Prawer who reviewed my English and Claudia Nicoletti for her kind assistance.

My field research in Belgrade would not have happened without Ivan Jovanovic of the OSCE, who made it possible for me to understand the nuance and complexity of the national post-war prosecutions in the Balkans.

Many thanks also to my parents and my close friends, who made this book possible. I am especially grateful to Marc Ariel and Galia Friedeman, Fred Polliart, Ur Shlonsky, Bernard Dreano, Philippe Bourdier, Bernard Seyssel, David, and Bianca.

This book is dedicated to my girls Zoe and Maayane, who were born during this research, with the hope that as they grow, the world around them will turn into a just one.

Finally, my warmest thanks go to Bartolomeo Conti, my partner and love.

Table of Contents

List of Abbreviations

ATS	Alien Tort Statute
AUMF	Authorization for Use of United States Armed Forces
ECtHR	European Court of Human Rights
FSIA	Foreign Sovereign Immunities Act
FTCA	Federal Tort Claims Act
GSS	General Security Service
HCJ	(Israeli) High Court of Justice
HLC	(Belgrade) Humanitarian Law Centre
ICC	International Criminal Court
ICJ	International Court of Justice
ICRC	International Committee of the Red Cross
ICTY	International Criminal Tribunal for the former Yugoslavia
IDI	Institut de Droit International
IHL	International Humanitarian Law
MCA	Military Commissions Act 2006
NGO	Non-Governmental Organization
NIAC	National Iranian American Council
OPT	Occupied Palestinian Territories
OWCP	Office of the War Crimes Prosecutor
STL	Special Tribunal for Lebanon
UCMJ	Uniform Code of Military Justice
WCC	War Crimes Chamber

Table of Cases

Greece

Israel

Italy

Japan

Serbia

Spain

United Kingdom

United States

Table of Legislation and Instruments

PEACE AGREEMENTS

TREATIES

UNITED NATIONS DOCUMENTS

General Assembly

Security Council

OTHER INSTRUMENTS

American Law Institute

Institut de Droit International

International Law Association

NATIONAL LEGISLATION

Canada

Introduction

International law regulates some of the most violent situations in which states and individuals can be involved. During times of armed conflict the state is empowered by law to use the most dramatic means available to achieve its military goals. The use of such means would be inconceivable in any other context. Such draconian power, if not regulated by binding rules, and subject to accountability, may have catastrophic consequences for the lives and security of a vast number of people. In view of the formidable power wielded by states, the theoretical assumption that states will voluntarily comply with international law, seems unconvincing. Naturally, national courts cannot be the only institution responsible for providing the necessary checks and balances over the state's exercise of its power during armed conflict. Indeed, the unique features of armed conflict place numerous obstacles in the path of the court attempting to oversee the state's exercise of its war time power. Yet, the enforcement of international law by courts seems essential, particularly in cases that require the application of International Humanitarian law (IHL).

Despite its necessity, IHL's weakest element remains the lack of its enforcement by the judiciary. The conduct of wars has traditionally been left to the discretion of the executive and its professional agencies. Their information is generally kept out of the public domain. This concealment prevents the effective crystallization of public opinion, impairs public ability to influence decision-making, and weakens the public demand for judicial scrutiny over armed conflict issues. These and other socio-psychological factors that favour unity and support for the state, (all of which typically emerge in times of crisis and violence) lead to a weakening of the checks and balances of the democratic system, not least its oversight by the judiciary.

However, times are changing, and as this work clearly illustrates, more and more IHL cases are coming before national courts.[1] With legislation codified at international level and a growing tendency to endorse it on a national level, this trend is

[1] This relatively new trend, which has become particularly prominent since the 1990s, is the result of a number of factors: (1) the creation of active international courts and tribunals in the 1990s with jurisdiction over serious IHL violations; (2) the emergence of a strong civil society and a number of professional, legally oriented non government organizations (NGOs). NGOs have become active in the international sphere—both in shaping public opinion's demand for scrutiny over armed conflicts and initiating legal procedures before national courts; (3) the training of an increasing number of international lawyers, journalists, diplomats, and academics; (4) growing domestic legislation that allows access to the courts; and (5) the development of progressive jurisprudence by a number of leading courts, which are cited across jurisdictions. See also, Eyal Benvenisti and George W. Downs, 'National Courts, Domestic Democracy, and the Evolution of International Law', *European Journal of International Law*, 20/1 (2009), 61.

of no surprise. It can reasonably be expected that this direction will continue. In light of this emerging and expanding trend, this book seeks to provide a theoretical framework for the analysis of national jurisprudence in the field of IHL.

The preliminary conditions necessary for the application of IHL by national courts depend on a number of *structural* conditions. One of these conditions is to have in place domestic legislation that allows for the application and enforcement of IHL. Another condition is for applicants to have access to the court. These structural requirements depend mainly on national legislation, and are not under review in this work.[2] Instead, this book focuses entirely on the *functional* role of national courts. If a court adjudicates a case involving IHL, it is assumed that these preliminary structural requirements will have been met. At that stage, the responsibility for applying IHL depends on national judges who operate within a political and socio-economical context, whose very limits they must respect in order to maintain their legitimacy. Thus, even if structurally, the relevant rule of IHL is guaranteed by appropriate legislation, it may well be that the *de facto* function of the court in IHL cases, which typically involves major political concerns, will not result in the normative application of the law. This is despite being formally expected to do so. A national court is supposed to function according to the rule of law, which requires it to be (or at least appear to be) independent, impartial, effective, equal and accessible.

The book aims at deconstructing this contradictory and often incoherent position in which national courts place themselves when applying IHL. It proposes a methodology for examining court decisions in order to decipher properly their functional role. Through a critical reading of case law from different democratic jurisdictions—whether criminal, civil or administrative cases, this book identifies a spectrum of functional roles that judges may assume. They can variously: serve as a legitimating agency of the state; avoid exercising jurisdiction for extra-legal considerations; defer the matter back to the other branches of government; enforce the law as required by the rule of law; or, develop the law and introduce ethical judgment beyond the positive application of the law. As the analyses will show, in IHL cases the way national courts function is neither predictable nor consistent.

The first four chapters of the book identify these different functional roles of courts, and locate them on a spectrum. The first chapter discusses the *apologist* role of courts, in which they serve as a legitimating agency for state action. The first case study shows how the Israeli High Court of Justice (HCJ) has actively contributed to the creation and legitimization of a segregated regime in the Occupied Palestinian Territories (OPT) by providing the state with the legal tools required to design and implement it. The second case study offers a critical examination of the jurisprudence of the Serbian War Crimes Chamber (WCC). The WCC is one of the few domestic courts in the world to prosecute its own nationals for war

[2] These preliminary structural demands were studied in a collective publication edited by Dinah Shelton (ed.), *International Law and Domestic Legal Systems, Incorporation, Transformation, and Persuasion* (Oxford: Oxford University Press, 2011).

crimes committed in a conflict that ended just a few years before the court's creation. More generally, it deciphers the legitimating role of a national court which exercises criminal jurisdiction over former government officials.

The second chapter presents the *avoiding* role of courts. Courts, motivated by policy considerations, avoid exercising their jurisdiction over a given case. This chapter first analyses at a theoretical level the construction of the act of state and political question doctrines. Secondly it observes the *de facto* selective application of these doctrines by different courts in the United States, Canada, and Israel.

The third chapter analyses both the *deferral* and the *normative application* roles of the court. It will be shown that the deferral techniques allow an important transition from the avoidance role (with respect to judicial review) towards the exercise of the most significant role of courts from the rule of law perspective: enforcer of IHL through its normative application. Two case studies are used to support this premise. The first case study focuses on the Guantanamo cases and examines the extent of the protections granted by courts to individuals in detention. The second deals with the limits on the state, imposed by the judiciary, on questions relating to the conduct of hostilities.

The fourth chapter identifies the *activist* role of courts. This is where national courts develop their own domestic law, without being explicitly entrusted to do so, in order to harmonize it with the requirements of international law. This chapter also discusses the *utopian* role of courts, in which courts introduce ethical judgments and develop international law in the name of a moral cause. The utopian role is explored by using the example of the Italian *Ferrini* case.

Having indentified the functional roles of courts, the book assumes also an external, political, 'good' outside this spectrum, which is the principles of the rule of law—to which courts should aspire. Using the methodology proposed will allow us then to criticize (both legally and politically) the different functions of national courts in the light of rule of law principles. In the fifth chapter, these different functional roles are assessed to see how they correspond to rule of law principles. More generally, it also appraises the contribution of national courts for generating commitment to the *international rule of law*. This analysis concentrates on the following elements:

(1) **Independency and impartiality**: Are courts misusing the law in order to maintain the state's position and to legitimize the state's illegal acts? To what extent do judges defer their decisions to the state? What facts are provided, and how are these assessed? Do courts use presumptions in favour of the state? Do courts engage in judicial activism or self-restraint in a manner that is consistent with their legal traditions, as in the context of judicial review of administrative decisions? Is it possible to discern an evolution in the willingness of courts to assert an independent position and to strengthen their authority in IHL cases? Is this evolution linear?

(2) **Access**: do judges employ doctrines that limit the admissibility or consideration of cases? Such doctrines employed include the non-justiciability of political questions doctrine or the practice of limiting the standing of the parties (which curbs the right of action of individuals and/or the competence of the court to

enforce IHL rules). Can new tendencies be observed, tendencies in which courts (a) attempt to extend the exceptions to the application of these traditional doctrines in order to justify their exercise of jurisdiction over cases; or (b) to explicitly reject their application altogether in light of the key principles of the rule of law, such as the right of access to a court?

(3) **Effectiveness:** IHL norms should be valid within the domestic legal system. Subjective factors are involved here, relating to the willingness of judges to apply IHL and to identify it as a valid norm which they are competent to apply. One example of this is where judges may provide for a restrictive or broad interpretation to the constitution that defines the validity of international law within domestic systems. Another example is the hierarchy of norms when there is conflict between domestic and IHL norms or to the identification of customary rules directly applicable in domestic systems. Second, the content of the norm should be applied effectively. The interpretation of the law should be in accordance with the ordinary meaning of its terms in their context and in light of its object and purpose as required by Article 31 of the Vienna Convention on the Law of Treaties. The subjective willingness of judges to do so may enter into the equation. Objective factors also come into play in the effective application of IHL. For example the skill of the judges and their knowledge of treaty and customary law, international and national jurisprudence, and academic writings.

(4) **Equality:** to what extent is the judicial function and judicial interpretation performed on an equal basis for all its subjects? Does it depend on the identity of the subjects litigating before the court, and factors such as their nationality or rank and position? Can a double standard be identified?

1. The political objective of the rule of law framework

Kelsen's statement that 'The idea of law, in spite of everything, seems still to be stronger than any ideology of power'[3] still seems to be pertinent. Indeed, the idea of law still seems to be stronger than any *other* ideology of power. Setting a system of social control in place is a political task. Basing it on the rule of law will limit the arbitrary exercise of political power, and will also minimize the danger that can be created by the power of law itself. Thus, the rule of law is a political ideal that supposes that it is *good to be ruled by law* as an alternative to any other form of governance or social control.[4] It sets conditions for rules and the legal structure, so that a community can be organized and ruled by the law. A legal system can meet these formal requirements to a greater or lesser degree.[5]

[3] Hans Kelsen, *Das Problem der Souveränität und die Theorie des Völkerrechts. Beitrag zu einer Reinen Rechtslehre* (Tübingen: JCB Mohr, (Paul Siebeck), 1920).

[4] W. Bradley Wendel, 'Legal Advising and the Rule of Law', in Kieran Tranter et al. (eds), *Reaffirming Legal Ethics: Taking Stock and New Ideas* (Abingdon: Routledge, 2010), 50.

[5] Andrei Marmor, 'The Ideal of the Rule of Law', in Dennis Patterson (ed.), *A Companion to Philosophy of Law and Legal Theory* (2nd edn, Oxford: Wiley-Blackwell, 2010), 666.

In this book, the rule of law should not be given its liberal meaning as a reflection of a dichotomy, which defines it simply as a formal legal principle, an objective legalistic standard as opposed to the subjective flexibility of politics;[6] 'nor should one confuse it with a formalist hope that if we design legal doctrines carefully enough, they can conclusively determine all important and contested cases or prevent all injustices and abuses'.[7] Rather, it should be understood as a political value to frame the organization of a given society by an ongoing process. As astutely noted by Balkin:

> the rule of law, like liberty or equality, is a political value. It is a value one struggles for and struggles with. It demands that legal institutions and professional culture should work to restrain the arbitrary and unjust exercise of power, and that we should build, preserve, and protect legal and social institutions to that end. Like most political principles, the principle of the rule of law does not determine the scope of its own extension; hence, it can be fought over and co-opted. But like other political principles – such as human dignity or equality – it is no less valuable to social life because it is underdetermined and co-optable.[8]

The national/international rule of the law, as a political structure, certainly allows political choices within its framework, yet, only to a certain extent. Going beyond the formal limits of the rule of law framework cannot be completely ignored and suggests a different political choice of global governance. Such a choice would be one which as a founding framework perpetuates the rule of power and arbitrariness over conceptions of equality before the law.[9]

At the same time, a commitment to the rule of law at the national and international level must be distinguished from compliance with the law.[10] Louis

[6] In his critique, Koskenniemi framed the term 'rule of law' in its traditional liberal definition—as representing a complete, hermetic distinction between itself—the law—and politics; a reflection of a dichotomy between law/politics, utopia/apology. See, for example, Martti Koskenniemi, *From Apology to Utopia—The Structure of International Legal Argument* (New York: Cambridge University Press, 2005), 88–9 and 613.

[7] Jack M. Balkin, 'Critical Legal Theory Today', in Francis J. Mootz (ed.), *On Philosophy in American Law* (New York: Cambrige University Press, 2009), 71.

[8] Balkin, 'Critical Legal Theory Today', 71–2 (n 7).

[9] An example is the American theory of exceptionalism, which denies the coercive dimension of international law given that 'The needs of the powerful are different from the needs of the weak; the powerful don't need to be concerned about penalties for violation that might dissuade the weak. Obligation is therefore a function of power and influence. A rule that obliges the weak may not oblige the powerful'. Michael J. Glennon, 'Force and the Settlement of Political Disputes' (Debate with Alain Pellet, The Hague Colloquium on Topicality of the 1907 Hague Conference, 7 September 2007), 5. Similarly, policy-oriented legal scholars of the New Haven School, argue that international law has no independent force, and they see international rules as mere guidelines for ways to cooperate with other states. 'The notion of law as a body of rules, existing independently of decision-makers and unchanged by their actions, is a necessary part of the intellectual and ideological equipment of the political inferior'. W. Michael Reisman, 'The View from the New Haven School of International Law', *American Society of International Law Proceedings of the Annual Meeting*, 86/118 (1992). These views cannot be seen as legitimated positions within the rule of law framework because their ideologies explicitly reject its foundations.

[10] Thus, for example, the *legal black hole* created in Guantanamo by the US government, or the segregation and domination of the Palestinian people maintained by the State of Israel—although justified by arguments grounded in international law—are manifest examples of the violation of the

Henkin's famous observation states that 'almost all nations observe almost all principles of international law and almost all of their obligations almost all of the time'.[11] What happens the rest of the time? Adjudicating on violations of the law is just an ordinary part of the routine work of courts. Breaches of international legal obligations are not an argument against the existence of the rule of law, but rather they reinforce its crucial importance and the role that courts play therein.

2. National courts and the international legal order: towards the rule of international law at the national level

'Applicability, 'enforceability', is not an exterior or secondary possibility that may or may not be added as a supplement to law. It is the force essentially implied in the very concept of justice as law . . . The word 'enforceability' reminds us that there is no such thing as law that doesn't imply *in itself, a priori, in the analytic structure of its concept,* the possibility of being 'enforced', applied by force'.[12]

According to the current international enforcement model, there are two main permanent international courts with jurisdiction over IHL cases. The first is the International Criminal Court (ICC), which is competent to determine individual criminal responsibility for IHL violations that amount to war crimes.[13] The second is the International Court of Justice (ICJ), which has jurisdiction to determine state responsibility and to interpret the law in the settlement of inter-state disputes and in the context of its Advisory Opinion function. The jurisdiction of both the ICC and the ICJ is restricted by the principle of state sovereignty. The ICC's jurisdiction is governed by the complementarity principle, attributing primary jurisdiction over international crimes to national courts.[14] The ICJ's jurisdiction is limited by the

law. Yet, non-compliance with the law, even when intentional, does not mean that a state operates within an environment free of the rule of law. The US and Israel are states bound by the idea of the rule of law—even at the international level—as evidenced by the numerous legal opinions penned by their legal experts in an attempt to provide *legal* legitimacy to their acts.

[11] Louis Henkin, *How Nations Behave: Law and Foreign Policy* (New York: Columbia University Press, 1979), 47.

[12] Jacques Derrida, 'The Force of Law: The Mystical Foundation of Authority', *Cardozo Law Review*, 11/920 (1990), 925–6. Coercion is a central feature of Kelsen's view of a legal order. According to Kelsen, what distinguishes law from other normative systems, such as morals, is the coercive force of law: Hans Kelsen, *Law and Peace in International Relations* (Cambridge, Mass.: Harvard University Press, 1942), 52. See, also, Antonio Cassese, *Violence and Law in the Modern Age* (Princeton: Princeton University Press, 1988), 4–7. In more pragmatic terms, Harold Hongju Koh recognizes the binding force of international law when it has been internalized into its domestic legal system. He calls for a transnational process in the form of domestication of international rules into domestic law. Harold Hongju Koh, 'International Law as Part of Our Law', *American Journal of International Law*, 98/1 (2004), 43; Harold Hongju Koh, 'Transnational Public Law Litigation', *The Yale Law Journal*, 100/8 (1991), 2360–6.

[13] Article 8 of the Rome Statute of the International Criminal Court (adopted 17 July 1998, entered into force 1 July 2002) 2187 U.N.T.S 3 (The Rome Statute).

[14] The principle of complementarity is defined in Article 17 of the Rome Statute and paragraph 10 of its preamble. Jann K. Kleffner, *Complementarity in the Rome Statute and National Criminal Jurisdiction* (Oxford: Oxford University Press, 2008), 95.

non-compulsory nature of that court and the necessity of state consent in order to proceed.[15] These limits reflect the traditional structure of the international legal order based on the principle of state sovereignty as laid down in Article 2(1) and 2 (7) of the 1945 United Nations Charter. Yet, the scope of the sovereign 'domestic jurisdiction' limitation is not necessarily an obstacle to the judicial enforcement model. The limited role of the international jurisdiction reinforces the important responsibility carried by national jurisdictions.[16]

Indeed, the judicial enforcement of IHL relies primarily on domestic courts. This structure was foreseen by the 1949 Geneva Conventions, which imposed an explicit obligation on state parties to incorporate the relevant IHL rules into domestic legislation.[17] The duty imposed upon states to enact IHL obligations into national legislation can be seen both as an expression of the principle of state sovereignty, and as a way of resolving the disparity that may exist between international and national law. The sovereign state will be normatively bound by

[15] Shabbtai Rosenne, *The Law and Practice of the International Court, 1920–2005*, Vol. II Jurisdiction (4th edn, Leiden: Martinus Nijhoff, 2006), 549–50.

[16] This argument was raised by Professor Falk in the 1960s: 'To achieve international order, it is therefore necessary to rely upon horizontal distribution of authority and power among independent states.... [I]t is likely that progress towards a more rational delimitation of jurisdiction will result from efforts to improve the horizontal method of allocating legal competence rather than from efforts to centralize authority[;]... from this viewpoint, one grows more cautious about investing a high percentage of one's enthusiasm... in attempts to narrow the scope of "domestic jurisdiction" in Article 2(7) of the UN Charter'. Richard Falk, *The Role of Domestic Courts in the International Legal Order* (Syracuse: Syracuse University Press, 1964), 22. Fifty years later, Nollkaemper observed that: 'Basing the primary role of national courts in the protection of the international rule of law on the principle of sovereignty presents something of a paradox. The principle of sovereignty has traditionally served so as to give states control over process of adjudication. In a Frankenstein-like reversal, it now provides a basis for courts to turn their dependent position into an independent power against the state.' Andre Nollkaemper, *National Courts and The International Rule of Law* (Oxford: Oxford University Press, 2011) 25–6.

[17] Common first paragraph of Articles 49/50/129/146 respectively to the Four Geneva Conventions of 1949 (adopted 12 August 1949, entered into force 21 October 1950) 75 U.N.T.S 85, and Article 85(1) of Protocol Additional to the Geneva Conventions of 12 August 1949, and relating to the Protection of Victims of International Armed Conflicts (adopted 8 June 1977, entered into force 7 December 1978) 1125 U.N.T.S 3 (hereinafter: the Additional Protocol I of 1977). Although the 1998 Rome Statute triggered a new wave of domestication of international crimes, including grave breaches of the Geneva Conventions, to date, not all states have complied with their obligations to adopt explicit IHL rules in their national legislation. See Knut Dörmann and Robin Geiβ, 'The Implementation of Grave Breaches into Domestic Legal Orders', *Journal of International Criminal Justice*, 7/4 (2009), 719; Jonathan I. Charney, 'International Criminal Law and the Role of Domestic Courts', *American Journal of International Law*, 95/1 (2001), 121. Other IHL provisions that impose an obligation to implement IHL clauses into domestic legislation include the use of the Red Cross emblem, the protection of cultural property and conventions regulating the use of weapons. See Articles 42, 44, 53 and 54 of the Convention (I) for the Amelioration of the Condition of the Wounded and Sick in Armed Forces in the Field (adopted 12 August 1949, entered into force 21 October 1950) 75 U.N.T.S 31, and Articles 44,45 of the Convention (II) for the Amelioration of the Condition of Wounded, Sick and Shipwrecked Members of Armed Forces at Sea (adopted 12 August 1949, entered into force 21 October 1950) 75 U.N.T.S 85. Article 28 of the Convention for the Protection of Cultural Property in the Event of Armed Conflict (adopted 14 May 1954, entered into force 7 August 1956); Article 15 of Second Protocol to the Hague Convention of 1954 for the Protection of Cultural Property in the Event of Armed Conflict (adopted 26 March 1999, entered into force 9 March 2004); and Article 9 of the Convention on Cluster Munitions, adopted 30 May 2008, entered into force 1 August 2010).

IHL obligations through the incorporation of international rules into its domestic legislation.[18] Thus, the role designed for national courts within the international legal order is not solely dependent upon international legislation. In fact, the function of national courts depends above all on the national empowerment of courts to apply IHL by the domestication of international obligations. National courts will not be able to derive jurisdiction from international law beyond that vested in them by national laws and their own national constitutional framework.[19]

In the current legal system, cases which claim violations of international law are typically raised before the forum of the wrongdoing state. Violations are not brought before those of third-party states because of state immunity and other judge-made doctrines. Thus, the present international legal order confers the primary responsibility for enforcing IHL obligations upon the national courts of the responsible state.[20]

Non-compliance with an IHL rule will trigger the state's international responsibility, so national courts, by their judicial review function shall ensure that domestic legislation and state's policies comply with the state's international obligations. This point can be inferred from Common Article 1 of the Four Geneva Conventions which states that 'The High Contracting Parties undertake to respect and to ensure respect for the present Convention in all circumstances'. It is also consistent 'with a general principle of interpretation common to most States of the world: that one should construe the national legislation of a State in such a manner as to align it as much as possible to international legal standards binding upon the State.'[21] Indeed, national courts are often the last opportunity for the state to comply with its international obligations before reaching an international tribunal. From a national rule of law perspective then, the interest of the state (and the judiciary) should be the genuine application of IHL.

[18] Harold Hongju Koh, 'Why Do Nations Obey International Law?', *The Yale Law Journal*, 106/8 (1997), 2653. See also Harold Hongju Koh, 'Why Transnational Law Matters', *Penn State International Law Review*, 24/4 (2006), 745.

[19] Nollkaemper, *National Courts*, 44–5 (n 16).

[20] For a discussion of the legal competence to review a third state's wrongful acts, see, e.g., Andre Nollkaemper, 'Internationally Wrongful Acts in Domestic Courts', *American Journal of International Law*, 101/760 (2007), 760–99; Malcom Evans, 'International Wrongs and National Jurisdiction' in Malcom Evans (ed.), *Remedies in International Law: the Institutional Dilemma* (Oxford: Hart Publishing, 1998), 173, 186–9 (which focuses on the lack of possibility for a state to be held liable before the courts of another state). Because of the (still very strong) conception of sovereignty and state immunity of jurisdiction before a third state's court, this is not common—at least not in the domain of IHL. However, practice shows that in certain cases a court could pronounce, even implicitly, on a third state's wrongful acts. For an example of an implicit statement of this kind, see the UK Court of Appeals decision in *R (Abbasi)* v. *Secretary of State for Foreign and Commonwealth Affairs* [2002] EWCA Civ 1598 [2003] UKHRR 76 CA, paragraph 106.

[21] Special Tribunal for Lebanon Appeals Chamber, *Interlocutory Decision on the Applicable Law: Terrorism, Conspiracy, Homicide, Perpetration, Cumulative Charging*, Case No. STL-11-01/I/AC/R176*bis*, 16 February 2011, paragraph 41.

3. National courts and the international rule of law: from the local to the global (and back to the local)

The methodology established in this book allows for the assessment of national courts in their commitment to the emerging concept of the *international rule of law*. When states expressed their willingness to empower national and international courts to enforce international law, they explicitly endorsed the ideal of the international rule of law. Thus, the application of IHL by national courts contributes not only to the growing process of generating respect for IHL at the national level, but also to the strengthening of the international rule of law on a global level.

Structurally, the international legal system differs greatly from the national one. The most apparent disparities are that at the international level there is no separate legislative authority, nor a central enforcement body, as is found in national democracies. It may be questionable, because of this difference, whether it is possible to *externalize*[22] the concept of the rule of law. That is, can we take a notion that originates in the context of domestic legal systems, and put it into the international sphere?[23] As Crawford has rightly observed: 'we have to be fully aware of the differences between domestic and international contexts—but also of the relativity of that distinction.'[24] Moreover, it seems that 'the problem is not so much one of conceptualization but of commitment'[25] which is, at least at the theoretical level, not the same thing at all. If it is true that subordinating arbitrary power to law is a political ideal that we are interested in promoting, it seems that the concept of the rule of law could (and should) be externalized to the international sphere, albeit subject to necessary adaptations.[26] Indeed, an international community not governed by the rule of law runs the risk of inconsistency,

[22] The term *externalized* is used by Stephane Beaulac. It refers to 'the process by which a feature or characteristic that exists within the inside set is projected or attributed to circumstances or causes that are present in the outside space according to an internal–external dichotomous structure.' Stephane Beaulac, 'The Rule of Law in International Law Today', in Gianluigi Palombella and Neil Walker (eds), *Relocating the Rule of Law* (Oxford: Hart Publishing, 2009), 204.

[23] See, for example, Arthur Watts, 'The International Rule of Law', *German Yearbook of International Law*, 36/15 (1993), 16; Beaulac, 'The Rule of Law in International Law Today', 204; James Crawford, 'International Law and the Rule of Law', *Adelaide Law Review*, 24/3 (2003), 5; Mattias Kumm, 'International Law in National Courts: The International Rule of Law and the Limits of the Internationalist Model', *Virginia Journal of International Law*, 44/19 (2003), 22; *Charles Sampford*, '*Reconceiving the Rule of Law* for a Globalizing World', in Spencer Zifcak (ed.), *Globalisation and The Rule of Law* (London: Routledge, 2005), 9–10.

[24] Crawford, 'International Law and the Rule of Law', 12 (n 23).

[25] Charles Sampford, 'Legal Ethics in a Post-Westphalian World: Building the International Rule of Law and other Tasks', in Kieran Tranter et al. (eds), *Reaffirming Legal Ethics—Taking Stock and New Ideas* (Abingdon: Routledge, 2010), 84.

[26] 'Under the principle of international legality, less powerful states tend to be more effectively protected against impositions by powerful states. Just as the rule of law became the battle cry for political reformers in much of Europe in the eighteenth and early nineteenth centuries to curb the arbitrary exercise of authority on the domestic level, so the international rule of law has been embraced in the twentieth century as a means of reining in the exercise of power by militarily and economically powerful actors on the international level.' Kumm, 'International Law in National Courts', 25–6 (n 23).

[D]oes international law apply the policy: the rule of law for others not for itself? . . . [I]n the long run national system founded on the rule of law cannot tolerate review by an international system not so founded [. . .] So we end by affirming the need for the rule of law as a virtue at the international level.[27]

The General Assembly has referred to the rule of law as an agenda item since 2006[28] and has adopted resolutions on the issue at subsequent sessions. For example, during the General Assembly's sixty-fourth session in 2009 on 'The rule of law at the international level', it was generally agreed that the rule of law is based on a number of core principles. The selective enforcement of international law was mentioned as an example of the failure to respect these basic principles.[29] The UN Secretary-General has issued a number of reports on the rule of law.[30] Similarly, the Security Council has held thematic debates on the rule of law and adopted a resolution stressing the importance of the rule of law in the context of the protection of civilians in armed conflict.[31]

Justice Higgins observed that 'despite this flood of reports, we still do not have a clear definition of what is meant by "the rule of law at the international level".'[32] At

[27] Crawford, 'International Law and the Rule of Law', 8–10 (n 23).

[28] UNGA Res. 61/39 (18 December 2006) UN Doc A/RES/61/39 on 'The rule of law at the national and international levels.' It reaffirms 'the need for universal adherence to and implementation of the rule of law at both the national and international levels and its solemn commitment to an international order based on the rule of law and international law, which together with the principles of justice, is essential for peaceful coexistence and cooperation among States.' All UN documents relating to the rule of law are available online at 'The UN and the Rule of Law' website <http://www.un.org/en/ruleoflaw/index.shtml>.

[29] The summary of the session is available at the General Assembly's official website <http://www.un.org/ga/sixth/64/RuleofLaw.shtml>. See, for example, the statement by the US delegation: 'The United States has reinvigorated its commitment to the rule of law at the international level, including in the arena of international humanitarian and human rights law and through its participation in the work of multilateral institutions. The Obama Administration signaled the seriousness of its commitment in these areas in its very first week of being in office. Among the President's first Executive Orders were orders that mandated the closure of the Guantanamo Bay detention facility, instituted searching reviews of U.S. detention and interrogation policies, closed CIA secret detention facilities, and caused all interrogations to be governed by the widely accepted guidelines set forth in the U.S. Army Field Manual . . . . In conclusion, the United States appreciates the Sixth Committee's interest in promoting respect for and adherence to the rule of law at the national and international level. We are strong proponents of respect for and adherence to the rule of law and look forward to working with others on practical measures to advance those objectives.' Statement made by Laura G. Ross, Senior Advisor to the Permanent Representative of the United States to the Sixty-fourth Session of the General Assembly, in the Sixth Committee, on Agenda Item 83: The Rule of Law at the National and International Levels (New York, 14 October 2009) <http://usun.state.gov/briefing/statements/2009/130581.htm>. More recently, see the 'Declaration of the High-level Meeting of the General Assembly on the Rule of Law at the National and International Levels' on 30 November 2012 (UNGA Res. 67/1 (30 November 2012) UN Doc A/RES/67/1).

[30] The first of these reports, 'The Rule of Law and Transitional Justice in Conflict and Post-Conflict Societies', offered a definition to the rule of law. Report of the Secretary-General, 'The Rule of Law and Transitional Justice in Conflict and Post-Conflict Societies' (23 August 2004) UN Doc S/2004/616, paragraph 6. For a more recent report see: Report of the Secretary-General, 'Delivering Justice: Programme of Action to Strengthen the Rule of Law at the National and International Levels' (16 March 2012) UN Doc A/66/749.

[31] See paragraph 11 of UNSC Res. 1674 (28 April 2006) UN Doc S/RES/1674.

[32] R. Higgins, 'The changing position of domestic courts in the international legal order', Speech at the First International Law in Domestic Courts Colloquium, The Hague, 17 March 2008, 1–3.

the same time, there is an emerging consensus that one of the core elements of the international rule of law requires an assertive role by the courts. Courts have a major role: these bodies, which are supposed to be independent, impartial, and accessible, are entrusted to guarantee the rule of law.[33] Indeed, as stated by the European Court of Human Rights, 'One can scarcely conceive of the rule of law without there being a possibility of having access to the courts.'[34] As the judicial enforcement of international norms remains the weakest element of the international rule of law, the proper function of national courts, which are major pillars of the international judicial mechanism, is therefore of supreme importance.[35]

Today, international law stands at a crossroads. It could provide a common legal basis for governing the international community within the rule of law framework. Alternatively it could serve as a tool to enable the exercise of a state's arbitrary power. If the arbitrary power is not constrained by a system of checks and balances, including by means of judicial review, international law could become a tool for generating abuses under the cloak of legality. However, within these opposite paths, the law offers other, more nuanced functions which could be seen to link them or to lead to new horizons. It is these functions which are explored in the following chapters.

[33] R. Higgins, 'The changing position of domestic courts in the international legal order', 1–3 (n 32); Nollkaemper, *National Courts* 58 (n 16).

[34] *Golder* v. *the United Kingdom* (Judgment), European Court of Human Rights No. 4451/70 (21 February 1975), paragraph 54.

[35] Watts, 'The International Rule of Law', 44 (n 23). See also 'In states that in all other aspects have a reputable quality of the rule of law, the powers of judicial review against the political branches often do not cover international law to the full extent.' Nollkaemper, *National Courts*, 50 (n 16) and the references he cites in fns 19 and 20.

1

The Apologist Role of National Courts: Legitimizing (Illegal) State Policy

One of the functions of national courts within a democratic system is the granting of legitimacy to the government and its policies. Sociology of law and political science research suggest that states need to rely on courts as a legitimizing agent.[1] According to Roger Cotterrell, courts are institutions that ensure the state's interest in maintaining the stability of the social and political order, 'first, by providing legal frameworks and legal legitimacy for *government* and government acts and, secondly, by maintaining the integrity of the *legal order* itself—the ideological conditions upon which legal domination depends.'[2]

Shapiro has demonstrated in a comparative study that governing authorities seek to maintain or increase their legitimacy through the courts and that courts have largely been subservient to the political sovereign. When governments acquired control over new territories, as in colonial situations, they would establish an effective judicial system to serve as a source of legitimacy for their rule. In effect they used courts as one of their many instruments for controlling conquered territories. Shapiro defined the role of the courts as 'a particular form of social control, the recruiting of support for the regime.'[3] That legitimacy is usually gained through the exercise of judicial review, which is the power of the court to veto a

[1] 'The political jurist begins with what any fool could plainly see if his eyes were not beclouded by centuries of legal learning, that judges and courts are an integral part of government and politics, would be meaningless and functionless outside of government and politics and are, therefore, first and foremost political actors and agencies' Martin Shapiro and Alec Stone Sweet, *On Law, Politics and Judicialization* (Oxford: Oxford University Press, 2002), 3.

[2] Roger Cotterrell, *The Sociology of Law* (London: Butterworths, 1984), 234, 245; Martin Shapiro, *Courts: A Comparative and Political Analysis* (Chicago: The University of Chicago Press, 1981), 17–28; Benvenisti, 'Judicial Misgivings', 174; Eyal Benvenisti, 'United We Stand: National Courts Reviewing Counterterrorism Measures', in Andrea Bianchi and Alexis Keller (eds), *Counterterrorism: Democracy's Challenge* (Oxford: Hart Publishing, 2008), note 63 and accompanying text; Eyal Benvenisti, 'National Courts and the "War on Terrorism"', in Andrea Bianchi (ed.), *Enforcing International Law Norms against Terrorism* (Oxford: Hart Publishing, 2004), 318.

[3] Shapiro, *Courts: A Comparative*, 297 (n 2). Shapiro perceives the prime historical and political function of courts as the one of *social control*: courts are the means by which the state rules *through* law. David D. Caron, 'Towards A Political Theory of International Courts and Tribunals', *Berkeley Journal of International Law*, 24/401 (2007), 407. Empirical studies suggest that courts systematically support a state's policies. See for example, Ronen Shamir, 'Landmark Cases and the Reproduction of Legitimacy: The Case of Israel's High Court of Justice', *Law & Society Review*, 24/3 (1990), 781.

statute or an administrative act or policy.[4] The doctrine of *ultra vires* allows courts to ensure that the executive obeys the law, otherwise their actions will be declared by the courts as void. However, the extent of judicial supervision under the doctrine of *ultra vires* will depend on the judges' exercise of their discretion in interpreting the law and establishing the facts. Exposing legal limitations that are imposed on judicial review and the general principles to which they are subject, shows that judicial review, (which on the face of it may appear to be an effective safeguard against excessive state authority) turns out to be just one more tool in the service of legitimizing the regime's political goals,

> [t]he doctrine ends in practice with a judiciary that will occasionally intervene against the most openly illegal conduct of local authorities but exercise very little supervision over the massive discretionary power of the central government.[5]

According to Cotterrell, the court was accorded competence to exercise judicial review over the political branches, and the level of independence required for the judiciary's authority in the eyes of the public was granted, precisely in order to provide this legitimating effect. It is a concession,[6] or a pact,[7] between the state and the judiciary. The judicial independence and judicial review competence are seen as 'two components of a "deal" between the court and the other branches of government'.[8]

While national courts grant legitimacy to the government and its policies, at the same time, the judiciary has to maintain its reputation as an independent institution in order to be perceived as legitimate in the eyes of the general public. Thus, the court within the state's democratic system is required to balance these two conflicting functions: the institutional necessity of any government 'to rely on the court as a legitimizing agent',[9] and the need for courts to be seen as independent actors. Shamir's argument is that courts, in order to legitimize state policies, must first secure their own legitimacy by showing that they are independent. This is achieved through the rare landmark cases in which they rule against the interest of the state. These exceptional decisions are usually not significant for their merits, as their impact in reality is often negligible[10] but rather for their

[4] Cotterrell, *The Sociology*, 17–28 (n 2).

[5] Shapiro, *Courts: A Comparative*, 118 (n 2).

[6] Shapiro, *Courts: A Comparative*, 232–6 (n 2).

[7] Thomas M. Franck, *Political Questions/Judicial Answers: Does the Rule of Law Apply to Foreign Affairs?* (Princeton: Princeton University Press, 1992), 10–12.

[8] Eyal Benvenisti, 'Judges and Foreign Affairs: A Comment on the Institut de Droit International's Resolution on "The Activities of National Courts and the International Relations of their State"', *European Journal of International Law*, 5/1 (1994), 425. In 1994, Benvenisti argued that apparently 'this "deal" does not appear to include the granting of judicial discretion in the sphere of foreign affairs.' Moreover, the courts accept this restriction on their powers, as it protects them from confrontation with the government or with public opinion, which may make them reluctant to demand scrutiny over international law.

[9] Benvenisti, 'United We Stand', 275 (n 2).

[10] 'By occasionally overruling or annulling governmental policies in some "landmark cases", the juridical apparatus asserts its independence from the polity.... [A]ntigovernment court decisions are often both painful for the government and discomforting for the judiciary. However, a by-product is that they often bring about a legitimating effect. Landmark decisions in which the jurisdiction of the

reinforcement of the legitimacy of the court itself by the very semblance of independency and impartiality. After establishing their own legitimacy as an institution which is not seen as linked to any political interests, courts' decisions can then be used to legitimate the majority of cases in which similar policies are approved.

1. Exposing the role of courts through a critical analysis of judicial decisions

Exposing the functional role of courts, especially the legitimating role, is not an easy task, particularly when dealing with democracies in which judicial bodies enjoy a significant degree of structural independence. In order to do so, the legal decisions rendered by judges, have to be critically read. The goal of this dissection of the legal text is to reveal the hidden politics of the law—it deconstructs the pretended universalism or neutrality, and exposes the particular politics which constitute the context in which the ruling was made.[11] Critical analysis shows how judges choose a political strategy through their use of seemingly *neutral* judicial methods and legal tools. Through a case by case analysis, it aims to relocate case law in its political context and reveal the role of judges in the context of a broader political mechanism, i.e. a political mechanism which involves structures of power and control—evidence that legal indeterminacy may also allow the use of law to legitimate oppression:

> The mainstream claims of objectivity, neutrality, and determinacy are not targeted for fun or mischief making, but because they function to disguise or evade responsibility—to focus attention on technical expertise rather than moral accountability.[12]

The critical analysis that I propose in this chapter, while focusing on the jurisprudence of the Israeli High Court of Justice (HCJ) and the Serbian War Crimes Chamber (WCC), places special emphasis on four aspects: interpretation, fact-finding, moving disputes from the courtroom into their political environment, and lastly, the effect of a court's political bias in the long run.

court is reasserted also reinforce the legitimacy of the court as an independent institution. Consequently, such decisions enhance the legitimacy of the government in general.' Shamir, 'Landmark Cases', 782–3 (n 3). See also Shapiro, *Courts: A Comparative*, 124 (n 2).

[11] Deconstruction started as a technique for reading texts connected to areas of philosophy of language and meaning as developed by Jacque Derrida and Paul de Man. For a comprehensive overview see Jack M. Balkin, 'Deconstructive Practice and Legal Theory', *Yale Law Journal*, 96/743 (1987), 743–86; Florian Hoffmann and Cornelia Vismann, 'Special Issue: A Dedication to Jacques Derrida', *German Law Journal*, 6/1 (2005).

[12] Jason Beckett, 'Critical International Legal Theory', Oxford bibliographies, online at <http://www.oxfordbibliographies.com/view/document/obo-9780199796953/obo-9780199796953-0007.xml>.

1.1 Interpretation: Who interprets the text makes the texts[13]

[C]ritique understands unreflective twentieth-century American legal discourse to be power disguised as truth. In this view, the judge orders social relations while "saying the law." When we focus attention on the saying, we are diverted from the ordering. This picture of legal hegemony suggests a form of critique. If we could "expose" what is "really going on" by attacking the ideas about truth that populate judicial discourse we could "delegitimize" judicial decision making.[14]

Interpretation is a central feature in adjudication of any sort, and certainly of judicial review. While filling content into vague statutory terminology, expressions such as 'necessity', 'proportionality', 'security', and 'public order', courts introduce a policy choice. When courts are granted the discretion to give meaning to terms that demand interpretation before application, each meaning given to these terms in a concrete dispute is necessarily a political choice, or a *construction*.[15] That process of interpretation is prior to and in service of substance.[16]

The provisions of international humanitarian law (IHL) were drafted by governments and were intentionally formulated in general and vague terms to enable them to cover a wide variety of situations and conflicts of interests. This vagueness allows governments wide discretion to pursue their political/security interests. When courts are asked to exercise their capacity of review, their interpretation of whether the agency's exercise of discretion was *reasonable,* is directed not only by the interpretation of these vague statutory terms. First, national courts are the organs that rule by their own interpretation of the law whether or not an IHL norm can be enforced by them. The national courts are the ones that determine if a provision is 'directly applicable', 'self-executing', 'customary', and so on. In addition, in their interpretation the courts are free to choose whether to refer to international jurisprudence or not, and, if so, what weight to

[13] David Kennedy, 'The Turn to Interpretation', *Southern California Law Review*, 58/251 (1985), 252. 'Deconstructionists regard interpretation more as a process of fabrication than of discovery', Paul Brest, 'Interpretation and Interest', *Stanford Law Review*, 34/765 (1982), 766; see also Michel Rosenfeld, 'Deconstruction and Legal Interpretation: Conflict, Indeterminacy and the Temptations of the New Legal Formalism', *Cardozo Law Review*, 11/1211 (1989–1990). According to Duncan Kennedy, as soon as we view adjudication as interpretation and not merely rule application 'we threaten the structures that distinguish law from politics.' Duncan Kennedy, *A Critique of Adjudication (fin du siècle)* (Cambridge, Mass.: Harvard University Press, 1997), 37. Kennedy pointed at the 'fundamental contradiction' that the legal indeterminacy allowed the use of law to legitimate oppression. Duncan Kennedy, 'The Structure of Blackstone's Commentaries', *Buffalo Law Review*, 28 (1979), 211–382.

[14] Kennedy, 'The Turn to Interpretation', 251–2 (n 13).

[15] Koskenniemi, *From Apology to Utopia—The Structure of International Legal Argument* (Cambridge University Press, New York, 2005), 38–40.

[16] Koskenniemi, *From Apology to Utopia*, 341 (n 15). According to Kennedy, each of the theories of adjudication has been a part of a broader political project. Yet, courts have not openly assumed their policy role, and discretion has been understood to take place 'within the existing law.' Kennedy, *A Critique of Adjudication*, 35 (n13). Unger shows that an interpretation of a law is not a result of necessity or expertise, but it is made necessary by extra-interpretative (or political) choices. Roberto Mangabeira Unger, *False Necessity: Anti-Necessitarian Social Theory in the Service of Radical Democracy: from Politics, a Work in Constructive Social Theory* (London: Verso, 2004).

attribute to these rulings. As there is no satisfactory regulation of the relationship between international and national courts, each national court will naturally choose the most politically convenient option.

1.2 Fact-finding: the politics of establishing the facts

Presumptions and burden of proof are just two examples of legal methods for manipulating factual issues to achieve policy goals.[17] Deconstructing the way facts are established suggests that courts, far from being 'revealers of the truth', may be functioning as collaborators in the state's portrayal of reality. For example, courts (on factual grounds) do not usually reverse decisions taken by the authority in areas under that authority's expertise. Courts usually abide by the agency's course of action as long as the agency can show some evidence in support of its decision. This outcome is the result of two legal presuppositions: first, the general presumption of honesty, good faith, and integrity afforded to agency officials, which assumes that the authority's factual claims are true. In judicial review cases, unlike cases in which it adjudicates the claims of two private parties, the courts do not assess where the predominance of evidence lies. The authority's version of the facts is given special presumptive weight, and it is the challenging party that has the burden of refuting this factual presumption that works in favour of the state agency. It becomes extremely difficult to prove that the authority's decision was arbitrary, as states are in an excellent position to conceal the facts of their misdeeds from courts and, unlike the other party, also possess all the resources necessary to do so. Therefore, the version of the facts presented by the state is supported by the courts in an almost unchallenged manner. Second is the presumption that the judiciary's lack of expertise in the agency's field prevents the court from intervening in a decision that was taken following the professional authority's assessment. As a result, as long as the state agency claims it was guided by *reasonable* considerations, it is likely that the decision will be upheld.

1.3 Moving disputes from the sterile courtroom into complex reality

Courts' decisions have to be read in their political context, with the aim of revealing the different interests of the parties, and exposing the political tendency of the court. Judgments are not just a mere application of *neutral* legal rules on facts detached from any environment. Although courts tend to strip cases out of their political environment, a dispute is a complex reality that involves a matrix of political actors and interests. In a court ruling this dispute is reduced to a calculated selection and evaluation of evidence, abstracted from its broader context, and transformed into an anonymous dispute on which so-called *neutral* legal codes are applied. This perception is wholly misleading. Legal decisions are not 'an independent or isolated

[17] Shapiro, *Courts: A Comparative*, 42 (n 2).

event but an integral part of a political process in which many agencies interact with one another.'[18] Therefore cases must be read within their political context.

1.4 Looking at cases in the context of a court's political bias in the long run

A judicial decision needs to be read in the light of the everyday work of the court over the long term and should not be examined as an isolated landmark case detached from the political line of the court. Courts usually render their decisions on a case by case basis, and do not impose general policies. This renders their political impact barely visible. Therefore, once the legal decision has been allocated to its own particular political context, it is necessary, at a second stage, to decrypt the more general political line of the court by reading together its different decisions and observing the court's policy over a number of years. In this way, it is not the rare landmark cases that indicate the court's function—rather the opposite. It is its routine work over the long run that reveals its true character.

2. The apologist role of the Israeli High Court of Justice

This case study examines the judicial review role of the Israeli High Court of Justice (HCJ) in its application of the law of military occupation—more specifically its treatment of Article 43 of the Hague Regulations. The first section outlines the competence of the Israeli HCJ; the second section provides a brief background of the law of military occupation; and the third section critically analyses HCJ jurisprudence from the early 1970s to the present day—examining its legitimating role.

2.1 The jurisdiction of the Israeli High Court of Justice and its policy of justiciability

The Israeli Supreme Court, sitting as the HCJ, has the authority to hear matters 'in which it deems it necessary to grant relief for the sake of justice and which are not within the jurisdiction of another court.'[19] Thus, it has no jurisdiction over civil and criminal cases, but is competent to review the legality of decisions and acts of

[18] Shapiro and Stone Sweet, *On Law, Politics*, 27, 168–9 (n 1).

[19] Article 15(c) of the Israeli Basic Law: the Judiciary (28 February 1984). Article 15(d) lists among its operational authority the competence: 1) to make orders for the release of persons unlawfully detained or imprisoned; (2) to order State and local authorities and the officials and bodies thereof, and other persons carrying out public functions under law, to do or refrain from doing any act in the lawful exercise of their functions or, if they were improperly elected or appointed, to refrain from acting; (3) to order courts and bodies and persons having judicial or quasi-judicial powers under law . . . to hear, refrain from hearing, or continue hearing a particular matter or to void a proceeding improperly taken or a decision improperly given. The Basic Law is available online at <www.knesset.gov.il/laws/speciaL/eng/basic8_eng.htm>.

the state, its agencies, and the armed forces.[20] Israel, which established a military government over the territories it occupies from the moment the occupation began,[21] almost immediately accepted the competence for judicial review of its highest judicial body over the acts of the military commander in the Occupied Palestinian Territories (OPT). Since the beginning of the military occupation in 1967, Palestinian residents and non-governmental organizations (NGOs) have been filing petitions to the HCJ, in which they challenge the legality of Israeli operations in the OPT. Yet, it was not self-evident whether the HCJ was actually competent to exercise extraterritorial jurisdiction over acts committed beyond the sovereignty of the State of Israel, and whether foreigners, particularly Palestinians, would have standing before this Israeli judicial institution.[22] In the early cases, as no challenge on jurisdiction was voiced by the state as a matter of policy,[23] the HCJ

[20] In the Israeli domestic legal structure the HCJ exercises exclusive jurisdiction. Its jurisdiction is exercised as first and last instance. The procedure is initiated by a petition directly filed by individuals or non-governmental organizations (NGOs). In general, the panel is composed of three justices, but for petitions of particular importance a larger panel of justices up to fifteen may preside.

[21] 'Proclamation Regarding Law and Administration (The West Bank Area) (No. 2)—1967' (7 June 1967) '*Collection Proclamation, Orders and Appointments of the I.D.F. Command in the West Bank Area* (Hebrew and Arabic) reproduced in *Israel Yearbook on Human Rights* 1 (1971), established the military government while keeping in force local law as required by Article 43 of the Convention (IV) respecting the Laws and Customs of War on Land and its Annex: Regulations concerning the Laws and Customs of War on Land (adopted 18 October 1907, entered into force 26 January 1910) *American Journal of International Law* 2, Supplement 90–117 (1908) (hereinafter: the Hague Regulations of 1907): "(2). The law that existed in the region on June 7, 1967 will remain in effect, to the extent that it contains no contradiction to this proclamation or to any proclamation or order issued by me, and with the revisions ensuing from the establishment of the Israel Defense Force's regime in the region." (3)(a). All authority of government, legislation, appointment and administration pertaining to the region or its residents will now be exclusively in the hand of the military commander and will be exercised only by him or by someone appointed by him for this purpose or by someone acting on his behalf.' Article 35 of the Military Proclamation No. 3 stated that 'the military courts and their directors should adhere to the Geneva Convention of 12 August 1949 concerning the protection of civilians during war and regarding all matters relating to judicial procedure. If there is a contradiction between this order and the above-mentioned convention then the regulation of the convention will take precedent.' Only four months later this provision was replaced by the Order Concerning Security Provision (amendment 9 to Military Proclamation 3) (Order No. 144) (22 October 1967). The New Article 35 regulated a completely different issue and stated that—'if an accused was sentenced to a term in prison, the time of detention should be reduced from the sentence.' The State denied the *de jure* application of the Geneva Conventions of 1949, recognizing only its *de facto* applicability, and declaring it will observe its humanitarian provisions. For the Israeli position, based on its interpretation of Article 2 of the Fourth Geneva Convention of 1949, and the rejection of this position by the international community, including the International Court of Justice (ICJ), see *Legal Consequences on the Construction of a Wall in the Occupied Palestinian Territory* (Advisory Opinion) ICJ Rep 2004, paragraphs 90–101. At the same time, however, the applicability of the Hague Regulations of 1907 was never contested.

[22] 'The Supreme Court of Israel is not an International forum.... [I]t is not self-evident that the Court's power of review extends to actions carried out by the military in areas that are not part of Israeli sovereign territory and in which the Israeli legal system does not apply.' David Kretzmer, *The Occupation of Justice: The Supreme Court of Israel and the Occupied Territories* (Albany: State University of New York Press, 2002), 19.

[23] Meir Shamgar, 'Legal Concepts and Problems of the Israeli Military Government—The Initial Stage', in Meir Shamgar (ed.), *Military Government in the Territories Administrated by Israel 1967–1980, The Legal Aspect,* (Jerusalem: The Hebrew University, The Harry Sacher Institute for Legislative Research and Comparative Law, 1982), 13, 43. Benvenisti, 'Judicial Misgivings Regarding

review over state acts in the OPT was a fait accompli.[24] Later, the HCJ ruled that since military commanders are public servants who belong to the executive branch of the state, and they 'fulfil public duties according to law', they are subjected to the jurisdiction of the HCJ. This is even if the acts were committed in the OPT.[25] The official position of the state not to contest the HCJ's jurisdiction, as expressed by the state legal advisor at that time, Meir Shamgar, was to prevent arbitrariness by the army and to preserve the rule of law. Yet, its role was also explained 'by the wish to intensify ties between the local residents and the Israeli military system, encouraging them to have faith in the Israeli system.'[26] This decision was not based solely on genuine respect for IHL and the rule of law. Rather, it was the best way to legitimize the policy of the government and the actions of the army in the eyes of its society, and the international community—both of which are accorded great importance by the Israeli HCJ.[27] The state's interest in relying on the HCJ as a legitimating agency was in all likelihood one of the factors that lead to the court's 'activism' and its remarkable reluctance to apply non justiciability doctrines. Before turning to analyse the HCJ jurisprudence perhaps it is useful to provide a brief background on the law of military occupation.

2.2 Background on the law of military occupation

The rationale of the law of military occupation is that it is a temporary situation, which lasts until a political agreement is reached. During this period, the occupant does not enjoy sovereign rights over the territories it occupies; as stated by Oppenheim, 'there is not an atom of sovereignty in the authority of the Occupying Power.'[28] At the same time, the occupying power is responsible for administering the local life of the population under its control, maintaining it as it was prior to the occupation as closely as possible, and for providing security. For this purpose, and for the duration of the occupation, the military commander centralizes in his hands all governmental powers: legislative, judicial, and enforcement authorities. However, in exercising these powers the occupying power should refrain from introducing changes that could influence the outcome of a future

the Application of International Norms: An Analysis of Attitudes of National Courts', *European Journal of International Law*, 4 (1993), 181 and fn 113.

24 See for example HCJ 337/71, *The Christian Society for the Holy Places* v. *Minister of Defense*, (1971) 26(1) PD 574 (English summary in *Israel Yearbook on Human Rights*, 2/354 (1972)).

25 HCJ 302/72, *Abu Hilou at al.* v. *Government of Israel*, (1972) 27(2) PD 169, 176.

26 Moshe Negbi, *Justice under Occupation: the Israeli Supreme Court versus the Military Occupation in the Occupied Territories* (Jerusalem: Cana Publishing House, 1981), 16–17 (in Hebrew) cited in Eyal Benvenisti, *The International Law of Occupation* (2nd edn, Princeton: Princeton University Press, 2004), 119.

27 Benvenisti, 'Judicial Misgivings', 181 (n 23). See also Kretzmer, *The Occupation of Justice*, 20 (n 22); Shamir, 'Landmark Cases', 795 (n 3).

28 Lassa Oppenheim, 'The Legal Relations between an Occupying Power and the Inhabitants', *Law Quarterly Review*, 33/363 (1917), 364 cited in Yoram Dinstein, *The International Law of Belligerent Occupation* (Cambridge: Cambridge University Press, 2009), 49.

political settlement, as reflected, for example, by the prohibition under IHL on the transfer of populations into the occupied territory.[29]

Article 43 of the 1907 Hague Regulations, 'the cornerstone of the law of occupation in the 20th century',[30] was recognized by the Nuremberg tribunals as constituting a customary rule.[31] Although it was drafted more than 100 years ago, being the first positive instrument of international law regulating the law of military occupation, it still constitutes the basic legal structure defining the scope of the occupying power's authority in occupied territories. As a matter of principle, Article 43 limits the power of the occupier, whose government is of a temporary nature. The purpose of the Article is to promote the maintenance of the *status quo*, while, at the same time, granting the occupying power the authority to introduce changes when required. According to Article 43 of the Hague Regulations, the structure of the occupier's authority comprises two elements: the authority to restore and ensure public order and civil life, and the authority to legislate.[32] '*Restore*' refers to re-establishing the pre-occupation condition of civilian life and security. This fits the concept of maintaining the *status quo*. At the same time, '*ensure*' indicates the responsibility of the occupying power for the future—as long as the occupation lasts. During this period, the occupying power is under an obligation to guarantee that the dynamic civil life (including its social and economic dimensions) will go on. As for the legislative authority, the basic principle articulated in Article 43 is that local law remains in force. It imposes a general obligation on the occupying power to respect, unless absolutely prevented, the law that was in force prior to the occupation, thus preventing the occupying power from extending its own legal system over the occupied territories and 'from acting as a sovereign legislator'.[33] However, as observed by many commentators, the precise scope of the authority granted by Article 43 is unclear.[34] One of the main causes of its vagueness is the

[29] Marco Sassòli, Antoine Bouvier and Anne Quintin, *How Does Law Protect in War?* (3rd edn, Geneva: International Committee of the Red Cross, 2011), 231–2; Adam Roberts, 'Prolonged Military Occupation: The Israeli-Occupied Territories Since 1967', *American Journal of International Law*, 84/1 (1990), 46–7; Adam Roberts, 'What is a Military Occupation?', *The British Yearbook of International Law*, 55/1 (1984), 249–305.

[30] Benvenisti, *The International Law*, 9 (n 26). The article states: 'The authority of the legitimate power having in fact passed into the hands of the occupant, the latter shall take all the measures in his power to restore, and ensure, as far as possible, public order and safety, while respecting, unless absolutely prevented, the laws in force in the country.'

[31] See 'Judicial Decisions: International Military Tribunal (Nuremberg) Judgment and Sentences', *American Journal of International Law*, 41/1 (1947), 248–9; *Legal Consequences on the Construction of a Wall*, paragraph 89 (n 21).

[32] Originally, in the Brussels Declaration, the content of Article 43 was formulated from two separate sections (Articles II and III) with each Article being read independently from the other: 'the ensuing of syntactic amalgamation of Brussels Articles II and III into a single Article 43 was not designed to disturb the substantive duality of the concepts involved'. The term 'public order and safety' as it appeared in the English version of the Article, was in fact translated from the original text in French—'*l'ordre et la vie publics*'. As the original French text encompasses a broader meaning, and in light of the legislative history, the English version should be understood as 'public order and civil life'. Dinstein, *The International Law*, 89–90 (n 28).

[33] Dinstein, *The International Law*, 668 (n 28).

[34] Marco Sassòli, 'Legislation and Maintenance of Public Order and Civil Life by Occupying Powers', *European Journal of International Law*, 16/4 (2005), 663.

terms 'unless absolutely prevented.' Since the occupier is almost never absolutely prevented from respecting local law, in the technical sense of the word, this term has no meaning of its own.[35] Therefore, its interpretation will be based on the conception that the occupier holds vis-à-vis its own role—passive guardian of the *status quo* or active ambassador of social and economic reforms. Indeed, as state practice has shown, Article 43 has proved to be 'an extremely convenient tool for the occupant: if it wished, it could intervene in practically all aspects of life; if it was in its interest to refrain from action, it could invoke the "limits" imposed on its power'.[36] The scope of interpretation given by scholars to this term also varies. It ranges from 'military necessity',[37] 'necessity,'[38] through 'reasonable test',[39] down to simply 'sufficient justification.'[40] Most authors agree that the interests of the local population as well as the interests of the occupying army should be taken into account when considering whether to prevent the application of local laws.[41]

2.2.1. *Prolonged military occupation*

Although the basic philosophy behind the law of military occupation is that it is a temporary situation, modern occupations have well demonstrated that '*rien ne dure comme le provisoire*'.[42] A significant number of post-1945 occupations have lasted more than two decades, such as the occupations of Namibia by South Africa and of East Timor by Indonesia, as well as the ongoing occupations of Northern Cyprus by Turkey and of Western Sahara by Morocco. The Israeli occupation of the Palestinian territories, which is the longest in all occupation's history, has already entered its fifth decade.[43]

[35] Benvenisti, *The International Law*, 13 (n 26). See also Edmund H. Schwenk, 'Legislative Power of the Military Occupant under Article 43, Hague Regulations', *Yale Law Journal* 54/2 (1944–1945), 397 and Ernst Feilchenfeld, *The International Economic Law of Belligerent Occupation* (Washington: Carnegie Endowment for International Peace, 1942), 89.

[36] Benvenisti, *The International Law*, 11 (n 26).

[37] Morris Greenspan, *The Modern Law of Land Warfare* (Berkley: University of California Press, 1959), 224; Michael Bothe, 'Occupation, Belligerent', in Rudolf Bernhardt (ed.), *Encyclopedia of Public International Law* (1997), iii, 765, Oppenheim and Kelzen, also see military necessity and the safety of the Occupying Power as the sole justification, under Article 43, to introduce changes in existing laws. Oppenheim, 'The Legal Relations', 365 (n 28); Hans Kelsen, *Principles of International Law* (New York: Rinehart & Company, 1952), 73.

[38] Dinstein, *The International Law*, 109 (n 28). Dinstein proposed a 'litmus test' to examine the sincerity of the occupying power's intentions when introducing new legislation—whether a similar law exists in its own legal system. Yet, as was recognized by several authors, this test seems to be of little relevance. Benvenisti, *The International Law*, 15–16 (n 26); Roberts, 'Prolonged Military Occupation', 94 (n 29).

[39] Myres S. McDougal and Florentino P. Feliciano, *Law and Minimum World Public Order: Transitional Coercion and World Public Order* (New Haven: Yale University Press, 1961), 767.

[40] Feilchenfeld, *The International Economic Law*, 89 (n 35).

[41] Sassòli, 'Legislation and Maintenance', 674, fn 80 (n 34). Benvenisti proposes a case by case analysis, in which the different interests and alternatives should be considered. Benvenisti, *The International Law*, 16 (n 26).

[42] Cited in Roberts, 'Prolonged Military Occupation', 47 (n 29).

[43] For other examples, see Roberts, 'Prolonged Military Occupation', 50–1 (n 29).

States have become increasingly involved in the economic activities, the regulation of the markets, and social welfare of its occupied territories. Consequently, the occupant had new interests in the resources of the land it occupied. Commentators have observed that contemporary occupations have changed in their nature. They are no longer a mere outcome of an armed conflict.[44] State practice has shown that contemporary occupations endure considerably longer. At the same time, control over these territories involves major political and economic interests resulting from control over foreign land and resources, and has a 'pejorative connotation'.[45] For these reasons most occupying powers do not recognize their new territory as occupied and avoid applying the law of military occupation.

Prolonged military occupation contains special circumstances that cannot be ignored. The longer the occupation lasts, the more the occupying power would have to be involved in different aspects of civil life, in order to maintain the welfare of the local population and to adapt to evolving circumstances. Thus, it may be obliged to introduce long-term changes to civilian infrastructure and services, and also in the local institutions dealing with health, education, and so on. Indeed, all authors agree that 'it would be wrong, and even at times illegal, to freeze the legal situation and prevent adaptations when an occupation is extended'.[46] As Roberts put it:

> Decisions may have to be taken about such matters as road construction, higher education, water use . . . although they involve radical and lasting change, cannot be postponed indefinitely. Nor can the setting up of political institutions be postponed indefinitely without creating the theoretical possibility (and in the West Bank and Gaza it is more than theoretical) that the law on occupations could be so used as to have the effect of leaving a whole population in legal and political limbo: neither entitled to citizenship of the occupying state, nor able to exercise any other political rights except of the most rudimentary character.[47]

Prolonged military occupation does not fit the basic assumption of temporality and maintenance of the *status quo*. Therefore is the law of military occupation as legislated for in the Hague Regulations, the Geneva Conventions, and their first additional protocol, a legal framework applicable to this situation? Or do these kinds of occupations constitute a special category of occupation, requiring different legislation? Most writers state categorically that the law is flexible enough to be adapted to prolonged occupations. Roberts argues that even if lengthy occupations give rise to special problems and 'do expose certain inadequacies in a body of law essentially intended for much briefer and more precarious periods of foreign military control',[48] the law is nevertheless flexible enough to be capable of being

[44] Roberts identified at least seventeen categories of different kinds of occupations. See Roberts, 'Prolonged Military Occupation' (n 29).

[45] Benvenisti, *The International Law*, 212 (n 26).

[46] Benvenisti, *The International Law*, 147 (n 26); 'Sooner or later, a prolonged military occupation faces the need to adopt legislative measures in order to let the occupied country evolve.' See also Sassòli, 'Legislation and Maintenance', 679 (n 34); Dinstein, *The International Law*, 120 (n 28).

[47] Roberts, 'Prolonged Military Occupation', 52 (n 29).

[48] Roberts, 'Prolonged Military Occupation', 273 (n 29). Roberts, 'What is a Military Occupation?' (n 29).

applied in a situation of prolonged occupation. Several authors argue that in an occupation that endures for many years, the military government must be given more flexibility in the application of its legislative power.[49] At the same time the risk of abuse of a possible extension of the occupying power's authority should not be ignored, 'as it is the occupying power that decides whether a legislative act is necessary, and its interpretation is not subject to revision during the occupation'.[50] Roberts is well aware of the danger of the use and abuse of the authority, and therefore concludes that some of the authorities should be limited, while others are extended.[51] As for Benvenisti, he proposes that since an extension could, in effect, 'grant the occupant almost all the powers a modern sovereign government would wield',[52] the solution of adapting to changing circumstances lies in encouraging the participation of the indigenous population and the ousted government—i.e., to delegate to them as many powers as possible and to consult with them on major initiatives that involve long term changes. This fits well with one of the major criticisms of the extension of authority of the occupying power, an authority which allows the occupying power to decide on the appropriate changes as part of a colonial vision—i.e., the authority of one who is in control 'knowing what is best' for the local population. This is clearly not the case, first because the occupying power usually comes from a different cultural, political, and economical background, and secondly because it is motivated by its own interests in introducing modifications.[53]

Thus, although doubts have been raised concerning the adequacy of the law of military occupation and the Hague Regulations in their application to contemporary occupations, it is commonly accepted that the law of military occupation should be adapted to contemporary situations. This can be done through the application of the existing legislation, which is sufficiently flexible.[54] At the heart of the debate is

[49] Dinstein, *The International Law* (n 28), 120. Robert Kolb, *Ius in Bello—Précis de Droit International des Conflits Armés* (2e édn, Bâle/Bruxelles: Helbing & Lichtenhahn/Bruylant, 2009), 186.

[50] Sassòli, 'Legislation and Maintenance', 674 (n 34).

[51] 'In a prolonged occupation there may be strong reasons for recognizing the powers of an occupant in certain specific respects: for example, because there is a need to make drastic and permanent changes in the economy or the system of government. At the same time, there may be strong reasons for limiting the occupier's powers in other respects'. Roberts, 'Prolonged Military Occupation', 53 (n 29).

[52] Benvenisti, *The International Law*, 246 (n 26).

[53] Kretzmer, *The Occupation of Justice*, 59 (n 22).

[54] Christopher Greenwood, 'The Administration of Occupied Territories', in Emma Playfair (ed.), *International Law and the Administration of Occupied Territories* (Oxford: Clarendon Press, 1992), 263. The academic debate was recently revived following the occupation of Iraq in 2003 by the US and the UK, and the emerging presence of peace keeping missions. See, e.g., Sassòli, 'Legislation and Maintenance', 661–94 (n 34); Marco Sassòli, 'Article 43 of the Hague Regulations and Peace Operations in the Twenty-First Century' (Program on Humanitarian Policy and Conflict Research at Harvard University, June 2004) (paper presented for Informal High-Level Expert Meeting on Current Challenges to IHL, Cambridge, 25–27 June 2004); Adam Roberts, 'Transformative Military Occupation: Applying the Laws of the War and Human Rights', in Michael N. Schmitt and Jelena Pejic (eds), *International Law and Armed Conflict: Exploring the Fault Lines: Essays in Honour of Yoram Dinstein* (Leiden: Martinus Nijhoff Publishers, 2007), 439–95; Nehal Bhuta, 'The Antinomies of Transformative Occupation', *European Journal of International Law*, 16/4 (2005), 735–9 and Yoram

the proper interpretation of the role of the occupying power: should it preserve the *status quo* as a trustee, or should it introduce changes for the benefit of the local population/its own interests?

Where does the proper balance lie?

2.3 The application of the law of military occupation by the Israeli HCJ

The HCJ has been applying and interpreting Article 43 since the early 1970s until today and it provides us with a rare opportunity to examine the role of a court in applying IHL over the long term, as well as the consequences of its jurisprudence.

Since the early years of the occupation, Israel has promoted a settlement policy and encouraged Israeli Jewish citizens to live in new communities in the OPT. Over the years, the Israeli and Palestinian populations living in separated cities and villages, situated side by side over the entire Occupied West Bank, have been placed under the jurisdiction of two different sets of laws. The Palestinians have been subjected to the law of military occupation[55] and to the jurisdiction of Israeli military courts.[56] On the other hand, Israeli settlers have been excluded from this territorial legal regime, and, although living beyond the territorial jurisdiction of Israel, they are subjected to a similar legal regime as in Israel. By critical analysis, this case study will show how the Israeli HCJ, through the selective use (and misuse) of the law of military occupation, and more specifically of Article 43 of the 1907 Hague Regulations, has not only legitimatized the creation of a segregation regime in the OPT, but has actively contributed to its formation by providing the state with the necessary legal tools required to design and implement it.

The analysis is set out as follows: the first section, 2.3.1 deconstructs the interpretation given to Article 43; sections 2.3.2 and 2.3.3 demonstrate the policy behind the establishment of the facts and the legal tests applied when establishing

Dinstein, 'Legislation Under Article 43 of the Hague Regulations: Belligerent Occupation and Peace building' (Program on Humanitarian Policy and Conflict Research at Harvard University—Occasional Paper Series, Fall 2004).

[55] The applicable law in the West Bank is composed of several layers. The law of military occupation imposes a general obligation on the occupying power to respect the law that was in force prior to the occupation, unless absolutely prevented from doing so (Article 43 of the Hague Regulations). In 1967, when Israel established a military government over the OPT, it indeed recognized the continued applicability of local law in Military Proclamation No. 2 of 7 June 1967. Proclamation Regarding Law and Administration (The West Bank Area) (No. 2)—1967 (7 June 1967), *Collection Proclamation, Orders and Appointments of the I.D.F. Command in the West Bank Area* (Hebrew and Arabic) reproduced in *Israel Yearbook on Human Rights*, 1 (1971). In addition, the law of military occupation authorizes the enactments of Israeli executive military orders (Art. 43 of the Hague Regulations and Art. 64 of the 1949 Geneva Convention IV). Following the establishment of the Palestinian Authority under the Oslo Accords of 1995, the Palestinian Authority was granted legislative authority in certain limited areas. Moreover, certain Israeli parliamentary acts have extraterritorial effect within the OPT, and thus are also applicable.

[56] See Yesh Din, 'Backyard Proceedings: The Implementation of Due Process Rights in the Military Courts in the Occupied Territories' (2007). Online at <http://www.yesh-din.org/site/images/BackyardProceedingsEng.pdf>. Sharon Weill, 'The judicial arm of the occupation: the Israeli military courts in the occupied territories', *International Review of the Red Cross*, 89/866 (2007), 395–420.

those facts. Section 2.3.5 puts the case study into its political context and the final section 2.3.6 examines the outcome of this jurisprudence in the long-term.

2.3.1 Interpretation

i. Prolonged military occupation

When the first cases were decided in the 1970s and early 1980s, the HCJ was forming its interpretation of Article 43 of the Hague Regulations within the context of prolonged military occupation—a term that first appears in 1972, only five years after the occupation started.[57] At first, the HCJ did not hold a unified stand vis-à-vis the interpretation of Article 43 and the role of the occupying power. The HCJ was called upon to interpret Article 43 of the Hague Regulations for the first time in March 1972, in a case that dealt with the legislative authority of the military commander to amend a local Jordanian labour law. Customarily, labour disputes of Palestinian civilians were heard at arbitration councils. The military order introduced a novel procedure to appoint arbitrators to these arbitration councils. According to the local Jordanian labour law of 1960, two of these appointments should have been done by the association of the employers and the employee. The military commander however amended the law and introduced a new procedure instead. The petitioners claimed that the military commander should have respected the local law in force and that this new legislation was beyond the power of the military authority according to Article 43. In its ruling, the HCJ first established that the French version of Article 43 is the authoritative one, and it ruled that the term *safety* should have been translated more precisely as *civil life*,[58] which was interpreted as 'the whole commercial, economic and social life'. The majority further ruled that in a situation of prolonged occupation, in which life does not stand still, the military government does not 'fulfil its obligation vis-à-vis the local population if the legislation is frozen and [the military government] refrains from adapting it to contemporary time.'[59] As for the statutory limit enacted in Article 43, the HCJ ruled that fulfilling the obligation to restore and ensure the welfare of the civilian population in prolonged occupations is the appropriate meaning that should be given to 'unless absolutely prevented'.

Thus, five years after the beginning of the occupation, the HCJ had already stripped the limit imposed by Article 43—*unless absolutely prevented*—to become simply the need to fulfil its obligation towards the local population, due to the special circumstances of prolonged occupation. The occupying power may introduce almost all changes to the local law as far as its intention is to adapt the law to

[57] HCJ 337/71, *The Christian Society for the Holy Places* v. *Minister of Defense* (1972), p. 582 (n 24). In HCJ 256/72, *Electricity Company for Jerusalem District* v. *Minister of Defense*, (1972) the court noted that 'today, we can not predict how prolonged the situation in the Region will be and what are the final agreements that will end the military government' (p.125).

[58] The HCJ referred to Schwenk, and interestingly, added: 'If I may comment on the English translation proposed by Schwenk himself, it also has flaws. In his translation of *sauf empêchement absolu* as *unless prevented*, he omitted one word: *absolutely*', HCJ 337/71, *The Christian Society for the Holy Places* v. *Minister of Defense*, 581 (n 24).

[59] HCJ 337/71, *The Christian Society for the Holy Places* v. *Minister of Defense*, 582 (n 24).

the changing needs of the local population. This authority is only limited by the *dominant factor test*: as long as the dominant consideration to change the legislation was for the *benefit of the local population*, and not the occupying power's own political interests, it is within the occupying power's competence to change it.[60]

The next relevant case, the first *Jerusalem District Electricity Company* case (1972), follows the above majority reasoning.[61] In this case, the electricity supply in the Palestinian city of Hebron was at issue. The military commander enacted an order granting the concession to an Israeli company. In its decision the HCJ ruled that the military commander had the authority to introduce such legislation as the 'welfare of the local population' requires an adequate supply of electricity, which the local supplier of electricity could not provide.[62] However, the HCJ's decision was not yet a unified one. In a very similar case, the second *Jerusalem District Electricity Company* case (1981), which dealt with the same issue only in a different zone, the HCJ ruled the opposite way.[63] Here, the court stated that the changes that the military commander wanted to introduce were too far-reaching. The court felt that the changes involved political considerations beyond economic or technological advantages, which may not be in the interest of the local population. Indeed, it is perfectly possible that 'the civilian population under belligerent occupation may prefer to have less electricity and enjoy more independence from the military government.'[64] Making them dependent on an electricity supplier originating with the occupying power probably does not represent their political interest.[65]

The two electricity cases represent two sharply differing judicial attitudes to assessing the interests of the local population, and the political consequences involved. In the second case, the HCJ was ready to accept that a political outcome may not be in the interests of the Palestinian population, and proceeded to void the authority of the military commander. This proved to be the last time that this would happen.

By 1983, the doctrine was set, and the 'benevolent occupant'[66] approach was confirmed. Justice Barak's broad interpretation was to become a cornerstone of ongoing interpretation, allowing almost unlimited possibility for changing the law and introducing long-term changes until today.

[60] As observed by Kretzmer, 'being "absolutely prevented" from changing local law means only that the law may not be changed unless there is a need to change it, and that the need is to be judged by the duty to endure public order and civil life.' Kretzmer, *The Occupation of Justice*, 63 (n 22).

[61] HCJ 256/72, *Electricity Company for Jerusalem District* v. *Minister of Defense*, (1972) 27(1) PD 124 (n 57).

[62] HCJ 256/72, *Electricity Company for Jerusalem District* v. *Minister of Defense*, 138 (n 57).

[63] HCJ 351/80, *Electricity Company for Jerusalem District* v. *the Minister of Energy and Infrastructure et al*, (1981) 35(2) PD 673.

[64] Yoram Dinstein, 'The Israeli Supreme Court and the Law of Belligerent Occupation: Article 43 of the Hague Regulations', *Israeli Yearbook on Human Rights*, 25/1 (1995), 11–12.

[65] Emma Playfair, 'Playing on Principle? Israel's Justification for its Administrative Acts in the Occupied West Bank', in Emma Playfair (ed.), *International Law and the Administration of Occupied Territories* (Oxford: Clarendon Press, 1992), 205, 216–20.

[66] Kretzmer identifies the 'benevolent occupant' and 'maintenance' approaches. See Kretzmer, *The Occupation of Justice*, 59 (n 22). To borrow Benvenisti's terms, they reflect two opposite rationales of the law of military occupation—*status quo* v. changes.

The Jami'at Ascan case (1983)

The *Jami'at Ascan* case dealt with the authority of the military government to introduce a long-term development project—a complex system of roads that would connect Israel to the West Bank—and the authority to expropriate private land for that purpose.[67] Dinstein rephrased the legal question as follows: 'Can an occupier create permanent facts on the ground, which can provoke fears of a "length annexation" by linking transportation routes of the occupied territory to traffic routes in the occupying country?'[68]

The petitioners, whose land was to have been expropriated for this purpose, claimed that this plan exceeded the authority of the military government for two reasons: first, the roads were not being constructed to serve the local population of the West Bank, but rather Israeli transportation needs: i.e. the roads were for Israeli residents coming from Israeli cities such as Tel Aviv to the West Bank and Jerusalem; and second, long-term projects introducing permanent changes that would endure after the occupation ended were beyond the authority of the military commander. It was the state's position that the road planning was initiated for the benefit of the local population who had been using a very old road system which no longer answered their current needs.

In this precedent-setting ruling, Justice Barak fixed the doctrine that frames the authority of Israel as Occupying Power in the context of its prolonged military occupation. It can be summarized as follows:

(1) The military commander's duty to ensure public order and civil life as a 'modern and civilized state of the twentieth century'[69] requires the introduction of long-term projects that may involve permanent changes. Justice Barak follows the reasoning first set out in 1972 in the *Christian society* case, whereby civil life encompasses all aspects of modern life—economic, social, education, health, transport, etc. As the military commander must provide for the changing needs of the local population, it can (and should) develop industry, agriculture, commerce, education, and introduce permanent changes.[70] Thus, Justice Barak explicitly rejected the *status quo* approach, and ruled that in situations of prolonged military occupation the interests of the civilian population deserve supplementary investments in all domains of life.

[67] HCJ 393/82, *Jami'at Ascan al-Mu'aliman Altauniya Almahduda Almasauliya Cooperative Society* v. *The Military Commander in the West Bank,* (1983) 37(4) PD 785 (excerpted in English in *Israel Yearbook on Human Rights*, 14/301 (1983)), paragraphs 1–4. For details on the roads, see Kretzmer, *The Occupation of Justice*, 96 (n 22).

[68] Yoram Dinstein, 'The Maintenance of Public Order and Life in the Administered Territories', *Tel Aviv Law Review*, 10/405 (1984), 409 (in Hebrew).

[69] HCJ 393/82, *Jami'at Ascan al-Mu'aliman Altauniya Almahduda Almasauliya Cooperative Society*, paragraph 21 (n 67).

[70] 'Long term investment that could bring permanent changes that could exist after the end of the occupation, are authorized, if they are for the benefit of the local population, without changing the fundamental institutions of the occupied region. This may well reflect the balance between the need of the Occupying Power that is responsible for the long-term interest of the local population, and takes into consideration the dynamics of life, and between the natural restrictions imposed on the military government as being temporary.' (paragraph 27).

(2) New laws and long-term changes can be introduced for two reasons: the security needs of the Occupying Power, or the welfare of the local population.[71] With this interpretation the court replaced the actual wording of Article 43, which imposes the obligation to restore and ensure *l'ordre et la vie publics*, while respecting the local law unless absolutely prevented. Thus, as noted by Kretzmer 'being "absolutely prevented" from changing local law means only that the law may not be changed unless there is a need to change it, and that the need is to be judged by the duty to endure public order and civil life.'[72]

(3) While the military commander cannot be guided by national economic or social interests of his own country alone, these can be secondary conditions, which would be assessed through the dominant factor test. In this case, although the state recognized that the planning would also serve Israelis, as the primary use of the roads would be for the local population of the OPT, it was not illegal.

Following this doctrine, the HCJ accepted the state's position and the expropriation of the land was approved.[73] Following these expropriations, Road 443 was built; it has become one of the most important traffic routes connecting the centre of Israel to Jerusalem. Today, it is estimated that approximately 40,000 Israeli residents use it on a daily basis.[74] In the wake of the Second Intifada in 2000, following several attacks on Israeli vehicles, Palestinians were increasingly prevented from using this road for security reasons. By 2002 the prohibition had become absolute, and Road 443 turned into an 'Israelis-only road' through *de facto* physical obstacles—iron gates, concrete blocks, or checkpoints.[75] The absolute ban on travel for Palestinian vehicles became statutory in August 2007 through the issue of a military order.[76] Thus, the occupied land that was expropriated twenty years earlier in order to build a modern and developed

[71] This interpretation is based on a famous quotation of Professor Dinstein (Yoram Dinstein, 'The Legislative Power in Administrated Territories', *Tel Aviv University Law Review*, 2/505 (1972), 509), cited in all the cases, in which the court applied Article 43. See, for example, HCJ 256/72, *Electricity Company for Jerusalem District* v. *Minister of Defense* (n 57); HCJ 393/82, *Jami'at Ascan al-Mu'aliman Altauniya Almahduda Almasauliya Cooperative Society*, paragraph 794 (n 67); HCJ 10356/02, *Hass* v. *IDF Commander in West Bank*, (2004), paragraph 8; HCJ 7957/04, *Mara'abe et al.* v. *Israel Prime Minister et al.*, (2005), paragraph 18.

[72] Kretzmer, *The Occupation of Justice*, 63 (n 22).

[73] HCJ 393/82, *Jami'at Ascan al-Mu'aliman Altauniya Almahduda Almasauliya Cooperative Society* (n 67).

[74] The Association for Civil Rights in Israel, *Route 443: Fact Sheet and Timeline*, May 2010. Online at <http://www.acri.org.il/en/2010/05/25/route-443-fact-sheet-and-timeline/>.

[75] 'I made Route 443 an Israelis-only road,' he said with satisfaction, while insisting it had been his decision. 'I ordered all the exits serving Palestinians to be barricaded.' IDF commander of the Ramallah region, Colonel Gal Hirsch, cited in Ofer Shelah and Raviv Drucker, *Boomerang—the Failure of Leadership in the Second Intifada* (Tel Aviv: Keter Publishers, 2005), 31.

[76] Security Provisions Order No. 378 (West Bank)—1970. Order concerning transportation and traffic (Road 443) (West Bank) 2007 dated 28 April 2007. The order was in force for one year and was extended for another year on 19 June 2008. Interestingly, the military order was issued only after the petition of the Association of Civil Rights in Israel was filed. See HCJ 2150/07, *Abu Safiya* v. *Minister of Defence*, (2009), paragraph 7. I am grateful to Adv. Limor Yehuda from the Association for Civil Rights in Israel who wrote the petition for providing me with information on the case. See also Guy Harpaz and Yuval Shany, 'The Israeli Supreme Court and the Incremental Expansion of the Scope of Discretion Under Belligerent Occupation Law', *Israel Law Review*, 43/03 (2010), 514–50.

system of roads for the benefit of the *local Palestinian population* has come to serve only the occupying power's population. In March 2007, the Association of Civil Rights in Israel (ACRI) petitioned the HCJ, arguing for the first time that the state policy amounted to an exercise of *apartheid.*

ii. The security consideration

In *Jami'at Ascan* (1983), Justice Barak pointed out that it was curious that the authorities did not mention the security need to build these roads and instead relied exclusively on the humanitarian needs of the local population. He questioned why they did not rely on the security argument as well.[77] Professor Dinstein, soon after the decision, also made the same criticism.[78] Both Justice Barak and Professor Dinstein were in fact advising the state: if the occupying power's good intentions for the local population may be suspect—why not simply rely on security arguments? This criticism did not fall on deaf ears. In most cases dealing with the authority set out in Article 43 that followed *Jami'at Ascan,* the state based its claims on security considerations.

According to Article 43, the occupying power is responsible for providing the security in the area. Yet, instead of having an Article 43 that authorizes changes for security needs of the occupying power forces, *when absolutely necessary,* the court transformed Article 43 into a provision that permits changes for security reasons—while this term has been extended to include all kinds of situations.[79]

First, this term has been broadly interpreted so that it includes the obligation to secure Israeli settlements, even if they were established in violation of IHL.[80] This interpretation contradicts the ICJ Advisory Opinion according to which measures taken to strengthen illegal settlements are themselves illegal.[81] If the goal is the protection of human life and not the policy of colonialism, then the settlers could be settled within the border of Israel, where their security is guaranteed.[82] The HCJ's

[77] HCJ 393/82, *Jami'at Ascan al-Mu'aliman Altauniya Almahduda Almasauliya Cooperative Society,* paragraph 15 (n 67).

[78] Dinstein, 'The Legislative Power', 507 (n 71).

[79] '[I]n exercising his authority pursuant to the law of belligerent occupation, the military commander must "ensure the public order and safety". In this framework, he must consider, on the one hand, considerations of state security, security of the army, and the personal security of all who are present in the *area.* On the other hand, he must consider the human rights of the local Arab population.' HCJ 7957/04, *Mara'abe et al.* v. *Israel Prime Minister et al.*, paragraph 18 (n 71).

[80] 'It is not relevant whatsoever to this conclusion to examine whether this settlement activity conforms to international law.... Even if the military commander acted in a manner that conflicted the law of belligerent occupation at the time he agreed to the establishment of this or that settlement—and that issue is not before us, and we shall express no opinion on it—that does not release him from his duty according to the law of belligerent occupation itself, to preserve the lives, safety, and dignity of every one of the Israeli settlers. The ensuring of the safety of Israelis present in the area is cast upon the shoulders of the military commander.' HCJ 7957/04, *Mara'abe et al.* v. *Israel Prime Minister et al.*, paragraphs 19–20 (n 71).

[81] *Legal Consequences on the Construction of a Wall,* paragraph 120 (n 21).

[82] Kretzmer and Shany both point to the difference between protecting individuals—which is legal, and protecting the settlements—which is illegal. D. Kretzmer, 'The Advisory Opinion: The Light Treatment of IHL', 99 AJIL (2005), 93, 97. Y. Shany, 'Capacities and Inadequacies: a Look at the Two Separation Barrier Cases', 38 ILR (2005) 230, at 243.

selective application of IHL on that point enabled the state to administrate the settlers through the use of the security element of Article 43.

As a matter of routine, different needs have been legally translated into a security issue. The military commander is not protecting the security of the settlers, as a mere reflection of their rights to life and to security. He is responsible more broadly to *secure* the implementation of the entire scope of their individual human rights. Settlers are also citizens of a democratic state, whose individual rights must be guaranteed. Article 43, through its security element, has been used as a legal tool to *enable* that large spectrum of Israeli needs ('human rights') in the name of security. Thus, fulfilment of the settlers' individual rights in the OPT, a clear political choice, is transformed in the court room into a question of security. This question would be decided in accordance with the rules of international law of military occupation. Justice Barak stated in 2005:

> We have reached the conclusion that the considerations behind the determined route are security considerations. It is not a political consideration which lies behind the fence route at the Alfei Menashe enclave [= a settlement], rather the need to protect the well-being and security of the Israelis (those in Israel and those living in Alfei Menashe, as well as those wishing to travel from Alfei Menashe to Israel and those wishing to travel from Israel to Alfei Menashe).[83]

President Beinisch declared in 2009:

> We ruled many times that the freedom of movement is a basic individual right, and that there is a duty to put all efforts in order to ensure its exercise also in the territories held by Israel under belligerent occupation.[84]

When the HCJ accepted the state's position and transformed a purely political choice into a security one, it enabled the state, through the application of the security element of Article 43, to carry out its settlement policy.

Many other cases illustrate the interpretation given to the scope of *security* under the responsibility of the military commander. In *Hass* and *Bethlehem*, the freedom of movement, property rights, and freedom of religion of the Jewish settlers and the Palestinians were at issue. The court's ruling was that both populations, both being *local*, are to have equal protection of their human rights.[85] At the same time, the inherent reality is that the settlers have an overwhelming need that required protection: namely, their security. Therefore, the initial authority to expropriate

[83] HCJ 7957/04, *Mara'abe et al.* v. *Israel Prime Minister et al.*, paragraph 101 (n 71).

[84] HCJ 2150/07, *Abu Safiya* v. *Minister of Defence*, paragraph 3.

[85] The inhabitants of the area have a constitutional right to freedom of religion and worship. This is the case for the Arab inhabitants and it is also the case for the Jewish inhabitants who live there: HCJ 10356/02, *Hass* v. *IDF Commander in West Bank*, paragraph 15; HCJ 1890/03, *Municipality of Bethlehem v Ministry of Defense*, (2005) 59(4) PD 736, paragraph 19: '[A]fter we have examined the nature and intensity of the violation to the freedom of movement in this case, we have reached the conclusion that the solution chosen by the respondents within the framework of the new order does indeed guarantee the essence of the realization of the freedom of worship without violating the essence of the freedom of movement. The respondent's decision within the framework of the new order succeeds in preserving the "essence" of both of these two liberties of equal weight, and this is therefore a reasonable balance that does not justify any intervention.'

Palestinian private land in order to enlarge a road built exclusively to enable settlers to have access to a holy place situated in the middle of a Palestinian neighbourhood was based on Article 43, for security reasons. The restriction of the right of movement of the Palestinians on that road was then balanced with the freedom of the Jewish population's freedom to worship. The illegality of the settlers' presence to even be there was completely ignored. This is a horizontal balance, based on Israeli constitutional law, which is practised in Israel in the context of conflicting rights between two equal rights-holding communities. Naturally applying this legal test is completely irrelevant in the OPT as these two communities are not equal in any way: it is the minority that militarily dominates the majority, and their entire legal status and set of rights is completely different.[86] Moreover, because of the court's inherent bias towards its own community, in the main it has been the rights of the Palestinians, the rights of an occupied people, which have been restricted in favour of the fulfilment of all kinds of rights of Jewish settlers. The argument has been that the security of these Jewish settlers was at issue.

At first, these *security* needs were mainly those of the settlers. With time, however, that interpretation would be enlarged to include more generally all Israelis, as illustrated by the *Road 443* (2009) case. Although mostly built within the OPT, it is estimated that the majority of the 40,000 drivers a day who use the road are Israelis residing in Israel. According to the High Court of Justice, the freedom of movement of Israelis not resident in the OPT on Road 443 must be guaranteed by the military commander as a security matter:

> [T]he population that had been using Road 443 [include] . . . Israeli citizens who are not residing in the Region, but have been using this road as a traffic route from the centre of Israel to Jerusalem. The obligation of the military commander to guarantee public order and safety under Article 43 of the Hague Regulations is broad. It does not protect only 'protected persons', but all the population present in the Region in any given time, including Israeli communities' residents and Israeli citizens who do not reside in the OT [emphasis added].[87]

Thus, the HCJ ruled that Israeli citizens are entitled to move freely within the OPT. In the exercise of their individual liberties, the military commander is under the obligation, according to Article 43, to ensure their security. For that purpose, the freedom of movement of the Palestinians may be limited in a proportional way.[88] The petitioners raised the preliminary questions of the general context of the occupation, the legitimacy of the Israeli use of its resource and their right to exercise their freedom of movement there. These questions were completely absent from the ruling. While the HCJ ruled that Israeli freedom of movement in the OPT has to be guaranteed, it in fact recognizes that the Israeli population have the right to benefit from OPT resources. The fulfilment of their right shall be *balanced* with the right of the Palestinians to use that road in

[86] Aeyal Gross, 'Human Proportions: Are Human Rights the Emperor's New Clothes of the International Law of Occupation?', *European Journal of International Law*, 18/1 (2007), 19.

[87] HCJ 2150/07, *Abu Safiya* v. *Minister of Defence*, paragraph 20.

[88] HCJ 2150/07, *Abu Safiya* v. *Minister of Defence*, paragraph 3 (Opinion of President Beinish); (Justice U. Vogelman, paragraphs 27–36 of the majority opinion).

the name of security: the military commander's own balance resulted in a total ban on Palestinian use of that road for almost a decade.[89]

Ironically, while most of the land in the OPT used for roads was expropriated for security reasons in order to protect the settlers, once built, they become a security threat to the State of Israel itself. Palestinian cars using a road connecting the West Bank to Israel were thought to be a terrorist threat. The military commander considered a 'fear of infiltration of terrorists to Israel as a result of traffic of Palestinian cars on the road'.[90] The solution against this threat, in the long run, has been the restriction of Palestinians' presence into defined and closed zones. Palestinians and settlers do not live in the same communities nor physically share the public common good. Once the land is expropriated for settlement construction or for paving roads, then, for security reasons, the access of Palestinians to these zones is restricted or entirely prohibited by military orders or physical barriers, or both.[91] For the sake of the security of the settlers, Palestinians have been gradually limited to living in defined areas, their freedom of movement in the West Bank has thereby become very restricted.

iii. The welfare of the *local population*

The second legitimate consideration according to which the Occupying Power may introduce new laws and other changes is 'the welfare of the local population'. In 1972, in the first electricity case, the HCJ ruled that 'the residents of Kiryat Arba [a Jewish settlement] should be regarded as having been added to the local population, and they are also entitled to an adequate supply of electricity.'[92] This ruling provided for the first time the legal basis to govern the illegal presence of the settlers. Since then, in the extensive jurisprudence of the HCJ, the *local population* or the *population of the Region* have been constantly referred to as including the Jewish settlers. Consequently, the 'humanitarian element' of Article 43, which was originally designed to protect the occupied people, also comes to protect the interests of the occupier. That interpretation had two implications. First, the equilibrium of Article 43, which balances humanitarian needs (of the occupied people) with security considerations (of the occupying forces), represents a shift in favour of the occupier and its population. The protection granted in the humanitarian element, which was intended to protect the people who originally occupied, must now be shared with the people of the occupying force. Thus, the interest of the original local population has to be restricted not only by the endless security concerns of the Israeli army, Israel, and the settlers (see the 'security element' in the previous section), but, in addition, by the need to protect the well-being of the Jewish settlers.

[89] Military Order on Traffic (Road 443) (West Bank)—2008, (19 June 2008) (on file with the author).

[90] HCJ 2150/07, *Abu Safiya* v. *Minister of Defence*, paragraph 23.

[91] As of September 2012, 542 obstacles, including roadblocks and checkpoints, obstruct Palestinian movement in the West Bank. UN Office for the Coordination of Humanitarian Affairs, 'West Bank: Movement and Access Update' (September 2012).

[92] HCJ 256/72, *Electricity Company for Jerusalem District* v. *Minister of Defense*, 138 (n 57).

Second, and more far reaching, in 1972 the HCJ provided the state with a legal tool to administer the settlers. The state was given the authority, through the application of the law of military occupation over Israelis, to issue whatever legislation was required through military orders, to provide the settlers with an Israeli environment within the OPT. This was done without any need to do it through a *de jure* annexation of the land (and more critically, its native people). The HCJ enabled it to be done while using IHL, via military orders. These enactments would regulate each detail of the needs of everyday life in the course of the next forty years.

2.3.2 Fact-finding

i. The 'dominant factor' test

The military commander may not be guided by national economic or social interests of his own country alone in order to introduce changes according to Article 43. The HCJ ruled that these can be only secondary considerations.[93] To establish whether the military government acted for security reasons or for the welfare of the local population, the court established the *dominant factor test:* as long as the security concerns or the welfare of the local population were the dominant consideration, even if other considerations were also taken into account, it is deemed to be acting within its authority.

How does the court detect which consideration was the dominant one? This is a fact-finding issue that involves assessment of the evidence. When security concerns are raised, the HCJ, as a matter of principle, attributes special weight to the claims of the state and the armed forces. The presumption is that the agency is acting in good faith: 'We have no reason not to give this testimony less than full weight, and we have no reason not to believe the sincerity of the military commander . . . our long-held view is that we must grant special weight to the military opinion of the official who is responsible for security'.[94]

Another presumption is that the court does not replace the agency's professional assessment. As a rule, in such a dispute on professional military questions, in which the court does not have any expertise of its own, the court will give considerable weight to the professional opinion of the military authorities. After all, the military has the professional expertise and the responsibility for security.[95] As the intentions presented by the state are difficult to challenge as a matter of evidence and as state agencies are attributed a greater weight for their versions of the facts through the

[93] Justice Barak in HCJ 393/82, *Jami'at Ascan al-Mu'aliman Altauniya Almahduda Almasauliya Cooperative Society*, 795 (n 67); see later, HCJ 2056/04, *Beit Zourik Village Council* v. *The Government of Israel*, (2004) 58(5) PD 807, paragraph 27.

[94] HCJ 2056/04, *Beit Zourik Village Council* v. *The Government of Israel*, paragraphs 28, 47.

[95] HCJ 1890/03, *Municipality of Bethlehem* v. *Ministry of Defense*, paragraph 19; HCJ 390/79, *Duikat* v. *Government of Israel*, (1979) 34(1) PD 1, 10 (English summary in *Israel Yearbook on Human Rights* 9 (1979), 345); HCJ 7015/02, *Ajuri* v. *The Commander of IDF Forces in the West Bank*, (2002), 56(6) PD 352, 375; HCJ 10356/02, *Hass* v. *IDF Commander in West Bank*, 458.

presumption that state agencies 'tell the truth', it becomes almost impossible to challenge the state's arguments.

Moreover, the *dominant factor* test allows political aims to be considered, as long as they are secondary. Thus, the HCJ could adopt the state's position, that the *dominant factor* was for security or welfare of the local population, without being required to completely camouflage the all too obvious political aims, and to risk appearing to legitimize an absurd position. The HCJ does not need to establish that the political aims were absent, but only that they were not the dominant ones. With the legal evidentiary presumptions in favour of the state, this has not been too difficult. In almost all cases the court's conclusion is that the *dominant factor* was not political but was relating to security concerns, even in the Road 443 case. The expropriation of the land was legitimized by the HCJ in *Jami'at Ascan* in the 1980s, while recognizing that,

> Although at the heart of the project lies the interest of the local population, the defendants do not ignore the fact that the planning project is linked to Israel, and represents a common project. It will serve not only the *population of the Region*, but also the Israeli residents and the traffic between Judea and Samaria and Israel.[96]

In its 2009 ruling, even though the Palestinians had been completely prevented from using that road for almost a decade, and Road 443 had become an Israeli-only road, the HCJ was still not prepared to see this situation as a consequence of a political decision: 'We do not have a reason to doubt the position of the military commander according to which he exercised its authority for security considerations, based on his responsibility to ensure security and order'.[97]

Thus, through the evidentiary presumptions in its favour, the security argument provided an effective legal tool to justify the different measures taken to introduce far-reaching changes for securing illegal settlements and their fluid traffic connections to Israel—that has never been found to be the 'dominant factor'. This was achieved at the massive expense of the safeguard of the Palestinians' rights: their property rights and right to free movement to name just a few.

ii. The proportionality test

The HCJ introduced the 'proportionality test' into its IHL analysis, a test which originates in Israeli administrative law.[98] This domestic test was imported into the IHL analysis, and became an integral part of it. The proportionality test enabled the

[96] HCJ 393/82, *Jami'at Ascan al-Mu'aliman Altauniya Almahduda Almasauliya Cooperative Society*, paragraph 5 (n 67).

[97] HCJ 2150/07, *Abu Safiya* v. *Minister of Defence*, paragraph 26 (unofficial translation). The court ruled that the military commander did exceed his authority (which was exercised for security reasons) because of the *result* of the decision (and not because of the *nature* of the decision). As the total ban led to a situation in which the road served only the occupying force's population—a situation that could not be approved in the initial expropriation in the 1980s—the authority to issue a total ban was found to be unlawful. While the dominant factor test was fine, the court was declaring the authority as unlawful as a result of a different test—the 'result' test.

[98] For a definition of the proportionality test see the HCJ 7957/04, *Mara'abe et al.* v. *Israel Prime Minister et al.*, paragraph 30 (n 71).

court to provide remedies to Palestinian individuals in extreme cases without having to challenge the entire policy, as the 'Wall' cases well illustrate.

The legal argument enabling the legitimization of the Wall was articulated by Justice Barak in *Beit Zourik* (2004). Barak initially ruled that in principle, the construction of the Wall was within the authority of the military commander. The court ruled that it had no reason to doubt the claim of the military commander that the Wall was constructed for security reasons, and not political ones, and was thus justified by Article 43 of the Hague Regulations. Having laid that foundation, the HCJ reviewed the specific segment's route, its planning and its construction, in light of the proportionality test. While the HCJ was ready to annul segments of the Wall when the authority of the commander was not exercised in a proportionate manner, it was not prepared to expose the political intention that stood behind the Wall as a whole. In none of the Wall cases was the authority challenged, nor the more general political policy exposed. Thus, instead of reviewing the legality of the entire policy, the HCJ reduced the legal question to an issue of proportionality of each segment of the route detached from the general political context. Thus, while each segment of the Wall, stripped from its entire context, is reviewed, the political intention of the *de facto* annexation is easier to ignore. Here lies the divergence between the ICJ and the Israeli HCJ on the legality of the Wall. Unlike the ICJ, Justice Barak chose not to review the legality of the Wall in its entire route, even though a petition of this nature was pending before the court. Instead he handed down a precedential ruling in the *Beit Zourik* case, which challenged a specific segment of the Wall.[99] This strategy (which would be followed in dozens of Wall cases) made it easier for the court to close its eyes and deny the *de facto* annexation by way of the Wall's route, legitimating the state's action.[100] With this de-contextualized approach, the HCJ provided legal justification for the construction of the Wall as a matter of principle, and supported the state's political plan to create a *de facto* border, annexing territories beyond the Green Line.[101]

[99] A general petition on the legality of the Wall was pending before the court. Yet, when the flow of petitions concerning the Wall, (which were at the centre of attention of the international community in light of the United Nations General Assembly request from the ICJ to pronounce itself on the legality of the Wall) arrived before the HCJ, Justice Barak took two decisions: (1) One chosen case will provide the precedent (2) all the Wall cases would be reviewed by the senior Judges, Justices Barak, Chechin and Benish. Shaul Arieli and Michael Sfard, *The Wall of Folly* (Tel Aviv: Yediot Sfarim, 2008), 157–60 (in Hebrew). The ICJ, on the other hand stated that the military commander has no authority to build the Wall in the route chosen as it amounts to *de facto* annexation (political consideration), and it aims at protecting the settlements, which are illegal. *Legal Consequences on the Construction of a Wall*, paragraphs 118–21 (n 21).

[100] As for political intention, 'the debate in Israel clearly demonstrates that the government did indeed have political intentions in setting the barrier's route'. Kretzmer, 'The Advisory Opinion', 92 (n 82).

[101] This recalls the strategy used by the HCJ to review the legality of the settlements. As the HCJ did not review the legality of the whole route of the Wall it was not ready to review in principle the legality of the settlement in light of Article 49(6) of the Fourth Geneva Convention of 1949 through different avoidance doctrines (see Chapter 2). However, it was ready to review the legality of specific requisition orders that involved private property rights, and to examine whether the expropriation of the land was carried out for security reasons, as required by Article 52 of the Hague Regulations of 1907. Again, the Court used the *dominant consideration* test, and was ready to accept that the

With respect to the proportionality test two points now need to be highlighted: first, the political choices of the test and secondly, the test's structural bias.

2.3.3 The political choices of the proportionality test

The facts chosen by the court to be used in the proportionality test reflect a political choice of the court. That construction will necessarily influence the outcome and general narrative of the court. The *Mara'abe* case (2005) illustrates clearly that the balance test is a policy choice as a matter of fact-finding. In this famous Wall case, the HCJ found that the military commander had the authority to build a wall according to Article 43.The authority was for security reasons, yet, the route chosen in that specific area was illegal, as the route was not proportional. While a similar precedent had been set previously, in June 2004 in *Beit Zourik* , the importance of that ruling lies in its timing. The judgment in *Mara'abe* was the first delivered after the ICJ's advisory opinion. There, Justice Barak provides an extensive analysis of the different opinions of both courts and attempts to explain their origin. In that context Barak notes that 'the difference between the factual bases upon which the courts relied is of decisive significance.'[102] This sentence could not be formulated any better. Indeed, in order to better understand the prism under which the lack of proportionality was found, it is necessary to examine the facts which were put in the proportionality balance test when the case was decided. More significantly, the facts which must be examined are those that were left out, being deemed irrelevant by the court.

The Alfei Menashe settlement, which has a population of approximately 5,700, is situated a few kilometres east of the Green Line. It is close to the Palestinian city of Qalqiliya (with a population of 40,000). The Wall in the area surrounds the settlement and created three enclaves: Qalqiliya, an enclave in the north; Habla, an enclave to the south; and five Palestinian villages with a total population of approximately 1,200, who found themselves trapped on the Israeli side with the settlement. A close look at the map reveals that for the protection of Alfei Menashe and its connection road to Israel, Qalqiliya which is entirely situated in the West Bank, became totally encircled by an eight-metre high wall and a 50-metre wide barbed-wire fence.[103]

The HCJ opened its judgment by ruling that the security of the settlers in the Alfei Menashe and their freedom of movement justified a construction of the wall. This was a measure to be taken under Article 43: it is not a political consideration which lies behind the fence route at the Alfei Menashe enclave, rather the need to protect the 'well being and security of the Israelis.'[104] In this case, it meant that the

settlements were necessary for the security of the State of Israel. See HCJ 606/78, *Ayyub* v. *Ministry of Defense*, (1978) 33 (2) PD 113, 121. An English summary is available at *Israel Yearbook on Human Rights*, 9 (1979), 337. HCJ 390/79, *Duikat* v. *Government of Israel*, 17. In that case the political intentions were exposed almost despite it: the settlers were part of the proceedings and declared that this was an ideology settlement.

102 HCJ 7957/04, *Mara'abe et al.* v. *Israel Prime Minister et al.*, paragraph 68 (n 71).

103 <http://www.passia.org/images/pal_facts_MAPS/Wall/WebPDF/QalqPs2.pdf>.

104 HCJ 7957/04, *Mara'abe et al.* v. *Israel Prime Minister et al.*, paragraph 101 (n 71).

'well being and security of the Israelis' was achieved through a de facto imprisonment of more than 40,000 Palestinians in the city of Qalqiliya and the other surrounding villages. After establishing the general authority to build security walls, the court proceeded to examine the question whether that authority had been exercised proportionately. While the court legitimizes the general authority of the military commander in light of IHL, the HCJ may still invalidate its decision as being disproportionate in light of Israeli administrative law. Indeed, even to an unprofessional observer, it may appear to be a disproportionate decision. And, indeed, the HCJ found it to be disproportionate. Yet, as surprising as it may appear from a simple look on the map the court's finding, which strengthens its reputation as an independent judiciary after the ICJ advisory opinion, dealt only with an almost insignificant part of the route of the Wall, the part where five small villages (a total of 1,200 inhabitants) were trapped within 'the Israeli side' of the wall. The city of Qalqiliya and its 40,000 inhabitants were not included in the proportionality test of the HCJ. The balance test was conducted between the settlement of Alfei Menshe (5,700 inhabitants) and the five small Palestinian villages, (1,200 inhabitants).[105] A more reasonable description of the facts would dictate a different balance: should the needs of a small number of settlers be guaranteed by the encirclement of 40,000 persons in the Palestinian city of Qalqiliya behind an eight-metre wall, which has only two exits controlled by the army that can be, and are, easily blocked? This proportionality issue remained somehow camouflaged, although it is the dominant political factor. The court's remedy was to move the wall's route in this specific segment to relocate these already abandoned five small Palestinian villages into the 'Palestinian side' of the Wall. The court's remedy therefore had a negligible impact on the ground. At the same time, the complete caging of a Palestinian city of 40,000 people, with only two or three gates to exit and enter, became indirectly legitimized by the court.

This is how the *security* of 5,700 settlers living in Alfei Menashe and their freedom of movement was legitimated by the HCJ. This came at the price of severe restrictions to the right of movement of 40,000 people. This fact was simply not put into Barak's balancing test. However, and even more astonishing, the situation in Qalqiliya is not absent from the court's ruling. It is described in detail, just not in the sections 'relevant' to the case. The story of Qalqiliya appears as an *obiter*, under a section of the ruling entitled 'The Advisory Opinion of the

[105] The relevant facts are described in paragraph 75: the Alfei Menashe enclave is an 11,000 dunam area (see the appendix to this judgment). It includes Alfei Menashe (population 5,650) and five Palestinian villages (Arab a-Ramadin (population approximately 180); Arab Abu Farde (population approximately 80); Wadi a-Rasha (population approximately 180); Ma'arat a-Dara (population approximately 250) and Hirbet Ras a-Tira (population approximately 400); total population of the five villages is approximately 1,200). The enclave is located on the "Israeli" side of the separation fence. The enclave and Israel are territorially contiguous, meeting at highway 55. Exit from the enclave into the *area*, by car and foot, is through one crossing ("crossing 109") to Qalqiliya. This crossing is open at all hours of the day. The separation fence also includes three gates (the Ras a-Tira gate; the South Qalqiliya gate; and the Habla gate). At first, we shall discuss petitioners' arguments and the state's response in detail. Then, we shall examine the arguments and the answers to them according to the standards determined in HCJ 2056/04, *Beit Zourik Village Council* v. *The Government of Israel*.

ICJ at the Hague and *The Beit Sourik Case*'. Here, the HCJ cited parts of the United Nations reports written by Professors Dugard and Ziegler, who constructed the factual basis for the ICJ's ruling.[106] Justice Barak's aim was to show how the two courts had two different fact-finding processes. Among other examples appears the example of Qalqiliya. Thus, Qalqiliya is not portrayed in this ruling as a relevant fact of the actual petition, but, in the *obiter*, to illustrate the facts that lay before the ICJ were lacking the security component.[107]

The fact that such an extreme situation as the Qalqiliya enclave could be legitimized while ruling on the disproportionality of a negligible part of the wall was also related to the legal procedure. The petitioners in this case were five small villages trapped on the Israeli side. The court could therefore ignore the northern enclave, in the name of the relevant facts. This is how human rights lawyers have come to wonder whether petitioning the HCJ serves the interest of the state more than the petitioners, even when the petitioners win their case.[108]

2.3.4. The proportionality test's structural bias

The bias of the proportionality test manifests itself in two ways. First, the proportionality test is measured within a colonial prism: Israelis' democratic social and political rights that should be guaranteed at the level of Western developed states are balanced against the rights of the Palestinians. In contrast with the Israelis, the Palestinians are an occupied, native people, deprived of civil rights. Their humanitarian needs, governed by IHL, are guaranteed by a minimum set of rights until the occupation ends. Thus, Alfei Menashe's Jewish residents need to have a protection of all kinds of rights, such as freedom of movement, property, social rights, and so on, according to Israeli democratic standards. The rights of Palestinians, on the other hand, are subordinated to the grant of rights by an occupying army. This is why the restriction on the freedom of movement of thousands of Palestinians becomes not only possible but also *proportional*. Second, in all proportionality balances there is an implicit bias, an implicit principle, according to which the protection of the rights of Israelis is more important; the equilibrium of the balance is initially shifted to prevail over another population. Otherwise, we could imagine the balance being done the other way round. Yet, because of this inherent bias,

[106] 'The report states that the Palestinians living in the enclaves are facing some of the harshest consequences of the barrier's construction and route. Thus, for example, the city of Qalqiliya is encircled by the barrier, with entrance and exit possible from only one gate. Thus the town is isolated from almost all its agricultural land. The villages surrounding it are separated from their markets and services.' (paragraph 40); '. . . almost completely imprisoned by the winding route of the wall, including 40,000 residents of Qalqiliya.' (paragraph 45).

[107] And here Justice Barak explains that: 'It was not mentioned that Qalqiliya lies two kilometers from the Israeli city of Kfar Saba; that Qalqiliya served as a passage point to Israel for suicide bomber terrorists, primarily in the years 2002–2003, for the purpose of committing terrorist attacks inside of Israel; the Trans-Israel highway (highway 6) [built beyond the green line] *whose users must be protected*, passes right by the city.' (paragraph 68).

[108] Michael Sfard, 'The Price of Internal Legal Opposition to Human Rights Abuses', *Journal of Human Rights Practice*, 1/1 (2009), 37–50; Al-Haq, *Legitimising the Illegitimate?* (Al-Haq Organisation, 2010), fn 106 and accompanying text.

reversing the positions of the balance is inconceivable. (Obviously, the court would not find it proportional to quasi-imprison 40,000 Israelis in order to secure the movement of 5,700 Palestinians. Similarly, it is not conceivable that it would find it proportionate to limit the movement of 5,700 settlers for a guarantee of movement of 40,000 Palestinians in the West Bank).

This inherent bias finds extensive expression in the *Road 443* case (2009). The proportionality test was defined in the following manner: Can the freedom of movement and the 'security need' to secure for the Israelis' use of the road be achieved in a manner less draconian than the imposition of a total ban on Palestinian use? In other words, was the commander able to achieve the same security need, (i. e. that of guaranteeing that 40,000 Israelis could continue to use that road built in the OPT on a daily basis in total security), in another way?[109] Thus, not only was the preliminary question of the legitimacy of the Israeli use of that road taken for granted, but there was also an implicit assumption that the protection of their right of movement in the OPT (portrayed as a security issue) should be entirely protected. It is only the right of movement of the Palestinians, which has a direct impact on their access to education, health, and work, as described in the ruling, which is to be restricted in the *balancing*. The proportionality test does not even consider limiting the Israeli use of the OPT resources. The question was how far the Palestinians' rights may be restricted. The ruling on the merits delivered by the court and its implementation only reinforces that observation. The HCJ deferred to the military commander the responsibility to find another *proportionate* solution. The deferral enabled the military to *de facto* keep the situation essentially intact.[110]

2.3.5. Political de-contextualization

Palestinians are rarely described as a national group. The term *Palestinians* is in most cases used to describe individuals who commit terror attacks. Both Palestinians in the Occupied Territories and the ones who became Israeli citizens in 1948 are labelled *Arab,* while the settlers are referred to as *Israeli* or *Jewish*.

> The Hague Convention authorizes the area commander . . . to ensure the needs of the local population in the area under belligerent occupation. The local population in this regard includes both the Arab and Israeli inhabitants.[111]

[109] The proportionality test was an obiter in the case, as the court found that the authority was denied, nevertheless most of the ruling of the case was dedicated to it (paragraph 36).

[110] The HCJ ruled that a total ban was beyond the authority of the military commander. The judgment came into effect five months from the date it was given, in order to allow the military commander to determine the necessary security arrangements, while leaving him a wide margin of discretion. See Amos Harel, 'Despite Court Ruling, Palestinian Use of Route 443 Likely to be Limited' *Haaretz* (10 May 2010) <http://www.haaretz.com/print-edition/news/despite-court-ruling-palestinian-use-of-route-443-likely-to-be-limited-1.289321>. As of June 2013 Palestinian cars can drive on the road, but just on a very short section of the road (Interview with Claudia Nicoletti, legal researcher, Al Haq—Palestinian non-governmental human rights organisation based in Ramallaha).

[111] HCJ 10356/02, *Hass* v. *IDF Commander in West Bank*, paragraph 8.

[The] respondent has the duty to defend the population – Arab and Jewish – in the territory under his military control.[112]

The de-stigmatization of colonizers into *Jewish* and the de-nationalization of the Palestinians into *Arabs* strips them from the political and legal context of the occupation. The two national groups, the occupied and the occupiers, living in the same place become equal: Jews and Arabs are supposedly entitled to the same treatment.[113] Yet there is no greater illusion than that. Their legal status is not equal in any way, and IHL was never intended for the protection of a community whose presence was illegal. The utopian situation, before the outbreak of the second *intifada* and the terror acts that have been committed since, was described in the following way by Justice Levy: 'Previously, the benefit of road 443 was shared by Israelis and Palestinians altogether. Palestinian cars were using that road for long years . . . no apartheid nor segregation existed but a situation of *sharing* [emphasis added].'[114]

2.3.6 Policy outcome in the long term: From military occupation to apartheid

The International Convention on the Suppression and Punishment of the Crime of Apartheid of 1973 declares that apartheid is a crime against humanity and that the acts 'resulting from the policies and practices of apartheid and similar policies and practices of racial segregation and discrimination' are international crimes.[115] It defines the crime of apartheid as covering 'inhuman acts committed for the purpose of establishing and maintaining domination by one racial group of persons over any other racial group of persons and systematically oppressing them.'[116] The acts that fall within the scope of the crime are listed in Article 2. They include *inter alia* torture, inhuman treatment and arbitrary arrest of members of a racial group; legislative measures that discriminate a racial group in the political, social, economic, and cultural fields; measures that divide the population along racial lines by the creation of separate residential areas for racial groups; the prohibition of

[112] HCJ 4219/02, *Gusin* v. *The Commander of IDF Forces in the Gaza Strip*, (2002) 56(4) PD 608, 611.

[113] HCJ 4219/02, *Gusin* v. *The Commander of IDF Forces in the Gaza Strip*, 16 (n 112).

[114] HCJ 2150/07, *Abu Safiya* v. *Minister of Defence*, paragraph 3 (Dissenting opinion Justice Levy).

[115] See Article 1 of the International Convention on the Suppression and Punishment of the Crime of Apartheid, General Assembly Resolution 3068 (XXVIII) of 30 November 1973. Article 85(4)(c) of Additional Protocol I recognized apartheid as a 'grave breach' of the Protocol; it is defined as a crime against humanity by the Rome Statute of the International Criminal Court in Article 7(2)(h). Thus, apartheid is intended to include other situations than South Africa, although originally the 1973 convention was drafted in light of this particular one. See the Report of the Special Rapporteur on the situation of Human Rights in the Palestinian Territories Occupied since 1967, UN Doc A/65/331 of 30 August 2010, paragraph 5.

[116] Article 2 of the International Convention on the Suppression and Punishment of the Crime of Apartheid. According to the United Nations Convention on the Elimination of All Forms of Racial Discrimination of 1969, the term 'racial discrimination' means any 'distinction, exclusion, restriction or preference based on race, colour, descent, or national or ethnic origin which has the purpose or effect of nullifying or impairing the recognition, enjoyment or exercise, on an equal footing, of human rights and fundamental freedoms in the political, economic, social, cultural or any other field of public life.'

interracial marriages; and the persecution of persons opposed to apartheid. While it is beyond the scope of this chapter to examine whether the Israeli practice in the West Bank amounts to the commission of the crime of apartheid,[117] it has shown how the HCJ has effectively contributed to the creation of the dual and segregated legal regime in the OPT.

i. *De facto* annexation of land via Article 43 and the physical separation of population

The long term result of the HCJ's legal construction is well illustrated in *Jami'at Ascan* (1983) and *Road 443* (2009).[118] The legal basis for expropriation of the land on which Road 443 was built was Article 43, justified by its humanitarian element—to build a modern traffic route for the benefit of the local population. The occupied land that was expropriated twenty years earlier in order to build a modern and developed system of roads for the benefit of the *local population* has come to serve only the Occupying Power's population, as a matter of privilege. In 1983, Justice Barak did not doubt the sincerity of the state's position:

> The military administration is not authorized to plan and build road systems in areas that are in military custody, if these are nothing other than a 'service path' to the sovereign country... our conclusion – which we have reached without reservation or doubt – is that Israel's considerations and civilian needs were not at the basis of the road plan.[119]

Today, it clearly appears that this choice for Justice Barak in 1983 was not a neutral one. It was a political choice with legal consequences. Indeed, the political intention

[117] For studies focusing on this question see John Dugard and John Reynolds, 'Apartheid, International Law, and the Occupied Palestinian Territory', *European Journal of International Law*, 24/3 (2013), 1–47, Virginia Tilley (ed.), *Beyond Occupation—Apartheid, Colonialism and International Law in the Occupied Palestinian Territories* (London: Pluto Press, 2012), 123–215; Russell Tribunal on Palestine, 'Findings of the South Africa Session: Are Israel's Practices against the Palestinian People in Breach of the Prohibition on Apartheid under International law' (Cape Town, 5–7 November 2011). See also the Report of the Independent International Fact-Finding Mission to Investigate the Implications of the Israeli Settlements on the Civil, Political, Economic, Social and Cultural Rights of the Palestinian People Throughout the Occupied Palestinian Territory, including East Jerusalem, UN Doc A/HRC/22/63 (7 February 2013), paragraph 49: 'The legal regime of segregation operating in the OPT has enabled the establishment and the consolidation of the settlements through the creation of the privileged legal space for settlements and settlers. It results in daily violations of a multitude of the human rights of the Palestinians in the OPT, including incontrovertibly violating their rights to non discrimination, equality before the law and equal protection of the law.' The Concluding Observations of the Committee on the Elimination of Racial Discrimination Doc CERD/C/ISR/CO/14–16 (9 March 2012), at paragraph 24: 'The Committee is extremely concerned at the consequences of policies and practices which amount to *de facto* segregation, such as the implementation by the State party in the Occupied Palestinian Territory of two entirely separate legal systems and sets of institutions for Jewish communities grouped in illegal settlements on the one hand and Palestinian populations living in Palestinian towns and villages on the other hand. The Committee is particularly appalled at the hermetic character of the separation of two groups, who live on the same territory but do not enjoy either equal use of roads and infrastructure or equal access to basic services and water resources'.

[118] For background see The Association for Civil Rights in Israel (ACRI), 'Ban on Palestinian Movement on Route 443: Background Information' (June 2009). Online at <http://www.acri.org.il/pdf/route443Aug09.pdf>.

[119] HCJ 393/82, *Jami'at Ascan al-Mu'aliman Altauniya Almahduda Almasauliya Cooperative Society*, 813 (n 67).

of the state in the 1980s to build highways to integrate the West Bank and Israel was not a hidden agenda.[120] Settlements cannot exist in isolation—they need to be connected to each other and to Israel.[121] As Dinstein predicted in the early 1970s, 'professed humanitarian concern may camouflage a hidden agenda, and it may be prudent to guard the inhabitants from the bear's hug of the Occupying Power'.[122] Indeed, this precedent-setting ruling paved the way for the expropriation of land required for the construction of a large number of highways which ultimately came to serve only Israelis.[123] Road 443 has become one of the most important traffic routes connecting the centre of Israel to Jerusalem. In December 2009, the High Court of Justice rendered its judgment in *Road 443*, explicitly recognizing the right of thousands of Israelis, not living in the West Bank, to be protected by Article 43 while using OPT resources. The court ruled that an eight-year total ban on Palestinian use was an *ultra vires* decision,[124] and demanded that the military commander find a more *proportional* solution. Despite that ruling, it nevertheless ruled that the Israelis residing within the green line had the right to use that road. While using it, they become themselves entitled to benefit from the protection of Article 43, at the expense of the right of the Palestinians to use their own resources. This use and misuse of the law of military occupation shows how the *de facto* annexation of the land and OPT resources operate in the long term.

Similarly, the 'Wall' cases, discussed in 2.3.2.ii, indicate the same result in the use of Article 43 as legitimating *de facto* annexation. The security element of Article 43 has been used by the HCJ in the following three ways: (1) it provided a broad (and distorted) interpretation of the term 'security' that includes the entire needs of settlers; (2) it applied the *dominant factor test* finding that the state was motivated by security consideration and not political motivation, and (3) it introduced the proportionality test to de-contextualize the political impact of the Wall. It is the combination of these three factors which serves to legitimize the findings in a string of cases dealing with the expropriation of land and the construction of the Wall.

[120] See for example the explanation to a plan for highways prepared by the World Zionist Organization cited in Kretzmer, *The Occupation of Justice*, 94 (n 22).

[121] UN Office for the Coordination of Humanitarian Affairs, 'The Humanitarian Impact on Palestinians of Israeli Settlements and Other Infrastructure in the West Bank' (July 2007), 58.

[122] Dinstein, 'The Legislative Power', 511, Dinstein, *The International Law*, 120–1 (n 28).

[123] Throughout the West Bank, additional roads—main roads and key arteries—that have always served the local population have been expropriated from the local residents and designated for the sole use of Israelis. A case regarding another road that has been closed to local residents is pending. HCJ 3969/06, *Mayor of the Village of Deir Samit et al.* v. *Commander of IDF Forces in the West Bank*, cited in HCJ 2150/07, *Abu Safiya* v. *Minister of Defence*, paragraph 97 (petition). Available in English at <http://www.acri.org.il/pdf/road443petition.pdf>. See also B'Tselem, 'Forbidden Roads: The Discriminatory West Bank Road Regime' (August 2004).

[124] On the merits the majority opinion held that the military commander was not authorized under Article 43 to impose a complete ban on the traffic of Palestinian vehicles on the road.The ban makes the road used solely for Israeli traffic rather than to serve the needs of the local population. 'The situation resulting from the sweeping travel ban on the villages' residents is that it is no longer a road that serves the local population, but a "service road" of the occupying state. An arrangement with such a result exceeds the military commander's authority, and contravenes international law on belligerent occupation'. HCJ 2150/07, *Abu Safiya* v. *Minister of Defence*, paragraph 26.

ii. Segregate legislation via Article 43

In the course of the past forty years, through the use of IHL, the HCJ has enabled a population to be kept under a military regime without any civil rights. On the other hand, through the misuse and selective application of the same law, it has justified the illegal presence of the settlers in the OPT. Although IHL prohibits the transfer of the occupier's own population to occupied territories, the HCJ has persistently avoided addressing this issue. The HCJ has ignored the illegality of the settlements, and has ruled that the settlers are a part of the *local population* for the purpose of Article 43. The HCJ has subjected them to the regime of Article 43, which authorizes the introduction of military legislation 'for the benefit of the local population'.[125] By providing this interpretation as early as 1972, the HCJ provided the state with an effective legal tool that enabled it to carry out the settlement policy and administer the presence of settlers in the OPT without having to enact Israeli extraterritorial legislation. The result of this policy was the creation of a distinct legal environment for the settlers—Israeli citizens would have been discouraged from living in settlements had they been subjected to the same territorial legal regime that was applied to the Palestinians (i.e., the law of belligerent occupation, pre-Israeli occupation Jordanian/British/Ottoman law, and Israeli military orders).

The HCJ's interpretation of Article 43, according to which the settlers make up a part of the local population, effectively introduced two 'local populations', the occupied and the colonizers, and paved the way for two sets of laws to be imposed over two separated populations. The living conditions desired for the Jewish local population, in accordance with the political and economic norms of the Western world, required a completely different kind of legislation. The Palestinians, as an occupied population, could stay deprived of any civil rights. Through the use of the law of military occupation, the Palestinian population could be kept under a military regime, while on the other hand, through the misuse and selective application of the same law, a distinct legislation could be created for the Israeli population.

Different methods have been employed by different legal institutions to provide the settlers with a legal environment and living conditions similar to those in Israel. This has been done without amounting to a *de jure* annexation of the land and more importantly its population of four million Palestinians. Some of these sophisticated legal manoeuvres exclude Jewish settlers from the applicable territorial legal regime in the OPT. For example, Israeli nationals are excluded from the jurisdiction of the military courts, and consequently, from the military criminal code and rule of procedure that is territorially applicable.[126] At the same time, the

[125] See Article 49(6) of the Fourth Geneva Convention of 1949, Article 85(4)(a) of Additional Protocol I of 1977 and Article 8(2)(b)(viii) of the Rome Statute. However, the HCJ persistently avoided addressing this issue (see further discussion on that point at Chapter 2 (n 179)), ruling recently that this question is *irrelevant*. HCJ 7957/04, *Mara'abe et al.* v. *Israel Prime Minister et al.*, paragraph 19 (n 71).

[126] This was done through a policy directed from the Ministry of Justice. The military police and prosecution authorities do not submit cases involving Israeli citizens to the military court system, but defer them to Israeli civil authorities. Sharon Weill, 'Reframing the Legality of the Israeli Military

HCJ has insisted on including the settlers as a part of the territorial *local population*. This was done in order to subject them to the regime of Article 43, which authorizes the introduction of military legislation 'for the benefit of the local population'. This kind of legislation became one of the main legal methods to provide the settlers in the OPT with an Israeli legal environment.

The military legislation enacted for the settlements and the settlers regulated their legal environment so that it conformed with the legal environment in Israel (as many of these orders explicitly incorporated Israeli legislation). A separate administration was established through local and regional councils.[127] The settlements also have their own courts. Through the extension of the jurisdiction of the Court of Domestic Affairs in 1983 by a military order,[128] these courts were bestowed with jurisdiction to apply twenty-nine Israeli laws, regulations of the military authorities concerning the administration of the local council, and regulations enacted by the council. In addition, Rabbinical Courts were established by military order 981 from April 1982 to regulate the personal status of the Jewish population. Many other military enactments deal with detailed needs of everyday life, which could not be provided for through the extraterritorial application of the entire corpus of Israeli law. The case of Radio 2 is illustrative of this point.[129] In this case, the military commander simply copied the Israeli statutory regulations on radio services into a military order he issued, in order to grant Israel Radio a concession to broadcast in the settlements. This is not a famous HCJ precedent-setting ruling, but just one of many examples that exist as a matter of routine. Yet, given that these orders are not regularly published in any official gazette, the massive legislation regime which has been taking place has been kept well hidden.[130]

The HCJ has recognized the extraterritorial applicability of Israeli constitutional law to settlers as Israeli citizens on a personal basis[131] and the extraterritorial jurisdiction of Israeli civilian courts on civil matters.[132] Moreover, the HCJ ruled that the extension of Israeli laws to the occupied territories was compatible with IHL. Their justification, while distorting the principle that the occupying power is prevented from expanding its own legislation into the occupied territories, was that the law of occupation does not govern the extension of laws by the occupant's government to its citizens in the occupied territories.[133]

Courts—Military Occupation or Apartheid?', in Abeer Baker and Anat Matar (eds), *Threat—Palestinian Political Prisoners in Israel* (London: Pluto Press, 2011), 136,140–1.

[127] Military Order n. 783 of 25 March 1979 established a local council for the administration of urban settlements.

[128] Benvenisti, *The International Law*, 138 (n 26).

[129] HCJ 8555/07, *Gush Shalom* v. *Minister of Communication*, (2008) (unpublished).

[130] Weill, 'Reframing the Legality', 141–2 (n 126).

[131] HCJ 1661/05, *Gaza Coast Regional Council* v. *The Knesset* (2005), 59(2) PD 481, paragraph 80.

[132] Those decisions were taken by the Ministry of Justice and the HCJ. See Benvenisti, *'The International Law'*, 129–33 (n 26).

[133] The HCJ reviewed the legality of the Income Tax Ordinance (Amendment No. 32) Law—1978, which expanded its application over Israeli residents in the region: HCJ *K.P.A Co.*v. *State of Israel*, (1984) 38 (1) PD 813, 819. For more details on the Israeli law applicable extraterritorially to the OPT see Chapter 2, section 2.3.2.

In *Road 443*, Israel's highest court explicitly divided the people living under its control into *categories*:

[The population] can be divided into three categories: Residents of the villages, who are Protected Persons as defined by the Fourth Geneva Convention [= Palestinians]; The second, residents who live in Israeli communities in the Region [= settlers[134]]. These residents are part of the local population, even if they are not Protected Persons. In addition to these two groups, Israeli citizens who are not residing in the Region.[135]

Normally, when a court is explicitly dividing people into different categories—each subject to a different legal regime—the alarm bells ought to be ringing. Yet, President Beinisch held in her separate opinion in *Road 443* that the comparison made by the petitioners between preventing the traffic of Palestinians on Road 443 and the crime of apartheid was so radical that it should not have been raised at all. However, had the majority opinion not only provided a description of each population category, but also an analysis of the legal status of each category and their resulting rights, the comparison with apartheid would not seem so radical as it may appear at first glance. In fact, Adam Roberts' warning that the law of military occupation could potentially pave the way for a kind of apartheid[136] has been realized over the years with the active contribution of the HCJ. The HCJ's refusal to address the legality of the settlements, coupled with the misuse of Article 43 in protecting the settlers, has given rise to a legal framework that enables the creation of a segregated legal regime. The creation of such a framework, under the cloak of lawful IHL measures, has enabled the state to establish two separate legal regimes without opting for a *de jure* annexation. The separate legal regimes have been created without explicitly appearing as an *apartheid* system. It has been done simply by the apparent application of the law of military occupation—legitimated by the HCJ, and indirectly by the international community who holds the HCJ and its judicial review system in high esteem.

3. The apologist role of the Belgrade War Crimes Chamber[137]

The second case study looks at the function of the Serbian War Crimes Chamber (WCC). The role of the WCC in adjudicating war crimes committed during the Balkan wars and, more generally, the role of a national court in exercising its

[134] Interestingly the HCJ does not use the word *settlements*, which may have a bad connotation, but the word *communities* (*hityashvout* in Hebrew), which signifies in the Israeli Zionist national narrative the positive and constructive movement of the Jewish population.

[135] HCJ 2150/07, *Abu Safiya* v. *Minister of Defence*, paragraph 20.

[136] Roberts, 'Prolonged Military Occupation', 52 (n 29): 'the law on occupations could be so used as to have the effect of leaving a whole population in legal and political limbo: neither entitled to citizenship of the occupying state, nor able to exercise any other political rights except of the most rudimentary character.... the law on occupations might provide, paradoxically, the basis for a kind of discrimination that might bear comparison with apartheid.'

[137] The War Crimes Chamber of the Belgrade District Court established in 2003 was renamed as the Higher Court in 2010. I use the term War Crimes Chamber, except for cases decided after 2010.

competence over former government officials in criminal cases is examined.[138] The case study analyses the first two decisions of the WCC, which reflect more generally the ability and willingness of the court to apply IHL in its particular post-conflict context. This analysis offers an insight into the functioning of the WCC; how it applied IHL, referred to international jurisprudence, and established the facts in light of the post-conflict national narrative. These three factors are compared in two cases, one where it was free from any political pressure, and one where it had to face considerable political constraints.

3.1 Historical background to the Court

The WCC is one of the few domestic courts in the world to prosecute its own nationals for war crimes committed in a conflict that ended just a few years before its creation. The atrocities in the wars in the former Yugoslavia were unprecedented in Europe since World War II and had provoked a strong international reaction. In 1993, the United Nations Security Council established the International Criminal Tribunal for the former Yugoslavia (ICTY) to try those responsible for such crimes.[139] Article 9 of the ICTY Statute establishes its jurisdiction with superiority over the national jurisdiction. However, the statute did not limit the responsibility of national jurisdictions to repress international crimes committed during the armed conflict.[140] During the conflicts in the 1990s and in the first few years after the overthrow of the Milošević regime in October 2000, trials for war crimes in Serbia were rare exceptions. Impunity was almost a political and social norm.[141] As state officials were behind many of the atrocities, they were more concerned about covering up such crimes than in prosecuting them. Ten years after the ICTY was created, as a result of internal political changes, along with strong external pressures, the Serbian War Crimes Chamber was established within the District Court of Belgrade.[142] On 1 July 2003 the Serbian Parliament adopted the Law on

[138] This case study is largely based on field research I conducted in the Belgrade WCC during September 2007 and on an article I co-authored with Ivan Jovanovic, head of the war crimes domestic trials unit at the Organization for Security and Co-operation in Europe (OSCE). (Sharon Weill and Ivan Jovanovic, 'National War Crimes Prosecution in Post-Conflict Era and Pluralism of Jurisdictions: the Experience of the Belgrade War Crimes Chamber' in Andre Nollkaemper, Cedric Ryngaert and Edda Kristjánsdóttir (eds), *Importing International Law in Post-Conflict States: The Role of Domestic Courts* (Antwerp: Intersentia, 2012), 241–68.

[139] See the Statute of the International Tribunal for the Prosecution of Persons Responsible for Serious Violations of IHL Committed in the Territory of the Former Yugoslavia since 1991 established pursuant to UN Security Council Resolution 827 (25 May 1993), UN Doc S/Res/827 (1993) (hereinafter: the ICTY Statute).

[140] 'It was not the intention of the Security Council to preclude or prevent the exercise of jurisdiction by national courts'. Report of the UN Secretary-General pursuant to paragraph 2 of Security Council Resolution 808 (1993) (3 May 1993) UN Doc S/25704, paragraph 64.

[141] The few trials in Serbia were to a large extent assessed as being conducted at below acceptable standards and sentences given were inappropriately low. See Report by the OSCE Mission to Serbia and Montenegro, 'War Crimes before Domestic Courts' (Belgrade, October 2003). Online at <www.osce.org/documents/fry/2003/11/1156_en.pdf>.

[142] For additional background see Mark S. Ellis, 'Coming to Terms with Its Past—Serbia's New Court for the Prosecution of War Crimes', *Berkeley Journal of International Law*, 22 (2004), 165–94.

Organisation and Competence of Government Authorities in War Crimes Proceedings ('War Crimes Law').[143] This law set up the War Crimes Chamber and the Office of the War Crimes Prosecutor (OWCP), and established their jurisdiction. The War Crimes Chamber is a specialized department established within the District Court in Belgrade since 2003.

A number of factors made the Serbian government decide, at the end of 2002, to initiate domestic prosecution of war crimes. Potential accession to and important economic assistance from the European Union brought with it considerable diplomatic pressure. Financial and international political support from the US came with conditions attached.[144] Internally, after the fall of Milošević an active civil society in Serbia played an important role in raising public support for accountability for war crimes. Moreover, it was in Serbia's political interest to improve its image abroad, to send signals of commitment to the rule of law, and to distance itself from the Milošević regime. By supporting domestic trials, it was hoped that these courts could substitute for the prosecution at the ICTY. According to the ICTY completion strategy[145] transfer of indictments against low-level accused and incomplete investigations to the national courts in the former Yugoslavia would be effected. This would be on the condition that there was a credible domestic legal system with well-trained staff and proper legislation.[146]

The model that was chosen for prosecuting war crimes in Serbia was the establishment of a national specialized judicial chamber and prosecutor's office.[147] The international community, mainly the Organization for Security and Co-operation in Europe (OSCE) Mission to Serbia, the US Embassy in Belgrade, and independent international experts, exerted a decisive influence on the final outcome of the creation of these specialized judicial agencies in Serbia.[148] It was a compromise made in order to strengthen the independence and competence of

[143] 'Law on Organisation and Competence of Government Authorities in War Crimes Proceedings', *Official Gazette of the Republic of Serbia [no. 67/2003*, with subsequent amendments in *Official Gazette 135/2004, 61/2005, 101/2007*. Online at <www.osce.org/documents/fry/2005/11/18508_en.pdf> (hereinafter: The War Crimes Law).

[144] For example, the US, which financed a new building for organised crime trials, conditioned its support by requesting that this new infrastructure had to be used for war crimes trials as well.

[145] 'Ninth Annual Report of the International Criminal Tribunal for the Former Yugoslavia submitted to the UN General Assembly', Fifty-seventh Session, UN Doc A/57/379 – S/2002/985 (2002); UNSC Res. 1503 (28 August 2003) UN Doc S/RES/1503 (2003), paragraph 6.

[146] Statement by Ms Carla del Ponte, ICTY Chief Prosecutor, to the OSCE Permanent Council (Vienna, 4 November 2003) PC.DEL/1278/03. Online at <http://www.osce.org/pc/13283>.

[147] Some authors classify the WCC as a 'court established by a state with international support'. Robert Cryer, Hakan Friman, Darryl Robinson, Elizabeth Wilmshurst, *An Introduction to International Criminal Law and Procedure* (Cambridge: Cambridge University Press, 2007), 161–2. Other courts that have dealt with war crimes are either hybrid (Sierra Leone, Cambodia, Kosovo, or, previously, East Timor), domestic courts with international presence (Bosnia and Herzegovina), or they are regular national courts without exclusive jurisdiction (such as in Croatia, Montenegro, Macedonia).

[148] OSCE Mission to Serbia and Montenegro, 'Strategy on Support to the National Judiciary in Conducting War Crimes Trials' (Belgrade 11 April 2003) (on file with the author). Ellis, 'Coming to Terms with Its Past—Serbia's New Court for the Prosecution of War Crimes' *Berkeley Journal of International Law*, 22 (2004), 165–84.

such institutions, while preserving them within the parameters of the existing structure of the national judiciary and criminal legislation. The participation of international judges and prosecutors in trials, as suggested by international experts, was rejected by the Serbian authorities. The government wanted to demonstrate that the Serbian judiciary was capable of handling such cases, in line with international standards, with its own human resources. The inclusion of international staff in the legal process was rejected on the basis that it might be seen as another ICTY-like court, imposing justice and prompting public animosity in Serbia.

WCC judges are selected from regular criminal law judges in Serbia, and assigned to the WCC for a renewable term of four years.[149] There are eight judges on the WCC, and the Chamber sits in trial panels of three professional judges. The OWCP of the Republic of Serbia is a specialized prosecutorial office. The OWCP is headed by the War Crimes Prosecutor, elected in 2003 directly by the Serbian Parliament, unlike other prosecutors in the country who were, at the time, appointed by the government.[150] The War Crimes Law includes specific provisions obliging all state bodies and institutions to provide information and documents or render any other assistance to the War Crimes Prosecutor at his request.[151] This special status of the OWCP, especially prompted by the participation of international experts, was to provide for a prosecutor with wide competencies and a strong independent position.[152]

3.1.1 Jurisdiction

The War Crimes Chamber and the War Crimes Prosecutor's Office have exclusive jurisdiction in Serbia over war crimes, whenever they have been committed.[153] The WCC can try persons for any crime within its *ratione materiae* jurisdiction committed in the wars in the former Yugoslavia, regardless of nationality of the victim or the perpetrator.[154] Serbia is a party to the 1949 Geneva Conventions and their Additional Protocols. The applicability of international law is set by the 2006 Serbian Constitution. International law is defined by the Constitution to be a part of the internal legal order and superior to national laws. Treaties, however, according to the Serbian Constitution of 2006, cannot overrule any constitutional provision.[155] The Constitution confirms the direct applicability of international law, and therefore treaties do not need to be endorsed via domestic legislation in

149 'Law on Organisation and Competence of Government Authorities in War Crimes Proceedings', Articles 10(2) and (3).

150 'Law on Organisation' Articles 4(4) and 5(1) (n 149).

151 'Law on Organisation', Article 7 (n 149).

152 Ellis, 'Coming to Terms with Its Past', 180 (n 148).

153 'Law on Organisation', Article 3 (n 149).

154 'Law on Organisation', Articles 2(1), 4(1) and 9(1) (n 149).

155 Constitution of the Republic of Serbia (adopted 30 September 2006, entered into force 8 November 2006), Article 16(2) and Articles 194(4) and (5). The same provision existed in the former constitution of the Federal Republic of Yugoslavia (in force from 1992 to 2003) and the Constitutional Charter of Serbia and Montenegro (from 2003 to 2006).

order to have a legal effect.[156] The Criminal Code of the Federal Republic of Yugoslavia ('FRY Criminal Code') was in force from 1992 and is the applicable criminal code for crimes committed in the Balkan wars in the 1990s.[157] There are fourteen international crimes from the FRY Criminal Code falling under the jurisdiction of the WCC, but the most frequently applied is the offence of War Crimes against Civilians (Article 142 FRY Criminal Code).[158] The definition of the crime in Article 142 begins with a chapeau and continues with an exhaustive list of underlying acts of commission.[159] The chapeau reads: 'Whoever, in violation of the rules of international law in time of war, armed conflict or occupation... orders... or commits' any of the enumerated underlying acts. It contains the key condition that, in order to convict a person it has to be proved that a criminal act listed in the provision was committed. The criminal act has to be in violation of the rules of international law applicable during armed conflict. The prosecution and the court have to examine and find a violation of an IHL rule in order to apply Article 142. The chapeau requirement of Article 142 does not only simply allow for the use of international law as a source of norms; it actually requires courts to rely on international law and to introduce it into the case as a part of the element of the crime. It has therefore been portrayed as a 'dynamic reference to international law by national criminal law provisions'.[160]

3.2 The role of the Belgrade war crimes chamber in prosecuting war crimes

Within its first decade of operation, as at June 2013, the War Crimes Prosecutor's Office issued forty-five indictments against 151 individuals for crimes committed in the course of armed conflicts in Croatia, Bosnia and Herzegovina, and Kosovo. The WCC rendered final judgments in thirty-four cases: fifteen accused persons

[156] Article 142(2) of the Constitution of the Republic of Serbia states that the courts shall adjudicate 'on the basis of the Constitution, law, ratified international treaties and generally accepted rules of international law.' Article 1(2) of The Law on Judges (2008), applicable as of January 2010, also authorizes judges to give decisions by applying 'ratified treaties and generally accepted rules of international law.'

[157] Criminal Code of the Federal Republic of Yugoslavia, *Official Gazette of the FRY* Nos. 35/92, 37/93, 24/94, 61/01. Upon the creation of the State Union of Serbia and Montenegro in 2003, this code was transformed into the Basic Criminal Code of the Republic of Serbia, *Official Gazette of the Republic of Serbia* No. 39/03, but the content of the provisions relevant for this analysis remained the same.

[158] Other crimes in Chapter XVI of the FRY Criminal Code include genocide (Article 141), war crimes against the sick and wounded, war crimes against prisoners of war, and different violations of IHL such as marauding, use of prohibited means of warfare, destruction of cultural and historical monuments, misuse of international emblems and others.

[159] Such underlying acts include subjecting civilian population to killings, torture, inhuman treatment, biological experiments, immense suffering or violation of bodily integrity or health, forcible prostitution or rape, intimidation and terror, taking of hostages, unlawful deportation or displacement, unlawful arrests and confinement, forced labour, attacks on objects protected by international law, indiscriminate attacks upon civilian objects etc.

[160] Helmut Kreicker, 'National Prosecution of Genocide from a Comparative Perspective', *International Criminal Law Review*, 5/313 (2005), 313–28.

were acquitted and sixty-eight were found to be guilty and were sentenced.[161] Twenty-nine of the cases involved ethnic Serbs tried for war crimes committed in Croatia, Bosnia and Herzegovina, and Kosovo. In addition, investigations have been opened against at least 110 individuals, most of them Serbs.[162]

The following sections 3.2.1 and 3.2.2 examine the first two decisions given by the WCC and try to analyse the WCC's role in applying IHL. This is assessed by looking at two aspects: (1) The WCC's objective ability to apply IHL: whether the judges have the necessary expertise and knowledge of IHL (including treaty law and international customary law as well as international and national court decisions and academic writings); and (2) its subjective willingness to enforce IHL: whether the court enforces the law without applying double standards, and whether the judicial system is independent, i.e., to what extent local or international political interests influence the judicial decision-making. Section 3.3 discusses the prosecution office policy not to prosecute high ranking officers.

3.2.1 The case of Anton Lekaj

Anton Lekaj, a Kosovar Albanian and a member of the former Kosovo Liberation Army (KLA), was the first person tried by the WCC to be convicted in a final decision. He was found guilty of war crimes against a civilian population during the armed conflict in Kosovo and, on 18 September 2006, sentenced to thirteen years in prison.[163] This first case was a relatively easy one, not only because the WCC was judging 'the enemy' and not a national of its own (i.e. it was not encumbered by domestic political inconvenience) but also because the factual and procedural issues were straightforward.

On 7 July 2005 Anton Lekaj was accused of committing unlawful confinement, rape, inhuman treatment, torture, and murder, between 12–16 June 1999, in the region of the city of Đakovica in Kosovo, during the armed conflict. According to the indictment, Lekaj, along with other KLA members, captured thirteen non-Albanian civilians (twelve Roma and a Serb) in the middle of a wedding parade and confined them for four days and nights in a basement of a hotel, where they were tortured and sexually assaulted. According to the 1992 FRY Criminal Code, which was in force at the time the alleged acts were committed, the prosecution had to prove that the alleged criminal acts were listed in Article 142 of the Code (War Crimes against Civilians), and that they were committed in violation of a rule of

[161] See the website of the War Crimes Prosecutor's Office <http://tuzilastvorz.org.rs/html_trz/predmeti_cir.htm>.

[162] Of the total number of 114 accused, 91 of them (80 per cent of the total number of accused) are ethnic Serbs. As at the beginning of November 2010, there have been nine first instance trials, with 50 defendants before the War Crimes Chamber. Interview with Trial Monitors of the OSCE Mission to Serbia (Belgrade, 17 November 2010).

[163] War Crimes Chamber of the Belgrade District Court, *Anton Lekaj*, (Judgment) Case No. K.V. 4/05, 1st Instance Verdict (18 September 2006) (in Serbian, unofficial translation in English on file with the author). The ruling was confirmed by the Serbian Supreme Court on 5 April 2007.

international law applicable during armed conflict. Thus, the accusations were based on both the national criminal code and on IHL.[164]

i. The qualification of the conflict and the applicable treaty law

The WCC based its jurisdiction on Article 3 of the War Crimes Law that grants jurisdiction over war crimes committed anywhere in the former Yugoslavia, regardless of the nationality of the accused or of the victim.[165] As a starting point, the WCC defined the nature of the conflict. An accurate qualification of the conflict is of major importance as the applicable IHL treaty law depends on this preliminary determination. The WCC found that in the period relevant to the facts, 12–16 June 1999, two armed conflicts existed—a non-international armed conflict between the KLA and the Federal Republic of Yugoslavia (FRY) and Serbian police forces, and an international armed conflict between NATO and the armed forces of the FRY.[166] This analysis of the facts, which broke down the conflict into its components, follows the doctrine of IHL which recognises that two types of conflicts may exist simultaneously, or that a conflict may be of a mixed character. In such a situation, the law of international armed conflict applies to the fighting between the armed forces of two states. The law of non-international armed conflict applies to the fighting between the government and rebel forces.[167] Yet, while the WCC rightly assessed that the armed conflict in Kosovo was composed of two parallel conflicts, it failed to apply properly the relevant legal framework consequent to this finding. The WCC simultaneously applied both sets of laws to Lekaj's alleged crimes[168]—an impossible situation according to IHL. An act can be connected to either an international armed conflict or to a non-international armed conflict, but not to both at the same time. A more accurate ruling would have been to qualify the acts of Lekaj as being part of the non-international armed conflict and consequently to apply the law applicable to such type of conflict only.

In order to avoid the task of qualifying the conflict, the WCC could have referred solely to customary law rules applicable to both kinds of armed conflicts. Yet, although customary international law may be relied upon by Serbian courts in

[164] International rules mentioned in the indictment included provisions from the Fourth Geneva Convention of 1949 and both Additional Protocols of 1977: Article 2(1) of the Fourth Geneva Convention of 1949 (definition of international armed conflict), Article 3 of the Fourth Geneva Convention of 1949 (non international armed conflict) and Article 27(1) and (2) of the Fourth Geneva Convention of 1949. Article 51 (protection of the civilian population), Article 75 (fundamental guarantees) and Article 76 (protection of women) of the Additional Protocol I of 1977, Article 4(1) and (2)(a, e) and Article 13 of the Additional Protocol II of 1977.

[165] *Anton Lekaj*, (Judgment) Case No. K.V. 4/05, 43.

[166] *Anton Lekaj*, (Judgment) Case No. K.V. 4/05, 8.

[167] See, eg, Marco Sassòli, 'The Legal Qualification of the Conflicts in the Former Yugoslavia: Double Standards or New Horizons for IHL?' in Wang Tieya and Sienho Yee (eds), *International Law in the Post-Cold War World: Essays in Memory of Li Haopei* (London: Routledge, 2001), 314.

[168] The WCC applies simultaneously Article 27 of the Fourth Geneva Convention of 1949, the Additional Protocol I of 1977, the Additional Protocol II of 1977 and Article 3 of the Fourth Geneva Convention of 1949. The Supreme Court of Serbia upheld such an approach when confirming Lekaj's conviction. Supreme Court of Serbia, *Anton Lekaj* (Appeals Judgment) Case No. Kž. I RZ 3/06 (26 February 2007) (in Serbian), 7.

establishing the content of international norms that were violated, by virtue of the chapeau of Article 142 FRY Criminal Code, the WCC did not make any reference to this source of law—not in this case and not in any other. In this regard, the WCC differed from the approach taken by the ICTY, which had not made an explicit qualification of the conflict since the intervention of NATO. In the two first ICTY judgments given in Kosovo, the *Limaj* and *Haradinaj* cases, the ICTY dealt only with what it considered as a non-international armed conflict. This was because the facts were related to events that took place in 1998, before NATO's bombing campaign.[169] It was only on 26 February 2009 in the *Milutinovic* case, that the ICTY rendered a judgment dealing with crimes committed after the beginning of the international armed conflict. In this case the Chamber established that there was an armed conflict starting in 1998, continuing into 1999, and ending with the cessation of the NATO bombing, but without qualifying it in further detail. As the ICTY indictment did not charge grave breaches of the Geneva Conventions, but only violations of customary law applicable to all conflicts, there was no need for the ICTY to determine whether the armed conflict was internal or international.[170]

ii. Protected persons status

As the acts of Lekaj were linked to a non-international armed conflict, the special protected persons regime, regulated in Article 4 of the Fourth Geneva Convention was not applicable. Yet the WCC first finding was that the victims, FRY nationals from Kosovo, were protected persons:

> Such acts of the defendant constitute grave breaches of international humanitarian law as the defendant was a belligerent of the armed conflict (member of the KLA), while the victims were civilians who have not directly taken part in the hostilities, and who were under the status of protected persons pursuant to the Fourth Geneva Convention on protection of civilians during war of 12 August 1949. . . .[171]

The legal status of protected persons grants enemy nationals special protection during international armed conflict. With the aim of adapting the law to the specific conflict in Bosnia, and to include as many civilians as possible under the special protection regime, the ICTY in the *Tadic* case, after qualifying the conflict as international, interpreted the definition of protected persons in a broad manner. The ICTY ruled that the nationality requirement should be interpreted as an

[169] The ICTY case *Prosecutor* v. *Haradinaj et al.*, (Judgment, Trial Chamber) ICTY IT-04-84-T (3 April 2008) concerns crimes allegedly committed in Kosovo between 1 March and 30 September 1998. On the basis of the evidence before it, the ICTY Trial Chamber found that a non-international armed conflict existed in Kosovo from and including 22 April 1998 onwards. The case of *Limaj* includes crimes committed during May–July 1998. During this period the Trial Chamber found the existence of a non-international armed conflict. See *Prosecutor* v. *Limaj et al.*, (Judgment, Trial Chamber) ICTY IT-03-66-T (30 November 2005), paragraph 173.

[170] *Prosecutor* v. *Milutinovic et al.*, (Judgment, Trial Chamber) ICTY IT-05-87 (26 February 2009), paragraph 1217.

[171] Page 26 of the judgment.

allegiance test.[172] When the WCC ruled that civilians of Kosovo, who were FRY nationals, were protected persons, it seemed to apply the *Tadic* allegiance test without explicitly mentioning it. Indeed, the WCC stated on several occasions that the victims had been loyal to the adverse party of the armed conflict.[173] By using the term 'loyal', the WCC appeared implicitly to assert that the allegiance, and not the nationality test, is the legal test applicable to determine who is a protected person. As the allegiance test had been applied only by the ICTY, and not without criticism,[174] it would have been useful for the WCC to have elaborated on this issue and provided an explicit stance on this question.

iii. Conviction

The WCC found that the acts of Lekaj that included rape, murder, torture, and illegal detention violated both the rules of international armed conflict and non-international armed conflict.[175] Although this finding is not accurate, and only the rules of non-international armed conflict apply, i.e. common Article 3 of the Geneva Conventions and Additional Protocol II, the final result remained the same: Lekaj's acts were all illegal according to the law of non-international armed conflict, and therefore were subject to Article 142 of the FRY Criminal Code.

The trial of Lekaj was handled relatively quickly without encountering internal political obstacles. The Belgrade Humanitarian Law Centre, which monitors war crimes trials and represents the victims in most cases, was at first critical of the fact that the case was held before a Serbian court and not before a court in Kosovo. At the end of the trial though it concluded that a fair trial was conducted, and the main problem encountered was the number of witnesses from Kosovo refusing to testify in Belgrade.[176] Indeed, it may not be a coincidence that the first conviction of the WCC was an Albanian from Kosovo in a case in which the victims were Serbs. As the WCC has jurisdiction over crimes regardless of the nationality of the perpetrator, this choice contributed to legitimatize its social standing, before sitting in judgment against Serbians for war crimes—which is today still politically and emotionally very sensitive.

[172] *Prosecutor* v. *Tadic*, (Judgment, Appeals Chamber) ICTY IT-94-1-A (15 July 1999), paragraphs 166 and 168. Likewise, *Prosecutor* v. *Delalić et al. (Čelebići case)*, (Judgment, Appeals Chamber) ICTY IT-96-21-A (20 February 2001), paragraphs 73 and 98; *Prosecutor* v. *Blaskic*, (Judgment, Appeals Chamber) ICTY IT-95-14-A (29 July 2004), paragraph 634.

[173] 'The victims were civilians [..] who did not represent any real threat to the safety of the defendant and other KLA members. The only reason for their treatment in such manner was their ethnicity [..] under the assumption that they collaborated with Serbs [..] and hence KLA members considered them *disloyal* to them.' *Anton Lekaj*, (Judgment) Case No. K.V. 4/05, 39.

[174] See Marco Sassòli and Laura M. Olson, 'The Judgment of the ICTY Appeals Chamber on the Merits in the Tadic Case', *International Review of the Red Cross*, 82/839 (2000), 741.

[175] The WCC mentions Article 3(1) and Article 27 (1) and (2) of the Fourth Geneva Convention of 1949, Articles 51, 75 and 76 of the Additional Protocol I of 1977, Article 4 (1) and (2) and Article 13 of the Additional Protocol I of 1977. *Anton Lekaj*, (Judgment) Case No. K.V. 4/05, 39.

[176] Humanitarian Law Center press release, 'The Trial of Anton Lekaj was Fair Although Conducted Before a Non-Jurisdictional Court' (23 September 2006). Online at <http://www.hlc-rdc.org/?p=12873&lang=de>.

3.2.2 The Scorpions *case*

Unlike *Lekaj*, the *Scorpions* case was a trial with significant political overtones, as it had the potential of involving Serbia with the Srebrenica genocide.[177] The WCC certainly did not ignore this fact. The case dealt with war crimes committed in July 1995 against civilian prisoners brought from Srebrenica to a place near the town of Trnovo in south-east Bosnia. The arrest of the accused in Serbia came immediately after release of a video which showed the brutal shooting of prisoners from Srebrenica by members of the paramilitary unit the 'Scorpions'.[178] The video had been filmed by one of the members of the Scorpions, and ten years later, in 2005, it was screened for the first time before the ICTY. Reactions in Serbia to the screening of the video were immediate. The footage was aired on most of the television stations across the Balkans as well as around the world and had a strong impact on Serbian public opinion. Serbian authorities arrested the paramilitary members shown in the video, including the Scorpions' commander, and their trial commenced on 20 December 2005.

The video became the key evidence in the criminal trial of the Scorpions in Belgrade, but not only there. Between 2005 and 2007, this video evidence was at the centre of major international proceedings before two international jurisdictions—the ICTY and the ICJ—in cases relating to the genocide committed in Srebrenica. These cases raised not only complex legal questions, but also significant political issues. The Scorpions case represents a particular legal situation, in which different international and national jurisdictions dealt with similar facts, and provides us with a rare opportunity to examine their interplay. The next section discusses the international courts' findings on the Scorpions unit which were given before the Belgrade court's decision.

i. The Scorpions video before the ICTY and the ICJ

The Scorpions video was screened for the first time during the cross examination of a defence witness on 1 June 2005 before the ICTY Trial Chamber of the Milošević trial. Carla Del Ponte, the ICTY Chief Prosecutor at that time, describes the screening:

> The film shows a Serbian Orthodox priest blessing members of the paramilitary unit known as the Scorpions... which was affiliated with the Serbian Ministry of the Interior... The monitors showed the six young prisoners led up a hill and into a clearing with tall grass. Two by two, they were shot from behind....[179]

[177] On 2 August 2001 Bosnian Serb Army General Radislav Krstic was the first person to be convicted of genocide by the ICTY. The Appeals Chamber ruled that Krstic should have been convicted only of aiding and abetting genocide, but it confirmed the finding that genocide had taken place in Srebrenica.

[178] The video footage shows six prisoners being brought out of a truck and then led up a hill and into a clearing where they are shot from behind, two by two, by the Scorpions. The entire version of the film is available at <www.bosniafacts.info/web/trnovo_execution_video.php>.

[179] Carla Del Ponte and Chuck Sudetic, *Madame Prosecutor: Confrontations With Humanity's Worst Criminals and the Culture of Impunity* (New York: Other Press, 2009), 322. See also page 32096 of the

By showing the video, the prosecution strategy aimed to prove that the Scorpions had taken an active part in the Srebrenica massacres, and to establish that they had acted as *de facto* agents of the Serbian Ministry of the Interior.[180] If the control by Serbia over the Scorpions was proven, Milošević could be held criminally responsible for committing the genocide in Srebrenica through the doctrine of command responsibility and/or his participation in a joint criminal enterprise as a co-perpetrator.[181] The ICTY Chief Prosecutor affirmed that the prosecution had obtained the necessary evidence to establish, according to the overall control test,[182] the link between the Scorpions and the central command in Belgrade. She referred especially to the secret minutes of the FRY Supreme Defence Council.[183] The minutes and other secret files were provided to the ICTY by the Serbian authorities on condition that they would remain confidential and used only at the trial before the ICTY. Therefore, the ICTY had afforded this evidence protective measures for 'national security criteria', according to Article 54 bis of the ICTY rules of procedures, in a confidential decision of 5 June 2003.[184] As Milošević died in March 2006, a few months before the close of the hearings in his trial, a final ruling on this question was never given. Since that time, the evidence has remained in ICTY's files without having been made public.[185]

In parallel, the ICJ had to determine whether Serbia bore state responsibility for genocide in Bosnia and Herzegovina. Bosnia presented the video of the Scorpions to the court in January 2006:

transcript of the hearing in the *Prosecutor* v. *Slobodan Milošević*, ICTY IT-02-54 *'Kosovo, Croatia and Bosnia'* on 1 June 2005 (The Milošević transcript): 'M. Nice [ICTY prosecutor]: I'm suggesting this film shows Scorpions executing prisoners from Srebrenica. Mr Stevanovic [defense witness]: I am upset, I have to say that this is one of the most monstrous images I have ever seen on a screen. Of course I have never seen anything like this in live.' Online at: <http://icr.icty.org/LegalRef/CMSDocStore/Public/English/Transcript/NotIndexable/IT-02-54/TRS2375R0000127803.doc>.

180 The Milošević Transcript, 40251, 40260, 40267.

181 *Prosecutor* v. *Slobodan Milošević*, (Amended indictment, Bosnia and Herzegovina) ICTY IT-02-54-T (22 November 2002), paragraph 32. For further analysis see Elies van Sliedregt, 'Joint Criminal Enterprise as a Pathway to Convicting Individuals for Genocide', *Journal of International Criminal Justice*, 5/1 (2007), 184–207.

182 The ICTY set the 'overall control' test to establish which organ constitutes a *de facto* state agent in *Prosecutor* v. *Tadic*, paragraph 160. This test differs from the test established by the ICJ.

183 Del Ponte and Sudetic, *Madame Prosecutor*, 173, 202, 357 (n 179). This was also affirmed by Florence Hartmann, a former spokesperson of the ICTY Office of the Prosecutor, in Florence Hartmann, *Paix et Châtiment. Les guerres Secrètes de la Politique et de la Justice Internationales* (Paris: Flammarion, 2007), 103–4, 114–22.

184 Hartmann, Paix et Châtiment, 122 (n 183). On 14 September 2009 Florence Hartmann was convicted of contempt of the Tribunal by the ICTY for revealing these facts. *The Case against Florence Hartmann*, (Judgment on Allegations of Contempt) ICTY IT-02-54-R77.5 (14 September 2009).

185 Yet, the ICTY Chamber found that there was prima facie evidence to establish Milošević's responsibility in committing genocide. *Prosecutor* v. *Slobodan Milošević*, (Decision on Motion for Judgment of Acquittal, Trial Decisions) ICTY IT-02-54-T (16 June 2004).

There was no denial of the fact of the relocation of the "Scorpions" to Trnovo. The Applicant during the oral proceedings presented video material showing the execution by paramilitaries of six Bosnian Muslims, in Trnovo, in July 1995.[186]

The applicants aimed to prove the *de facto* link between the unit and the Serbian state. It was the applicants' position to attribute the acts of the Scorpions, including the massacres at Srebrenica, to the FRY according to the principles of state responsibility. Unlike the ICTY, the ICJ applied the effective control test to define who was a *de facto* state agent, as it had already established in the *Nicaragua* case.[187] Bosnia requested the ICJ to call upon Serbia and Montenegro, to produce 'the "redacted" sections of documents of the Supreme Defence Council of the Respondent, i.e. sections in which parts of the text had been blacked out so as to be illegible'.[188] The ICJ refrained from doing so, arguing that Bosnia 'has extensive documentation and other evidence available to it, especially from the readily accessible ICTY records'.[189] Judge Al Khasawneh in his dissenting opinion labelled this reasoning as 'worse than its failure to act', and he added that 'it is a reasonable expectation that those documents would have shed light on the central questions of intent and attribution'.[190] Also Kandic points out that it is not clear why the ICJ did not engage in revealing all the necessary evidence.[191] On 26 February 2007, the ICJ held in its judgment that the act of genocide at Srebrenica could not be attributed to the FRY as, among other things, it had not been proven that the Scorpions were acting under its effective control.[192]

It remains unknown whether the evidence held by the ICTY would have satisfied the ICJ's effective control test and established the status of the Scorpions as *de facto* agents of the FRY (and whether this finding would have resulted in

[186] *Case Concerning the Application of the Convention on the Prevention and Punishment of the Crime of Genocide (Bosnia and Herzegovina* v. *Serbia and Montenegro)* (Judgment), ICJ Report 2007, 43, paragraph 289.

[187] *Case Concerning Military and Paramilitary Activities in and against Nicaragua (Nicaragua* v. *United States of America)* (Judgment), 27 June 1986. In *Case Concerning the Application of the Convention on the Prevention and Punishment of the Crime of Genocide* (n 186), the Court tried to reconcile its previous *Nicaragua* judgment and the ICTY *Tadic* judgment, by stating that the test applicable to determine state's responsibility (effective control) can differ from the one that determines individual criminal responsibility (overall control) (*Case Concerning the Application of the Convention on the Prevention and Punishment of the Crime of Genocide*, paragraphs 402–405). This approach was previously rejected by the ICTY in *Prosecutor* v. *Tadic*, paragraph 104. See also Antonio Cassese, 'On the Use of Criminal Law Notions in Determining State Responsibility for Genocide', *Journal of International Criminal Justice*, 5/4 (2007), 875–87; Marco Sassòli and Laura M. Olson, 'Prosecutor v. Tadic (Judgment), Case No. IT-94-a-A. 38 ILM 1518 (1999)', *American Journal of International Law*, 94/3 (2000), 575.

[188] *Case Concerning the Application of the Convention on the Prevention and Punishment of the Crime of Genocide*, paragraphs 44, 205 (n 186).

[189] *Case Concerning the Application of the Convention on the Prevention and Punishment of the Crime of Genocide*, paragraph 206 (n 186).

[190] Dissenting opinion of Judge Al Khasawneh, paragraph 35. See also dissenting opinion of Judge Mahiou, paragraph 56.

[191] 'Why the ICJ did not engage in a thorough investigation, of the status of the Scorpions, why it did not deal with these papers which contain the data [..] why the judges did not look for additional evidence providing the participation of the MUP of Serbia in Trnovo'; Humanitarian Law Center, 'Regional Debate on the Judgment by the ICJ on Genocide' (Transcript) (29 June 2007), 37.

[192] *Case Concerning the Application of the Convention on the Prevention and Punishment of the Crime of Genocide*, paragraph 395 (n 186).

establishing the responsibility of the FRY for the Srebrenica genocide). At the same time, according to Carla Del Ponte and Florence Hartmann (the former spokesperson of the ICTY Prosecutor's Office) the protection provided to the FRY's Defence Council minutes (on the basis of national security) was related to the fact that the ICJ were dealing with the genocide case at the same time. While the Serbian government accepted that it had to provide the evidence related to the trial of Milošević, one of Serbia's main concerns was that if it were found by the ICJ to be responsible for genocide, the compensation that it could be required to pay would destroy the country's economy. Therefore, the Serbian government wanted insurance that the evidence could not be used in the ICJ proceeding.[193] This revelation well illustrates that political pressures bring international courts to make compromises too, and that fact-finding is not merely a neutral task of revealing the truth, but often involves political decisions.[194] Such pressures at international level, which can be fairly expected to be even more influential on the national jurisdiction, frame the limits of the rule of law within the international legal order, and demonstrate the deficiency of the potential impact of these international jurisdictions on the Belgrade court. This deficiency occurred not only because of the factual background that remained blurred following the ICTY protective measures, but, more worryingly, because of the international jurisdictions' divergence at the doctrinal level. Both the ICTY and ICJ were required to rule if the paramilitary unit was a *de facto* organ of the state of the Federal Republic of Yugoslavia. The Belgrade WCC had to rule on the same issue. As remarkable as it may seem, far away from the Hague, each international jurisdiction, ICTY and the ICJ, applied a different legal test to establish whether the Scorpions were a *de facto* state organ. As a result, the legal message sent from the Hague is that the legal test to determine a *de facto* state organ depends on the jurisdiction that is required to apply it. Which of these tests is supposed to be applied by the national court in Belgrade? As this answer was not provided by the Hague, Belgrade could simply choose the test that brought about the more convenient political result.

ii. The *Scorpions* case before the Belgrade WCC

On 10 April 2007, less than two months after the ICJ rendered its judgment, the WCC convicted four members of the Scorpions, including their commander, but found no link between the Scorpions to the FRY, as was claimed by the victims.[195] In the indictment it was alleged that the crime had taken place on 16 or 17 July

[193] Del Ponte and Sudetic, *Madame Prosecutor*, 356–7 and Hartmann, *Paix et Châtiment*, 159–62 (n 183).

[194] Shapiro, *Courts: A Comparative*, 42 (n 2).

[195] War Crimes Chamber of the Belgrade District Court, *Slobodan Medić et al. (Scorpions case)*, (Judgment) Case No. K.V. 6/2005 (10 April 2007). Slobodan Medić, the commander of the Scorpions, and Branislav Medić, were sentenced to 20 years in prison. One of the accused who pleaded guilty, was sentenced to 13 years, and the last one, convicted for aiding and abetting, was sentenced to five years' imprisonment, the minimum sentence prescribed for war crimes. In 2008, the Supreme Court reduced the term of imprisonment of Branislav Medić from 20 to 15 years. For criticism on the level of punishments see Bogdan Ivanišević, 'Against the Current—War Crimes Prosecutions in Serbia (2007)', *International Center for Transitional Justice* (2008), 17.

1995, that the accused, Slobodan Medić, commander of the Scorpions unit, had received an order by his superior from the Army of Republika Srpska to execute the prisoners, and that the prisoners who were shot had been brought from Srebrenica. However, in its ruling, the WCC portrayed the acts documented in the video as an isolated incident. The broader context of the war and the massacres in Srebrenica, were totally lacking. The WCC ruled that it could not establish if the unit had received an order from a higher command than Republika Srpska. Also not established was the exact date of the commission of the crime, and whether the victims arrived from Srebrenica. This was despite the fact that the victims' family members who testified confirmed that all the victims had been from Srebrenica and they had disappeared shortly after Serbian forces had entered the town on 11 July 1995. Unlike the ICTY, which qualified the conflict in Bosnia in some of its judgments as international, whereas in others did not qualify it at all, the WCC categorized the conflict in Bosnia in 1995 as a non-international armed conflict.[196] In its conclusion it also ruled that the Scorpions had been subordinated only to the army of the Bosnian Serb entity Republika Srpska. It clearly established that the army of Republika Srpska had no connection with the FRY, without specifying what legal test it applied in reaching this conclusion. According to the court, no proof was shown in its formation, organization or function which pointed to the Scorpions being a special unit of the Ministry of the Interior of Serbia.[197] While an accurate legal analysis would have required a reference to one of the doctrines, it referred only to whether the evidence was reliable:

> There have been no written proofs shown to the Court as an official act, to point at the formation, organization and function, as well as status or belongings of this unit, on the basis of what it could have been determined that the unit "Scorpions" was formed as a special unit of MUP of Serbia . . . None of the authority organs who mentioned the link between the "Scorpions" and the MUP of Serbia delivered to the Court any official documents whether the original or not, but only operative information . . . the Court couldn't establish any link between the "Scorpions" and the MUP of Serbia in this specific period.[198]

[196] See *Slobodan Medić et al. (Scorpions case)*, paragraph 13.3. After establishing in *Tadic* that the FRY exercised overall control of the army of Republika Srpska, the ICTY qualified the conflict in Bosnia as an international armed conflict. In *Milošević*, the ICTY prosecution also qualified the conflict as an international armed conflict, see *Prosecutor* v. *Milošević*, (Second Amended indictment) ICTY IT-02-54-T (22 November 2002). Yet, the ICTY qualification of the conflict as international was not without controversy. See Theodor Meron, 'Classification of Armed Conflict in the Former Yugoslavia, Nicaragua's Fallout', *American Journal of International Law*, 93/2 (1998), 237–9. See also Sassòli and Olson, 'Prosecutor v. Tadic (Judgment)', 575.

[197] *Slobodan Medić et al. (Scorpions case)*, paragraph 13.4. According to the Belgrade Humanitarian Law Center, 'in reaching its Decision the Trial Chamber was clearly influenced by political rather than judicial reasons. This is reflected in its intention to adjust its position to that of Serbia's authorities with respect to the genocide in Srebrenica in the context of the International Court of Justice decision'. Humanitarian Law Center, 'War Crimes Trials in Serbia' (December 2007), 7–8. Online at <www.hlc-rdc.org/uploads/editor/War%20Crimes%20Trials%20in%20Serbia%20Report.pdf>.

[198] Paragraph 13.4 of the WCC decision. According to the Belgrade Humanitarian Law Center 'The Trial Chamber accepted [..] that the Scorpions unit is considered to be a paramilitary formation. Such an allegation is contrary to the evidence, primarily the documents of the ICTY, which were presented as evidence before the Trial Chamber, the statement of witness Tomislav Kovač, a former Minister of Interior of the Republika Srpska, who did not dispute the claim that he and his colleagues

Although it convicted four Serbs originally from Croatia who were members of the paramilitary unit the 'Scorpions',[199] the WCC ruled that being under the sole command of the army of *Republika* Srpska, no link between the paramilitary unit and the state of Serbia could be established. The Scorpions' crimes were portrayed as an isolated act, unconnected with the ongoing Srebrenica genocide.[200] According to the Belgrade Humanitarian Law Center (HLC), the testimonies of the victims' families, confirmed that all the victims were from Srebrenica and that they had disappeared shortly after Serbian forces entered the town on 11 July 1995 and,

> the position of the Trial Chamber can only be explained by political motives whose objective is to separate the execution of the six Bosniak civilians from the killing of 8,000 Bosniaks from Srebrenica in the period from 11 July to 19 July 1995.[201]

In this case, although the convicts were Serbs, the WCC ruling was in line with the political interest of the state. It did not engage in connecting their acts with the broader context of genocide which was going on at that time and place, nor did it establish any link with the central command in Belgrade. At the same time, the national court was not operating in a legal vacuum. On the contrary, the international jurisdictions themselves, the ICJ and ICTY, provided the legal tools on doctrinal and factual levels to reach this politically convenient ruling.

3.3 Prosecution policy between 2003–2013

The OWCP established in 2003 is reluctant to indict high-ranking officials. This reluctance is based on the unwillingness to prosecute on the basis of command responsibility, which is absent from the FRY Criminal Code applicable to war

signed telegrams and reports describing the Scorpions unit as a MUP Serbia Unit or a unit of the Department of Internal Affairs of the Republic of Serbia. [..] In reaching its Decision the Trial Chamber was clearly influenced by political rather than judicial reasons. This is reflected in its intention to adjust its position to that of Serbia's authorities with respect to the genocide in Srebrenica in the context of the International Court of Justice Decision.' 'War Crimes Trials in Serbia' (December 2007), 7–8 (n 197).

199 *Slobodan Medić et al. (Scorpions case)*. Slobodan Medic, the commander of the Scorpions, and Branislav Medić, were sentenced to 20 years in prison. One of the accused who pleaded guilty, was sentenced to 13 years, and the last one, convicted as an accomplice, was sentenced to five years' imprisonment, the minimum sentence prescribed for war crimes. In 2008, the Supreme Court reduced the term of imprisonment of Branislav Medić from 20 to 15 years. For critics on the level of punishments, see Ivanišević, 'Against the Current', 17, (n 195); 'War Crimes Trials in Serbia' (December 2007), 7 (n 197).

200 On 2 August 2001 Bosnian Serb Army General Radislav Krstic was the first person to be convicted of genocide by the ICTY. According to the Trial chamber it had been proved 'beyond any reasonable doubt that a crime of genocide was committed in Srebrenica.' The Appeals Chamber ruled that Krstic should have been convicted only of aiding and abetting genocide, but it confirmed the finding that genocide had taken place in Srebrenica.

201 'War Crimes Trials in Serbia' (December 2007), 7 (n 197); see also Ivanišević, 'Against the Current', 16, (n 195). It is interesting to note that another domestic court was dealing with the Scorpions video. In 2005 the Court of Zagreb, one of the four specially designated courts in Croatia for war crimes cases, tried Slobodan Davidovic, a Serb from Croatia, who was one of the members of the Scorpions shown in the footage. He was sentenced for the same crime to 14 years' imprisonment.

crimes prosecutions in Serbia. The new Serbian criminal code of 2006 includes command responsibility.[202] The OWCP refuses to rely on the principle of command responsibility based on the argument that it violates the principle of non-retroactivity of harsher criminal law. At the same time, command responsibility could be 'imported' and applied by Serbian courts through international law—which is a binding law.[203] The sole case leading to a conviction on the basis of command responsibility is the *Zvornik II* case, despite command responsibility not being mentioned expressly in the judgment. In 2010, Branko Popović was sentenced by the Belgrade High Court to 15 years' imprisonment because he failed to prevent crimes committed by his subordinates against Bosnian Muslim hostages. As the commander of the Zvornik Territorial Defense, he was found guilty for 'aiding and abetting by omission', i.e. his conviction relied on the command responsibility principle.[204]

However the OWCP did not change its strategy. The *Zvornik II* judgment continues the policy of only indicting (and ultimately convicting) immediate perpetrators and not prosecuting those higher in the responsible chain of command. Since the establishment of the OWCP in 2003, two cases have dealt with low-ranking officers (the *Lovas* and *Ćuška* cases) and only one with a mid-ranking officer (the *Suva Reka* case). The first judgment was handed down in April 2009 in the *Suva Reka* case, leading to the acquittal of the main accused. The second judgment was handed down in June 2012 in the *Lovas case*, and the highest-ranking officer in this case was sentenced to ten years' imprisonment. The *Ćuška* case is still on trial.

3.3.1 The Suva Reka *case (2009)*

In the *Suva Reka* case, Radoslav Mitrović, commander of the detachment of the Special Police Unit of the Ministry of Interior (Republic of Serbia) was acquitted on 23 April 2009.[205] He was indicted, along with other members of the Special Police Unit, for having committed war crimes during the Kosovo conflict, in Suva Reka. They were accused of having unlawfully killed on 26 March 1999 fifty Albanian civilians, including nineteen juveniles and women. The War Crimes Department of the Belgrade Higher Court acquitted Mitrović, along with Nenad Jovanović[206] and Zoran Petkovic,[207] on the grounds that it could not be proved beyond reasonable doubt that they had committed the crimes they were charged with. The fact that the OWCP dropped charges against Ramiz Papić, a police officer of

[202] Article 384 of the 2006 Serbian Criminal Code.

[203] See Article 142 of the FRY Criminal Code discussed at 3.1.1.

[204] For a more detailed analysis, Humanitarian Law Center, 'Trials for War Crimes and Ethnically Motivated Crimes in Serbia in 2010', 10–13. Accessible at <http://www.hlc-rdc.org/wp-content/uploads/2012/06/Reports-on-war-crimes-trials-in-the-Republic-of-Serbia-2010.pdf>. I wish to thank Carine Placzek from the Belgrade Humanitarian Law Center for her research assistance on that topic.

[205] *Judgment K.V.2/2006*. See Humanitarian Law Center, 'Trials for War Crimes and Ethnically Motivated Crimes in Serbia in 2010', 41–58 (n 204).

[206] Deputy Police Commander of the Department of Interior in Suva Reka.

[207] Member of the Territorial Defence in Suva Reka.

the Department of Interior in Suva Reka was very controversial. Only four defendants,[208] who were not even low-level perpetrators, were convicted for the murder of the fifty civilians. Appeals were filed against the decision and on 30 June 2010, the Belgrade Appellate Court[209] dismissed the appeals, confirming the conviction of three of them,[210] and confirming the acquittal of Mitrović, Jovanović and Petković. According to the HLC, this case is illustrative of the OWCP's persistent refusal to prosecute high-level commanders. In the present case, not a single member of the Ministry of Interior nor officers of the Yugoslav People's Army were indicted, when they could have been prosecuted on the basis of command responsibility.[211] The HLC noticed that similar events occurred in Suva Reka involving the same commanders of the Special Police Unit, as well as members of the Ministry of Interior and the Yugoslav People's Army. Between 22–25 March, forty-three Albanian civilians were killed in Suva Reka, i.e. just a few days before the killing of the fifty civilians involved in the case against Radoslav Mitrović. According to the HLC,

> it remains unclear how the prosecutor responsible for prosecuting cases of war crimes requested an investigation and then filed an indictment against persons responsible for the killing of 50 civilians committed on 26th March 1999, but failed to take the same action for the killings of 43 Albanian civilians which were committed by the same commanders and executors on the previous days—22nd and 25th March 1999.[212]

The OWCP's actions can hardly be justified on legal grounds, and clearly demonstrate the unwillingness to prosecute high-ranking commanders.

3.3.2 The Lovas *case (2012)*

The *Lovas* case,[213] is a complex case dealing with war crimes committed against the Croatian civilian population between October and November 1991 in Lovas, Croatia. For the first time the court itself criticized the OWCP for not prosecuting high-ranking members of the Yugoslav People's Army.

In June 2012 the Belgrade Higher Court did convict middle-rank officers for committing war crimes against the Croatian civilian population. Željko Krnjajić, the commander of the Tovarnik police station, who had been in command of an armed group composed of twenty officers from the police station and a number of

[208] Radojko Repanović, Commander of the Police Department in Suva Reka, Slađan Čukarić, a police officer from a regular police unit, Mirislav Petković, a police officer from a reserve police unit in Suva Reka, and Milorad Nišavić, a member of the State Security Agency (DB) branch department in Suva Reka.

[209] *Judgment K-Po2 4/2010.*

[210] Radojko Repanović was tried by another trial chamber, which also convicted him on 15 December 2010 for war crimes against civilians (*Judgment K-Po2-49/2010*).

[211] Humanitarian Law Center, 'Report on War Crimes Trials in Serbia in 2012', 43. Online at <http://www.hlc-rdc.org/wp-content/uploads/2013/02/Report-on-war-crimes-trials-in-Serbia-in-2012-ENG-FF.pdf>.

[212] 'Report on War Crimes Trials in Serbia in 2012' (n 211).

[213] *Judgment K-Po2-22/10*. See also 'Report on War Crimes Trials in Serbia in 2012', 53–61 (n 211). The indictment is available at <www.tuzilastvorz.org.rs>.

volunteers, was sentenced to ten years' imprisonment; Miodrag Dimitrijević, the most senior officer in Lovas in 1991, was sentenced to ten years' imprisonment, and Ljuban Devetak, the highest *de facto* commander of the militia group, was sentenced to twenty years' imprisonment.[214] At the same time, the court ruled that these acts were perpetrated under the orders of the Second Proletarian Guard Motorized Brigade of the Yugoslav People's Army. The court emphasized that higher-ranking officers should have been convicted:

> the command of the Second Proletarian Guard Mechanized Brigade of the JNA was to be held primarily responsible for the attack on Lovas, the manner it was carried out and everything that had happened during the said attack, despite the fact that none of its members was indicted for it.[215]

According to the court, convincing pieces of evidence emerged during the proceedings demonstrating the personal responsibility of the commander of that brigade Dušan Lončar, a colonel of the Yugoslav People's Army. But, despite the existence of convincing evidence the OWCP did not indict Dušan Lončar or any member of the Yugoslav People's Army in the chain of command.[216]

3.3.3 The Bytyqi *case (2012)*

The reluctance of the OWCP to prosecute higher-ranking officers is demonstrated in cases such as the *Bytyqi* case[217] and the *Beli Manastir* case.[218] The *Bytyqi* case concerned crimes committed by commanders of the 124th Intervention Brigade of the Serbian Ministry of Interior's Special Police Units during the Kosovo conflict in 1999. Sreten Popović, commander of the Operational Pursuit Group of the 124th Brigade, and Miloš Stojanović, commander of a squad in this platoon, were accused of aiding and abetting war crimes against prisoners of war—namely the killing of the Bytyqi brothers. According to the HLC, such events could not have happened without the knowledge of senior officers of the Ministry of Interior. However, those higher-level commanders were not indicted by the OWCP.[219] The OWCP only indicted Sreten Popović and Miloš Stojanović—lower-ranking commanders.

Moreover, the Belgrade Higher Court had to acquit Popović and Stojanović as the prosecution failed to prove the allegations. The court underlined that because of inconsistencies and contradictions in the OWCP indictment itself, it was not possible to prove where the Bytyqi brothers were murdered and who killed them.

214 *Judgement K-Po2-22/10.*
215 'Report on War Crimes Trials in Serbia in 2012', 53 (n 211).
216 'Report on War Crimes Trials in Serbia in 2012', 59 (n 211).
217 *Judgment K-Po2 51/2010.*
218 *Judgment K-Po2 45/2010.* On the *Bytyqi* case, see 'Report on War Crimes Trials in Serbia in 2012', 50–52 (n 211).
219 'Report on War Crimes Trials in Serbia in 2012', 52 (n 211).

3.3.4 The Beli Manastir *case (2012)*

Similarly, this case illustrates the unwillingness of the OWCP to prosecute higher-ranking officers and to bring indictments on the basis of command responsibility. In the *Beli Manastir* case, on 19 June 2012 the court convicted Zoran Vukšić (twenty years), Slobodan Strigić (ten years), Brank Hrnjak (five years) and Velimir Bertić (eighteen months) for war crimes committed against the civilian population in the Croatian town of Beli Manastir between August and December 1991. Notwithstanding these convictions, the OWCP failed to indict higher-level commanders, although the court ruled that Vukšić's superiors were aware of crimes being carried out but failed to prosecute perpetrators, allowing further atrocities to be committed.

According to the HLC:

> It is not clear why the TRZ [Office of the War Crimes Prosecutor] has not prosecuted these officials to date, although the facts established during this trial suggest that all legal prerequisites have been met for such an action. The court is bound to act within the limits of the indictment of the TRZ, which de facto creates a criminal case and, in particular, defines its scope, by determining which persons are to stand trial. The way in which the TRZ acted in this case, shows that the TRZ has continued with the practice of prosecuting only direct perpetrators and not those who, as their superiors, were at least as responsible for the crimes as the direct perpetrators.[220]

3.4 Patterns and trends

The analysis of the *Lekaj* and *Scorpions* cases shows that both served the interests of the state well. In easy cases, such as the *Lekaj* case, the WCC legitimizes its institutional function in the eyes of its own society and the international community. This legitimacy is important for the interests of Serbia in its post-conflict era. Indeed, one of the fears raised by a judge of the WCC was the following:

> The existence of political will [to prosecute war criminals] should not be confused with illegitimate political pressure to obtain convictions. This is exactly the danger of war crimes trials carried out in the legal systems of countries in transition. War crimes convictions are often seen as the most powerful manifestation of a society's readiness to come to terms with the past. This approach, if taken to extremes, can create a paradoxical situation in which confronting crimes could be carried out by means of new and illegal acts that would, in the case of court proceedings, violate the right to a fair trial, and as a further consequence undermine the independence of the judiciary.[221]

At the same time, in hard cases, such as the *Scorpions* case, the court could not establish direct involvement of the prior government in the commissioning of the genocide in Srebrenica. This also fits the interest of the government: some of the

[220] 'Report on War Crimes Trials in Serbia in 2012', 70 (n 211).

[221] Miodrag Majić and Dušan Ignjatović, 'Ten Lessons from Serbia's Experience in War Crimes Issues', FICHL Policy Brief Series No. 9 (2012). Miodrag Majić is a judge at the Belgrade War Crimes Chamber.

officials are still in the same positions as before the change of the regime. More generally the society has not yet accomplished the revision of its national historical narrative and maintains a high level of sensitivity on this issue. As at May 2013, all cases so far have punished low-ranking soldiers. One might conclude that the reluctance of the OWCP to prosecute high-ranked military and police officials is a result of political pressures or self-imposed restraints. Prosecution of immediate low-level perpetrators appears to be more opportune.

3.4.1 The ability of the WCC to apply international law

The *Lekaj* and *Scorpions* cases reveal two observations related to the capacity of the WCC to apply international law as required by the rule of law doctrine. First, it can be noted that the level of IHL expertise of the judges falls short. In the Serbian legal framework, in which the WCC is explicitly required by the Serbian criminal code to apply international law in order to convict alleged war criminals, knowledge of international law is a fundamental requirement from a domestic perspective. Yet, as demonstrated in *Lekaj*, international treaty law is not accurately applied and references to international jurisprudence and customary law are lacking. At the same time, judges refer to international treaty law, although not always explicitly or accurately, and perceive it as an authoritative legal framework. Such poor application of international law is down to two issues: lack of skills and deference to a legal tradition that often sees international law merely as a required referencing formality. The WCC's poor application of international law is thus due to lack of expertise rather than as a result of a negative stance towards international law or the ICTY, on whose experience and evidentiary material the WCC relies heavily.[222] This problem could be ameliorated by improving the skills and knowledge of legal practitioners and by developing a legal culture in which judgments address not only factual, but also legal questions.

A second observation relates to the capacity of the court to reconcile political goals with valid international legal arguments. National courts in post-conflict situations are supposed to combat impunity; international law is supposed to provide them with a neutral framework to do this task. At the same time, political choices made by judges while interpreting the law or establishing the facts are an integral part of the rule of law as long as the law is not distorted and the legal framework is respected. While both international and local courts may be influenced by political pressure and interests, as the *Scorpions* case demonstrates, the striking difference between them is their material capacity to incorporate these political goals into the legal framework of international law. For example, it can be argued (although not affirmatively confirmed) that the ICTY and the ICJ relied on two distinct control doctrines in order to reach a desired conclusion in light of the evidence at their disposal. At the same time, each jurisdiction provided an extensive legal argument in support of their political choice. By contrast, the WCC relied

222 Weill and Jovanovic, 'National War Crimes Prosecution in Post-Conflict Era', 264 (n 138).

almost exclusively on fact-finding and did not develop any legal justification on a doctrinal level. While the WCC's final conclusion is predictable as a matter of policy, the absence of doctrinal argument seems to be related to the judges' professional deficiency, as the court could have easily relied on the ICJ ruling to attain the result it opted for. Yet, having relied on a poor legal basis, the apologist role of the court is more evident.

3.4.2 The willingness of the WCC to apply international law

In a post-conflict society, rule of law reform needs to be capable of serving justice on all sides of the conflict—however unpalatable politically. It is fundamental that the law is enforced in an equal manner, without having national interests prevail, which could lead to a double standards application. Having said that, one should be conscious of the limits of the court as a state institution. When the legislative framework promotes equal enforcement of international law—as it does in the case of Serbia—it is fundamental to observe whether international law is enforced in an equal manner irrespective of who is the victim and perpetrator, or whether the courts use double standards in their application of international law. In the case of the latter, does the double standard phenomenon result from institutional deficiency of the judiciary and lack of independence? Or does it arise from a policy of restraint of the courts that is, to a certain extent, predictable and inevitable in order to safeguard their legitimacy at the domestic level? The trial of Lekaj, in which the court was judging the conduct of what the majority in Serbia perceived as the enemy side, was handled relatively quickly, without encountering internal political obstacles. One has to bear in mind that only a few cases were completed in several years as a number of them were remanded for re-trial as a result of decisions by the previous Supreme Court of Serbia, which were considered by many observers as dubious.[223] It may not be a mere coincidence that the first conviction of the WCC confirmed on appeal was an Albanian from Kosovo in a case in which the victims included a Serb. While this choice could be perceived as a double standards attitude exercised by the court, its motivation could have related to legitimate institutional considerations: this first case could contribute to the perception of legitimacy of the court within Serbian society. Given the political and emotional sensitivity of war crimes prosecutions against Serbs, still in existence today, a legitimacy needed to be acquired in order to secure its future institutional function.

At the same time, the *Scorpions* case portrays well the limits of the Belgrade court. Although the WCC convicted four Serbian members of the Scorpions paramilitary unit, the WCC ruling was in line with the political interest of the state; it did not engage in connecting the defendants' acts with the broader context of genocide that

[223] There are reports suggesting that the decisions of the Supreme Court in quashing several first instance convictions against Serb defendants went against facts established at the trial in an attempt to avoid taking unpopular responsibility to confirm convictions of Serbs. Ivanišević, 'Against the Current', 18–19 (n 195); Human Rights Watch, 'Unfinished Business Serbia's War Crimes Chamber' (HRW Report, 28 June 2007), 30–1.

was going on at the time, nor establish any link with the command in Belgrade. The Scorpions' crimes were portrayed as an isolated act, lacking any reference to the ongoing Srebrenica genocide.[224] Yet, the outcome of the ruling was predictable and it seems that such restrictions on the rule of law are still inevitable. In the Balkans' post-conflict political context, it is hardly imaginable that a national court would reach a ruling that would allow an admission of genocide in opposition to the state's official narrative. National courts of democratic states with a long tradition of judicial independence have developed different self-restraint doctrines—such as the act of state doctrine or the political question doctrine (discussed in the next chapter)—in order to avoid giving rulings on issues with colossal political consequences. Emerging democratic states in a post-conflict era have to deal with sensitive issues of reconciliation on a daily basis. Not only that, they have to surmount numerous economic obstacles as well. Their courts are supposed to take these fragilities into account, probably more and certainly not less than any other court in a stable and powerful state. Therefore, in post-conflict societies, the judiciary alone cannot provide the required justice reform unless it is supported by other mechanisms that reinforce its local position.

4. Concluding observations

As this chapter shows, courts legitimize states' acts and policies even if this involves a distortion of the law. It is suggested that this kind of application of the law must remain outside the valid choices available under the rule of law. Misuse of international law by national jurisdictions may have far-reaching negative consequences beyond the specific facts of the case over the long term. Such misuse as this promotes development of bad law, which runs the risk of being cited and adopted by other national jurisdictions. Given that political objectives are to a certain degree irresistible, especially when dealing with armed conflicts, the following chapters propose other ways, which may be more acceptable from the rule of law perspective, to address these political constraints.

[224] As the NGO observing the trial reported: 'the position of the Trial Chamber can only be explained by political motives whose objective is to separate the execution of the six Bosniak civilians from the killing of 8,000 Bosniaks from Srebrenica in the period from July 11 to July 19, 1995.' 'War Crimes Trials in Serbia' (December 2007), 7, fn 82 (n 197); see also Ivanišević, 'Against the Current', 16, (n 195).

2

The Avoiding Role of National Courts: Law as a Political Doctrine

> [International] courts have examined the legal aspects of the conduct of armies. . . . Why do those questions, which are justiciable in international courts, cease to be justiciable in national tribunals?
>
> Justice Barak, Israeli High Court of Justice (HCJ)[1]

Access to court is a constitutional right in democratic states, and an important pillar of the rule of law. Yet, although '[t]here is always a legal norm according to which the dispute can be solved',[2] judges in domestic courts have developed avoidance doctrines. These doctrines work by allowing courts to refrain from exercising their established jurisdiction. As a result, states are shielded from the judicial scrutiny of domestic courts. These doctrines include the US 'act of state doctrine', which was labelled by Lord Nicholls as a 'self-denying principle'[3] and the 'political question doctrine', better known in the UK as the '*Buttes* non-justiciability principle'. Similarly, the domestic doctrines on immunity, such as the UK 'act of state' and 'combat immunity' serve to achieve an equivalent goal.[4] These justiciability doctrines are invoked in the preliminary stages of proceeding. By their application, or their rejection, the courts design their own role in applying IHL because when a legal question remains outside of the courts' jurisdiction, the question is then left in the political arena. These doctrines allow courts to decline jurisdiction in questions involving matters of IHL—often referred to by courts, not as a branch of law but as a *foreign policy* matter—a category referred to as 'highly suspect' by Thomas Franck.[5]

[1] HCJ 769/02, *The Public Committee against Torture in Israel et al.* v. *The Government of Israel et al.*, (2006), paragraph 53 (In English at <http://elyon1.court.gov.il/files_eng/02/690/007/a34/02007690.a34.pdf>).

[2] HCJ 769/02, *The Public Committee against Torture in Israel*, paragraph 48 (n 1).

[3] *R* v. *Bow Street Metropolitan Stipendiary Magistrate Ex parte Pinochet Ugarte (No.1)* (1998) 3 WLR 1456 (HL 1998), 117.

[4] However, the international rule on state immunity is of a different nature. Unlike the act of state or the political question doctrines, state immunity is not a domestic judge-made rule on justiciability (or admissibility) but an international procedural law rule that limits courts' jurisdiction. The international rule on state immunity is based on the founding principle of equality and sovereignty of nations set out in the UN Charter. See Andrea Bianchi, 'Serious Violations of Human Rights and Foreign States' Accountability Before Municipal Courts' in Lal Chand Vohrar (ed.), *Man's Inhumanity to Man. Essays in Honour of Judge Antonio Cassese* (The Hague/London/Boston: Kluwer Law International, 2003), 164. For a further discussion on international state immunity and domestic immunity doctrines, see Chapter 5.

[5] Franck, *Political Questions/Judicial Answers: Does the Rule of Law Apply to Foreign Affairs?* (Princeton: Princeton University Press, 1992), 8.

Recourse to avoidance doctrines may be justified in light of the difficulty in evaluating evidence in foreign cases and in applying legal standards to policy questions. There is too the issue of whether judges have the requisite expertise in these matters and the institutional fear of judges that a decision will be ignored by the executive.[6] However, avoidance usually also serves political goals which are not always visible. When courts choose not to pronounce on the legality of a state's action, or not to denounce its possible illegality, they do not confer explicit legitimacy upon the executive nor grant legal justification to its acts. Rather, they shield the state from judicial review and allow it to pursue its political objectives free of legal constraints. Yet, when a case is declared by the court as non-justiciable, it appears that the judiciary is not only deferring to the political branch, but is also, implicitly, condoning the action. Deeper examinations of cases in which these doctrines are not applied—either by their rejection or by defining their exceptions—support this assumption. Studies have shown that a court is more likely to render a decision on the merits in cases involving foreign relations or military affairs, when the case results in a finding in favour of the state.[7]

The first part of the chapter presents the origin and development of two of these avoidance techniques: the act of state and the political question doctrines. Their rationales, scope of application, and exceptions that have been constructed by the courts over the years, are discussed. The second part of the chapter critically analyses different case law within the given political context in which they were decided. It is demonstrated how these doctrines are applied in practice. The aim of the chapter is to show how the use of avoidance doctrines raises problems—from the rule of law perspective—particularly for access to the court and remedies for law violations, scrutiny over the executive's acts, and the unequal application of the doctrines in the first place.

1. The construction of avoidance doctrines

> The act of state doctrine depends on public policy as perceived by the courts.[8]
>
> Lord Steyn, UK House of Lords

1.1. The act of state doctrine

The act of state doctrine is a justiciability doctrine developed by judges in US and UK courts and applied in the courts of other states.[9] In its traditional formulation

[6] Franck, *Political Questions/Judicial Answers*, 45–60 (n 5).

[7] Jeff L. Yates and Andrew B. Whitford, 'Presidential Power and the US Supreme Court', *Political Research Quarterly*, 51/2 (1998), 539–50. See 2.1.2.iii, the analysis of the *Agent Orange Litigation* case.

[8] *R* v. *Bow Street Metropolitan Stipendiary Magistrate Ex parte Pinochet Ugarte (No.1)* (Lord Steyn), paragraph 4 (n 3).

[9] Ian Brownlie, *Principles of Public International Law* (7th edn, New York: Oxford University Press, 2008), 504; Antonio Cassese, *International Law* (2nd edn, New York: Oxford University Press, 2005), 99. In *Habib* v. *Commonwealth of Australia*, FCAFC 12 (25 February 2010), the court discusses in length the applicability of the doctrine in Australia.

the doctrine prevents courts from inquiring into the validity of the public acts of a foreign sovereign state committed within its own territory. The classical definition in American jurisprudence was formulated by Justice Fuller in *Underhill* v. *Hernandez* (1897):

> Every sovereign state is bound to respect the independence of every other sovereign state, and the courts of one country will not sit in judgment on these acts of the government of another done within its own territory. Redress of grievances by reason of such acts must be obtained through the means open to be availed of by sovereign powers as between themselves.[10]

The modern notion of act of state doctrine emerged from three other US Supreme Court cases decided between 1964 and 1976, most notably the case of *Banco Nacional de Cuba v. Sabbatino.*[11] These were civil cases that dealt with the nationalization of American assets by Cuba in the aftermath of the Cuban revolution. Nonetheless, the principles enunciated in *Sabbatino* have been cited in all the cases in which the act of state doctrine has been invoked. The cases, whether in the US or around the world, have not necessarily been expropriation cases. More recently, in *Kirkpatrick,* the US Supreme Court ruled that the act of state doctrine 'requires that, in the process of deciding, the acts of foreign sovereigns taken within their own jurisdictions shall be deemed valid'.[12]

The doctrine has its roots in 'sound policy reasons'.[13] Based on the traditional assumption that the nation should *speak in one voice*—that of the government—in matters concerning foreign affairs, the act of state doctrine is designed to avoid 'embarrassing' the executive in its conduct of foreign relations and to reflect the proper separation of powers between the judicial and political branches of government.[14] Originally, in The *Underhill* case, the doctrine was founded on the principles of comity, sovereignty, and the equality of nations. In more recent decisions there has been a shift in focus about preserving the relationships between

[10] *Underhill* v. *Hernandez,* 168 U.S. 250 (1897), 252. See also from the same period *Oetjen* v. *Central Leather Co.*, 246 U.S. 297 (1918), 303–4. The roots of that doctrine are found in England as early as 1674, *Blads* v. *Bamfield,* 3 Swan 603, 604 (1674); *Duke of Brunswick* v. *King of Hanover,* 2 HLC 1(1848), 22. The leading English case is *Luther* v. *Sagor,* 3 K.B. 532 (1921), 548. For a detailed historical review see Michael Zander, 'The Act of State Doctrine', *The American Journal of International Law,* 53/4 (1959), 826, 828–33; Michael J. Bazyler, 'Abolishing the Act of State Doctrine', *University of Pennsylvania Law Review,* 134/325 (1986), 331–44.

[11] *Banco Nacional de Cuba* v. *Sabbatino,* 376 U.S. 398 (1964). *Sabbatino* is the landmark case from contemporary jurisprudence on the act of state doctrine that provides its formulation and interpretation in the US (§443(a) *Restatement [Third] of Foreign Relations Law of the United States*). The two cases that followed *Sabbatino* are *First National City Bank* v. *Banco Nacional de Cuba,* 406 U.S. 759 (1972) and *Alfred Dunhill of London, Inc.* v. *Republic of Cuba,* 425 U.S. 682 (1976).

[12] *Environmental Tectonics Corp.* v. *W. S. Kirkpatrick Inc.*, 110 S.Ct. 701 (1990), 707.

[13] *Banco Nacional de Cuba* v. *Sabbatino* (Dissenting opinion of Judge White) (n 11).

[14] For the origin of this concept see Lawrence Collins, 'Foreign Relations and the Judiciary', *International and Comparative Law Quarterly,* 51/3 (2002), 485–510. Richard Falk, *The Role of Domestic Courts in the International Legal Order* (Syracuse: Syracuse University Press, 1964), 92 (questioning why the 'national interest' is necessarily that the nation would speak in one voice); Jeffrey Davis, *Justice across Borders: The Struggle for Human Rights in U.S. Courts* (Cambridge: Cambridge University Press, 2008), 140.

branches of government in a system of separation of powers, namely that the judiciary should not intervene in domains within the realm of the executive.[15] However, this separation of powers rationale could lead to the opposite conclusion: the application of an avoidance doctrine may in itself violate the separation of power principle since the policy choice over the scope of jurisdiction belongs to the legislature and not to individual judges. Moreover, the separation of powers between the executive, legislative, and judicial branches of a government requires courts to exercise their jurisdiction on cases independently from the interest of the executive branch. By avoiding cases, courts allow the executive not to be checked and balanced by the judiciary as required by the separation of power principle. Indeed, the separation of power rationale was identified 'more as an excuse than a reason for the judicial disinclination to implement international norms.'[16]

In the UK, the doctrine of non-justiciability applicable to acts of foreign executives corresponds to the US act of state doctrine. It dictates that English courts, in general, will not inquire into the validity of acts performed in the sovereign capacity of foreign states.[17] It was formulated in *Buttes Gas & Oil* v. *Hammer*, which ruled that courts should abstain from adjudicating any case in which a court has 'no judicial or manageable standards by which to judge [these] issues.'[18] According to Singer, the doctrine has rather been viewed as a comity principle between nations with respect to sovereign immunity.[19]

Sabbatino did not lay down an 'inflexible and all-encompassing rule'[20] for the application of the doctrine. Instead it established a number of factors to be

[15] In *Sabbatino* the US Supreme Court stated that the doctrine 'arises out of the basic relationships between branches of government in a system of separation of powers'; 'The act of state doctrine embodies the purely prudential concern that judicial inquiry into the validity of a foreign nation's sovereign acts may interfere with Executive and Congressional foreign policy efforts.' *Banco Nacional de Cuba* v. *Sabbatino*, 423 (n 11). See also *Environmental Tectonics Corp.* v. *W. S. Kirkpatrick Inc.*, 1058 (n 12).

[16] Benvenisti, 'Judicial Misgivings Regarding the Application of International Norms: An Analysis of Attitudes of National Courts', *European Journal of International Law* 4/2 (1993), 174–5. See also 'Note: Judicial Enforcement of International Law Against the Federal and State Governments', *Harvard Law Review*, 104/6 (1991), 1285–7.

[17] As a matter of terminology a distinction should be made with the US and UK act of state doctrine. The English act of state relates to the non-justiciable nature of the Crown's acts abroad. It is a form of domestic state immunity ('An action done outside the jurisdiction by the Crown in exercise of the royal prerogative can give no rise to a claim. The plea of act of state does not make an unlawful act lawful: it prevents the courts from having cognisance of it'—*Nissan* v. *Attorney General*, (1970) AC 179; *All England Law Reports*, 1/629 (1969), paragraph 235). The US and the UK act of state are two distinct doctrines. This was emphasized by the House of Lords in *R* v. *Bow Street Metropolitan Stipendiary Magistrate Ex parte Pinochet Ugarte (No.1)*: '[the non justiciability principle is] referred to as "the Act of State" doctrine, especially in the United States. But Act of State is a confusing term. It is used in different senses in many different contexts. So it is better to refer to non-justiciability.' (n 3) Thus, the US act of state doctrine is known in the UK as the *Buttes* non-justiciability principle.

[18] 'These are not issues upon which a municipal court can pass. Leaving aside all possibility of embarrassment in our foreign relations (which it can be said not to have been drawn to the attention of the court by the executive) there are [..] no judicial or manageable standards by which to judge these issues [..] the court would be in a judicial no-man's land.' *Buttes Gas and Oil Co.* v. *Hammer (No. 3)*, (1982) AC 888 UKHL, 931, 938.

[19] Michael Singer, 'The Act of State Doctrine of the United Kingdom: An Analysis, with Comparisons to United States Practice', *American Journal of International Law*, 75/2 (1981), 291, 296.

[20] *Banco Nacional de Cuba* v. *Sabbatino*, 428 (n 11).

considered on a case-by-case basis, leaving a wide margin of appreciation for the court to decide on the matter. Thus, the extent to which a domestic court should suspend its normal jurisdiction in order to avoid conflict with relevant executive policy is based on a balance test taking into consideration the following factors:

(1) The international consensus on the international rule at issue. Richard Falk, in support of this factor, argued that any invalidation of a foreign act of state by a domestic court—based upon a non-consensus rule of international law—would be more a political decision than an authoritative judicial opinion.[21]

(2) The impact on foreign relations. Where the impact on foreign relations of the international issues presented is minimal, the justification for application of the act of state doctrine is weak and it is more appropriate for the judiciary to render a decision in the case.[22]

(3) The continued existence of the government. If the government which perpetrated the challenged act of state no longer exists, the danger of interference with the executive's conduct of foreign policy is less than in a case where the act of state is that of the current foreign government.

These 'Sabbatino factors' have been systematically considered by US courts and other national courts in deciding whether to exercise their jurisdiction. In parallel, exceptions to the application of the doctrine have been developed, so courts can avoid the application of the doctrine and exercise their normal authority.

1.2 The political question doctrine

In the US the political question doctrine requires abstention on the court's part 'in issues of political delicacy in the field of foreign affairs'.[23] Henkin formulated this doctrine as relating to 'some issues, which prima facie and by usual criteria would seem to be for the courts, will not be decided by them but, extra-ordinarily, left for political decision'.[24] In US literature, two approaches to the political doctrine can be identified.

[21] Falk, *The Role of Domestic Courts*, 75 (n 14).

[22] 'Some aspects of international law touch much more sharply on national nerves than do others; the less important the implications of an issue are for our foreign relations, the weaker the justification for exclusivity in the political branches.' *Banco Nacional de Cuba* v. *Sabbatino*, 428 (n 11); See also *Doe* v. *Unocal Corp.*, 110 F. Supp. 2d. 1294 (C.D. Cal. 2000), 354.

[23] Malcolm N. Shaw, *International Law* (5th edn, Cambridge: Cambridge University Press, 2003), 169. *Tel Oren* v. *Libyan Arab Republic*, 726 F.2d 774, (D.C. Cir. 1984), 803: 'Questions touching on the foreign relations of the United States make up what is likely the largest class of questions to which the political question doctrine has been applied.' Louis Henkin, 'Is There a "Political Question" Doctrine?', *Yale Law Journal*, 85/5 (1976), 600: see also *Oetjen* v. *Central Leather Co.*, paragraph 302 (n 10); *Kadic* v. *Karadzic*, 70 F.3d 232 (2d Cir. 1995), 248–9.

[24] Henkin, 'Is There a "Political Question" Doctrine?', 599 (n 23). 'The foreign relations of the United States have provided a second group of leading cases commonly cited as instances of judicial abstention because the issues were political . . . They are decisions of a kind for which the Judiciary has neither aptitude, facilities nor responsibility and which has long been held to belong in the domain of political power not subject to judicial intrusion or inquiry.' (600).

The *classical* formulation of the doctrine is a constitutionally based theory focusing on the principle of separation of powers.[25] Under this view of the doctrine, judicial abstention is required by the constitution: it is a doctrine rooted in the text and structure of the constitution. For Wechsler, the principal representative of that approach, the courts have no basis for abstaining other than in cases in which the constitution could be interpreted as requiring them to abstain.[26] As this rationale blurs the distinction between questions of jurisdiction/competence and justiciability,[27] some scholars have questioned whether a separate doctrine is actually needed. In his famous critique, Henkin made the important distinction between questions in which the court lacks jurisdiction because the matter was confined by the constitution to the executive, and (political) questions left to the executive by deference as being non-justiciable.[28]

The *prudential* or the *functional* approach, by contrast, argues that courts should apply the political question doctrine in order to avoid cases that may undermine their institutional legitimacy. This stance, represented by Alexander Bickel, is based on notions of expediency. Unlike the former view of the doctrine, the prudential approach holds that courts have the discretion to use this tool in order to protect their legitimacy. Courts have to avoid conflict with the political branches in controversial cases even when the constitution does not contemplate such a delegation. Clear factors for applying this view are lacking—it is a policy that should be applied by the judges as matter of wisdom.[29] As noted by Bickel, 'there is something different about it, in kind, not in degree, from the general "interpretive process"; something greatly more flexible, something of prudence, not construction and not principle.'[30] Henkin, quite cynically noted that Bickel 'would probably support abstention whenever he and the courts agreed that abstention was "wise," in the public interest most broadly conceived.'[31] American literature has observed that the courts are inconsistent with respect to the rationales used to justify their application of the political question doctrine in cases involving US foreign policy.[32] While Bickel's prudential stance 'did not try to "domesticate" his prudential concerns into guidelines',[33] the US Supreme

[25] David D. Cole, 'Challenging Covert War: The Politics of the Political Question Doctrine', *Harvard International Law Journal*, 26/1 (1985), 164.

[26] Herbert Wechsler, 'Toward Neutral Principles of Constitutional Law', *Harvard Law Review*, 73/1 (1959), 9.

[27] Wayne McCormack, noted that 'a decision to allow one political branch to have the final say on an issue... is itself an interpretation of constitutional law'. Wayne McCormack, 'The Political Question Doctrine-Jurisprudentially', *University of Detroit Mercy Law Review*, 70/793 (1993), 798.

[28] Henkin, 'Is There a "Political Question" Doctrine?', 600–2 (n 23).

[29] Alexander M. Bickel, *The Least Dangerous Branch—The Supreme Court at the Bar of Politics* (New Haven/London: Yale University Press, 1962), 184; Fritz W. Scharpf, 'Judicial Review and the Political Question: A Functional Analysis', *Yale Law Journal*, 75/517 (1966), 538, 566–83.

[30] Alexander M. Bickel, 'The Supreme Court, 1960—Term Foreword: The Passive Virtues', *Harvard Law Review*, 75/1 (1961), 46.

[31] Henkin, 'Is There a "Political Question" Doctrine?', 603 (n 23).

[32] Jonathan I. Charney, 'Judicial Deference in Foreign Relations', *American Journal of International Law*, 83/4 (1989), 805; Rebecca L. Brown, 'When Political Questions Affect Individual Rights: The Other Nixon v United States', *Supreme Court Review*, 125 (1993), 152–3; Michael E. Tigar, 'Judicial Power, The "Political Question Doctrine", and Foreign Relations', *UCLA Law Review*, 17/[i] (1969–1970), 1135, 1146, 1163.

[33] Henkin, 'Is There a "Political Question" Doctrine?', 603 (n 23).

Court in the precedent setting decision *Baker* v. *Carr* preferred the view that 'judicial action must be governed by standard, by rule.... [L]aw pronounced by the court must be principled, rational, and based upon reasoned distinction.'[34] Therefore, in order to avoid any appearance of arbitrariness in the application of the political question doctrine, the court established the rules of non-justiciability of the political question doctrine. These rules have reference to six considerations which should be evaluated on a case by case basis:

Prominent on the surface of any case held to involve a political question is found a textually demonstrable constitutional commitment of the issue to a coordinate political department; or a lack of judicially discoverable and manageable standards for resolving it; or the impossibility of deciding without an initial policy determination of a kind clearly for non-judicial discretion; or the impossibility of a court's undertaking independent resolution without expressing lack of the respect due coordinate branches of government; or an unusual need for unquestioning adherence to a political decision already made; or the potentiality of embarrassment from multifarious pronouncements by various departments on one question.[35]

The US Supreme Court's guidelines leave a wide margin of discretion for courts to decide to abstain for policy reasons. While Jack Goldsmith astutely observed that *Baker*'s discussion of the prudential factors gave courts a discretionary tool 'to abstain whenever they decide, based on an independent analysis of US foreign relations, that an adjudication would harm U.S. foreign relations or the political branches' conduct of those relations',[36] the US Supreme Court preferred to underline the separation of powers principle as the rationale for the political question doctrine, declaring that 'non justiciability of a political question is primarily a function of separation of powers'.[37] This rationale, however, is not unequivocal. If the constitution grants discretion to the executive in foreign affairs (issues that may not be reviewed by the judiciary branch), then this is not an issue of abstention, but of constitutional interpretation concerning courts' jurisdiction. The

[34] *Baker* v. *Carr*, 369 U.S. 186 (1962), 217. Indeed, according to Shapiro and Sweet, courts, in order to achieve their institutional legitimacy, must be perceived as neutral and independent, and therefore, 'if courts are political, that fact needs to be hidden by the judges themselves.' Shapiro and Stone Sweet, *On Law, Politics and Judicialization* (Oxford: Oxford University Press, 2002), 6.

[35] *Baker* v. *Carr*, 217 (n 34). The court instructed that each case requires 'a discriminating analysis of the particular question posed, in terms of the history of its management by the political branches, of its susceptibility to judicial handling in the light of its nature and posture in the specific case, and of the possible consequences of judicial action.' (211–12).

[36] Jack Landman Goldsmith, 'The New Formalism in United States Foreign Relations Law', *University of Colorado Law Review*, 70/4 (1999), 1395, 1402. Other scholars, critical of the courts' treatment of foreign relations cases, have called for abandonment of the doctrine. See, Franck, *Political Questions/Judicial Answers*, 4–5 (n 5); Harold Hongju Koh, *The National Security Constitution: Sharing Power After the Iran-Contra Affair* (New Haven: Yale University Press, 1990), 158, 221–4.

[37] *Baker* v. *Carr*, 210 (n 34). See also *First National City Bank* v. *Banco Nacional de Cuba*, 785–93 (n 11)—(Judge Brennan dissenting) (noting that the act of state doctrine, as articulated in *Banco Nacional de Cuba* v. *Sabbatino* is equivalent to the political question doctrine) (n 11); *Trajano* v. *Marcos*, 878 F.2d 1439 (9th Cir. 1989) ('The act of state doctrine is the foreign relations equivalent of the political question doctrine'). See also *Credit Suisse* v. *United States Dist. Ct.*, 130 F.3d 1342 (9th Cir. 1997), 1346; *Tel Oren* v. *Libyan Arab Republic*, 726 F.2d 774, 803. Yet, one should be cautious when using this argument, for it is not an issue of lack of jurisdiction.

abstention doctrine becomes relevant in situations where the courts have jurisdiction to review the acts of the executive (as an expression of the rationale of separation of power), but choose not to exercise it because the issue concerns a political question. In this context the separation of power principle, will, on the contrary, dictate a legal review instead of an abstention.If the court has competence to act as a watchdog over the executive, by avoiding carrying out that task, the court undermines the purpose of the separation of power principle.

1.2.1 UK 'forbidden areas'

In the UK, the doctrine of non-justiciability applies to both domestic and foreign executive acts. Concerning the former, which is the equivalent of the US political question doctrine, domestic executive acts include executive functions under the 'Royal Prerogative'. These include issues involving foreign and military affairs, for example concluding treaties, declaring war, mobilizing the armed forces, recognition of governments, and the attribution of diplomatic immunity. The House of Lords recognized that there were certain areas which remain outside the area of justiciability such as 'the most important prerogative powers concerned with control of the armed forces and with foreign policy.'[38] Generally, prerogative decisions involving government policy are not justiciable 'as taking one course rather than another does not normally involve questions to which, if disputed, the judicial process is adapted to provide the right answer.'[39] In English courts the certificate of the Secretary of State is conclusive in these matters in order to avoid the embarrassment of conflicting opinion between the courts and the executive.[40] As a classic example of 'the forbidden areas', Lord Richards mentions the *Campaign for Nuclear Disarmament* case.[41] In that case, the applicants requested the court to declare that the state would be acting in breach of customary international law were it to take military action against Iraq without a further security council resolution: 'in my judgment I said it was "unthinkable that the national courts would entertain a challenge to a Government decision to declare war or to authorise the use of armed force against a third country".'[42] Further, in *R* v. *Jones and Others*, protestors against the war in Iraq were charged with various criminal offences. In their defence they argued that they had been acting to prevent the commission of the crime of aggression. The House of Lords ruled that aggression is not a crime under domestic law and therefore could not serve as a defence for the protestors. Among other considerations that led the court to this ruling was the argument that the crime of

[38] *Council of Civil Service Unions* v. *Minister for the Civil Service*, (1985) AC 374, 398. See also in *R (Abbasi)* v. *Secretary of State for Foreign and Commonwealth Affairs*, [2002] EWCA Civ 1598, [2003] UKHRR 76 CA, paragraph 106: 'the court cannot enter the forbidden areas, including decisions affecting foreign policy'. See also *R* v. *Foreign Secretary ex p. Everett*, (1989) 1QB 811, 820.

[39] *Council of Civil Service Unions* v. *Minister for the Civil Service*, 411(n 38).

[40] Brownlie, *Principles of Public*, 49–50 (n 9).

[41] *R (Campaign for Nuclear Disarmament)* v. *Prime Minister and Others*, (2002) EWHC 2777 (Admin).

[42] Lord Richards, 'The International Dimension of Judicial Review', *The 2006 Gray's Inn Reading* (7 June 2006), paragraphs 7, 10–11.

aggression would take national courts into areas where, under 'well established rules' they will be 'very slow to review the exercise of prerogative powers in relation to the conduct of foreign affairs and the deployment of the armed services'.[43]

1.3 The exceptions: from political to legal questions?

1.3.1 Deference to state position

One of the first exceptions to the act of state doctrine in the US is known as the *Bernstein* exception, after the name of the case.[44] Bernstein, a German Jew, brought a claim before a US court after World War II, to recover properties that had been expropriated by the Nazis. The second Circuit refrained from exercising its jurisdiction over the claim because of the act of state doctrine. After Bernstein obtained a letter from the State Department declaring that it was the executive's policy to relieve American courts from the restraints of the act of state doctrine in cases involving Nazi expropriation, the Second Circuit changed its initial decision. Since then, the 'Bernstein exception' has meant that when the state informs a court by letter that it has no objection to a decision on the merits, the courts are prevented from applying the act of state doctrine. In the *First National City Bank* case, Justice Rehnquist found the directive from the executive sufficient to prevent application of the act of state doctrine. He referred to the separation of powers argument of *Sabbatino* as the rationale for the application of the doctrine and stated that the only purpose of the doctrine was to prevent embarrassment to the executive. Thus, the different result of the application of the doctrine (*Sabbatino*) and its non-application (*City Bank*) 'is primarily attributable to the different positions taken by the executive in the two cases.'[45] This exception has been widely criticized by judges and scholars. Justice Brennan stated in *City Bank*:

> The consequence of adopting the '*Bernstein*' approach would only be to bring the rule of law both here at home and in the relations of nations into disrespect. Indeed, the fate of the individual claimant would be subject to the political considerations of the Executive Branch. [...] No less important than fair and equal treatment to individual litigants is the concern that decisions of our courts command respect as dispassionate opinions of principle. Nothing less will suffice for the rule of law. Yet the '*Bernstein*' approach is calculated only to undermine regard for international law.[46]

[43] *R* v. *Jones (Appellant)*, (2006) UKHL 16, paragraph 30. See also *R* v. *Jones (Appellant)*, (2005) EWHC 684 (Admin) where the court examined if the crime of aggression constituted a crime within the meaning of section 3 of the Criminal Law Act 1967, and if so, whether non-justiciable doctrines are applicable in criminal trials. In criminal proceedings, usually initiated by the state prosecution, the political question doctrine is irrelevant. Political considerations are taken into account at the prosecution office, before reaching the court.

[44] *Bernstein* v. *N.V. Nederlandische—Amerikaansche Stoomvaart-Maatschappij*, 210 F.2d 375 (2d Cir. 1954).

[45] Bazyler, 'Abolishing the Act', 340 (n 10).

[46] See *First National City Bank* v. *Banco Nacional de Cuba*, 790–3 (n 11) (Justice Brennan dissenting). Falk stated that intervention in international law cases 'is itself a deprecation of the commitment to international law. The prestige of international law in domestic courts is undermined

This exception has not been validated by the US Supreme Court and its continuing authority is doubtful. However, the US government continues to direct the judiciary through *amicus briefs*. Lower courts were instructed by the Supreme Court in *Sosa* to give *serious weight* to the state's position in relation to the application of the act of state doctrine in Alien Tort Statute (ATS) cases.[47] Thus the criticism, voiced by Justice Brennan forty years ago in *City Bank* seems to be still relevant: automatically accepting the state's position would be to renounce the court's role in the separation of powers doctrine and allow politics to rule instead of the law.

1.3.2 Flagrant violations of human rights and humanitarian law

US jurisprudence has established that an exception to the application of the doctrine should be made where there is a flagrant violation of international law.[48] In this spirit, the Restatement (Third) of Foreign Relations Law of the United States (Revised) states:

> a claim arising out of an alleged violation of fundamental human rights—for instance, a claim on behalf of a victim of torture or genocide—would (if otherwise sustainable) probably not be defeated by the act of state doctrine, since the accepted international law of human rights is well established and contemplates external scrutiny of such acts.[49]

Recent decisions have developed this exception, even if on the merits the courts have proved to remain much more reluctant. A line of US cases established that *jus cogens* violations and other flagrant violations of human rights and IHL should not be barred by the act of state doctrine, because these acts cannot be seen as sovereign acts of the state. This position was first developed in cases dealing with torture. In *Filártiga* (1980) the Court of Appeal of the Second Circuit held that the act of state doctrine does not apply to acts of torture under the appearance of law as this cannot be an official act of state.[50] Similarly, in *Trajano* v. *Marcos*, the court ruled that the alleged acts of torture and rape cannot be seen as official acts:

if its application depends upon a prior political authorization'. Falk, *The Role of Domestic Courts*, 93, 136–7 (n 14).

[47] *Sosa* v. *Alvarez-Machain et al.*, 542 U.S. 692 (2004).

[48] This could be seen as a formulation of the 'consensus exception' formulated in *Banco Nacional de Cuba* v. *Sabbatino* (n 11) see Gregory H. Fox, 'Re-examining the Act of State Doctrine: An Integrated Conflicts Analysis', *Harvard International Law Journal*, 33/2 (1992), 531; Malvina Halberstam, 'Sabbatino Resurrected: The Act of State Doctrine in the Revised Restatement of U.S. Foreign Relations Law', *American Journal of International Law*, 79/1 (1985), 85–6. See also Justice White in his dissenting opinion in *Banco Nacional de Cuba* v. *Sabbatino*, 444: 'These cases [prior decisions of the Court] do not strongly imply or even suggest that the Court would woodenly apply the act of state doctrine and grant enforcement to a foreign act where the act was a clear and flagrant violation of international law.'

[49] American Law Institute, 'Restatement of Foreign Relations Law of the United States', (1987), paragraph 443.

[50] 'We doubt whether action [of torture] by a state official in violation of the Constitution and laws of the Republic of Paraguay, and wholly ratified by that nation's government, could properly be characterized as an act of state.' *Filártiga and Filártiga* v. *Pena-Irala*, 630 F.2d 876 (2d Cir 1980), paragraph 39.

Because nations do not, and cannot under international law, claim a right to torture or enslave their own citizens . . . the Court need not apply the act of state doctrine in this case.[51]

This position was reaffirmed in the context of alleged war crimes in *Karadzic*,[52] and more recently in *Rio*, where the US court of Appeal of the Ninth Circuit also found that racial discrimination, being *jus cogens*, cannot constitute an official sovereign act, and precludes the applicability of the act of state doctrine.[53]

As for the exception to the application of the political question doctrine, the US Supreme Court noted in *Baker* that not every case touching foreign relations involves a non-justiciable political question, and that the determination should be done on a case by case basis.[54] In this way, courts are left with a large margin for discretion—a discretion that has been gradually expanded to include review over IHL issues. In *Karadic*, the Court of Appeals of the Second Circuit followed that line, ruling that 'the doctrine is one of political questions, not one of political cases'.[55] In *Ibrahim* v. *Titan Corp.*, the Ninth Circuit stated that 'the fact that an action is "taken in the ordinary exercise of discretion in the conduct of war" does not put it beyond the judicial power' and ruled that military decisions, whether taken in peace or war time, can be reviewed by the court if a citizen was injured.[56] The post 11 September jurisprudence has largely contributed to that growing tendency. The US Supreme Court in *Hamdi* (2004) rejected the government's separation of powers argument and made clear that the constitution's allocation of war powers to the executive does not exclude the courts from every dispute connected to it. It stated that 'We have long since made clear that a state of war is not a blank check for the President when it comes to the rights of the Nation's citizens.'[57] And indeed, two years later in *Hamdan* the US Supreme Court not only exercised its authority (which required far reaching legal determinations e.g. the qualification of the conflict and the applicability of the Geneva Conventions to the non-state armed group, questions that until then had been avoided and deferred to the State) but it ruled on the merits that there was a violation of IHL.[58]

[51] Cited in *Doe* v. *Unocal Corp.*, 963 F. Supp. 880 (C.D. Cal. 1997), 894–5.

[52] 'We doubt that the acts of even a state official, taken in violation of a nation's fundamental law and wholly ratified by that nation's government, could properly be characterized as an act of state.' *Kadic* v. *Karadzic*, 70 F.3d 232 (2d Cir. 1995) 250 (n 23). See for other examples: *Linder* v. *Portocarrero*, 963 F.2d 332 (11th Cir. 1992), 336; *Flatow* v. *Islamic Republic of Iran*, 999 F. Supp. 1 (D.D.C. 1998), 24; *Xuncax* v. *Gramajo*, 886 F. Supp. 162 (D. Mass. 1995), 1859; *Forti* v. *Suarez-Mason*, 672 F. Supp. 1531 (N.D. Cal. 1987), 1541.

[53] This case involved illegal acts committed by the Papua New Guinea Defence Force during the civil war in Bougainville: 'because "[i]nternational law does not recognize an act that violates *jus cogens* as a sovereign act," the alleged acts of racial discrimination cannot constitute official sovereign acts, and the district court erred in dismissing these claims under the act of state doctrine.' *Sarei et al.* v. *Rio Tinto, PLC and Rio Tinto Limited*, 456 F.3d 1069 (9th Cir. 2006), paragraph 67. For more examples, see the ATS case study section 2.1.

[54] *Baker* v. *Carr*, 211 (n 34).

[55] *Kadic* v. *Karadzic*, 249 (n 23).

[56] *Ibrahim* v. *Titan Corp.*, 976 F.2d 1328 (9th Cir. 1992), 1332.

[57] *Hamdi* v. *Rumsfeld*, 542 U.S. 507 (2004), 536.

[58] For a deeper discussion on the *Salim Ahmed Hamdan* v. *Donald H. Rumsfeld et al.*, 548 U.S. 557 (2006), see Chapter 3. See also *Boumediene* v. *Bush*, 553 U.S. 723 (2008), 765: 'Abstaining from questions involving formal sovereignty and territorial governance is one thing. To hold the political branches have the power to switch the Constitution on or off at will is quite another. The former

1.3.3 The UK public policy exception: human rights violations and flagrant breaches of public international law

British judges have developed the 'public policy exception'. In *Oppenheimer* (1976) the House of Lords refused to recognize racially discriminatory Nazi laws, stating that a law of this sort constitutes 'so grave an infringement of human rights that the courts of this country ought to refuse to recognise it as a law at all.'[59] This obiter was the principal basis of the key decision in *Kuwait Airways No. 4* (2000). This case was the first in which the English Court of Appeal recognized that the public policy exception to the act of state doctrine encompasses clear breaches of international law—in this case, the unlawful use of force.[60] While there was formerly very little authority to support the existence of a public policy exception of this kind,[61] the UK House of Lords affirmed this ruling in 2002. It described the public policy exception as 'well established in English law'.[62] Lord Steyn saw the public policy exception as a natural development of the reasoning in *Oppenheimer* holding that 'the Court of Appeal was right to extend the public policy exception beyond human rights violations to flagrant breaches of public international law. It does not follow, however, that every breach of international law will trigger the public policy exception.'[63]

Thus, while caution has to be exercised when faced with an allegation that a foreign sovereign state was in breach of its international obligations, the decisions of the House of Lords in *Kuwait Airways* established that an English court may find a

position reflects this Court's recognition that certain matters requiring political judgments are best left to the political branches. The latter would permit a striking anomaly in our tripartite system of government, leading to a regime in which Congress and the President, not this Court, say "what the law is".'.

59 *Oppenheimer* v. *Cattermole (Inspector of Taxes)*, (1976) AC 249 UKHL, 277–8. The context of the dispute was not the applicability of the act of state doctrine, but whether Mr Oppenheimer had, by reason of German nationality law, lost the right to double taxation relief in England which was available to those of dual British and German citizenship.

60 *Kuwait Airways Corporation* v. *Iraqi Airways Company*, (2000) EWCA Civ 284, paragraphs 317–323, 372. Following Iraq's invasion in Kuwait in 1990 and its purported annexation, both of which were condemned by the UN Security Council (UNSC), the Iraqi forces seized ten commercial aircraft belonging to Kuwait Airways Corporation (KAC). Iraq then adopted a domestic enactment that dissolved KAC and transferred all its property worldwide. The court held that it was entitled to refuse recognition of the Iraqi resolution, because it was in breach of clearly established principles of international law, most notably UNSC resolutions.

61 Martin Davies, 'Kuwait Airways Corp v Iraqi Airways Co.—The Effect in Private International Law of Breach of Public International Law by a State Actor', *Melbourne Journal of International Law*, 2/2 (2001), fn 50. See also Janeen M. Carruthers and Elizabeth B. Crawford, 'Kuwait Airways Corporation v. Iraqi Airways Company', *International and Comparative Law Quarterly*, *52/3* (2003), 761–74.

62 *Kuwait Airways Corporation* v. *Iraqi Airways Company & Anor*, (2002) UKHL 19, paragraph 18.

63 *Kuwait Airways Corporation* v. *Iraqi Airways Company & Anor*, paragraph 114 (n 62). See also Lord Hope, paragraphs 138–140. *Kuwait Airways* was described by O'Keefe as 'reflective of the English courts' commendable move in recent times towards a more direct engagement, where English law permits, with the UK's international engagements.' Oxford Reports on International Law in Domestic Courts, 'Analysis of O'Keefe' (30 November 2006). Online at <http://www.oxfordlawreports.com>.

case justiciable with regard to what it perceives as a foreign state's clear breach of international law, particularly in the context of human rights. In *R (on the application of Abbasi)* v. *Secretary of State for Foreign and Commonwealth Affairs*, a few months after the House of Lords rendered its decision in the *Kuwait* case, the English Court of Appeal, dealing with its first Guantanamo case, stated that 'where fundamental human rights are in play, the courts of this country will not abstain from reviewing the legitimacy of the actions of a foreign sovereign state'.[64] Interestingly in a later Guantanamo case decided in Australia in 2007, the judge noted that:

Their Lordships twice expressed deep concern that in apparent contravention of fundamental principles of law, Mr Abbasi may be subject to indefinite detention by the United States authorities with no opportunity to challenge the legitimacy of his detention before any recognised court or tribunal. Their Lordships referred to what appeared to be 'a clear breach of a fundamental human right'. This latter expression echoes the language in *Kuwait Airways*.[65]

The Australian federal court further ruled to include a grave infringement of human rights such as detention at Guantanamo Bay for more than five years without valid charges as an exception to the act of state doctrine:

In *Kuwait Airways*, a clear acknowledged breach of international law standards was considered sufficient for the court to lawfully exercise jurisdiction over the sovereign act of the Iraq State. In that case, the clear breach of international law was the wrongful seizure of property. It is clear in the case before me that the deprivation of liberty for over five years without valid charge is an even more fundamental contravention of a fundamental principle, and is such an exceptional case as to justify proceeding to hearing by this Court.[66]

The judicial review over UK prerogative power has also evolved. In this regard it is necessary to refer to the landmark decision in *Council of Civil Service Unions* v. *Minister for the Civil Service*, which established that the mere fact that a power derived from the Royal Prerogative did not necessarily exclude it from the scope of judicial review. As stated by Lord Richards 'recent cases show that the forbidden areas of foreign policy and the like are much narrower than one might have thought, and that the *CCSU* case has opened up very considerable scope for judicial review in these fields.'[67] The House of Lords emphasized that the controlling factor in considering whether a particular exercise of prerogative power is subject to review is not its source, but its subject matter.[68]

[64] *R (Abbasi)* v. *Secretary of State for Foreign and Commonwealth Affairs*, paragraph 53 (n 38).

[65] *Hicks* v. *Ruddock et al.*, (2007) FCA 299 (8 March 2007), paragraph 78.

[66] *Hicks* v. *Ruddock et al.*, paragraph 91 (n 65). See also *Habib* v. *Commonwealth of Australia* [2010] FCAFC 12; Batros and Philippa Webb, 'Accountability for Torture Abroad and the Limits of the Act of State Doctrine: Comments on Habib v. Commonwealth of Australia' *J. Int'l Crim. Just.* 8 (2010), 1153.

[67] Richards, 'The International Dimension', paragraph 7 (n 42).

[68] *Council of Civil Service Unions* v. *Minister for the Civil Service*, 398 (n 38): 'It is not an answer to a claim for judicial review to say that the source of the power of the Foreign Office is the prerogative. It is the subject matter that is determinative.'

2. The avoiding role of courts in practice: a contextual analysis

In practice, courts in different states function in a similar way; they avoid politically sensitive cases through the application of self developed doctrines. Courts will attempt to establish a legal framework for the application of an avoidance doctrine or its exception. However, it is not always possible to predict whether the courts will render a judgment on its merits or abstain on grounds of non-justiciability, given the extra-legal considerations involved in the decision. Avoiding rendering a judicial decision in a case would inevitably be a political choice and not a legal one as from a legal point of view, the option of giving a ruling is equally possible. A court may avoid exercising its jurisdiction in a case or alternatively may not apply the avoidance doctrine. It all depends on different legal traditions and institutional position, relations with the executive, and the claim under review.

This chapter presents an analysis of case studies that illustrate how courts from different jurisdictions apply avoidance doctrines. It seeks to expose the policy goals served through their application or rejection. The first case study examines the application of the act of state and the political question doctrines by US courts in Alien Tort Statute (ATS) cases that deal with IHL. It reveals a double standard in the courts' decisions, based largely on the state's position whether to enforce the law or not. The analysis focuses on three kinds of case law: cases against US officials, cases against US allies, and lastly cases against the officials of *other* third states. The second case study shows how courts from different states adopt different positions on whether the policy of targeted killings is a justiciable issue. This case study illustrates that the application of the avoidance doctrine is a policy choice of courts and not a normative obligation through which they define their role in enforcing IHL over their own government. On the other hand, as the third case study shows, there are certain issues which national courts from different states invariably prefer to avoid. The question of legality of the Israeli settlements is explored in relation to the jurisprudence of the Israeli HCJ and the *Bil'in* case in Canada.

The aim of the critical analyses of these three case studies is to draw conclusions about the judiciary's role in avoiding the application of IHL, in light of the rule of law principles namely access to court and equity.

2.1 The use of avoidance doctrines in ATS cases

Since the revival of the ATS in 1980 with the Second Circuit's landmark decision in *Filártiga*, US courts apply international law, including IHL, directly. Enacted in 1789, the ATS grants federal courts in the United States jurisdiction over 'any civil action by an alien for a tort only, committed in violation of the law of nations or a treaty of the United States'.[69] Yet, the ATS was largely dormant for 200 years until

[69] 'US Code—Section 1350: Alien's action for tort' (28 U.S.C. § 1350).

Filártiga. Since then, dozens of claims have been filed in different US federal courts.[70] ATS litigation has flourished and has evolved to encompass 'historical justice cases' against former foreign dictators and claims against non-state actors most notably, private corporations and military companies.[71] Recent rulings of the Courts of Appeals of the Second and Eleventh Circuits, however, indicate that the actual trend seems to limit the reach of the ATS litigation, to questioning jurisdiction over corporations[72] and the development of the obligation to exhaust local remedies 'in appropriate cases'.[73] This trend reached a new peak in 2013 with the US Supreme Court limiting the ATS's extraterritorial scope, and consequently the courts' jurisdiction to hear cases on violations committed outside the US.[74] These limits may also be attributed to a shift in the nature of the defendants in the ATS cases—away from cases against dictators, as in the early *Filártiga* and *Marcos*

[70] Between 2001 and 2007, forty decisions were rendered by courts of appeal and 107 by district courts. Davis, *Justice across Borders*, 128 (n 14).

[71] The Court of Appeals of the Second Circuit held in 1995 for the first time that war crimes may be asserted against non-state actors under the ATS. See *Kadic* v. *Karadzic*, 232, 244 (n 23). This ruling opened the door for suits to be brought against corporations and private military companies. By 2004, more than eighty cases had been brought against corporations. For example, in *Khulumani* v. *Barclay National Bank, Ltd*, 504 F.3d 254 (2d Cir. 2007), the court accepted jurisdiction over corporations' liability for aiding and abetting the South African apartheid regime. More recently, see the cases of *Presbyterian Church of Sudan et al.* v. *Talisman Energy Co.*, 582 F.3d 244 (2nd Cir. 2009), 254–5; *Abdullahi* v. *Pfizer, Inc.*, 562 F.3d 163 (2d Cir. 2009), 173 and *Sinaltrainal* v. *Coca-Cola Co.*, 578 F.3d 1252 (11th Cir. 2009), 1266–7. Kate Gallagher identified four kinds of litigation against corporations: (1) cases in which multinationals were accomplices to human rights violations committed by a state, known to have a poor human rights record, in order to pursue their economical interests (as *Wiwa* v. *Royal Dutch Petroleum Co.*, 226 F.3d 88 (2nd Cir. 2000)); (2) Corporate cases alleging the commission/complicity of war crimes (*Corrie* v. *Caterpillar, Inc.*, 403 F. Supp. 2d 1019 (W.D. Wash. 2005)); *Corrie* v. *Caterpillar, Inc.*, 503 F.3d 974 (9th Cir. 2007); (3) labour-related case (*Aldana* v. *Del Monte Fresh Produce*, 416 F.3d 1242 (11th Cir. 2005)); and (4) relatively new attempts to sue for environmental damage (*Flores* v. *Southern Peru Copper Corp.*, 406 F.3d 65 (2nd Cir. 2003)), and *Abdullahi* v. *Pfizer, Inc.*; Katherine Gallagher, 'Civil Litigation and Transitional Business—An ATS Primer', *Journal of International Criminal Justice*, 8/3 (2010), 750, 752–4. For cases against private military companies see *Xe Services Alien Tort Litig.*, 665 F. Supp. 2d 569 (E.D.Va. 2009) and *Ibrahim* v. *Titan Corp.*, 556 F. Supp. 2d 1(D.D.C. 2007); *Saleh et al.* v. *Titan Corp. et al.*, 580 F.3d 1 (DC Cir. 2009).

[72] On 11 September 2009, the Court of Appeals for the District of Columbia ruled in *Saleh et al.* v. *Titan Corp. et al.*, (n 71) that claims of torture and war crimes could not be brought against private military contractors because they are not state actors. In *Royal Dutch*, the Second Circuit followed this reasoning and ruled that corporations are not liable under international law (*Kiobel* v. *Royal Dutch Petroleum*, 621 F.3d 111 (2nd Cir. 2010)). This question was appealed to the US Supreme Court. Quite surprisingly, the US Supreme Court avoided ruling on that question. This was despite the US supporting the plaintiffs in their brief submitted to the court, by ordering in March 2012, shortly after the oral hearing, a new question to be determined by the court –'[w]hether and under what circumstances the ATS ... allows courts to recognize a cause of action for violations of the law of nations occurring within the territory of a sovereign other than the United States.' That time, the US brief was in support of limiting the extraterritorial scope of the ATS. Interestingly, the later brief was not signed by the US legal advisor Harold Koh, unlike the first one, which was in support of the petitioners. (Transcripts of the oral proceedings, the supporting brief of the US government and the order to reargue are available at the CCR website at <http://www.ccrjustice.org/ourcases/current-cases/kiobel>.) On 17 April 2013 the majority found there was a presumption against extraterritorial application of the ATS—thereby ending the *Kiobel* litigation—without ruling on the responsibility of a corporation under international law.

[73] *Sarei et al.* v. *Rio Tinto, PLC and Rio Tinto Ltd*, 550 F.3d 822 (9th Cir. 2008), 823.

[74] *Kiobel* v. *Royal Dutch Petroleum*, 569 U. S. (2013) (17 April 2013).

cases—to litigation against powerful political and economical defendants: US private companies, US officials, and allied states.

Not surprisingly, when cases started to go against the interests of the US Department of State, as reflected in their *amicus* briefs, courts have relied more and more on avoidance doctrines. Indeed, the policy of avoidance was directed by the US Supreme Court itself. In *Sosa* (2004), the first Supreme Court ruling on the ATS, cautious language was used concerning its applicability, urging lower courts to exercise restraint,[75] and instructing federal courts to give *serious weight* to the executive's view of the case's impact on foreign policy.[76]

A 2004 survey of ATS cases found that approximately four out of five cases brought under the ATS since 1980 have been dismissed on the basis of various avoidance doctrines.[77] Thus, even where jurisdiction under the ATS is established, suits for civil damages for serious violations of IHL committed abroad still face the barrier of avoidance doctrines: the political question doctrine, *forum non conveniens*, the act of state doctrine, and domestic rules on sovereign immunity. ATS cases provide an important source of jurisprudence governing the exercise of these doctrines.

2.1.1 Deferral to the state

In ATS cases dealing with IHL the courts tend not to upset the US State Department. It appears that the application of avoidance doctrines in ATS cases is more reflective of state directed policy than of a normative implementation of neutral factors. The state's main argument for judicial avoidance of sensitive cases is the constitutional argument based on the separation of powers. The argument is that courts should not interfere in matters which have considerable ramifications for foreign relations of the state, for which the executive branch is responsible. Notwithstanding, a closer examination of ATS cases and the relations between the court and the executive reveals an opposite reality, one in which the court is often used by the government as a tool for conducting its foreign affairs. By means of a double standard guidance to the court—which depends on the nationality of the respondent, and which is more often than not respected by the judiciary—the state aims to maintain its reputation as a worldwide human rights defender while at the same time shielding its own officials and allies from judicial scrutiny.

How does it work? When judges are concerned about the implications of an ATS case for US foreign relations they can invite the Department of State to submit its views on the question. In some cases, the state intervenes and submits a statement

[75] 'Since many attempts by federal courts to craft remedies for the violation of new norms of international law would raise risks of adverse foreign policy consequences, they should be undertaken, if at all, with great caution.' *Sosa* v. *Alvarez-Machain et al.*, 2744 (n 47). For an analysis of *Sosa*, see Naomi Norberg, 'The US Supreme Court Affirms the Filartiga Paradigm', *Journal of International Criminal Justice*, 4/2 (2006), 387–400.

[76] *Sosa* v. *Alvarez-Machain et al.*, 733, fn 21 (n 47).

[77] Lee K. Boyd, 'Universal Jurisdiction and Structural Reasonableness', *Texas International Law Journal*, 40/1 (2004), 46–58.

of interest on its own initiative.[78] Interestingly, landmark ATS cases, where the court did not avoid the exercise of its jurisdiction, did in fact reflect the State Department's position. The litigation in *Filártiga,* the first successful torture case brought to the court under ATS was supported by the state. The Department of State and Department of Justice submitted a joint *amicus* brief expressing their support for adjudication stating (in 1980!) that 'an individual's fundamental human rights are in certain situations directly enforceable in domestic courts'.[79] In *Marcos,* the Department of State under the Reagan administration did not request application of the act of state doctrine because of the 'very barbarousness of certain of the alleged acts'.[80] The Clinton administration supported the two first precedent cases against non-state actors. It supported the proceedings against Karadzic, head of the Republika Srpska for war crimes committed during the armed conflict in Bosnia although the Dayton peace agreements were being negotiated at the time the State's statement of interest was submitted to the court. The Clinton administration did not perceive the proceedings as an obstacle to peace negotiation (as was later proclaimed in *Rio* by the Bush administration in the context of peace agreements negotiated in Papua New Guinea). In *Unocal,* one of the first corporation cases, the plaintiffs alleged they had suffered human rights abuses including forced labour, forced expulsion of villagers, murder, rape, and torture during the construction of a gas pipeline by the Myanmar military. The US company Unocal Corporation and French Total were alleged to be complicit in these abuses and the State Department supported the plaintiffs in its statement of interest submitted to the district court in 1997. However, when the case was heard by the appellate court, the administration, this time under President Bush, modified its position in the brief submitted in 2003. It questioned whether US courts had jurisdiction in extraterritorial cases.[81] The tendency of courts to limit the applicability of the ATS was directly linked to the Bush administration's opposition

[78] See, for example, in the cases of *Trajano* v. *Marcos* and *Kadic* v. *Karadzic* (n 23). However, it is not always the case. According to Jeffrey Davis, of twenty-two cases in which the State Department under the Bush Administration intervened, only in seven cases was it asked to do so. The other cases in which it intervened were on its own initiative. He furthermore found out that of a total of seventy-seven decisions issued by the circuit courts of appeal in ATS cases, the executive intervened in seventeen cases, and at district level, in twenty out of 156 cases—while the Bush administration intervened the most so far: out of a total of thirty-seven cases in which the US participated, twenty-two were during the Bush administration (five of the six cases in appeals). See Davis, *Justice across Borders,* 113–18, 125 (n 14). See also Adam N. Schupack, 'The Arab-Israeli Conflict and Civil Litigation against Terrorism', *Duke Law Journal,* 60/207 (2010), 245.

[79] Brief for the United States as *Amicus Curiae* in *Filártiga and Filártiga* v. *Pena-Irala,* 3 (n 50). During the Bush administration, the State Department would claim that the ATS does not apply extraterritorially.

[80] Brief for the United States as *Amicus Curiae* in *Trajano* v. *Marcos,* 4. Yet, the state did not recognize jurisdiction *ratione materiae. Republic of the Philippines* v. *Marcos,* 806 F.2d 344 (2nd Cir. 1986), (refusing to apply act of state doctrine). Summarized in *American Journal of International Law,* 81/417 (1987).

[81] Brief for the United States as *Amicus Curiae* in *Doe* v. *Unocal Corp.,* 395 F.3d 978 (9th Cir. 2003), 2. Finally, the parties reached a confidential settlement in which Unocal agreed to compensate the plaintiffs, and the case was closed on 13 April 2005. The case's documents are all available at: <http://www.earthrights org/legal/doe-v-unocal>.

to ATS cases. Studies have shown that the Bush administration intervened in twenty-two ATS cases—all of which were in support of the defendants.[82] After the Supreme Court precedent *Sosa,* the Bush administration based its attack against ATS cases on five foundations: political question doctrine, act of state doctrine, foreign officials entitled to sovereign immunity, and two other lines related to denial of jurisdiction—extraterritorial jurisdiction and subject matter.[83] The ultimate denial of extraterritorial application of the ATS was recognized by the Supreme Court in April 2013 in *Kiobel.*[84]

It should however be noted that courts have not always followed the position of the state. An example repeatedly cited in academic literature and case law to illustrate this claim is the *Rio* case,[85] although that case merits closer observation. It dealt with a claim against a private company that allegedly committed human rights violations in respect of the operation of a copper mine in Papua New Guinea. Following the district court request for guidance from the State Department, the State Department filed a statement of interest. The statement argued that continued adjudication of the claim 'would risk a potentially serious adverse impact on the peace process, and hence on the conduct of our foreign relations' and that Papua New Guinea, a 'friendly foreign state' had 'perceive[d] the potential impact of this litigation on US-PNG relations, and wider regional interests, to be "very grave"'.[86] The Court of Appeals, while citing the Supreme Court decision in *Sosa,* recognized the 'serious weight' that should be attributed 'to the Executive Branch's view of the case's impact on foreign policy', but did not accept the state's position. The court recognized *jus cogens* violations to be an exception to the rule that justified application of the act of state doctrine.[87] This was an extremely important statement that could have had an important impact on the ground, had the case not been dismissed on comity grounds.

i. From double standards application towards a unified position?

When former dictators were found liable for gross violations of international law, the State Department's interest in promoting its image as a defender of global human rights was best served by allowing the court to exercise its natural judicial function to the fullest extent. This was reflected in the US *amicus curiae* brief submitted in *Filártiga*: 'A refusal to recognize a private cause of action in these circumstances might seriously damage the credibility of our nation's commitment to the protection of

[82] According to Beth Stephens, this attitude is consistent with the Bush administration's multiple efforts to eliminate judicial review over the executive since 11 September 2001: 'The Bush administration's opposition to human rights litigation coincides with the filing of lawsuits against politically powerful defendants: corporations, foreign government officials and the US government itself... although couched in terms of separation of powers the campaign seeks to protect allies from accountability for egregiously wrongful behaviour.' Beth Stephens, 'Upsetting Checks and Balances: the Bush Administration's Efforts to Limit Human Rights Litigation', *Harvard Human Rights Journal,* 17/169 (2004), 179.

[83] Davis, *Justice across Borders,* 127 (n 14).

[84] On the position of the Obama government in that case—see note 72.

[85] *Sarei et al.* v. *Rio Tinto, PLC and Rio Tinto Limited* 456 F.3d 1069 (9th Cir. 2006).

[86] Cited in the Judgment of the United States Court of Appeal, *Sarei et al.* v. *Rio Tinto, PLC and Rio Tinto Limited.,* paragraph 12 (n 85).

[87] *Sarei et al.* v. *Rio Tinto, PLC and Rio Tinto Limited.,* paragraph 60 (n 85).

human rights.'[88] More recently, this has occurred in a brief signed by Harold Koh in the name of the Obama administration submitted to the Supreme Court in the *Samantar* case: 'The United States condemns grave human rights abuses of the kind alleged in the complaint in this case, and it has a strong foreign policy interest in promoting the protection of human rights.'[89]

On the other hand, such litigation may be counterproductive, notwithstanding the gravity of the violation, if it is addressed to US allies. This was the claim made by the Bush administration in a case involving allegations against American oil corporation, Unocal, and the Myanmar military. Forced labour and human rights violations were allegedly committed during the construction of an oil pipeline,

> Although often asserted against rogues and terrorists, these claims are without bounds, and can easily be asserted against allies of our Nation . . . This Court's approach to the ATS bears serious implications for our current war against terrorism, and permits claims to be easily asserted against our allies in that war.[90]

Thus, a selective application of the ATS emerges, one that follows the prevailing political interest of the state in the particular case. However, with the growing quantity of litigation, 'easy cases', which could previously have been obvious candidates for the application of the law, have now become politically sensitive; they raise the spectre of establishing precedents that could be implemented against US officials or allies. Therefore it may be expected that the government, and by extension the courts, will avoid the enforcement of ATS legislation altogether. From the perspective of the rule of law, this may be a better choice if the law is not universally and equally applied. This new tendency may be observed in the proceedings of the *Samantar* case. That case concerned allegations of torture and extrajudicial killings committed by the former Somali Prime Minister. The respondents, who were persecuted by the Somali government during the 1980s, filed a damages action alleging that the defendant exercised command and control over the military forces committing the abuses. The allegations were also that he knew or should have known of these acts, and that he aided and abetted in their commission. The US Supreme Court was asked to determine whether a foreign state's immunity under the Foreign Sovereign Immunities Act (FSIA) extended to (1) an individual acting in his official capacity on behalf of a foreign state and (2) whether an individual who is no longer an official of a foreign state at the time a suit is filed retains this immunity.[91] Of interest are the briefs submitted to the Supreme Court

[88] Brief for the United States as *Amicus Curiae* in *Filártiga and Filártiga* v. *Pena-Irala*, 22–3 (n 50).

[89] Brief for the United States as *Amicus Curiae* supporting Affirmance at <http://www.scotusblog.com/wp-content/uploads/2010/01/08-1555_us-amicus-supporting-affirmance.pdf>. The US Supreme court rendered a decision in line with the State position on the issue of immunity. See also Memorandum for the United States submitted to the Court of Appeals for the Second Circuit in *Filártiga and Filártiga* v. *Pena-Irala*, reprinted in *ILM*, 19/585 (1980).

[90] Brief for the United States of America as *Amicus Curiae* at 2–4 (filed 8 May 2003), *Doe* v. *Unocal Corp.*, 395 F.3d 978 cited in 'Department of Justice Position in "Unocal"', *American Journal of International Law*, 97/3 (2003), 704.

[91] *Samantar* v. *Yousuf*, 130 S.Ct. 2278 (2010). See Brief for the United States supporting Affirmance at <http://www.scotusblog.com/case-files/cases/samantar-v-yousuf/>.

by the Zionist Organization of America and the Kingdom of Saudi Arabia. Both were in support of the defendant, and neither had any connection to Somalia or to the case, apart from their own narrow interest in preventing an exception to state immunity.[92] Saudi Arabia stated that it was an ally state of the US and that the allegations against it and its officials in the involvement of the 11 September attack were 'fabricated':

> Saudi Arabia has been and is a pivotal ally of the United States. . . . in light of the possibility that litigation in U.S. courts will be used as a means to harass or embarrass Saudi Arabia and its officials in other matters (even as the political branches of the United States work toward even stronger diplomatic and economic ties with Saudi Arabia), Saudi Arabia retains a strong interest in the issues of sovereign immunity raised here.[93]

The briefs of the Zionist Organization of America stated that:

> The decision of the Fourth Circuit that permits civil lawsuits to be brought against current and former government officials notwithstanding the immunity that their governments have under the Foreign Sovereign Immunities Act will, if not reversed by this Court, encourage the institution of many unfounded lawsuits in United States courts against present and former government officials of the State of Israel.[94]

Thus, in the eyes of the above parties, while the Supreme Court was deciding a case concerning a Somali dictator for allegedly having committed grave violations of international law, it should not neglect the consequences of its ruling for ally states. The US Administration, 'while having strong interest in promoting Human Rights', had made it clear that it was up to the executive and not the judiciary to decide on immunity issues. The Supreme Court ruled accordingly: while the FSIA of 1976 was found to be inapplicable to current or former officials of foreign nations being applicable only to states, common law immunity—which defers the definition of its scope to the state—could be asserted.

2.1.2 ATS cases against US officials

According to a survey conducted by Davis, when ATS cases are brought against US officials they typically fail because of a variety of avoidance doctrines and defences that allow judges to dismiss the case at a preliminary stage of the proceedings. For example, Davis found that in all cases against US officials in which the political question doctrine was raised, the case was dismissed on this ground.[95] Most of the

[92] Both briefs are at <http://www.scotusblog.com/case-files/cases/samantar-v-yousuf/>.

[93] Brief of the Kingdom of Saudi Arabia as *Amicus Curiae* in Support of Petitioner (7 December 2009), 2–3.

[94] Brief of the Zionist Organization of America, The American Association of Jewish Lawyers and Jurists, Agudath Israel of America, and the Union of Orthodox Jewish Congregations of America in Support of Petitioner (7 December 2009), 2.

[95] 'Clearly courts have granted broad deference to the US government in cases challenging abuse committed in the exercise of US foreign policy. . . . plaintiffs are more successful to overcome the political question doctrine when it is asserted by a non US government defendant, or by the US

cases against US officials dealing with the 'War on Terror' were dismissed on immunity grounds. Other doctrines used are the state secret and political question doctrines.[96] To date, ATS plaintiffs have not yet succeeded in overcoming these barriers and have not received rulings on merits.[97]

A number of cases have sought to challenge the legality of the treatment of the detainees held by US forces in Guantanamo and Abu Ghraib in the context of the so-called 'War on Terror'. The conduct alleged in these cases, if proven, amounts to torture. These include, as described in one of the cases 'hooding, forced nakedness, housing in cages, deprivation of food, forced body cavity searches, subjection to extremes of heat and cold, harassment in the practice of their religion, forced shaving of religious beards, placing the Koran in the toilet, placement in stress positions, beatings with rifle butts, and the use of un-muzzled dogs for intimidation.'[98] While the US failed to conduct criminal investigations for these allegations against any of those who were higher up in the chain of command,[99] the victims launched civil claims for damages based on different causes of action including the ATS. The first cases analysed in this section—*Rasul* v. *Rumsfeld* (that on appeal became *Rasul* v. *Myers*) and *Re: Iraq* and *Afghanistan Detainees Litigation*[100]—were both dismissed on immunity grounds and seem to reflect accurately the general attitude of US courts in addressing such questions.

i. Rasul v. Rumsfeld

In this case four former Guantanamo detainees, UK nationals, were seeking damages for their arbitrary detention and torture. The complaint was based on several causes of action—violations of ATS, the Geneva Conventions, the Fifth and

government as an amicus party.' Davis, *Justice across Borders*, 102, fn 384 (n 14). These cases are not limited to IHL but also include human rights violations.

[96] See, for example, *El-Masri* v. *United States*, 479 F.3d 296 (4th Cir. 2007), 300, 313 (dismissing plaintiff's complaint on the basis of the invocation of the state-secrets doctrine by the United States without considering whether his allegations that he was detained and interrogated 'pursuant to an unlawful policy and practice . . . known as "extraordinary rendition".' See also *Mohamed* v. *Jeppessen Dataplan, Incinclud.*, 579 F.3d 943 (9th Cir. 2009) (dismissing on the basis of the state-secrets doctrine a suit against a Boeing subsidiary for its role in the extraordinary rendition programme of the CIA).

[97] In one of the cases against a state's contractor a settlement was achieved. Blackwater Worldwide, a private company that operated in Iraq, was sued for war crimes committed during the armed conflict in Iraq. The US government submitted its response to Blackwater's motion on 8 October 2009, stating that if the contractors committed the alleged conduct, they were not acting as US employees and therefore they were not entitled to immunity. On 21 October 2009, a few days after the US government submitted its response to Blackwater's motion to dismiss, the District Court for the Eastern District of Virginia rendered a memorandum opinion based on the state position. Accordingly the claim does not raise a 'non justiciable political question' as the allegations cannot be attributed to the government: *Xe Services Alien Tort Litig.*, 6 January 2010. Soon after a confidential settlement was concluded.

[98] *Rasul* v. *Rumsfeld*, 414 F. Supp. 2d 26 (D.D.C. 2006), 26.

[99] Katherine Gallagher, '*Universal Jurisdiction in Practice: Efforts to Hold Donald Rumsfeld and Other High-Level United States Officials Accountable for Torture*', *Journal of International Criminal Justice*, 7/5 (2009), 1098–9. In the absence of domestic accountability criminal complaints were filed in Germany, France, and Spain, on the basis of universal jurisdiction. See also the CCR website <http://ccrjustice.org/case-against-rumsfeld>.

[100] *Re Iraq and Afghan Detainees Litigation,* 479 F. Supp. 2d 85 (D.D.C. 2007).

Eighth Amendments to the US Constitution, and the Religious Freedom Restoration Act. In a memorandum opinion issued on 6 February 2006, the District Court of Columbia dismissed the ATS and Geneva Conventions claims on immunity grounds. The dismissal was based on the Federal Employees Liability Reform and Tort Compensation Act of 1988, known as the 'Westfall Act'.[101] Under this Act, federal government officials may not be held liable for damages for acts carried out within the scope of their employment. The scope of their employment is defined by the Restatement (Second) of Agency as conduct 'of the same general nature as that authorized, or incidental to the conduct authorized',[102] leaving 'serious crimes' beyond that scope.[103]

It would have been reasonable to expect a court to hold that acts of torture, which are illegal under US federal and international humanitarian and human rights law, would fall outside of the scope of official employment. For example, in another ATS case—against a foreign official—the court held that torture does not constitute an 'official act' as it is in violation of state law.[104] However, the District Court of Columbia and the Court of Appeals preferred a wide interpretation of the *Restatement*. Both instances held that the alleged acts of torture that include 'interrogation techniques such as the use of stress positions, intimidation by the use of dogs, twenty-hour interrogation sessions, shaving of detainees' facial hair, isolation in darkness and silence and the use of "mild non-injurious physical contact"'[105] (which has to be assumed as true at this stage of the proceedings) all

[101] *Rasul* v. *Rumsfeld* (Order Granting Motion to Dismiss on International and Constitutional Claims). For the other claims that were dismissed as well see Bardo Fassbender, 'Can Victims Sue State Officials for Torture? Reflections on Rasul v. Myers from the Perspective of International Law', *Journal of International Criminal Justice*, 6/2 (2008), 347–69.

[102] Restatement (Second) of Agency, 228–30. The Federal Tort Claims Act (FTCA) provides the exclusive remedy for torts by officials committed within the scope of their employment: upon certification by the Attorney General that the defendant employee was acting within the scope of his employment any civil action or proceeding commenced upon such claim in a United States district court shall be deemed an action against the United States. It mandates that the US be the defendants instead of the individual officials, and that a plaintiff must first submit an administrative claim to the appropriate government agency and have it denied before filing a suit at court. To define whether an act falls within the scope of employment, a four-factor test drawn from the Restatement is applied: (a) it is of the kind he is employed to perform; (b) it occurs substantially within the authorized time and space limits; (c) it is actuated, at least in part, by a purpose to serve the master, and (d) if force is intentionally used by the servant against another, the use of force is not unexpectable by the master.

[103] Jaykumar A. Menon, 'Guantanamo Torture Litigation', *Journal of International Criminal Justice*, 6/2 (2008), 331.

[104] The US District Court for the Northern District of California rendered a default judgment against Liu Qi, Mayor of Beijing, for his role in the torture of Falun Gong. Both the Chinese government and State Department submitted statements urging that the case be dismissed. The State Department stated, among other things, that the suit risked interfering with the US Government's relations with China, and raised the possibility of retaliatory suits by other countries against US officials. The court held that Liu Qi did not enjoy sovereign immunity under the FSIA. Liu Qi acted outside the scope of his authority as torture was in violation of Chinese law. *Doe* v. *Lui Qi*, 349 F. Supp. 2d 1258 (N.D. Cal 2004), 1287. The state demanded the dismissal of the case on the basis of act of state doctrine and political question grounds. However, the judge rendered a declaratory judgment, justifying it on the fact that the US had repeatedly complained to China regarding its policy towards Falun Gong. Thus the court assumed that a declaratory judgment could not have an influence on foreign relations.

[105] *Rasul* v. *Myers*, 512 F.3d 644 (D.C. Cir. 2008), 4.

fall within the scope of the state's officials' employment because these were 'incidental to the conduct authorized'.[106] Moreover, the first instance judge notes that 'torture is a foreseeable consequence of the military's detention of suspected enemy combatants' emphasizing that 'the heightened climate of anxiety, due to the stresses of war and pressures after September 11 to uncover information leading to the capture of terrorists, would naturally lead to a greater desire to procure information and, therefore, more aggressive techniques for interrogations.' The court also found that the defendants were acting 'to further the interests of their employer, the United States' and that the plaintiffs have not 'proffered any evidence that would lead this court to believe that the defendants had any motive divorced from the policy of the United States to quash terrorism around the world.'[107] The Court of Appeals followed this line and stated that 'While it may generally be unexpected that seriously criminal conduct will arise "in the prosecution of the business", here it was foreseeable that conduct that would ordinarily be indisputably "seriously criminal" would be implemented by military officials responsible for detaining and interrogating suspected enemy combatants.'[108] Thus, in order to accord immunity to state officials, US courts went as far as to rule that torture committed by the US officials is 'incidental' and 'foreseeable', explicitly establishing that torture is to be expected of the United States during detention of suspected enemy combatants. Having found that the Federal Tort Claims Act (FTCA) is applicable, the courts of both instances affirmed that neither the claims based on ATS nor the Geneva Conventions can be raised because the plaintiffs had failed to exhaust their administrative remedies as required by the FTCA.[109]

ii. Re: Iraq and Afghanistan Detainees Litigation

The same immunity was granted in the *Re: Iraq and Afghanistan Detainees Litigation*. In this case, a group of Iraqi and Afghani citizens claimed that they had been tortured and abused by US military officials in Iraq and Afghanistan. Their claim was based on the ATS and the Geneva Conventions, stating that the Westfall Act did not apply to intentional torts that violate *jus cogens* norms. The court rejected

[106] *Rasul* v. *Rumsfeld*, 33 (n 98). See also the ruling of the Court of Appeals: The defendants respond that '[w]here high-level military officials are charged with winning the war on terror, and specifically with detaining and obtaining information from suspected terrorists, the officials' policies on detention and interrogation, and their supervision of the implementation of those policies, is at least "incidental" to those duties.' *Rasul* v. *Myers*, 657 (n 105).

[107] *Rasul* v. *Rumsfeld*, 34–6 (n 98).

[108] *Rasul* v. *Myers*, 661 (n 105). The Court of Appeals dismissed the plaintiffs' appeal against the decision of the District Court. It affirmed that the Westfall Act makes the Federal Tort Claims Act the exclusive remedy for any damages action for torts committed by a federal official 'while acting within the scope of his office or employment'—as it had been in this case.

[109] See n 102. However, the co-counsel for the plaintiffs, Jaykumar A. Menon, raised a view that any claim by Guantanamo detainees under the FTCA is likely to be futile as the FTCA does not waive sovereign immunity for 'any claim arising in a foreign country', nor for certain 'intentional torts.' Therefore 'the Court's ultimate ground of dismissal—failure to exhaust remedies under the FTCA—[is] somewhat misleading. Instead of using the Westfall scope of employment analysis for its intended purpose (namely, determining who should be liable, an employee or the "boss"), the Court has used it to deny liability altogether.' Menon, 'Guantanamo Torture Litigation', 340.

this claim and ruled that there was no per se rule that violations of *jus cogens* norms of international law were ever within the scope of employment. Thus, it held that the defendants were entitled to immunity for ATS claims pursuant to the FTCA, as the acts of detaining and interrogating enemy aliens were within the defendants' scope of employment. Torture was either of the same general nature that they were authorized to perform or incidental to authorized conduct. Consequently, the defendants were entitled to immunity for the alleged international law violations even if these amount to *jus cogens* violations.

In addition to invoking the ATS as authority for a cause of action for alleged violations of Geneva Convention IV, the plaintiffs also asserted that the treaty itself grants a private right to sue.[110] Unlike the Court in *Rasul* that dealt with both claims under the immunity defence, here the court ruled that Geneva Convention IV is not self-executing and it cannot be judicially enforced via private lawsuits in federal courts.

Vance and Ertel v. Rumsfeld

In the case of *Vance and Ertel* v. *Rumsfeld* the plaintiffs, who alleged torture, were US citizens, and indeed—at least at first instance level— while distinguishing it from *Rasul* and *Re Iraq* the decision on motion to dismiss resulted in a different outcome.[111] The avoidance doctrines raised by the state were dismissed and on its role during times of war the court declared:

> [W]e are not convinced that dismissing the claim of these two *American citizens* is a proper exercise of judicial authority. Instead, we believe 'a state of war is not a blank check' for the President or high-ranking government officials when it comes to the rights of the American citizens . . . When an American citizen sets out well-pled allegations of torturous behaviour by executive officials abroad, we believe that courts are not foreclosed from denying a motion to dismiss such allegations at the very first stage of the trial process.[112]

This case may indicate that the court is more reluctant to apply avoidance doctrines when it deals with the protection of fundamental rights during armed conflict of its own citizens—a trend which has been clearly established in foreign courts dealing with Guantanamo torture cases.[113] Yet, this case has to be read within a more

[110] The plaintiffs referred to Articles 3, 27, 31, 32, 118 and 119 of the Fourth Geneva Convention of 1949 as self-executing provisions and relied principally on the decision in *Jogi* v. *Voges*, 425 F.3d 367 (7th Cir. 2005), to validate this contention. See *Re Iraq and Afghan Detainees Litigation*, paragraph 57 (n 100).

[111] *Vance and Ertel* v. *Rumsfeld et al.*, 694 F. Supp. 2d 957 (N.D. Ill. 2010), 23.

[112] *Vance and Ertel* v. *Rumsfeld et al.*, 31–3. See by contrast *Al-Aulaqi* v. *Obama*, 727 F. Supp. 2d 1 (D.D.C. 2010) in which the review of the legality of the targeted killing of an American citizen was avoided by the court.

[113] The Supreme Court landmark *Guantanamo habeas corpus* cases (*Rasul* v. *Bush*, 542 U.S. 466 (2004) and *Boumediene* v. *Bush*), went even further to accept that the right to habeas corpus extends extraterritorially to aliens. In *Rasul* the Supreme Court found that, because the habeas statute drew 'no distinction between Americans and aliens held in federal custody, there is little reason to think that Congress intended the geographical coverage of the statute to vary depending on the detainee's citizenship.' (481). See George P. Fletcher, 'Citizenship and Personhood in the Jurisprudence of War: Hamdi, Padilla and the Detainees in Guantanamo Bay', *Journal of International Criminal Justice*,

general context: it is one of the very rare cases in which a court of first instance agreed to examine the allegations of torture against US officials on the merits, and the decision to reject the motion to dismiss is currently before the US Court of Appeals for the Seventh Circuit.[114] The litigation itself is still a long way off.

While courts may avoid rendering a judgment, they may nonetheless explicitly disapprove of the government's policy. See for example the statements of Judge Urbina, who in order to provide immunity to state officials, ruled in *Rasul* that torture is incidental and foreseeable:

> Most disturbing, however, is . . . [that] the plaintiffs assert that their captors became the beasts they sought to suppress.
>
> [in footnote:] It would indeed be ironic if, in the name of national defense, we would sanction the subversion of one of those liberties . . . As Mahatma Ghandi stated, '[w]hat difference does it make . . . whether the mad destruction is wrought under the name of totalitarianism or the holy name of liberty and democracy?'[115]

And in *Re Iraq*, as observed by Erin Culbertson and Dinah Shelton: 'While this court felt compelled to dismiss the action, it expressed considerable sympathy for the plaintiffs throughout the opinion, for example by referring to the "horrifying torture allegations" in the "lamentable" case, and by providing considerable detail as to the abuse inflicted.'[116] This trend may be a signal to the government that while the court is still cautious about ruling on the merits against state acts committed during the conduct of war, times are changing. Where previously the US legal tradition would confine issues relating to foreign relations to the executive branch, it may adopt a more active attitude to IHL issues in the future.

iii. The *Agent Orange Litigation*: avoiding avoidance doctrines

In *Agent Orange Litigation* the plaintiffs, Vietnamese nationals and the Vietnam Association for Victims of Agent Orange/Dioxin, suffered from health problems caused by exposure to herbicides.[117] They sued a number of corporations that had produced and supplied the US government with chemical herbicides that contained dioxin. Dioxin allegedly caused serious damage to human health and the environment, when used by the US armed forces during the war in Vietnam. The plaintiffs relied on a long list of domestic statutes and international law references, most

2/4 (2004), 953–66. Yet lower US courts still make the distinction between the right to habeas corpus and the prohibition of torture—a distinction which is hard to defend from an international law stand—as torture constitutes a *jus cogens* violation.

[114] Another similar ruling was rendered by US District Judge Jeffrey S. White of the District Court of Northern California in the case brought by Padilla. On 12 June 2009 Justice White allowed a lawsuit against former Justice Department official John Yoo to go forward, based on the fact that Yoo wrote official memos justifying 'coercive interrogation' of detainees including Padilla (*Padilla* v. *Yoo*, 633 F. Supp. 2d 1005 (N.D. Cal. 2009)). The White decision is now under review in the Ninth Circuit Court.

[115] *Rasul* v. *Rumsfeld*, 27, fn 1 (n 98).

[116] Oxford Reports on International law in Domestic Courts, Analysis of Erin Culbertson and Dinah Shelton (21 July 2008). Online at <www.oxfordlawreports.com>.

[117] *Re 'Agent Orange' Product Liability Litigation*, 373 F.Supp. 2d 7 (EDNY 2005).

notably IHL. Their claim was that the defendants had conspired with the United States in violation of international law to manufacture, sell, and supply these toxic herbicides to the United States government for use as chemical weapons in Vietnam during the period of 1961–1975.[118]

The preliminary claims raised by the defendants argued were (1) that corporations acting as government contractors are immune under the government contractor defence (which protects government contractors from product liability claims if they can demonstrate that they followed the government's instructions); (2) that the claim was a non-justiciable political question and that the court should defer to the executive's determination at the time that the actions were lawful. In support of the defendants' preliminary claims the Bush administration filed a statement of interest supporting the defendants' motion to dismiss the claims under the ATS as non-justiciable political questions because those claims required an inquiry into executive judgments relating to the prosecution of a war. The Bush administration claimed that the case raised non-justiciable political questions that would require the court to pass judgment upon the validity of the president's decisions regarding combat tactics and weaponry during a time of armed conflict. Such judicial review would encroach on the executive's commander-in-chief authority, and run foul of basic principles of separation of powers and the political question doctrine. It stated that allowing the claim to proceed would interfere with the relationship with Vietnam, and that this litigation could open the US courts to all of the nation's past and future enemies. In addition, the state argued that the court should defer to the executive's interpretation of the relevant treaties and customary international law. This was in accordance with the US's use of chemical herbicides in Vietnam which did not violate any applicable rules of international law.

The court found the state position on non-justiciability to be 'not persuasive', and contrary to the government's stand it ruled that the claims were justiciable. It also ruled that the corporations were not immune as the contractor defence was inapplicable to allegations of war crimes. In defining its role the court adopted a remarkably active position:

> Justiciability is not eliminated because of possible interference with executive power even in wartime . . . given the importance of international law today in preventing abuse by nations and individuals, and the importation of that law into ruling federal law, the political question doctrine does not bar this suit . . . It raises issues that courts are structured and empowered to decide—the nature and applicability of substantive international law and

[118] The acts described allegedly constitute war crimes in violation of the ATS, customary international law, the Geneva Protocol for the Prohibition of the Use in War of Asphyxiating, Poisonous or Other Gases, and of Bacteriological Methods of Warfare (adopted 16 June 1925, entered into force 8 February 1928) 26 U.S.T. 571; Article 23 of the Hague Regulations of 1907; The Fourth Geneva Convention of 1949; Agreement for the Prosecution and Punishment of the Major War Criminals of the European Axis and Charter of the International Military Tribunal at Nuremberg (adopted and entered into force 8 August 1945) 82 U.N.T.S 280; the United Nations Charter; UNGA Res. 2603-A (16 December 1969) UN Doc A/RES/2603(XXIV)A; Customary international law.

domestic tort law.... What international law is and how it applies present questions of the meaning of substantive law, and the interpretation of these questions is a task entrusted to the courts. That judicial power cannot be frustrated by the overly broad preemption doctrine espoused by defendants.[119]

On the question of deferral the court also took a firm position:

The President of the United States has no power to violate international law or to authorize others to do so. The Nuremberg decisions made it clear that a head of state and those responding to his orders are bound by international law... The government's further contention that the courts should defer to the executive's interpretation of international law insofar as it suggests that the executive's statement of the law is controlling, is rejected, even though the courts will often be influenced by the executive's interpretation since its expertise in international law is substantial.

Thus the court rejected the defendants' non-justiciability and immunity claims, and took a very active stand on the appropriate role of the judiciary in adjudicating cases dealing with decisions and acts performed during armed conflict, in firm opposition to the views of the state. Seemingly, this represents a landmark decision on avoidance doctrines. Yet, these claims must be put in context. On the merits, the court rejected the plaintiffs' claims and ruled that IHL, at that time, did not prohibit the use of this kind of weapon. Thus, in deciding to exercise its competence the court in fact legitimized the state's use of herbicides in Vietnam prior to 1975. The important question to examine is if on the merits the finding had been different, and the court was about to rule that the government had used an illegal weapon and committed a war crime, would the court have been equally willing to exercise its judicial function in such an active manner? Would the judge have still relied so heavily on Second World War precedents including the *Eichmann* case, the Nuremberg trials, and responsibility of Hitler as commander?[120] Or, would the judge have preferred to avoid the case, as being politically sensitive? The answer to these questions has to remain unknown. However, as argued by Jeff Yates and Andrew Whitford, when the state has not violated the law, courts will be more willing to adjudicate the case.[121] Quite surprisingly an echo of this reflection may be found in the judgment itself where the court stated: a court cannot 'decide whether there is a textually demonstrable commitment or judicially manageable standards without first taking a peek at the very merits it purports to be avoiding. In effect, the court says that it must first decide the merits in order to avoid deciding the merits'.[122]

[119] *Re 'Agent Orange' Product Liability Litigation*, paragraph 183 (n 117).

[120] In *Re 'Agent Orange' Product Liability Litigation*, paragraph 216 (n 117), the court refers to the superior order defence. It states that although acting under Hitler's orders had not served as a defence at Nuremberg, spraying of herbicides being by orders of the president, could not serve as a defence. It referred also to the *Eichmann* case.

[121] Yates and Whitford, 'Presidential Power', 539–50 (n 7).

[122] *Re 'Agent Orange' Product Liability Litigation*, paragraph 156 (n 117) (citing Louis M. Seidman, 'This Essay is Brilliant/This Essay is Stupid: Positive and Negative Self-Reference in Constitutional Practice and Theory', *UCLA Law Review*, 46/[i] 501 (1998), 501, 528–30).

Thomas M. Franck in his book *Political Questions/Judicial Answers* provides other examples of federal courts taking an 'active position' when their ruling on the merits is in favour of the state. The *Holtzman* litigation which challenged the legality of US bombing in Cambodia during the Vietnam War is one example. The Second Circuit ruled that this was a non-justiciable political question, but then, as observed by Frank, the court 'went on to say: "we cannot resist..." examining congressional appropriations that would legitimate the President's actions.' Another illustration is the case dealing with missing persons in Vietnam, whose relatives sought an order to compel the president to intensify efforts to find them according to a domestic US act. While the court 'dutifully intoned that "conduct of foreign policy" is "an area traditionally reserved to the political branches"', the judge nevertheless determined that the president had wide discretion at his disposal.[123] In conclusion, Franck notes that: 'the jurisprudence has a powerful whiff of hypocrisy: Judges say they will abstain but fail to do so; judges proclaim the separation of powers but almost always decide in favor of the government in a process where the players—the government and those challenging its actions—appear not to be playing on a level field.'[124]

2.1.3 ATS cases against US allies

The varied avoidance doctrines used in cases involving US officials have been employed in a similar manner to avoid jurisdiction in cases involving the responsibility of officials from US ally states. In *Ya'alon*,[125] the plaintiffs sued the Israeli General Moshe Ya'alon, a former head of Israeli army intelligence. The action was brought under the ATS and the Torture Victim Protection Act of 1991 and alleged war crimes and extrajudicial killing for the shelling of a UN compound in Qana, Lebanon, in 1996 in which more than 100 Palestinian civilian refugees were killed. During the proceedings the Israeli government submitted a letter to the court stating that Ya'alon's actions were within the course of his official duties. The appellants argued that the FSIA did not apply to former government officials,[126] and that even if it did, a fundamental violation of international law could never be within the scope of official authority. The Circuit Court, however, found that Ya'alon was immune from suit under the FSIA and affirmed that an individual could qualify as an agent for the purposes of the FSIA.[127] The Circuit Court also rejected the plaintiffs' claim that the FSIA did not apply to foreign officials once they have left office. In addition, it declined to create a *jus cogens* exception to the

[123] Franck, *Political Questions/Judicial Answers*, 27–30, (n 5) discussing *Smith* v. *Reagan*, 844 F.2d 195 (4th Cir. 1988). *Holtzman* v. *Schlesinger*, 361 F.Supp. 553 (E.D.N.Y 1973); *Holtzman* v. *Schlesinger*, 484 F. 2d 1307 (3d Cir. 1973). These cases do not deal specifically with ATS, but with the application of other laws in the context of armed conflict.

[124] Franck, *Political Questions/Judicial Answers*, 30 (n 5).

[125] *Belhas* v. *Ya'alon*, 515 F.3d 1279 (D.C. Cir. 2008).

[126] *Belhas* v. *Ya'alon*, 1286 (n 125).

[127] This finding was overruled by the US Supreme Court two years later in *Samantar* v. *Yousuf*, in which the court held that the FSIA does not grant immunity to individuals. However it left open the question of whether officials were entitled to common-law immunity. *Samantar* v. *Yousuf*, 2292–3 (n 91) (holding that a Somali official was not entitled to immunity for his official acts under the FSIA).

FSIA in the absence of specific congress authorization,[128] although other courts in cases against other states, such as the Philippines, had recognized violations of *jus cogens* norms as an exception to FSIA immunity.[129] While courts have found the FSIA inapplicable in suits against certain states' officials based on violations of *jus cogens* norms, it granted immunity to Israeli officials and it seems that other federal courts are also unlikely to recognize a *jus cogens* exception in cases against close ally states.

In *Matar* v. *Dichter*,[130] the former director of the General Security Services was sued for planning and directing the commission of a war crime in the targeted killing of Salah Shehadeh. The complaint, filed in December 2005, alleged that by committing war crimes and other violations of international law, Dichter was liable for damages pursuant to the ATS. The State Department expressed the view that the FSIA grants sovereign immunity to countries, not to individuals, yet Dichter was still entitled to common law immunity which the FSIA did not displace. The Court of the Second Circuit ruled, in accordance with the US State Department's position, that even if the FSIA is not applicable, former officials are still entitled to common law immunity as long as their acts were within their official capacity. It recognized immunity of former foreign officials for 'acts performed in his official capacity': an immunity 'based on acts—rather than status—does not depend on tenure in office'.[131]

In allocating common law immunity to Dichter the court recognized that the alleged war crimes were performed within Dichter's official capacity, as explicitly confirmed by the State of Israel. It is interesting to note that this is exactly how the court of first instance distinguished this case from the ones in which a *jus cogens* violation did remove an official's immunity: 'none of the cases cited by Plaintiffs involve a situation where, as here, the foreign government has expressly ratified the defendant's actions and affirmed that the defendant was acting pursuant to his official duties.'[132] Oddly, the court ruled that to shield state officials from accountability for war crimes it is sufficient to present a mere declaration of the government that these were executed as a part of an official policy. Would this rationale be applicable to all states? Not necessarily. In the case of *Siderman de Blake* v. *Argentina*, for example, the Circuit Court stated that '[i]nternational law does not recognize an act that violates jus cogens as a sovereign act.'[133]

In addition to immunity, in *Matar* v. *Dichter*, the US's position was that the case should be dismissed on political question grounds. The district court was ready to follow this approach and to dismiss the case on those grounds. In doing so, the court adopted a strikingly deferential attitude. The plaintiff's referral to *Kadic* was labelled as 'misplaced' for the simple reason that in *Kadic* the State Department had

[128] *Belhas* v. *Ya'alon*, 1287–8 (n 125).

[129] *Hilao* v. *Estate of Marcos*, 25 F.3d 1467 (9th Cir. 1994), 1472; *Chuidian* v. *Philippine National Bank*, 912 F.2d 1095 (9th Cir. 1990), 1106.

[130] *Matar* v. *Dichter*, 500 F. Supp. 2d 284 (S.D.N.Y. 2007). On appeal *Matar* v. *Dichter*, 563 F.3d 9 (2nd Cir. 2009).

[131] *Matar* v. *Dichter*, 563 F.3d 9, 13–15 (n 130).

[132] *Matar* v. *Dichter*, 296 (n 130).

[133] *Siderman de Blake* v. *Republic of Argentina*, 965 F.2d 699 (9th Cir. 1992), 718–19.

'expressly disclaimed any concern that the political question doctrine should be invoked... the opposite is true here, as the State Department had advocated forcefully for the dismissal of this action'.[134]

The *Corrie* v. *Caterpillar*[135] case was dismissed on purely political question grounds. In this case it was not an Israeli official who was sued, but a private US company that supplied bulldozers to the Israeli army, which were allegedly used to commit war crimes. As the United States government had paid for the bulldozers as part of its aid to Israel and as the executive and legislative branches had approved the US policy of selling weapons and other goods to Israel, the court found that this case formed part of the non-justiciable political question doctrine. Furthermore, the court found that the act of state doctrine applied because the plaintiffs were asking the court to pass judgment on official military acts of Israel.[136]

In contrast with these cases, which involve the responsibility of Israel, in many other suits courts have imposed liability on the Palestinian Authority (PA), the Palestinian Liberation Organization (PLO) and Iran for acts of terrorism.[137] As pointed out by Adam N. Schupack, in civil cases involving the Israeli-Arab conflict, the courts have not applied the political question doctrine in a uniform fashion: 'Suits against the PA, PLO, and Iran have resulted in large judgments, while courts have dismissed suits against Israel, Israeli leaders, and Caterpillar. [...][T]his contrast represents an injustice that undermines the legitimacy of such suits and the notion that litigants who are victims of Israeli actions can rely upon U.S. courts to dispense justice.'[138]

2.1.4 ATS cases against other third states' officials

The case that is probably the best example of a situation in which a US court attributed compensation for victims during an ongoing armed conflict is the *Kadic* case. This was a suit brought by Bosnian nationals against Radovan Karadzic, the leader of the Bosnian Serb entity, for committing, inter alia, war crimes during the armed conflict in Bosnia and Herzegovina. Not only did the Second Circuit Court

134 *Matar* v. *Dichter*, 302 (n 130).

135 *Corrie* v. *Caterpillar, Inc.*, 503 F.3d 974 (9th Cir. 2007).

136 On appeal, the Ninth Circuit first held that the political question doctrine is a 'jurisdictional limitation imposed on the courts by the Constitution,' not just a prudential doctrine adopted 'by the judiciary itself.' *Corrie* v. *Caterpillar, Inc* (n 135). The court then applied the *Baker* factors, and found that the case did present a political question: 'The decisive factor here is that Caterpillar's sales to Israel were paid for by the United States [..] [T]hese sales were financed by the executive branch pursuant to a congressionally enacted program calling for executive discretion as to what lies in the foreign policy and national security interests of the United States [..] Allowing this action to proceed would necessarily require the judicial branch of our government to question the political branches' decision to grant extensive military aid to Israel. It is difficult to see how we could impose liability on Caterpillar without at least implicitly deciding the propriety of the United States' decision to pay for the bulldozers which allegedly killed the plaintiffs' family members.' For an analysis of the case see: Baars, G. 'Corrie et al v Caterpillar: Litigating Corporate Complicity in Israeli Violations of International Law in the U.S. Courts', *Yearbook of Islamic and Middle Eastern Law*, 2005/6 (2007).

137 Schupack, 'The Arab-Israeli Conflict', 207, 214–28 (n 78). The cases mentioned include those brought under the Anti Terrorist Act 1990.

138 Schupack, 'The Arab-Israeli Conflict', 245 (n 78).

not avoid rendering a ruling (indeed, it rendered a ruling in a particularly sensitive period of an ongoing conflict when peace agreements were being negotiated),[139] it also conducted an analysis of what were then innovative IHL issues. The court examined whether a violation of Common Article 3 of the Geneva Conventions constitutes a war crime as well as whether the court may exercise jurisdiction over non-state actors under the ATS.[140] The court opened the section of its ruling in which it discussed justiciability with the following statement:

> We recognize that cases of this nature might pose special questions concerning the judiciary's proper role when adjudication might have implications in the conduct of this nation's foreign relations. We do not read *Filártiga* to mean that the federal judiciary must always act in ways that risk significant interference with United States foreign relations. To the contrary, we recognize that suits of this nature can present difficulties that implicate sensitive matters of diplomacy historically reserved to the jurisdiction of the political branches.[141]

The court then considered whether, even though the jurisdictional threshold was satisfied other considerations 'relevant to justiciability weigh against permitting the suits to proceed'. Before addressing the political question and act of state doctrines in this particular case it emphasized that '[N]ot every case "touching foreign relations" is non-justiciable', and that: '[T]he doctrine is one of "political questions", not one of "political cases".' When the court moved to examine the *Baker factors* it cited as a reference a case against the PLO.[142] As for the act of state doctrine the court stated that it 'doubt[s] that the acts of even a state official, taken in violation of a nation's fundamental law . . . could properly be characterized as an act of state'. Finally, the court emphasized that in this case the statement of interest of the US State Department has 'expressly disclaimed any concern that the political question doctrine should be invoked to prevent the litigation of these lawsuits', thereby enabling it to reject the non-justiciability claims. It is beyond the scope of this section to examine why the Clinton administration found that there were no foreign relations ramifications that prevented this case from proceeding, when the same administration had been negotiating the Dayton Agreements with the defendant. Whatever were the interests of the US State Department, it may be reasonably assumed that without that consent the court would have abstained from delivering a ruling in such a politically sensitive period.

The preferable approach as to whether or not to avoid a case is to be widely cited in future cases: '[The court should] weigh carefully the relevant considerations on a

[139] The case was argued on 20 June 1995 and decided on 13 October 1995, while the Dayton Peace agreement was signed in December 1995. Karadzic was served with the Plaintiffs' complaint on two occasions during visits to NYC for negotiations at the UN. See Theodore R. Posner, 'Kadic v. Karadzic, 70 F.3d 232 (18 June 1996)', *American Journal of International Law*, 90/4 (1996), 659. See how the court opens its ruling: 'Most Americans would probably be surprised to learn that victims of atrocities committed in Bosnia are suing the leader of the insurgent Bosnian-Serb forces in a United States District Court in Manhattan.'

[140] *Kadic* v. *Karadzic*, 242–4 (n 23). [141] *Kadic* v. *Karadzic*, 249 (n 23).

[142] 'The department to whom this issue has been "constitutionally committed" is none other than our own—the Judiciary.' *Klinghoffer* v. *PLO*, 937 F.2d 44 (2nd Cir. 1991), 49.

case-by-case basis. This will permit the judiciary to act where *appropriate*.'[143] In this way, since the revival of the ATS in 1980, US federal courts have acted when it was deemed *appropriate*. As a result two contradictory trends coexist in the jurisprudence—one avoiding, the other activist. While 'often a court will treat the political-question doctrine as applicable to a case for reasons that fail to distinguish it from similar litigation in which judges felt entitled to decide without deferring to the doctrine',[144] opposing jurisprudence has developed. Courts are therefore able to rely on convenient jurisprudence to decide on a *state by state* basis whether it is *appropriate* to adjudicate and to apply IHL or whether it is *appropriate* to avoid rendering justice, most often in accordance with the US State position.

2.2. The use of avoidance doctrines in the US and Israeli targeted killing cases

The different roles and positions of the courts regarding the exercise of their jurisdiction during conduct of hostilities cases is well illustrated in the targeted killing cases. These were decided before the US District Court and the Israeli HCJ.

2.2.1 The targeted killing case before the US District Court of Columbia

The United States has adopted a secret policy of targeted killings since the attacks of 11 September 2001, in which drones and airstrikes are used for targeted killings in Afghanistan, Iraq, and allegedly in other territories too.[145] During the 2010 annual meeting of the American society of international law, the US Department of State legal advisor, M. Harold Koh, affirmed that the Obama administration 'is committed to ensuring that the targeting practices . . . are lawful'.[146] In his speech, Koh offered legal justifications for targeted killings. These were based both on the US's right to self-defence and IHL that was applicable to the armed conflict with *al-Qaeda*, the Taliban, and associated organizations. Philip Alston, the UN Special Rapporteur on extrajudicial, summary or arbitrary executions, who conducted a study on targeted killings, noted in his report that these justifications do not address

> some of the most central legal issues including: the scope of the armed conflict in which the US asserts it is engaged, the criteria for individuals who may be targeted and killed, the

[143] *Kadic* v. *Karadzic*, 249 (n 23).

[144] Franck, *Political Questions/Judicial Answers*, 8 (n 5).

[145] Council of Europe, 'Secret Detentions and Illegal Transfers of Detainees Involving Council of Europe Member States', Rapporteur Mr Dick Marty, Doc. 11302 Rev. (2007), paragraphs 58–64; Report of the Special Rapporteur on Extrajudicial, Summary or Arbitrary Executions, Philip Alston, Addendum, Study on Targeted Killings, UN Doc A/HRC/14/24/Add.6 (28 May 2010), 7–8. See for a general discussion on the legality of targeted killings: Robert Chesney, 'Who May Be Killed? Anwar al-Awlaki as a Case Study in the International Legal Regulation of Lethal Force', *Yearbook of IHL*, 13 (2011).

[146] Harold Hongju Koh, 'The Obama Administration and International Law', US Department of State (25 March 2010). Online at <http://www.state.gov/s/l/releases/remarks/139119.htm>.

existence of any substantive or procedural safeguards to ensure the legality and accuracy of killings, and the existence of accountability mechanisms.[147]

Shortly after, on 30 August 2010, the American Civil Liberties Union and the Center for Constitutional Rights filed a suit in the US District Court of Columbia in the name of Nasser Al-Aulaqi against President Obama and others, challenging their decision to authorize the targeted killing of Al-Aulaqi's son, a US citizen, in Yemen. They claimed that the US policy of targeted killing violates the Constitution and international law,[148] and requested the court to declare that according to US constitutional law and international law, the US government is prohibited from carrying out the targeted killing of citizens where no armed conflict exists.[149] The state requested the dismissal of the case, invoking various different avoidance doctrines including lack of standing, political question and state secrets privilege, basing itself on the separation of power rationale and the court's inability to evaluate military issues:

> The particular relief plaintiff seeks would constitute an *ex ante* command to military and intelligence officials that could interfere with lawful commands issued by the President, who is constitutionally designated as Commander-in-Chief of the armed forces and constitutionally responsible for national security . . . Enforcement of such orders would necessarily require the Court to supervise inherently predictive judgments by the President and his national security advisors as to when and how to use force overseas against that organization. Courts are not equipped to superintend such questions . . .
>
> the very determination of whether and in what circumstances the United States' armed conflict with al-Qaeda might extend beyond the borders of Iraq and Afghanistan is itself a non-justiciable political question.[150]

The US District Court of Columbia granted the state's motion to dismiss on the grounds that Al-Aulaqi's father lacked standing and that the claims concerned political questions and were therefore not justiciable. The court took the view that the questions posed required both 'expertise beyond the capacity of the judiciary' and the need for 'unquestioning adherence to a political decision by the executive' and an assessment of 'strategic choices directing the nation's foreign affairs [that] are constitutionally committed to the political branches.'[151] Ruling

[147] Report of the Special Rapporteur on Extrajudicial, Summary or Arbitrary Executions, Philip Alston, paragraph 22 (n 145).

[148] All the documents related to this case are available at <http://www.ccrjustice.org/targetedkillings>.

[149] The cause of actions were based on the constitution violation of the Fourth and Fifth Amendments, protecting the right to life and the due process, and the ATS, through which the claimants refer to international human rights and humanitarian law, accordingly there is a prohibition to kill outside of an armed conflict 'without judicial process in circumstances in which they do not present concrete, specific, and imminent threats to life or physical safety, and where there are means other than lethal force that could reasonably be employed to neutralize any such threat.' Complaint for Declaratory and Injunctive Relief (30 August 2010), 10 <http://ccrjustice.org/files/Al-Aulaqi%20v.%20Obama%20Complaint.pdf>.

[150] Opposition to Plaintiff's Motion for preliminary Injunction and Memorandum in Support of Defendants' Motion to Dismiss, 19, 22. Online at <http://www.aclu.org/national-security/al-aulaqi-v-obama-opposition-plaintiff-s-motion-preliminary-injunction-and-memoran>.

[151] *Al-Aulaqi* v. *Obama*, 727 F. Supp. 2d 1 (D.D.C. 2010), 76–7. Online at <http://www.ccrjustice.org/files/2010.12.07_Al-Aulaqi%20Decision_0.pdf>. See also at page 80: 'Because decision-making in the realm of military and foreign affairs is textually committed to the political branches,

that it is a non-justiciable political question, the court of first instance left the question of the legality of a targeted killing of an American citizen in light of his constitutional rights outside the realm of judicial scrutiny: 'Because these questions of justiciability require dismissal of this case at the outset, the serious issues regarding the merits of the alleged authorization of the targeted killing of a U.S. citizen overseas must await another day or another (non-judicial) forum.'[152]

As this case involved politically sensitive questions that concern an ongoing military policy with a potentially strong impact on US conduct in its fight against terrorism worldwide, institutionally a lower level court probably could not have decided otherwise. Yet, surprisingly, even the court itself felt uneasy with its own judgment:

> [I]t does not appear that any court has ever – on political question doctrine grounds – refused to hear a US citizen's claim that his personal constitutional rights have been violated as a result of US government action taken abroad...
>
> To be sure, this Court recognizes the somewhat unsettling nature of its conclusion – that there are circumstances in which the Executive's unilateral decision to kill a US citizen overseas is "constitutionally committed to the political branches" and judicially unreviewable.[153]

The court was also ready to acknowledge that it is a 'drastic measure' for the US to employ lethal force against one of its own citizens abroad, even if that citizen is an active part of a terrorist group. At the same time, it went no further than to express its discontent from that result. Attorney Pardiss Kebriaei from the Center of Constitutional Rights, who represented the victim in this case, commented that 'The court's holding on the political question doctrine is indeed "unsettling".... The court refused to hear a claim on behalf of a US citizen under threat of death by his own government that his personal constitutional rights have been violated—exactly what the court itself acknowledges it appears no court has ever done.'[154]

2.2.2 The targeted killing case before the Israeli High Court of Justice

The Israeli HCJ responded differently to the question of the justiciability of targeted killings and more generally regarding its willingness to review conduct of hostilities issues. In 2000, Israel made public its policy of 'targeted killings' of alleged terrorists in the Occupied Palestinian Territories (OPT), justifying them as being preventive acts.[155] The targets have included members of various groups, including Fatah, Hamas, and Islamic Jihad, who, according to

and because courts are functionally ill-equipped to make the types of complex policy judgments that would be required to adjudicate the merits of plaintiff's claims, the Court finds that the political question doctrine bars judicial resolution of this case.'

[152] *Al-Aulaqi* v. *Obama*, 4 (n 151). For the discussion on the political question doctrine see pages 65–80 of the case.

[153] *Al-Aulaqi* v. *Obama*, 74 and 78 (n 151).

[154] 'Court Dismisses Targeted Killing Case On Procedural Grounds Without Addressing Merits', Center for Constitutional Rights (7 *December 2010).*

[155] E.g., 'Press Briefing by Colonel Daniel Reisner, Head of the International Law Branch of the IDF Legal Division' (15 November 2000).

the state, were involved in attacks against Israeli civilians.[156] Means used for targeted killings include drones, snipers, missiles shooting from helicopters, killings at close range, and artillery.

The legality of the Israeli policy of targeted killing in the OPT was challenged before the HCJ. The petitioners submitted that by the end of 2005 close to 300 members of alleged terrorist organizations had been killed in targeted killings as well as approximately 150 civilian, who were close to the scene of the killing. Hundreds of others have been wounded.[157] The petitioners' claim was that the targeted killing policy is illegal as it violates international humanitarian and human rights law—both the rights of those targeted, and the rights of innocent civilians caught in the targeted killing zone. A considerable part of the state's response was dedicated to preliminary arguments, claiming that the policy of targeted killings employed by the army is a non-justiciable issue.

> [T]he IDF combat activity in the framework of the combat events occurring in the *area*, which are of operational character *par excellence*, are not justiciable... the dominant character of the issue is not legal, and the attribute of judicial restraint requires that the court refrain from stepping down into the combat zone and from ajudging the operational acts *par excellence* which are occurring in that zone... clearly, the subject's status as "nonjusticiable" does not mean that means of supervision and control on the part of the executive branch itself are not employed on this issue... the units of the army have been instructed by the Attorney General and the Military Advocate General to act on this issue, as in others, strictly according to the provisions of international law regarding laws of conflict, and they comply with that instruction.[158]

In the *Targeted Killings* case rendered in 2006, Judge Barak discussed the role of non justiciability doctrines in the Israeli legal system at length. He distinguished between two types of non-justiciability: normative and institutional. Normative non-justiciability means that there are no legal standards for deciding a case. According to Barak this type of non-justiciability does not exist as 'there is always a legal norm according to which the dispute can be solved'. Barak provides the simple example that if there is no law prohibiting a behaviour then it is legal. Likewise, if the legal framework establishes that a certain domain is under the executive discretion, then this is the legal norm that would resolve the issue. By contrast, the institutional non-justiciability means that the dispute should not be decided in a court according to the law as a matter of policy:

> That non-justiciability deals with the question whether the law and the court are the appropriate framework for deciding in the dispute. The question is not whether it is possible to decide in the dispute according to the law, in court. The answer to that question

[156] O. Ben-Naftali and K. Michaeli, 'We Must Not Make a Scarecrow of the Law: A Legal Analysis of the Israeli Policy of Targeted Killings', *Cornell International Law Journal*, 36/233 (2003), 247–50.

[157] HCJ 769/02, *The Public Committee against Torture in Israel*, paragraph 1 (n 1). According to the Israeli NGO B'Tselem, between 2002 and May 2008 at least 387 Palestinians were killed as a result of targeted killing operations. Of these, 234 were the targets, while the remainder were collateral casualties.

[158] HCJ 769/02, *The Public Committee against Torture in Israel*, paragraph 47 (n 1).

is in the affirmative. The question is whether it is desirable to decide in the dispute—which is normatively justiciable—according to legal standards, in court. That type of non-justiciability is recognized in our law.[159]

Probably in line with Bickel' s propositions, the Israeli High Court did not provide a clear list of factors to be applied and recognized that there is no consensus as to the scope of the institutional non-justiciability doctrine. More specifically concerning the targeted killing case, Justice Barak rejected the state's non-justiciability claim on four grounds. The first ground was that the Israeli High Court tends not to apply the non-justiciability doctrine where it might prevent the review over basic rights, such as the right to life.[160] Second, according to Justice Barak, the court may apply the non-justiciability doctrine when the dominant character of the disputed question is political or military, but when its dominant character is legal, the doctrine is inapplicable. In this case, Barak found that although the judgment is likely to have political or military implications, nonetheless, the question whether the 'state policy of preventive strikes which cause the death of terrorists and at times of nearby innocent civilians' is a question of legal character:

The questions disputed in the petition before us are not questions of policy. Nor are they military questions. The question is whether or not to employ a policy of preventative strikes which cause the deaths of terrorists and at times of nearby innocent civilians. The question is—as indicated by the analysis of our judgment—legal; the question is the legal classification of the military conflict taking place between Israel and terrorists from the *area*; the question is the existence or lack of existence of customary international law on the issue raised by the petition; the question is of the determination of the scope of that custom, to the extent that it is reflected in §51(d) of *The First Protocol*; the question is of the norms of proportionality applicable to the issue. The answers to all of those questions are of a dominant legal character.[161]

The third ground advanced by Justice Barak is that if international courts are entitled to review the legality of the conduct of armies, national courts should conduct the same examination. When Justice Barak asks, 'Why do those questions, which are justiciable in international courts, cease to be justiciable in national tribunals?'[162] he may be hinting to the government that while it claims non-justiciability, it should in fact agree that it is preferable for the question to be reviewed by an Israeli jurisdiction rather than an international one. Lastly, judge Barak noted that according to international customary law the conduct of the army performing preventive acts which cause the deaths of terrorists and of innocent bystanders required an *ex post* examination, which must be objective. Therefore the court concluded that 'in order to intensify that character, and ensure a maximum of

[159] HCJ 769/02, *The Public Committee against Torture in Israel*, paragraphs 48–49 (n 1).

[160] HCJ 769/02, *The Public Committee against Torture in Israel*, paragraph 50 (n 1): 'The petition before us is intended to determine the permissible and the forbidden in combat which might harm the most basic right of a human being—the right to life. The doctrine of institutional non-justiciability cannot prevent the examination of that question.'

[161] HCJ 769/02, *The Public Committee against Torture in Israel*, paragraphs 51–52 (n 1).

[162] HCJ 769/02, *The Public Committee against Torture in Israel*, paragraph 53 (n 1).

that required objectivity, it is best to expose that examination to judicial review'. At the same time it said that this judicial review 'is not a review instead of the regular monitoring by the army officials, who perform that review in advance'.[163]

Interestingly, the reasoning in the Israeli and the American decisions could each have reached an opposite result in these specific cases. In the American case the claim involved an allegation of a violation of constitutional rights of a US citizen.[164] The Israeli petition concerned a policy of general nature (and was not a concrete case), which had been previously ruled to be non-justiciable.[165] Yet, their decisions reflect their different attitudes to adjudication of conduct of hostilities cases and their internal institutional position on this matter.[166] Courts avoid or adjudicate cases in a manner that corresponds to their relationship with the government and their degree of independency vis-à-vis the political branches. Their willingness to exercise jurisdiction therefore differs from state to state. It is not related to the legal question itself, namely whether there are applicable 'judicial standards' or not, because as shown here, while in one jurisdiction the issue is not justiciable, in another it is.

2.3 Avoiding the review of the legality of Israeli settlements in the Occupied Palestinian Territories

This case study illustrates how different jurisdictions avoid the same question. It outlines the limits of national jurisdictions, and the inevitable necessity of international courts to address certain issues.

2.3.1 The Israeli HCJ

A number of avoidance doctrines have been employed over the years by the Israeli HCJ in order to avoid review of one of the most politically sensitive questions in Israel. The legality of the settlements in light of Article 49(6) of the Fourth Geneva Convention is perhaps the state's most striking violation of IHL. When the first series of cases dealing with settlements was brought before the court in the early 1970s, the HCJ was ready to review the legality of the requisition orders issued by the military commander with respect to Article 52 of the Hague Regulations. It was not prepared to pass judgment on the general legality of the settlement policy. It ruled that Article 49(6) of the Fourth Geneva Convention did not constitute a

[163] HCJ 769/02, *The Public Committee against Torture in Israel*, paragraph 54 (n 1).

[164] See, for example, *Hicks* v. *Ruddock et al.*, (n 65), *Habib* v. *Commonwealth of Australia* (n 66) and the *Amnesty International Canada* v. *Canada (Minister of National Defence)*, (2008) FC 336, (2008) 4 FCR 546. In these cases the claims were based on violations of the constitution, and the courts ruled that avoidance doctrines cannot be applied.

[165] See HCJ 4481/91, *Bargil* v. *The State of Israel* (1993) 47(4) PD 210, challenging the legality of the settlements policy.

[166] See also *El-Shifa Pharmaceutical Industries Company* v. *United States*, 402 F. Supp. 2d 267 (D.D.C. 2005) and *El-Shifa Pharmaceutical Industries Company* v. *United States*, 559 F.3d. 578 (D. C. Cir. 2009) (finding that questions regarding the legality of targeting decisions involving military attacks ordered by the president were immune from judicial review under political question doctrine).

customary rule, and therefore could not be directly enforced by Israeli courts.[167] It was during these early cases that the High Court of Justice formulated its policy: while it would not review the legality of the settlements in principle in light of Article 49(6) of the Fourth Geneva Convention, having established that it was not part of customary law, and therefore not enforceable by Israeli courts, it was ready to defend the property rights of the petitioners and to review the legality of the requisition orders in light of Articles 46 and 52 of the Hague Regulations—which were recognized as being part of customary law following Prof. Dinstein's guidance.[168] In the *Beit El* case Justice Witkon noted that property rights are justiciable:

> [I]t is clear that issues of foreign policy—like a number of other issues—are decided by the political branches, and not by the judicial branch. However, assuming... that a person's property is harmed or expropriated illegally, it is difficult to believe that the court will whisk its hand away from him, merely since his right might be disputed in political negotiations.[169]

In *Elon Moreh* Justice Landau likewise recognized that:

> A military government wishing to impinge upon the property right of an individual must show a legal source for it, and cannot except itself from judicial supervision over its acts by arguing non-justiciability.[170]

Thus, during this short period the HCJ rendered judgments on merits in cases that questioned the legality of the requisition orders used by the state to obtain possession of land to build settlements. It avoided ruling on the legality of the settlements themselves. The HCJ completely disregarded the question of the legality of construction of exclusive Jewish communities on occupied land, over which the Israeli legal regime is extra territorially applied. Similarly it failed to judicially review the legality of the Israeli government's encouragement (by way of tax reductions) of its own population to relocate in communities established on occupied land and to issue a ruling on whether this violates Article 49(6) of the Fourth Geneva Convention. Already in the 1970s the decision not to review the settlement policy was not only a question of whether Article 49(6) was customary

[167] The Israeli legal system is a dualist system: while international treaty law must be endorsed by parliamentary legislation in order to be enforced by a domestic court, customary law becomes the law of the land directly, insofar as there is no other contradicting legislation. The Geneva Conventions of 1949 were ratified by Israel in 1951 but the Israeli Parliament has never adopted endorsing legislation of the Convention. Therefore only IHL customary law may be enforced by Israeli domestic courts. Today, in light of the ICRC customary law study and the Rome Statute it is possible that a different conclusion could be reached by the Israeli HCJ regarding whether Article 49(6) of the Fourth Geneva Convention represents customary law or not. See Jean-Marie Henckaerts and Louise Doswald-Beck, *Customary IHL—Volume I: Rules* (Cambridge: Cambridge University Press, 2005). Rule 130 ('States may not deport or transfer parts of their own civilian population into a territory they occupy') and Articles 8(2)(b)(viii) of the Rome Statute ('The transfer, directly or indirectly, by the Occupying Power of parts of its own civilian population into the territory it occupies, or the deportation or transfer of all or parts of the population of the occupied territory within or outside this territory'). At the same time, as demonstrated, it is unlikely that an Israeli court will engage in such a finding for policy reasons.

[168] HCJ 606/78, *Ayyub* v. *Ministry of Defense*; HCJ 390/79, *Duikat* v. *Government of Israel*.

[169] HCJ 606/78, *Ayyub* v. *Ministry of Defense*, 124.

[170] HCJ 390/79, *Duikat* v. *Government of Israel*, 15.

and enforceable in Israeli domestic courts, but, more importantly, a question that the court preferred not to answer:

> [T]his court must refrain from considering this problem of civilian settlement in an area occupied from the viewpoint of international law... however, I agree that the petitioners' complaint is generally justiciable, since it involves property rights of the individual...[171]

The message sent to the government in these cases is clear—while the HCJ would not prevent the execution of the settlements' policy by adjudicating on its legality in accordance with Article 49(6), it would nevertheless be willing to review the requisition orders that infringed the Palestinian property rights.[172] Consequently, quite courageously, in *Elon Moreh* the court ordered for the first (and last time) the dismantling of a settlement (that was rebuilt near-by shortly after) because it found that the requisition order was illegal. The order had been issued for primarily political, and not military, reasons. In the aftermath of *Elon Moreh* Israel changed its policy and declared that settlements would henceforth be built exclusively on public—and not private—land.[173] Despite its irrelevance from the perspective of IHL, from a domestic perspective this policy enabled the state to continue settlement activity. The Israeli HCJ indicated that it would not review the legality of the general policy, but would only act in order to protect private property rights. From the moment that the state accepted this court-imposed limitation, the court has continued to respect its self-imposed limitations, i.e. until this very day it has reserved judgment on the legality of the settlement policy.

In *Arayeiv* an attempt was made to challenge the state's policy of building settlements on public land.[174] The state had declared that the settlements were built on public land meaning that the petitioner could not claim personal injury, and therefore that he lacked standing. The HCJ accepted the state's position, and dismissed the petition based on the avoidance doctrine of standing. More than ten years later, in 1991, the Israeli Peace Now movement filed a petition that directly questioned the legality of the settlements policy. This time the HCJ rejected the petition both because of the lack of standing and the absence of a concrete property dispute as well by reason of the political nature of the settlement question, which made it non-justiciable.[175] This argument had already been raised in the 1970s, but as the early cases had dealt with disputes of private property rights, the HCJ

[171] Justice Landau at page 128, cited at *Bil'in (Village Council) and Yassin et al.* v. *Green Park International, Inc. et al.*, (2009) QCCS 4151, paragraph 269. See also HCJ 390/79, *Duikat* v. *Government of Israel*, 4–5 cited in *Bil'in (Village Council) and Yassin et al.* v. *Green Park International, Inc. et al.*, paragraph 281. HCJ 606/78, *Ayyub* v. *Ministry of Defense*, 124.

[172] Years later, the same policy would be applied by the HCJ in the Wall cases.

[173] Kretzmer, *The Occupation of Justice: The Supreme Court of Israel and the Occupied Territories* (Albany: State University of New York Press, 2002), 89.

[174] The petitioner questioned whether the construction of settlements on public land violates Article 55 of the Hague Regulations. Under Article 55, the Occupying Power has the duty to administrate public property in accordance to the rules of usufruct, i.e., the Occupying Power can enjoy the fruits of the land, but cannot change its capital nature.

[175] HCJ 4481/91, *Bargil* v. *The State of Israel.* Cited in *Bil'in (Village Council) and Yassin et al.* v. *Green Park International, Inc. et al.*, paragraph 264.

nevertheless agreed to hear the petitions as an exception to the general rule, that the issue of the settlement is a political question.

Justice Shamgar set the non-justiciability test: when the dominant character of the disputed question is political or military, it is appropriate to prevent adjudication. However, when that character is legal, the doctrine of non-justiciability should not apply.

The standard applied by the court is a legal one, but public law issues also include political aspects, within the different meanings of that term. The question which must be asked in such a case is, generally, what is the *predominant* nature of the dispute. As explained, the standard applied by the court is a legal one, and this is the basis for deciding whether an issue should be considered by the court, that is, whether an issue is predominantly political or predominantly legal. In the case before us, it is absolutely clear that the predominant nature of the issue is political, and it has continued to be so from its inception until the present.[176]

Justice Goldberg followed the same reasoning:

In my opinion, the crux of the matter is whether this dispute should properly be determined by the court, *notwithstanding* our ability to rule on it as a matter of law. In other words, does this case fall into the category of the few cases where this Court will deny a petition for lack of institutional justiciability. I believe that we must answer this question in the affirmative. This is not because we lack the legal tools to render a judgment, but because a judicial determination, which does not concern individual rights, should defer to a political process of great importance and significance.[177]

Recently, the question of the legality of the settlements was revived through the petitions filed to the Israeli HCJ concerning the legality of the Wall. When the ICJ gave its Advisory Opinion on the Wall, an examination of the legality of the settlements was a fundamental factor for determining the illegality of the Wall.[178] The Israeli HCJ in contrast, persistently avoids addressing this issue, ruling that the legality of the settlement is an *irrelevant* question.[179]

By delivering a ruling on the settlement policy, the court risks losing its legitimacy in the eyes of Israeli society. The executive might not respect its judgment and the legislator would probably overrule the judgment anyway.

The HCJ has repeatedly stated that the Israeli settlements are 'controlled by the law of belligerent occupation. Israeli law does not apply in this area . . . the lives of the settlers are arranged, mainly, by the security legislation of the military

[176] HCJ 4481/91, *Bargil* v. *The State of Israel*—Justice Shamgar, paragraph 5. Cited partly in *Bil'in (Village Council) and Yassin et al.* v. *Green Park International, Inc. et al.*, paragraph 262.

[177] HCJ 4481/91, *Bargil* v. *The State of Israel*, 11.

[178] *Legal Consequences on the Construction of a Wall in the Occupied Palestinian Territory*, (Advisory Opinion) ICJ Rep 2004, paragraph 120.

[179] HCJ 7957/04, *Mara'abe et al.* v. *Israel Prime Minister et al.*, paragraph 19: 'The military commander is authorized to construct a separation fence in the area for the purpose of defending the lives and safety of the Israeli settlers in the area. It is not relevant whatsoever to this conclusion to examine whether this settlement activity conforms to international law or defies it, as determined in the Advisory Opinion of the International Court of Justice at the Hague.' See also HCJ 8414/05, *Yassin, Bil'in Village Council Chairman* v. *The State of Israel, et al.*, (2007), paragraph 28.

commander.'[180] Yet, one must refer to the broader picture. To provide Jewish residents with the same socio-economic environment as in Israel, the Israeli parliament enacted several laws that apply as a matter of personal and extraterritorial jurisdiction. These include laws regulating civil life such as fiscal laws, the Knesset Elections Law, and the National Insurance law.[181] The most significant extraterritorial legislation was the extension of validity of the Emergency Regulations Law (West Bank and Gaza—Criminal Jurisdiction and Legal Assistance) of 1984. Today it contains seventeen laws, their scope was extended to include Israelis or Jewish residents in the OPT.[182] The extension of Israeli laws to the OPT was approved by the HCJ in the *Shaer* case.[183]

2.3.2 The Quebec Superior Court, Canada

The Palestinian village of Bil'in is situated in the Israeli-Occupied West Bank, about 12km west of Ramallah and 5km north of Jerusalem. Beginning in the 1980s, and more significantly in 1991, fifty-six per cent of Bil'in's land was expropriated by the State of Israel to build the settlement of Modi'in Illit. Modi'in Illit is Israel's largest West Bank settlement in terms of population, and is designated to accommodate 150,000 residents. As the village of Bil'in could not find redress before Israeli courts,[184] it decided to file a civil action in Canada against the

[180] HCJ 6339/05, *Matar* v. *The Commander of IDF Forces in the Gaza Strip*, (2005) (unpublished). The same idea is expressed in HCJ 10356/02, *Hass* v. *IDF Commander in West Bank*, 455, HCJ 7957/04, *Mara'abe et al.* v. *Israel Prime Minister et al.*, paragraph 18. In the *Shaer* case the petitioner, an Israeli-Jewish national, claimed that the military commander was not competent to arrest him as his authority applied only to the Palestinian population. The court rejected this claim, and ruled that regarding the security of the region the commander's authority applied to all the residents of the region. According to the HCJ, the assumption that the military commander's authority applied selectively to only a section of the residents of the region 'is, evidently, contradicting basic norms'. HCJ 2612/94, *Shaer* v. *The Military Commander,* (1994) 48(3) PD 675, 679.

[181] Benvenisti, *The International Law of Occupation* (2nd edn, Princeton: Princeton University Press, 2004), 129–33.

[182] The seventeen laws listed in the annex of Regulation 6B of the 'Law for Amending and Extending the Validity of Emergency Regulations (West Bank—Jurisdiction in Offenses and Legal Aid)'—2007, and which apply extraterritorially to the OPT are the following: Entry to Israel Law, 1952; Defense Service Law [Combined Version], 1986; Bar Association Law, 1961; Income Tax Ordinance; Population Registry Law, 1965; Work Service in Time of Emergency Law, 1967; National Insurance Law [Combined Version], 1968; Psychologists Law, 1977; Registering Equipment and Mobilizing it for the Israel Defense Force, 1987; Traffic Ordinance; Traffic Regulations, 1961; State Health Insurance Law, 1994; the Hague Convention Law (Returning Abducted Children), 1991; Inheritance Law, 1965; Adoption of Children Law, 1981; Legal Competence and Guardianship Law, 1962; Surrogate Motherhood Agreements (Approval of Agreement and Status of Newborn) Law, 1996. Israeli residents are defined in Article 6B as 'a person whose place of residence is in the Region and who is an Israeli citizen, or who is entitled to immigrate to Israel under the law of Return 1950, and had his residence been in Israel that person would have been included under the same expression' [the last phrase meaning Jews who reside in the Region but are not Israelis]. For an unofficial translation see <http://nolegalfrontiers.org/en/israeli-domestic-legislation/isr1>.

[183] HCJ 2612/94, *Shaer* v. *The Military Commander* (n 180).

[184] To date, the legal path of the village of Bil'in has already gone through four petitions. Three of them have dealt with the legality of the constructions conducted in the settlement of Modi'in Ilit from a domestic planning law perspective, HCJ 143/06; HCJ 3998/06; HCJ 1526/07. The HCJ ruled, *inter alia,* that the local council of the settlement Modi'in Ilit provided construction permits for the

Canadian companies and their director who were building new neighbourhoods in the settlement of Modi'in City on Bil'in's land. On 7 July 2008, Bil'in Village Council and its elected head, Ahmed Yassin (from now on referred together as 'Bil'in'), brought a suit before the Superior Court of Quebec against the Canadian companies Green Park International, Inc., Green Mount International, Inc. and Annette LaRoche, the companies' sole director (together the 'Defendants'), all of them domiciled in Quebec.[185] In the suit Bil'in claims that the defendants by

illegally constructing residential or other buildings and marketing and selling condominium units and/or other built up areas on the land, to the civilian population of the State of Israel on the municipal lands of Bil'in',[186] aided, abetted, assisted and conspired with the State of Israel in carrying out an illegal purpose, that is, the transfer of the Occupying Power's own population into the territories it occupies in violation of Article 49(6) of the Fourth Geneva Convention. In addition, as the State of Israel contracts with private firms to build homes and other structures in the settlements, these firms, through soliciting, marketing, and selling these properties to Israeli civilians, aid and assist the State in committing a war crime, as defined by Article 85(4) (a) of Additional Protocol I and Article 8(2)(b)(viii) of the Rome statute. As all these international law provisions have been incorporated into Canadian domestic law the defendants' acts are in violation of international and Canadian domestic law.[187]

building company although the plans were not yet authorized by the planning authorities, thus construction was illegal. Yet, although the HCJ awarded unusually high costs for the petitioners, it found that the late approval retroactively cured the defects. Adv. Sfard, the lawyer who represented Bil'in, stated that it was 'a retroactive clearance of the biggest illegal construction that ever occurred in the West Bank.' Arieli and Sfard, *The Wall of Folly*, (Tel Aviv: Yediot Sfarim, 2008) 357. In all these cases, a Canadian company, the Green Park Inc. Company was a respondent. Following their request, the Green Park Inc. Company became a respondent in HCJ 8414/05 as well, in February 2006 as they claimed to be the private owner of the land. The state claimed that it was 'state land' (HCJ 8414/05, *Yassin, Bil'in Village Council Chairman* v. *The State of Israel, et al.*, paragraphs 23 and 39). The Green Park Inc. Company are one of the defendants in the claim submitted in Canada, see below. A fourth case challenged the legality of the Wall. Many other Palestinian communities affected by the Wall filed petitions to the Israeli HCJ on its legality. Bil'in is one of the rare cases in which the Israeli HCJ ruled in favour of the petitioners and declared that the Wall's route was illegal and needed to be changed. The ruling was based on the fact that the route of the Wall was intended to include territory for future expansion of the settlement Modi'in Illit. The East Mattityahu neighbourhood was to be built by the Canadian company, a consideration that was found to be illegal by the HCJ. See HCJ 8414/05, *Yassin, Bil'in Village Council Chairman* v. *The State of Israel, et al.*, paragraphs 35, 41. The construction of the Wall in Bili'n began in 2005. By 2007, the villagers began organizing almost daily demonstrations in protest against the Wall and the settlement being built on their land. The people of Bil'in have received support from other Palestinian, Israeli, and international peace activists, and it became the symbol of the non-violent resistance against the Israeli occupation. HCJ 8414/05, *Yassin, Bil'in Village Council Chairman* v. *The State of Israel, et al.*, (15 December 2008)—decision on contempt of court in which the petitioners were awarded costs, for the delay in the execution of the ruling.

185 Amended Complaint (7 July 2008) and 'Second Further Amended and Particularized Motion Introducing a Suit (Article 110 Code of Civil Procedure)' (12 June 2009).

186 Amended Complaint, paragraph 9 (n 185).

187 The Geneva Conventions of 1949 and their Additional Protocols provisions are incorporated in the Geneva Convention Act of 1985, (R.S.C., 1985, c. G-3) and the Rome Statute is incorporated in the Canadian Crimes Against Humanity and War Crimes Act of 2000, (S.C. 2000, c. 24). Section 6(1) (c) of the Canadian Crimes Against Humanity and War Crimes Act (S.C. 2000, c. 24) provides that:

It was noted by Bil'in in its action that Canada's official position on the Israeli settlements in the Palestinian West Bank is that they are illegal. This position is in line with the ICJ, various United Nations Security Council and General Assembly Resolutions, and Statements by the High Contracting Parties to the Geneva Conventions on the issue.[188]

For the civil claim to succeed, Bil'in had to establish that the violations amount to a civil wrong in Quebec. Indeed, violations of international law that are classified as crimes in domestic law are automatically also classified as civil wrongs. In addition to showing that the violations constituted civil wrongs in Quebec, the complaint went on to plead that the acts complained of constituted a common law tort under Canadian federal law. For this purpose, Bil'in argued that the defendants knowingly inflicted reasonably foreseeable losses by their acts, or at least that they either wilfully or negligently aided, abetted or assisted Israel in pursuing an illegal purpose. Finally, it was argued that as the matters at issue were not justiciable before the Israeli courts, and because the defendants are domiciled in Quebec, the Superior Court of Quebec was the appropriate forum. The remedies Bil'in demanded included permanent injunction and punitive damages. Bili'n also asked the court to declare the conduct of the defendants as being contrary to the international and Canadian laws mentioned, and to order the removal from Bil'in lands 'all building structures, equipment and material and to return the lands to the condition that they were in prior to the building construction'.[189] The defendants filed a series of preliminary motions, demanding the immediate dismissal of the action claiming no cause, immunity, *res judicata*, standing, and *forum non conveniens*.

On 18 September 2009, the Superior Court of Quebec gave its ruling on jurisdiction and rejected all preliminary claims raised by the defendants except the last one. It thus chose to follow the approach of the Israeli HCJ and avoided rendering justice on the issue of Israeli settlement in the OPT. The decision of the court should come as no surprise. An attentive reader of the judgment could already have predicted the outcome of this ruling in the first lines of the sixty-seven page decision. The judge cites a statement of UN Secretary General Ban Ki Moon from February 2007:

> The Palestinian people still yearn for the freedom and dignity denied them for decades. The Israeli people yearn for long term security. Neither can achieve their legitimate demands without a settlement of the conflict. Today, we are at a critical juncture in efforts to move beyond crisis management and renew efforts towards genuine conflict resolution.[190]

By citing a political body, and not a legal authority such as the ICJ, the judge seems to have determined the court's own role: issues related to the Israeli-Palestinian

'Every person who, either before or after the coming into force of this section, commits outside Canada (c) a war crime, is guilty of an indictable offense and may be prosecuted for that offense in accordance with section 8'.

[188] Amended Complaint, paragraph 22(a) (n 185).

[189] Amended Complaint, paragraph 35 (n 185).

[190] *Bil'in (Village Council) and Yassin et al.* v. *Green Park International, Inc. et al.*, paragraph 4 (n 171).

conflict are of a political and not a legal nature. The judiciary should avoid ruling on these issues which remain under the auspices of a 'conflict resolution'.

On the merits, the Quebec Superior Court accepted, for the first time in Canada, that the commission of a war crime constitutes a civil wrong in Canadian law.[191] In addition, the court held that a person (including a legal person) may also commit a civil wrong by knowingly participating in a war crime in a foreign country.[192] However, it dismissed the case on the grounds of *forum non conveniens*. It rejected the plaintiff's arguments that as Israeli courts refuse to adjudicate on the basis of Article 49(6) of the Fourth Geneva Convention, it renders Israeli fora to be 'inappropriate and manifestly inconsistent with public order as understood by international relations'. The Canadian court examined over more than fourteen pages of its ruling Israeli settlement cases from the early 1970s until today.[193] This was a scope of analysis of a foreign court's jurisprudence rarely done before. After this examination, it ruled that the HCJ 'would not refrain to adjudicate on a politically controversial matter if it were properly brought before the court'.[194] Therefore it concluded that it was *compelled* to avoid the case:

> This is one of those exceptional situations where the Superior Court is *compelled* to decline jurisdiction on the basis of forum non conveniens, as the plaintiffs have selected a forum having little connection to the Action, in order to inappropriately gain a juridical advantage over the defendants, and where the relevant connecting factors, considered as a whole, clearly point to the Israeli High Court of Justice as the logical forum and the authority in a better position to decide.[195]

The appeal against the court decision was rejected, and as this action cannot be heard before Israeli courts, the victims were once again left without redress. The court's self restraint policy is predictable as a matter of policy vis-à-vis Israel, an allied state. Indeed it is highly questionable whether a Canadian court could be involved in such a legal adventure. Yet, the court's legal reasoning is incorrect with respect to several issues.

(1) As discussed, Israeli courts would not, and cannot, enforce Article 49(6) of the Fourth Geneva Convention. Domestic political constraints prevent any possible adjudication of the settlement issue. Decrypting these conditions is not an easy task for a foreign court, but is nevertheless a necessary factor to be considered if one is to reach a correct legal conclusion.

[191] *Bil'in (Village Council) and Yassin et al.* v. *Green Park International, Inc. et al.*, paragraph 175 (n 171).

[192] *Bil'in (Village Council) and Yassin et al.* v. *Green Park International, Inc. et al.*, paragraph 176 (n 171). For an analysis see James Yap, 'Corporate Civil Liability for War Crimes in Canadian Courts: Lessons from *Bil'in (Village Council) v. Green Park International Ltd*', *Journal of International Criminal Justice, 8/2 (2010)*, 631–48.

[193] *Bil'in (Village Council) and Yassin et al.* v. *Green Park International, Inc. et al.*, paragraphs 242–289 (n 171).

[194] *Bil'in (Village Council) and Yassin et al.* v. *Green Park International, Inc. et al.*, paragraph 282 (n 171). See also at paragraph 288.

[195] *Bil'in (Village Council) and Yassin et al.* v. *Green Park International, Inc. et al.*, paragraph 335 (n 171). On the 28th of February 2013 an individual complaint was submitted to the Human Rights Committee under the Optional protocol to the International Covenant in Civil and Political Rights, claiming that Canada has violated its extra-territorial obligation by failing to ensure effective remedies. (*Mr. Mohammed Ibrahim Ahmed Abu Rahma et al.* v. *Canada*, Communication No. 2285/2013).

(2) This case represents a civil claim, over which the Israeli HCJ should not have jurisdiction. According to the territorial legal system, the district court in Ramallah should have jurisdiction over a civil case that involves a Palestinian plaintiff and a foreign company operating in the West Bank. The applicable civil law is Jordanian law and PA legislation.[196] From the standpoint of Israeli law, if a civil claim originates in the OPT, beyond the territorial jurisdiction of the State of Israel, Israeli civil courts can nevertheless exercise their jurisdiction as if the claim originated in Israel. According to the Israeli rules of civil procedure, Israeli courts are entitled to render judgments on merits in civil cases, if they exercise (a) personal jurisdiction over the defendant (the service of process was effected), (b) local jurisdiction (venue) and (c) jurisdiction over the subject matter.[197] In order to facilitate these jurisdictional requirements for claims originating in the OPT, several amendments to Israeli laws and regulations were introduced. For personal jurisdiction, the service of judicial documents in the OPT could be made according to the ordinary civil procedure rules as it is inside Israel.[198] As the West Bank was not *de jure* annexed to Israel, it has not been under the local jurisdiction of any Israeli district court. Therefore, in order to extend the local jurisdiction of Israeli district courts over the West Bank, in 1979 the Israeli Minister of Justice introduced an amendment to the venue provisions, granting local jurisdiction to the Jerusalem District Court.[199] Thus, according to Israeli law, in the case of Bil'in, the Jerusalem District Court would have been able to exercise jurisdiction if the defendants had been present in Area C, and if it had been possible to effect service of the summons. Not surprisingly, conflicts of jurisdiction between Israeli and Palestinian courts are normally resolved according to the interest of the Israeli side. Although the OPT have been traditionally considered as jurisdictional entities separate from the State of Israel, they have always been controlled by it.[200]

However, the territorial and personal expansion of Israeli law to the West Bank is in violation of IHL. According to the law of military occupation, the occupying power is prevented from extending its own legal system over the territories it occupies.[201] As explicitly stated by the ICJ in its Advisory Opinion on the Wall,

[196] According to Article 43 of the 1907 Hague Regulations, the West Bank should be governed by the courts and laws that were in force prior to the occupation, i.e., Jordanian law, and, in addition, by legislation enacted by the military commander. Military Proclamation No. 2 of 7 June 1967, endorsed the principle reflected in Article 43 of the Hague Regulations, and preserved the law and court system existing in the OPT prior to the occupation. Since the establishment of the PA, in certain zones legislation of the PA also comes into force. The 1995 interim agreement transferred several powers, including legislative authorities to the PA, according to three areas of control that were established. See Article XIII, Section 1 of the 'Israeli–Palestinian Interim Agreement on the West Bank and the Gaza Strip' (Washington DC, 28 September 1995). Local civil law remains in force.

[197] Michael M. Karayanni, 'Choice of Law under Occupation: How Israeli Law Came to Serve Palestinian Plaintiffs', *Journal of Private International Law*, 5/1 (2009), 43.

[198] Israeli Rules of Civil Procedure (Service of Documents in the Administered Territories) 1969.

[199] Today it is legislated for in Rule 6 of the Israeli CPR (1984).

[200] Karayanni, 'Choice of Law under Occupation', 27, 30 (n 197).

[201] See n 196.

Israeli settlements in the OPT have been established in breach of IHL.[202] The expansion also violates the general principles of public international law, including the illegality of any territorial acquisition resulting from the threat or use of force. Therefore, as Israel's extension of its own domestic civil law and courts' jurisdiction over the West Bank is illegal from an international law standpoint, is it really adequate for a Canadian court to decline jurisdiction in favour of that jurisdiction? Is the Israeli HCJ 'the *logical forum* and the authority in a *better position* to decide'? Wouldn't this position be in itself 'manifestly inconsistent with public order as understood by international relations'?

3. Concluding observations

Courts attempt to establish a legal framework for the application and rejection of the avoidance doctrines, in the form of guidelines and rules. However, as shown any judicial decision as to their application or rejection would essentially be a political one.

A contextual analysis of the ATS cases shows how, in accordance with state directives, domestic doctrines of non-justiciability and immunity are applied with double standards. The study demonstrated that when a court applied the ATS cases in favour of the victims, it was also in accordance with the state's position. The US courts tend to defer IHL issues to the executive. This is probably because of its tradition to 'speak in one voice' on foreign relations issues. However, the US state has contradictory interests: it seeks to promote its own image as protector of human rights, battling against humanitarian violations in the world; at the same time, it seeks to ensure that its own officials and allies will not be held accountable for the same violations. These considerations come together to produce a selective application of the avoidance doctrines (and of the ATS), one that follows the state's direction.

As demonstrated by the second case study, the US and Israeli targeted killing cases, avoidance doctrines have no definite borders. This is notwithstanding the judicial enumeration of 'neutral' factors for their application. On the same legal question, courts will apply avoidance doctrines in different ways when the decision of the court is motivated by a policy choice and not a legal one.

Finally, the decision by the Canadian court discussed in the third case study provides us with another illustration of how a national court functions when it is required to apply IHL. It can function as an active agent of the international legal order, which enforces international law. Alternatively, it may refrain from doing so by applying doctrines such as standing or justiciability, in order not to interfere in its own government's international policies or in matters pertaining to the sovereignty of third states. Through the application of the *forum non conveniens* doctrine, the judge denied jurisdiction to the Canadian court. In this way, the plaintiffs were

[202] *Legal Consequences on the Construction of a Wall in the Occupied Palestinian Territory*, paragraph 120 (n 178).

prevented from having a judicial decision ruling whether they were entitled to damages by reason of the alleged violation of Article 49(6) of the Fourth Geneva Convention. In Israel, the settlement question is probably a typical case in which the domestic judiciary resorts to avoidance doctrines. Within the Israeli political environment it seems that no matter what avoidance doctrine or legal justification is employed, Israeli courts are not willing to enforce Article 49(6) of the Fourth Geneva Convention and will continue to avoid dealing with that issue. When IHL enforcement is avoided in such a systematic way not only by Israel but by other national jurisdictions as well, from the rule of law and law enforcement perspectives, only one avenue remains available: an international court.

3

The Normative Role of National Courts: From Deferring to Limiting

> It can be seen that the approach of the courts has been very far from insular or narrow. There has been a readiness to tackle issues arising across the world and involving complex and sensitive questions of public international law. (...) In those fields [foreign affairs and military conflict] there are, inevitably, certain forbidden areas – areas where the courts themselves have accepted that it is not appropriate for them to intervene. But that should not be allowed to obscure the fact that modern judicial review is operating in a way that exposes ministers and their officials to close and effective judicial scrutiny, to which the human rights legislation has given additional impetus.[1]
>
> Lord Richards (UK House of Lords)

> Judicial branches of government, although charged with the duty of standing between the government and individuals, are often too deferential to the executive in time of peace. How then would the same judges act in a time of crisis? The role of the courts in time of crisis is less than glorious.[2]
>
> Lord Steyn (UK House of Lords)

The positions of these two judges working in the same court, appear to be somewhat contradictory. Nonetheless, they reflect the same contemporary reality: a growing trend towards the exercise of judicial review in what have traditionally been 'forbidden areas'. Domestic courts are demonstrating a growing determination and willingness to exercise their role of 'law enforcer' for violations of IHL during armed conflict. Yet, given the novelty of this trend,[3] as well as the political sensitivity of cases involving armed conflicts issues, change is unlikely to occur overnight. It is a process in which courts need to establish their own legitimacy within their societies as well as exercising a margin of independence vis-à-vis the authorities. Therefore, while courts are increasingly willing to exercise their jurisdiction over questions of IHL, and choose not to avoid them as they have done

[1] Richards, 'The International Dimension of Judicial Review', *The 2006 Gray's Inn Reading* (7 June 2006), 10.

[2] Johan Steyn, 'Guantanamo Bay: The Legal Black Hole' *Twenty-seventh F.A. Mann Lecture—British Institute of International and Comparative Law* (25 November 2003).

[3] See, for example, Benvenisti, 'Judicial Misgivings Regarding the Application of International Norms: An Analysis of Attitudes of National Courts', *European Journal of International Law* 4/2 (1993), 183.

previously, they are still reluctant to overturn an executive decision on the merits and tend to show significant deference for the executive's discretion.

1. The deferral role of the courts: from avoidance towards application

Exercising judicial review through the use of deferral techniques allows the judiciary to redefine its role as law enforcer in armed conflict issues. In doing so, the judiciary is seen to be applying its influence, while not exceeding its institutional capacities. In light of the redefinition of their role, the borders of their institutional limits have been modified, as has the public demand for scrutiny during armed conflict. The interaction of these two factors in states in which the judiciary has traditionally been independent of the political branches, has led to a growing willingness of courts to apply IHL instead of avoiding it.

1.1 The 'ladder theory'

The 'ladder theory' posits that judicial review over the state can be expressed in different levels of judicial responses. Each involves varying degrees of the use of the deferral technique.[4] The judicial review ladder can be described in the following way:

Level (1) A court clarifies the considerations that need to be taken into account in the exercise of the state's discretion, and then refers the matter back to the executive for reconsideration of its action in light of the court's assessments;

Level (2) A court triggers a judicial dialogue with the legislative branch while referring the issue for the latter's decision, seeking clarification of the scope of authorization granted;

[4] Benvenisti while setting the 'ladder theory', proposes that the judicial review process be considered as being composed of two layers. The first or 'institutional tier' examines whether the state was authorized by the law—constitution, statutes, or administrative regulations—to perform the act under review. Whether 'the authorizing' legal source also includes IHL rules, not transformed into domestic law, depends on the constitutional framework that regulates the relations between the international and national law of each state. In the second, or 'substance tier,' courts examine the facts of the specific case under review and determine whether the state has exercised its authority within the boundaries set in the authorizing law. Here the court may be required to balance policy considerations. Less controversial, in the sense of being less interventionist in the democratic process, will be for the courts to declare a state's act to be illegal under the first layer, because determining the institutional authority to act is 'a question that is no doubt the domain of the courts.' Benvenisti, 'United We Stand: National Courts Reviewing Counterterrorism Measures' in A. Bianchi and A. Keller (eds), *Counterterrorism: Democracy's Challenge* (Hart Publishing, Oxford, 2008), 257. When intervening in policy considerations the courts are usually more reluctant, and, if they do intervene, they tend to offer a detailed justification for their intervention.

Level (3) A court refers the matter to the legislature, but simultaneously imposes limitations on legislative discretion or requires the legislature to explicitly state its intention to depart from an international law obligation.

In the last levels (4) and (5) courts enter the domain of involving the most significant exercise of judicial authority, namely that of limiting the legislative branch through constitutional review.

Level (4) Courts would declare a part of a provision to be unconstitutional, but will allow the legislator to adjust the law with constitutional limits;

Level (5) The most interventionist level will declare a law to be unconstitutional and in excess of the legislator's authority, and therefore invalid.

As this theoretical framework shows, the deferral role finds expression in varying degrees of application of the law and deference to the state. The prevailing degree of political opposition to judicial intervention will determine whether courts will ascend or descend the judicial review ladder, seeking to share responsibility for its results with the other political branches. This gradualist approach offers the courts the practical possibility of adjudicating IHL cases despite their fragile position vis-à-vis the executive and public opinion during armed conflict. It enables courts to review the legality of the acts of the state. If necessary, because of institutional concerns, courts may defer the remedy or may refer to the political branches to exercise discretion in applying the law. Thus, through deference techniques they have begun to apply IHL instead of avoiding it. However, on the merits decisions may still remain in the hands of the executive. As Lord Justice Richards observed at the end of his lecture on UK modern judicial review,

> A cynic might say in the light of these cases that things have not changed greatly since the days when the prerogative powers in relation to the conduct of foreign affairs were not susceptible to judicial review at all. The courts have asserted a jurisdiction to intervene but all the claims to which I have referred have failed.[5]

Indeed, these observations might not be limited to cynics. However, in the long run, the fact that courts assert jurisdiction and reject the traditional avoidance doctrines is a turning point in the functioning of national courts and in their application of IHL. Moreover, it may represent a point of no return. Once a national court has exercised its jurisdiction over armed conflict issues, it can be expected that they are not going to avoid such intervention in future. Thus, even if contemporary courts' rulings on the merits produce rulings similar to those that resulted from judicial avoidance, this move should not be underestimated. Having opened the gates of judicial review, courts have initiated a process in which they establish their legitimacy and independence. As courts have established their independence in the domestic domain (such as human rights protection during peacetime), 'ascent' of the 'ladder' of judicial review is thus only a matter of time. Moreover, when courts exercise their jurisdiction, they send powerful messages to their governments. Governments begin to realize that next time a judicial review

[5] Richards, 'The International Dimension', 7 (n 1).

matter is brought, the courts may be more assertive. Even if still refraining from entirely enforcing the law and granting an explicit and binding remedy, courts in the course of their review indirectly impose greater pressure on a government's discretion.

The following sections examine that process, the move from avoiding towards application through the graduate use of the deferral technique. The extent of the discretion allowed to the state is examined using the ladder theory in two kinds of cases: those involving the protection of individuals in detention, and those concerning the conduct of hostilities. By this analysis, the positive and negative outcomes of the deference technique are highlighted.

2. The protection of individuals in detention and the 'war on terror'

For the protection of individual rights, usually of their own nationals, courts from different jurisdictions have found a prudent but practical way of tackling 'forbidden areas'. Detention is a subject directly linked to the protection of individuals' rights afforded in all Western democracies. Given the protracted nature of the "War on Terror" and of allegations concerning violations of the international rules of detention, the issue has been too fundamental to avoid. At the same time, inasmuch as it involves major foreign policy or IHL issues, courts have chosen to affirm their authority by reviewing the state's actions (thereby rejecting non-justiciability claims). They have, however, been cautious in granting a remedy on the merits and have referred decisions back to the executive. The following section presents a graded series of examples of jurisprudence from different jurisdictions related to detention. In these cases, the state's requests to avoid jurisdiction were rejected, and the courts engaged in varying degrees in limiting the power or actions of the states concerned.

2.1 Level one on the 'judicial review ladder': the *Abbasi case* (UK Court of Appeal, 2002)

> Where fundamental human rights are in play, the courts of this country will not abstain from reviewing the legitimacy of the actions of a foreign sovereign state.[6]

In *Abbasi* the court (1) progressively departs from the traditional 'one voice' (that of the government) approach and rejects the non-justiciability claims, which is a major preliminary step towards the application of IHL by national courts; (2) sends signals of its disapproval of the policy; and (3) on the merits, it still defers the matter entirely back to the state's sole discretion.

[6] *R (Abbasi)* v. *Secretary of State for Foreign and Commonwealth Affairs*, [2002] EWCA Civ 1598, [2003] UKHRR 76 CA, paragraph 53.

2.1.1 The facts

The *Abbasi* case is probably the most significant illustration of this 'first step' judicial review. Rendered by the English Court of Appeal in 2002, it was the first 'war on terror' case dealt with by a higher court of a US allied state. Abbasi, a British national, was captured by US forces in Afghanistan during the armed conflict there. In January 2002, he was brought to Guantanamo Bay. By the time of his appeal before the court he had been held captive for eight months without access to a lawyer, a court or any other form of tribunal. He sought judicial review over the UK's decision not to afford him diplomatic protection, and for the court to compel the UK foreign office to make representations on his behalf to the US. Abbasi claimed that his fundamental right not to be arbitrarily detained was being infringed and that the state owed him a duty under English public law to take positive steps to redress this violation.

2.1.2 Rejecting two non-justiciability claims

The first non-justiciability claim raised by the UK was that the relief sought by the claimant was founded on the assertion that the US government was acting unlawfully. As English courts, they should not examine the legitimacy of action taken by a foreign sovereign state—in this case the legality of the detention of prisoners at Guantanamo. In a nutshell, the claim was not justiciable as 'for the court to rule on that assertion would be contrary to comity and to the principle of State immunity'.[7] Although the state recognized that in *Oppenheimer* and *Kuwait* the House of Lords had established exceptions to the non-justiciability principle, these exceptions were relevant only 'in exceptional circumstances' and were not applicable in this case. It could have been expected that the English court would avoid jurisdiction over a case that involved serious violations committed by an allied state, at the beginning of an ongoing conflict (less than a year after 9/11) to which the UK was a party. However, the court took a stance in contrast to the state's position. It found that the non-justiciability principle was not applicable because of the importance of the right of habeas corpus.

> Albeit that caution must be exercised by this court when faced with an allegation that a foreign state is in breach of its international obligations, this court does not need the statutory context in order to be free to express a view in relation to what it conceives to be a clear breach of international law, particularly in the context of human rights.[8]

The second non-justiciability claim was that the conduct of the UK Secretary of State in his decision not to render diplomatic assistance to Mr Abbasi, was a matter that could not be reviewed by a court. It was a decision based on foreign policy considerations which were the exclusive domain of the political branch.[9]

[7] *R (Abbasi)* v. *Secretary of State for Foreign and Commonwealth Affairs*, paragraphs 28–57 (n 6). This claim corresponded to the US act of state doctrine, see Chapter 2.

[8] *R (Abbasi)* v. *Secretary of State*, paragraph 57 (n 6).

[9] *R (Abbasi)* v. *Secretary of State*, paragraphs 68–106 (n 6). This claim corresponds to the US political question doctrine, see above at Chapter 2.

This claim was also rejected by the court on the grounds that the law of judicial review had developed and included 'the invasion of areas previously immune from review, such as the exercise of the prerogative.'[10] In this context, the court stated that the issue of justiciability depends, not on general principle, but on subject matter and suitability in the particular case: 'It is not an answer to a claim for judicial review to say that the source of the power of the Foreign Office is the prerogative. It is the subject matter that is determinative.'[11] Here, the citizen's legitimate expectation was that his request would be considered, and in that consideration all relevant factors would be reviewed by the court.

2.1.3 Deferring to the state's discretion

On the merits, however, the court was less affirmative, deferring entirely to the executive's judgment: 'whether to make any representations in a particular case, and if so in what form, is left entirely to the discretion of the Secretary of State'. And with regard to the right to habeas corpus, the court declared that it can offer no direct remedy as 'the United States Government is not before the court, and no order of this court would be binding upon it', and that the respondent in this case, the UK, 'has no direct responsibility for the detention.'[12]

2.1.4 Sending explicit signals of disapproving the policy

The remedy was entirely deferred to the state by granting it a very broad margin of discretion. At the same time though, the court openly questioned the legality of the detention in Guantanamo in what was, at that time, an unprecedented manner:

> In apparent contravention of fundamental principles recognised by both jurisdictions and by international law, Mr Abbasi is at present arbitrarily detained in a 'legal black-hole' [...] What appears to us to be objectionable is that Mr Abbasi should be subject to indefinite detention in territory over which the United States has exclusive control with no opportunity to challenge the legitimacy of his detention before any court or tribunal.[13]

Moreover, the court directly addressed US courts, in a remarkable attempt to enter into dialogue with and guide the American judges, who were supposed to rule on the right of habeas corpus of British citizens detained in Guantanamo:

> On the face of it we find surprising the proposition that the writ of the United States courts does not run in respect of individuals held by the government... It is important to record that the position may change when the appellate courts in the United States consider the matter.[14]

[10] *R (Abbasi)* v. *Secretary of State*, paragraph 81 (n 6).
[11] *R (Abbasi)* v. *Secretary of State*, paragraph 106 (n 6).
[12] *R (Abbasi)* v. *Secretary of State*, paragraph 67 (n 6).
[13] *R (Abbasi)* v. *Secretary of State*, paragraphs 64, 66 (n 6).
[14] *R (Abbasi)* v. *Secretary of State*, paragraphs 15, 66 (n 6). See also paragraph 18: 'There have been widespread expressions of concern, both within and outside the United States, in respect of the stand taken by the United States government in cases such as *Hamdi*.'

Even if the litigation did not succeed, most cynics, including the present author, would recognize that the British court went far beyond its usual prudent line in declaring that Abbasi was arbitrarily detained and in labelling Guantanamo Bay a 'legal black-hole'.[15] *Abbasi* is important in two respects. First, because the court did not avoid exercising its competence to review the case. It expanded the exceptions previously established in two 'easy cases'—*Oppenheimer* ('grave infringement of human rights' committed during the 1939–1945 War) and *Kuwait* ('breaches of clearly established principles of international law' during the Iraqi invasion of Kuwait)—to include violation of the right of habeas corpus during the ongoing armed conflict between the US, UK, and their allies with Afghanistan. The ongoing conflict is a situation far less politically convenient than the two other precedents. Even if the court proved to be still reluctant to intervene on the merits, once it has exercised its competence and rejected the avoidance doctrines, the results on the merits may also be different in the future. Second, its decision not to avoid judicial review in this case allowed the court, if not to render a remedy on the merits, to engage in an audacious judicial dialogue with US courts on the policy of detention in Guantanamo Bay during the early days of the 'war on terror'. It is difficult to estimate the weight of this decision and its influence on US jurisdiction. When the decision in *Abbasi* was rendered in 2002 the question was still pending before the US Court of Appeals for the District of Columbia Circuit. A year later, on 11 March 2003, the US Court of Appeals did not follow the British court's stance. It dismissed the claimant's action. The US Supreme Court overruled the lower court's decision in *Rasul* v. *Bush* in 2004.[16] While *Abbasi* was mentioned in several *amici curiae* briefs submitted to the court, in its ruling the Supreme Court did not make any reference to *Abbasi*. It is quite possible that this may indicate that in the eyes of the American judiciary the UK court went beyond the limits of the usual comity between states' respective judicial institutions. At the same time, as noted by a commentator, the influence of *Abbasi*'s decision over the destiny of the British detainees in Guantanamo cannot be overestimated: 'headline-grabbing statements on the arbitrary detention and ill treatment of those individuals detained in Guantanamo set the tone of public debate.'[17] And Philippe Sands, counsel in *Abbasi* for the plaintiff, notes:

> The Court's judgment added great authority to those who were relying on international law to challenge the conditions of the Guantanamo detainees. . . . To a significant extent the judgement of the Court of Appeal has set the tone for British public opinion on the issue of Guantanamo.[18]

15 *R (Abbasi)* v. *Secretary of State*, paragraph 64 (n 6).

16 See, *Al Odah* v. *United States*, 321 F.3d 1134 (D.C. Cir. 2003) and *Rasul* v. *Bush*, 542 U.S. 466 (2004).

17 Colin R. G. Murray, 'The Ripple Effect: Guantanamo Bay in the United Kingdom's Courts', *Pace International Law Review Online Companion*, 1/9 (2010), 42.

18 Philippe Sands, 'The "Political" and the "Legal": Comments of Professor Tushnet's Paper', *International Journal of Law in Context*, 3/4 (2007), 319, 322.

Thirdly, by its harsh criticism of US government actions in Guantanamo, the court is sending a clear signal to the UK executive. Indeed, the court continued to grant complete discretion to the executive. Nonetheless, if the latter fails to be sufficiently attentive to the court's signals, then in the next case to come up for judicial review the court might well be more affirmative. The UK government knows that the court is willing to exercise its authority in Guantanamo cases. And indeed, by January 2005, following diplomatic pressure, *Abbasi* and the three other British citizens still detained at Guantanamo were transferred to UK custody.[19] It can reasonably be assumed that *Abbasi* was among the factors that influenced that decision.

2.2 Level two on the 'judicial review ladder': the *Hamdan* case (US Supreme Court, 2004)

> We have assumed [. . .] that Hamdan is a dangerous individual whose beliefs, if acted upon, would cause great harm and even death to innocent civilians [. . .] But in undertaking to try Hamdan and subject him to criminal punishment, the Executive is bound to comply with the Rule of Law that prevails in this jurisdiction.[20]

In *Hamdan* the court (1) rejects the avoidance doctrines; (2) declares the state's action to be illegal under IHL and domestic law; and (3) defers to the executive the possibility to seek from the legislative branch an approval for derogating from IHL.

2.2.1 Facts and previous proceedings

Hamdan, a Yemeni national, was captured in 2001 in Afghanistan during the armed conflict between the US and Afghanistan. In 2002, Hamdan was transferred to the military detention camp at Guantanamo Bay. In July 2003, he was deemed eligible by the US president to be prosecuted before the military commissions, which had been established by the same president.[21] A year later he was charged with conspiracy, inter alia to commit attacks on civilians. Hamdan filed a petition for habeas corpus claiming that being prosecuted before military commissions

[19] Murray, 'The Ripple Effect', 25 (n 17).

[20] *Salim Ahmed Hamdan* v. *Donald H. Rumsfeld et al.*, 548 U.S. 557 (2006), at p. 72 of the decision.

[21] The White House, 'Military Order—Detention, Treatment, and Trial of Certain Non-citizens in the War Against Terrorism' (13 November 2001). Online at <http://georgewbush-whitehouse.archives.gov/news/releases/2001/11/20011113-27.html>. This was enacted pursuant to US Congress' 'Authorization for Use of Military Force, § 2(a), Public Law 107-40, 115 Stat. 224' (enacted 18 September 2001) authorizing the President to 'use all necessary and appropriate force against those nations, organizations, or persons he determines planned, authorized, committed, or aided the terrorist attacks that occurred on September 11, 2001, or harbored such organizations or persons, in order to prevent any future acts of international terrorism against the United States by such nations, organizations or persons.' The commission rules were then regulated in US Department of Defense, 'Military Commission Order No. 1' (31 August 2005). Online at <http://www.defense.gov/news/Sep2005/d20050902order.pdf>. After the US Supreme Court granted a writ of certiorari in this case, Congress enacted the Detainees Treatment Act of 2005.

rather than facing a court martial would violate US domestic law—the Uniform Code of Military Justice (UCMJ) and the Third Geneva Convention. More specifically, Hamdan claimed that the military commissions lacked authority to try him on two bases: (1) conspiracy to commit a war crime is an offence that is not a violation of the law of war; and (2) the military commission procedures violate basic rules of military and international law, such as the principle that a defendant should have access to the evidence against him.

On 8 November 2004, the District Court for the District of Columbia granted the petition in part. It ruled that the third Geneva Convention is judicially enforceable. As long as Hamdan's prisoner of war status was in doubt, he must be tried by court martial. In addition, the first instance court ruled that the prosecution before military commission violated both the Third Geneva Convention and the UCMJ. On 15 July 2005, the Court of Appeals reversed the District Court's opinion. It held that the Congress had authorized the establishment of the military commissions through the Authorization for Use of United States Armed Forces (AUMF). It further ruled that the Geneva Conventions do not confer enforceable rights before US courts, and even if they did, the Third Geneva Convention does not apply to al-Qaeda and its members as these failed to comply with the requirements of Article 4.

2.2.2 Rejecting the state's request to avoid the case

Before the Supreme Court, the state claimed that the court should abstain and await the final outcome of ongoing military proceedings before entertaining a review on those proceedings.[22] Moreover, it pointed out that 'abstention is especially appropriate here because the armed conflict against Al Qaeda remains ongoing.'[23] The US Supreme Court rejected the state's motion to dismiss, until the ongoing proceedings before the commissions were over, as being 'unpersuasive':

> Hamdan and the Government both have a compelling interest in knowing in advance whether Hamdan may be tried by a military commission that arguably is without any basis in law and operates free from many of the procedural rules prescribed by Congress for courts-martial—rules intended to safeguard the accused and ensure the reliability of any conviction. While we certainly do not foreclose the possibility that abstention may be appropriate in some cases seeking review of ongoing military commission proceedings (such as military commissions convened on the battlefield), the foregoing discussion makes clear that, under our precedent, abstention is not justified here.[24]

[22] 'All of the reasons that this court has held abstention to be appropriate in similar circumstances counsel, a fortiori, against interlocutory review of this petition. Considerations of separation of powers, deference to military proceedings, avoiding abstract questions and unnecessary decisions all favour deferring judicial review, including review by this court until after the commission proceedings run their course.'—Brief for the Respondents in Opposition No. 05-184 (September 2005), 23. Online at <http://www.law.georgetown.edu/faculty/nkk/documents/HamdanBrief.opp.pdf>.

[23] Brief for Respondents No. 05-184 (September 2005), 7.

[24] *Salim Ahmed Hamdan* v. *Donald H. Rumsfeld et al.*, 25 (n 20). Note that Justice Scalia, with whom Justice Thomas and Justice Alito join, dissented, stating that he would abstain from exercising the court's equity jurisdiction as requested by the state.

As observed by one commentator,

> to reach the merits was a notable assertion of judicial authority.... [T]he Court could readily have gone the route of abstention, as did the D.C. Circuit below, in a well-ploughed tradition of avoiding the merits in cases involving sensitive issues of national security.[25]

2.2.3 On the merits: declaring state act illegal in light of IHL

On the merits, the Supreme Court ruled that the procedures of the commissions set by the president violate, inter alia, Common Article 3 of the Geneva Conventions.[26] In so ruling, the court rejected the position of the state in several aspects. First, the state's qualification of the armed conflict as being international and its position that the Geneva Conventions do not apply to the armed conflict with al-Qaeda were both rejected, as was its stance that these assessments should be deferred.[27] The US Court of Appeals accepted the state's position and ruled,

> the President's decision to treat our conflict with the Taliban separately from our conflict with al Qaeda is the sort of political-military decision constitutionally committed to him. To the extent there is ambiguity about the meaning of Common Article 3 as applied to Al Qaeda and its members, the President's reasonable view of the provision must therefore prevail.[28]

The Supreme Court, however, did not accept that the qualification of the conflict and the applicability of the Geneva Conventions to the conflict between al-Qaeda and the US, merited deference to the executive. This was seen as a legal question that a court can and should examine. Thus, these questions, traditionally given to the sole discretion of the state, were not just reviewed by the Supreme Court, but

[25] Peter J. Spiro, 'Hamdan v. Rumsfeld. 126 S.Ct.2749', *American Journal of International Law*, 100/4 (2006), 892.

[26] The court further ruled that the procedural rules of the commissions (such as the non-disclosure of evidence to the defence and the trial in absentia) violate Article 36 of the UCMJ, which requires that the rules of procedures must be uniform insofar as practical to the principles of law and the rules of evidence generally recognized in the trial of criminal cases in the United States district courts. While the court was ready to defer to the state the determination that it is 'impracticable to apply the rules and principles of law that govern the trial of criminal cases in the United States district courts' to Hamdan's Commission, the court ruled that 'nothing in the record demonstrates that it would be impracticable to apply court-martial rules here [...] The jettisoning of so basic a right cannot lightly be excused as "practicable".' *Salim Ahmed Hamdan* v. *Donald H. Rumsfeld et al.*, 61 (n 20).

[27] President Bush determined, in a memorandum to the Vice-President and others on 7 February 2002, that the armed conflict with al-Qaeda was not a non-international armed conflict, because the conflict was 'international in scope.' According to the state, Al Qaeda is not a High Contracting Party to the Geneva Convention. Common Article 2 to the Four Geneva Conventions of 1949 do not apply to the conflict between the US and Al Qaeda. See George W. Bush, 'Memorandum on Humane Treatment of al Qaeda and Taliban Detainees' (7 February 2002). Online at <http://www.washingtonpost.com/wp-srv/nation/documents/020702bush.pdf>. The state was also of the position that 'the decision whether the Geneva Convention applies to a terrorist network like Al Qaeda is [...] solely for the executive.' 'Writ of certiorari to the United States Court of Appeals for the District of Columbia Circuit' (February 2006), 38.

[28] *Hamdan* v. *Rumsfeld*, decision of the Court of Appeals for the District of Columbia Circuit, 415 F. 3d 33 (2005), 15–16 (citation omitted).

the state's position was actually rejected: the court ruled that the US was engaged in a non-international armed conflict and Common Article 3 of the Geneva Conventions was applicable to members of al-Qaeda.[29]

Second, the court notably rejected the long-held position of the state, echoed in *Johnson* v. *Eisentrager* whereby the Geneva Conventions are not judicially enforceable in domestic courts and that these legal instruments cannot be invoked by individuals.[30] Common Article 3 was not directly enforced, but applied through its domestic incorporation in Article 21 of the UCMJ, which set the obligation to respect the 'law of war'. Despite this, the court nevertheless relied on the Geneva Conventions to determine the legality of the military commissions established by the president.[31] Thus, without deciding more generally whether the Geneva Conventions were judicially enforceable in the absence of implementing legislation, the fact that the court relied on the Geneva Conventions to guarantee their rights, is novel.[32] Enforcing the Geneva Conventions, even via domestic legislation was not commonly done until *Hamdan*. Interestingly, John Yoo shows how *Eisentrager* was decided when a similar legislation, incorporating the 'law of war', existed:

[29] *Salim Ahmed Hamdan* v. *Donald H. Rumsfeld et al.*, 67 (n 20): 'The Court of Appeals thought, and the Government asserts, that Common Article 3 does not apply to Hamdan because the conflict with al Qaeda, being international in scope does not qualify as a conflict not of an international character [. . .] That reasoning is erroneous.' As observed by Benvenisti, 'United We Stand', fn 73 (n 4): 'until the *Hamdan* decision deference to executive treaty interpretation was near absolute, based on the theory that the President has both the constitutional responsibility for, and special competency in, foreign affairs.' For a critique of this judicial position: 'The *Hamdan* decision represents a remarkable and troubling departure from these longstanding precedents. Instead of deferring to the executive branch's reasonable interpretations, the Court adopted its own barely reasonable interpretations in order to invalidate the President's existing system of military commissions.' Julian G. Ku and John C. Yoo, 'Hamdan V. Rumsfeld: The Functional Case for Foreign Affairs Deference to the Executive Branch', *Constitutional Commentary*, 23 (2006), 143, 179. On the doctrine of deference, see also Robert Chesney, 'Unravelling Deference: Hamdan, the Judicial Power, and Executive Treaty Interpretations', *Iowa Law Review*, 92 (2006), 1723–82. Carlos M. Vázquez, 'The Military Commissions Act, the Geneva Conventions, and the Courts: A Critical Guide', *American Journal of International Law*, 101/1 (2007), 73–98. At page 78 Vasquez notes that *Hamdan* shows that it is 'the province of the judiciary to interpret treaties.'

[30] Harold Hongju Koh, 'Why Do Nations Obey International Law?', *The Yale Law Journal*, 106/8 (1997), 2350, 2363.

[31] Article 21 of the UCMJ states that: 'The provisions of this chapter conferring jurisdiction upon courts-martial do not deprive military commissions, provost courts, or other military tribunals of concurrent jurisdiction with respect to offenders or offenses that *by statute or by the law of war may be tried* by military commissions, provost courts, or other military tribunals.' The court ruled that it did not need to decide whether the Geneva Conventions of 1949 could be directly enforced by a US court, since Article 21 of the UCMJ authorizes trial by military commission only 'with respect to offenders or offenses that . . . by the law of war may be tried by military commissions'. Since the court has the authority to enforce the UCMJ, and the Geneva Conventions of 1949 are 'part of the law of war' referenced in Article 21, the court concluded that it had the authority to apply the Conventions. See also David Sloss, 'When Do Treaties Create Individually Enforceable Rights? The Supreme Court Ducks the Issue in Hamdan and Sanchez-Llamas', *Columbia Journal of Transnational Law*, 45/20 (2006–2007), 45; Hongju Koh, 'Why Do Nations Obey International Law?', 2363 (n 30).

[32] David Weissbrodt and Nathaniel H. Nesbitt, 'The Role of the United States Supreme Court in Interpreting and Developing Humanitarian Law', *Minnesota Law Review*, 95/4 (2011), 1339.

When *Eisentrager* was decided, the statutory predecessor to Article 21 contained exactly the same language regarding 'the law of war'. Thus, when the *Eisentrager* Court held that the Geneva Conventions were not judicially enforceable, military commissions were *already bound* by statute to comply with the laws of war.[33]

Third, in rejection of the state's position, the court ruled that the standards set by Common Article 3 of the Geneva Conventions are not met by the commissions. This is because they do not constitute a 'regularly constituted court' and they fail to provide the 'judicial guarantees which are recognized as indispensable by civilized peoples.' The court ruled that the requirements of Common Article 3 of the Geneva Conventions must be understood as incorporating at least the trial protections recognized by customary international law, as laid down in Article 75(4)(e) of Additional Protocol I. Interestingly the court refers to the Protocol's terms as reflecting customary international law, making it binding upon the US, even though the latter has not ratified the Protocol, and apparently also enforceable before US courts. At the same time, the court did not clarify why Additional Protocol I is applicable in a non-international armed conflict.

2.2.4 Deferring to the legislative branch

While the court ruled that the structure and procedure of the military commissions were illegal, the court still used the referral technique by emphasizing that the state can seek Congress' approval for derogating from the requirements of international law:

> Congress has denied the President the legislative authority to create military commissions of the kind at issue here. Nothing prevents the President from returning to Congress to seek the authority he believes necessary . . . [34]
>
> . . . absent express statutory provision to the contrary, information used to convict a person of a crime must be disclosed to him.[35]

Nevertheless the court sent an important signal to Congress: the court may eventually resort to an ultimate response—the review of the constitutionality of a future military commission.[36]

2.2.5 Follow-up after Hamdan

Following the US Supreme Court's decision in *Hamdan*, in order to maintain the military commissions, the US Congress passed the Military Commissions Act of 2006 (MCA). The Act created new military commission procedures, stripping the courts of habeas corpus jurisdiction with respect to non-US citizens determined

[33] Ku and Yoo, 'Hamdan V. Rumsfeld: The Functional Case', 110 (n 29).

[34] *Salim Ahmed Hamdan* v. *Donald H. Rumsfeld et al.* (n 20) (Opinion of Justice Breyer).

[35] *Salim Ahmed Hamdan* v. *Donald H. Rumsfeld et al.*, 72 (n 20).

[36] 'Because Congress has prescribed these limits, Congress can change them, requiring a new analysis consistent with the Constitution.' *Salim Ahmed Hamdan* v. *Donald H. Rumsfeld et al.*, 164 (n 20).

by the executive to be enemy combatants. The Act declared that: 'A military commission established under this chapter is a regularly constituted court... for purposes of common Article 3 of the Geneva Conventions' and further provided that the Conventions could not be invoked.[37] Moreover, it established that the commissions have the sole jurisdiction over habeas corpus cases.[38] In 2006, Benvenisti wrote that 'it is not clear whether the Court will respond to this challenge by climbing one of the two final, constitutional, rungs of the judicial review ladder'.

It did in fact take this step regarding the habeas corpus question. In *Boumediene*, rendered on 13 June 2008, the constitutionality of the MCA of 2006 was reviewed by the Supreme Court and declared un-constitutional. The question was whether the MCA of 2006, which deprived federal courts of jurisdiction over Guantanamo habeas corpus actions, violated the Suspension Clause of the Constitution.[39] The court held that the petitioners have the constitutional right of habeas corpus. Being detained in Guantanamo, they are not barred from invoking the Suspension Clause's protections. Section 7 of the MCA 2006 violated that provision by supplanting a federal habeas corpus jurisdiction with a constitutionally deficient substitute. The court noted that in *Hamdan* it had stated that '[n]othing prevent[ed] the President from returning to Congress to seek the authority he believes necessary', and it clarified that 'nothing in that opinion can be construed as an invitation for Congress to suspend the writ.'[40] Thus, in *Boumediene* the US Supreme Court ascended to the highest position on the ladder: it invalidated a law enacted by the legislative branch.

President Obama, shortly after taking office, suspended the military commissions. They were soon reintroduced through the 2009 Military Commission Act, which replaced the 2006 Act. Following *Boumediene*, the habeas corpus restriction which appeared in Section 7 of the 2006 MCA was removed. At the same time, *Hamdan* had a restricting effect on the definition of torture in the US War Crimes Act. The MCA of 2006 made several amendments to the War Crimes Act, so as to retroactively limit its scope. For example, it amended the War Crimes Act provisions concerning Common Article 3 so that only *specified* violations would be punishable (as opposed to

[37] The US 'Military Commissions Act' passed by the US Senate on 28 September 2006 and by the US House of Representatives on 29 September 2006. It is reproduced in Sassòli, Bouvier and Quintin, *How Does Law Protect in War?*, Case Study No. 265, 2380. See Article 948b of the US 'Military Commissions Act', paragraph (f) 'A military commission established under this chapter is a regularly constituted court, affording all the necessary "judicial guarantees which are recognized as indispensable by civilized peoples" for purposes of common Article 3 of the Geneva Conventions'; and paragraph (g): 'No alien unlawful enemy combatant subject to trial by military commission under this chapter may invoke the Geneva Conventions as a source of rights'.

[38] Section 7(e)(1) of the US 'Military Commissions Act' states that: 'No court, justice, or judge shall have jurisdiction to hear or consider an application for a writ of *habeas corpus* filed by or on behalf of an alien detained by the United States who has been determined by the United States to have been properly detained as an enemy combatant or is awaiting such determination'.

[39] The Military Commission Act (28 U.S.C. § 2241(e) (2006)). The Clause says: 'The privilege of the writ of Habeas Corpus shall not be suspended, unless when in cases of rebellion or invasion the public safety may require it.' Article I, § 9(2) of the Constitution of the United States of America (adopted 17 September 1787). This case did not rely on IHL.

[40] *Boumediene* v. *Bush*, 553 U.S. 723 (2008), 793–5.

any Common Article 3 violation, as it was defined before). These amendments, which were introduced in response to the court's ruling in *Hamdan*, are still valid.[41]

2.3 Higher up the 'judicial review ladder': the *Khadr* cases (Canadian Supreme Court, 2008/2010)

> The deference required by the principle of comity 'ends where clear violations of international law and fundamental human rights begin'.[42]

In the *Khadr* cases the court (1) rejects the avoidance doctrines; (2) declares the state's action to be ultimately illegal under constitutional law; and (3) defers only the decision on the appropriate remedy to the executive.

Khadr, a Canadian citizen, was arrested by US forces in Afghanistan before his 16th birthday, and had been detained since 2002 in Guantanamo Bay. His legal action involved a number of proceedings, including two cases before the Canadian Supreme Court. The first Supreme Court ruling of 2008 addressed the involvement of Canadian officials in his illegal detention in Guantanamo. The second case, from 2010, requested his repatriation to Canada. In both cases, the highest court of Canada affirmed the significance of international law, and at the same time it chose a practical method of intervention in this sensitive domain of foreign relations: after declaring the state officials' acts as unconstitutional, it granted the government entire discretion as to how to proceed for the remedy.

2.3.1 Canada (Justice) v. *Khadr (2008)*

In 2003, Canadian officials interrogated Khadr in Guantanamo Bay and shared the information obtained with US authorities. Faced with criminal charges before US military commissions and for the purpose of his defence, Mr Khadr petitioned the Canadian Minister of Justice for an order to disclose all documents pursuant to Section 7 of the Canadian Charter of Rights and Freedoms, including the interviews conducted in 2003. The Minister of Justice opposed the request, arguing that the Charter did not apply outside Canada. The claim was based on the Supreme Court precedent in *Hape*. That case ruled that in accordance with the principle of comity between nations, Canadian officials operating abroad were required to comply with local law, and therefore the Canadian Charter did not apply extraterritorially. Yet, as an exception to this principle, the court also established that if Canada was participating in a process that violated Canada's binding obligations under international law, the Charter would apply to the extent of that participation. Therefore, in order to decide if Canadian officials were bound by the Charter, the question pending

[41] For more details on the amendments to the War Crimes Act included in the MCA of 2006 see the CRS Report for Congress (29 January 2009) available at: <http://www.fas.org/sgp/crs/intel/RL33662.pdf>.

[42] *R* v. *Hape*, (2007) 2 SCR 292, 2007 SCC 26, paragraph 52, cited in *Canada (Justice)* v. *Khadr*, (2008) 2 SCR 125, 2008 SCC 28, paragraph 18. Online at <http://www.canlii.org/en/ca/scc/doc/2008/2008scc28/2008scc28.pdf>.

before the court was whether the process at Guantanamo Bay, in which Canadian officials conducted the interviews and handed them over to US officials, was a process that violated Canada's binding obligations under international law.

2.3.1.1 Rejecting avoidance doctrines

The state raised the non-justiciability claim 'whether it is appropriate for a Canadian court to pronounce on the legality of the process at Guantanamo Bay under which Mr Khadr was held at the time that Canadian officials participated in that process.'[43] The court ruled that it was not a question that needed to be addressed in this case as 'the United States Supreme Court has considered the legality of the conditions under which the Guantanamo detainees were detained' and held that 'the detainees had illegally been denied access to *habeas corpus* and that the procedures under which they were to be prosecuted violated the *Geneva Conventions*'.[44] In fact, the Canadian court broadened the exception of *Kuwait* based on the same reasoning. In *Kuwait airlines*, the UK House of Lords defined the non-justiciability exception as applying when it is 'a clear breach of international law.' In that case, it was the UN Security Council, which had recognized the Iraqi invasion of Kuwait as a clear breach of the law. In *Khadr,* the exception to the comity between states was based on a ruling of the state's domestic court. Insofar as the US Supreme Court declared the detention in Guantanamo as violating international law, Canadian courts (and maybe, more generally a third state's courts), could themselves use that declaration of illegality for the purpose of rejecting a non-justiciability claim, without violating the comity principle between nations.

2.3.1.2 On the merits: declaring the illegality of state act in light of international and constitutional law

Based on US Supreme court rulings in *Rasul* and *Hamdan* the Canadian Supreme Court found that the conditions under which Khadr was held in Guantanamo were in violation of international law. Accordingly, the court held that the participation of Canadian officials in the 'Guantanamo Bay process' constituted a 'clear violation of Canada's international human rights obligations', and that this was 'contrary to Canada's binding international obligations.'[45] The court therefore found that the Canadian Charter of Rights and Freedoms was applicable:

> We conclude that the principles of international law and comity that might otherwise preclude application of the *Charter* to Canadian officials acting abroad do not apply to the assistance they gave to U.S. authorities at Guantanamo Bay. Given the holdings of the United States Supreme Court, the *Hape* comity concerns that would ordinarily justify deference to foreign law have no application here. The effect of the United States Supreme Court's holdings is that the conditions under which Mr. Khadr was held and was liable for

[43] *Canada (Justice)* v. *Khadr*, paragraph 21 (n 42). [44] *Canada (Justice)* v. *Khadr* (n 42).

[45] *Canada (Justice)* v. *Khadr*, paragraphs 21, 25 (n 42). Interestingly the court did not refer to IHL violations, as expected, but to *human rights* or *international law* violations.

prosecution were illegal under both U.S. and international law at the time that Canadian officials interviewed Mr. Khadr and gave the information to U.S. authorities. Hence no question of deference to foreign law arises. The *Charter* bound Canada to the extent that the conduct of Canadian officials involved it in a process that violated Canada's international obligations.[46]

The US Supreme Court decisions had a decisive impact on the Canadian court. These cases provided the legal authority for the confirmation that international law was violated during the detention process of Khadr—a confirmation that is required for the application of the Canadian Charter extraterritoriality. In fact, the US Supreme Court rulings in 2004 (*Rasul*) and 2006 (*Hamdan*) enabled the Canadian Supreme Court in 2008 to apply the Canadian Charter extraterritorially (and perhaps retroactively) to the acts of Canadian officials in Guantanamo Bay in 2003. Thus, the *Khadr* decision imposed a significant limitation on the executive's authority.[47]

2.3.1.3 Deferring the remedy to the executive

After finding that the Canadian constitution applied in Guantanamo, the court ordered the Canadian government to disclose to Khadr the transcripts of the interviews and records of the information given to US authorities. Nonetheless, the court deferred the decision of what evidence to disclose to the state, pointing out that this disclosure was subject to the balancing of national security with other considerations and whether this disclosure 'would be injurious to international relations or national defence or national security, and whether the public interest in disclosure outweighs in importance the public interest in non-disclosure.'[48] At that point the question of balance would be performed by the state, yet the state received a clear signal that this discretion could be under future judicial review.

2.3.2 Canada (Prime Minister) v. *Khadr (2010)*[49]

In another series of litigation, Khadr requested his repatriation to Canada. This was sought as a remedy for Canada's violation of his constitutional right under

[46] *Canada (Justice)* v. *Khadr*, paragraph 26 (n 42).

[47] For an opposite conclusion see *Amnesty International Canada* v. *Canada (Minister of National Defence)*, (2008). There, the court of first instance ruled in March 2008 (before *Canada (Justice)* v. *Khadr*) (n 42) that protection under the Canadian Charter of Rights and Freedoms did not extend to Afghan detainees and did not apply to the conduct of Canadian forces in Afghanistan. In the appeal, which upheld the lower court's finding in December 2008, the court distinguished between *Khadr* and the Canadian forces in Afghanistan: 'Khadr stands therefore as a case where a Canadian citizen obtained disclosure of documents held in Canada and produced by Canadian officials for a breach of his rights under section 7 of the Charter by Canadian officials participating in a foreign process that violated Canada's international human rights obligations. The factual underpinning of this decision is miles apart from the situation where foreigners, with no attachment whatsoever to Canada or its laws, are held in CF detention facilities in Afghanistan.' *Amnesty International Canada and BCCLA* v. *Canada (Chief of the Defence Staff)*, (2008) FCA 401, (2009) 4 FCR 149, paragraphs 13–14.

[48] *Canada (Justice)* v. *Khadr*, paragraph 41 (n 42).

[49] *Canada (Prime Minister)* v. *Khadr*, (2010) SCC 3, (2010) 1 SCR 44. Online at <http://scc.lexum.org/en/2010/2010scc3/2010scc3.html>.

Section 7 of the Charter. The lower courts held that under the special circumstances of this case, Canada had a duty to protect Khadr under Section 7 of the Charter and ordered the government to request his repatriation.

2.3.2.1 Rejecting avoidance doctrines

The Canadian government submitted that its decision not to request the repatriation of Mr Khadr fell directly within the prerogative powers of the crown to conduct foreign relations. It argued that under the constitution of Canada courts have no power to intervene in this field. The court thus had to consider whether the remedy that Khadr sought—a repatriation request from Canada to the US government—was inappropriate because such an order to the government would touch upon the crown's prerogative power over foreign affairs. The Supreme Court accepted the government's position that the decision not to request Mr Khadr's repatriation was made in the exercise of the prerogative over foreign relations. However it concluded that the judiciary was empowered to review matters of foreign affairs in order to ensure their constitutionality:

> In exercising its common law powers under the royal prerogative, the executive is not exempt from constitutional scrutiny. [...] It is for the executive and not the courts to decide whether and how to exercise its powers, but the courts clearly have the jurisdiction and the duty to determine whether a prerogative power asserted by the Crown does in fact exist and, if so, whether its exercise infringes the *Charter* or other constitutional norms.[50]

At the same time the court mentioned that courts must remain 'sensitive to the fact that the executive branch of government is responsible for decisions under this power, and that the executive is better placed to make such decisions within a range of constitutional options.'[51]

2.3.2.2 On the merits: declaring the illegality of a state act and deferring the remedy to the executive

On the merits, the Supreme Court declared that Canada had infringed Mr Khadr's constitutional rights. At the same time, it decided that the lower courts' remedy ordering the government to request Khadr's repatriation gave 'too little weight to the constitutional responsibility of the executive to make decisions on matters of foreign affairs in the context of complex and ever-changing circumstances, taking into account Canada's broader national interests.'[52] The court was concerned about the lack of detailed information of any negotiations between Canada and the US that may have taken place and the need to respect the separation of powers between the courts and the executive. The court ruled that it would be more appropriate to leave it to the government to 'decide how best to respond to this judgment' and

[50] *Canada (Prime Minister)* v. *Khadr*, paragraph 36 (case references omitted) (n 49).
[51] *Canada (Prime Minister)* v. *Khadr*, paragraph 37 (n 49).
[52] *Canada (Prime Minister)* v. *Khadr*, paragraph 39 (n 49).

gave declaratory relief only.[53] As in the previous case, once again the court declared that the executive had exceeded its authority; yet, the remedy was again deferred to the executive's discretion.

2.3.3 Follow-up to the decision in Khadr

The follow-up to the Supreme Court's decision was that the executive made a request for the US government not to make use of any evidence received as a result of the interrogations of Khadr in 2003–2004 in which Canadian officials participated in the prosecution of Khadr before the military commission. The commission proceeding continued in the summer. Khadr pleaded guilty to a reduced charge and was sentenced to an agreed-upon eight years. The Canadian government did not go along with the proposed remedy of asking for Khadr's return prior to trial. This triggered a further case in the Canadian Federal Court that led to a new order to the government to make that request.The government successfully appealed the decision in the Federal Court of Appeal in mid-2010.[54] On 23 October 2010, Khadr pleaded guilty before a US military commission.[55] The US and Canada submitted a diplomatic note to Khadr in which it was agreed that after serving one year in Guantanamo, his request to be transferred to Canada to serve his remaining time there would be approved.[56] In June 2012 the United Nations Committee Against Torture released a report finding that Canada was complicit in rights violations against three Canadians who were held prisoner in Syria, and against Khadr, who was still being detained in Guantanamo Bay. The Committee condemned Canada for refusing to apologize and give compensation to the individuals who were tortured in Syria, and recommended that it do so immediately. The Committee also urged Canada to approve Khadr's request to be transferred from Guantanamo to Canada for the remainder of his sentence to avoid any future mistreatment. Khadr was also to be appropriately compensated for human rights violations that Canada's Supreme Court ruled he had actually suffered.[57] Khadr was transferred to the custody of the Canadian government in September 2012, nearly two years after being sentenced.

[53] *Canada (Prime Minister)* v. *Khadr*, paragraph 39 (n 49). See paragraph 46: 'In this case, the evidentiary uncertainties, the limitations of the Court's institutional competence, and the need to respect the prerogative powers of the executive, lead us to conclude that the proper remedy is declaratory relief.'

[54] Information given by Peter Carver, Centre of Constitutional Studies, University of Alberta, Canada, in an electronic interview (28 December 2010). In July 2010, a single Justice of the Federal Court of Appeal granted a stay of Justice Zinn's order pending the government's appeal, and made comments suggesting they had a strong appeal case. The Federal Court decisions can be found under 'Khadr' at the court's public website at <http://decisions.fca-caf.gc.ca/en/>.

[55] *United States of America* v. *Khadr*, (Stipulation of Facts) (13 October 2010).

[56] United States Department of State, 'Memorandum for Michael L. Bruhn—Executive Secretary—Department of Defence' (24 October 2010). Online at <http://www.law.utoronto.ca/documents/Mackin/Khadr_Diplomatic_Notes.pdf>.

[57] The Committee Against Torture, 'Concluding Observations: Canada, 48th Session', (25 June 2012), UN Doc CAT/C/CAN/CO/6, paragraph 16.

3. From deferring to legitimizing?

As discussed in the previous sections, the deferral technique allows the courts to slowly abandon their avoidance function in order to exercise their competence over IHL issues. However, the risk of the use of the deferral technique as a form of compromise and deference to the executive is that it will lead to an apologist role of courts by the misuse of the discretion allocated to the state. The Israeli *Torture* and *Targeted Killing* cases discussed next well illustrate this deficiency of the deferral technique.

3.1 The Torture case (Israeli HCJ, 1999)

> A democracy must sometimes fight with one hand tied behind its back. Even so, a democracy has the upper hand. The rule of law and the liberty of an individual constitute important components in its understanding of security. At the end of the day, they strengthen its spirit and this strength allows it to overcome its difficulties.[58]

3.1.1 Background

In 1987, the General Security Service (GSS) received an official mandate from the Israeli government to use a 'moderate degree of physical pressure' during interrogations of suspects involved in terrorist activities. This authorization was provided by the Landau Commission, an official commission headed by former president of the Supreme Court, Moshe Landau.[59] The authorization to use 'moderate degree of physical pressure' during interrogations was justified through the illustration of the 'ticking bomb' paradigm: a bomb is about to explode and cause the death of civilians, and the detainee has the information concerning the location of the bomb. The paradigm assumes that only by using physical interrogations will it be possible to reveal the information necessary to detonate the bomb and to save innocent lives. Its

[58] HCJ 5100/94, *Public Committee Against Torture in Israel* v. *the State of Israel*, (1999) 53(4) PD 817, paragraph 39 (in English at <http://elyon1.court.gov.il/files_eng/94/000/051/a09/94051000.a09.pdf>). This decision has been often referred to as a landmark decision by judges, academics, and state officials. See for example: 'In a landmark ruling, the Court maintained that as a democracy, Israel must wage its war against terrorism with self-restraint due to the need to safeguard human rights.' Israeli Ministry of Foreign Affairs, 'Judgments of the Israel Supreme Court: Fighting Terrorism within the Law' (2 January 2005), 24. Online at <http://www.mfa.gov.il/NR/rdonlyres/599F2190-F81C-4389-B978-7A6D4598AD8F/0/terrorirm_law.pdf>. However, a critic points out the limited scope of this ruling for the court which did not examine all the interrogation methods but only five, and for not obliging the state to disclose the secret guidelines. Ardi Emesis, '"Moderate" Torture on Trial: Critical Reflections on the Israeli Supreme Court Judgment Concerning the Legality of the General Security Service Interrogation Methods', *International Journal of Human Rights*, 5/3 (2001), 71, 73.

[59] 'Commission of Inquiry into the Methods of Investigation of the GSS Regarding Hostile Terrorist Activities' (October 1987). For excerpts of the official English translation see—*Israel Law Review*, 23 (2001), 146. The first part of the Landau Commission report was published, while its second part, in which the methods of interrogation that could be practised were described, remains confidential. In its report ('the Landau report') the commission stated that 'the exertion of a moderate degree of physical pressure cannot be avoided' and that without the use of physical methods of interrogation 'an effective interrogation is impossible.' At the same time the detailed guidelines of the approved methods remained secret.

legal basis was found in the necessity defence, a doctrine borrowed from criminal law, according to which under certain conditions of necessity, imminence, and proportionality one's criminal responsibility can be exempted. The Landau Commission introduced the necessity defence as a general legal authorization given in advance to carry out physical interrogations. This resulted, according to B'Tselem, in the use of physical methods amounting to torture against 850 persons a year.[60]

3.1.2 Declaring the illegality of a state act in light of international and domestic law

In 1999, thirteen years after the secret torture guidelines were issued by the state commission, the court delivered an important precedent in which it outlawed certain methods of interrogation that had been used against Palestinian detainees. The petitioners claimed that the methods amounted to acts of torture. The court ruled that these interrogation methods were illegal because they were practised solely on the basis of the government directives, without an authorizing law. In its decision the court stated that as interrogation inevitably infringes on an individual's freedom, 'in a country adhering to the rule of law, interrogations are not permitted in absence of clear statutory authorization.'[61] Moreover, the court made it clear that the statutory authorization must adhere to the requirements of Israeli constitutional law (the Basic Law: Human Dignity and Liberty).[62] The HCJ further ruled that the 'necessity defense' could not constitute a source of prior authorization for use of physical means during interrogations, thus rejecting the state position.[63] In an absence of any other authorizing law, according to the general regulations applicable to law enforcement officers, interrogators are only authorized to conduct *reasonable* interrogation. In that context the HCJ mentioned, while referring to international law, that,

> a reasonable investigation is necessarily one free of torture, free of cruel, inhuman treatment, and free of any degrading conduct whatsoever. There is a prohibition on the use of 'brutal or inhuman means' in the course of an investigation. [...] This conclusion is in accord with international treaties, to which Israel is a signatory, which prohibit the use of torture "cruel, inhuman treatment" and "degrading treatment." These prohibitions are "absolute." [...] The use of violence during investigations can lead to the investigator being held criminally liable.[64]

[60] B'Tselem, 'Routine Torture: Interrogation Methods of the General Security Service' (February 1998), 5, 16.

[61] HCJ 5100/94, *Public Committee Against Torture in Israel*, paragraph 18 (n 58).

[62] Basic laws are constitution-like provisions which enjoy a higher normative status than regular laws. Since 1995 following the Israeli HCJ precedent, *Bank Hamizrahi Hameuchad Ltd et al.* v. *Migdal Kfar Shitufi*, Israeli courts have the authority to review the constitutionality of laws in light of the Basic Laws. Article 8 of the Basic Law: Human Dignity and Liberty legislation sets the derogation clause. An act, which infringes the right to dignity and liberty may be passed, provided that the law "befit[s] the values of the State of Israel, is enacted for a proper purpose, and [infringes the suspect's liberty] to an extent no greater than required."

[63] HCJ 5100/94, *Public Committee Against Torture in Israel*, paragraphs 23, 35 (n 58).

[64] HCJ 5100/94, *Public Committee Against Torture in Israel*, paragraph 23 (n 58) (citations omitted). This is the only paragraph in which international law is mentioned. Unlike other cases in

3.1.3 Deference to the legislature

The legal basis for declaring the methods of interrogations illegal was the fact that the investigators were acting without an authorizing law. This situation could be legalized:

If the state wishes to enable GSS investigators to utilize physical means in interrogations, it must enact legislation for this purpose. [...] In such legislation, the legislature, if it so desires, may express its views on the social, ethical and political problems of authorizing the use of physical means in an interrogation. [...] Granting GSS investigators the authority to apply physical force during the interrogation of suspects suspected of involvement in hostile terrorist activities, thereby harming the suspect's dignity and liberty, raises basic questions of law and society, of ethics and policy, and of the rule of law and security. These questions and the corresponding answers must be determined by the legislative branch. This is required by the principle of the separation of powers and the rule of law, under our understanding of democracy.[65]

With this, the court deferred the possibility of codifying torture instead of preventing it, in defiance of the absolute prohibition in international law—an absolute prohibition that was recognized by the HCJ itself.[66] At the same time, signals were sent by the judgment that this legislation could be constitutionally reviewed by the HCJ in light of the Israeli constitutional law.[67]

which the HCJ refers to IHL or human rights law provisions, the ruling is based entirely on domestic constitutional law. This is odd as the petitioners, Palestinians from the OPT, benefit from the protection of the Fourth Geneva Convention of 1949 and human rights law and not from Israeli constitutional law. The extraterritorial application of Israeli constitutional law over Palestinians has never been recognized (it was recognized only for Israelis in the OPT, see HCJ 1661/05, *Gaza Coast Regional Council* v. *The Knesset (2005)*, 59(2) PD 481, paragraph 80). Interestingly in this case the acts of the investigators, and not the rights of the petitioners, are under review in light of the constitution. This is somewhat similar to *Amnesty International Canada* v. *Canada (Minister of National Defence)* before a Canadian court, which explicitly rejected that point. It ruled that even if the Canadian officials were bound by the constitution, it still does not necessarily imply that it is applicable extraterritorially in Afghanistan and that it provides a protection for the victims. It ruled that foreign detainees cannot enjoy the extraterritorial application of the Canadian constitution. Any allegation of torture should be based on the applicable law, which is IHL. See *Amnesty International Canada and BCCLA* v. *Canada (Chief of the Defence Staff)*, paragraph 36 (n 47).

[65] HCJ 5100/94, *Public Committee Against Torture in Israel*, paragraph 37 (n 58).

[66] HCJ 5100/94, *Public Committee Against Torture in Israel*, paragraph 23 (n 58).

[67] HCJ 5100/94, *Public Committee Against Torture in Israel*, paragraph 39 (n 58): '(the authorizing) legislation may be passed, provided, of course, that the law "befit[s] the values of the State of Israel, is enacted for a proper purpose, and [infringes the suspect's liberty] to an extent no greater than required." (This corresponds to a derogation clause as set out in Article 8 of the Basic Law: Human Dignity and Liberty.)' As Israeli constitutional legislation sets out a derogation clause, it does not correspond to the absolute international prohibition to torture, which reflects a *jus cogens* norm (*Prosecutor* v. *Furundžija*, (Judgment, Trial Chamber) ICTY IT–95–17/1-T (10 December 1998), paragraphs 137–138, 153; Article 2(2) of the Convention Against Torture and Other Cruel, Inhuman or Degrading Treatment or Punishment (adopted 10 December 1984, entered into force 26 June 1987) 1465 U.N.T.S 85, that allows no exceptions.

3.1.4 Deference to the executive

While the HCJ ruled that the necessity defence could not constitute an authorizing law allowing physical interrogation techniques, it recognized that this defence was available in the course of a criminal trial: 'if a General Security Service investigator, who applied physical interrogation methods for the purpose of saving human life, *is criminally indicted*, the necessity defense is likely to be open to him in the appropriate circumstances'.[68] Moreover, the HCJ went one step further in allowing an important deference to the executive, which would result in upholding the very same practice in the next decade. In a contradictory statement the HCJ ruled that '[t]he Attorney-General can establish guidelines regarding circumstances in which investigators shall not stand trial, if they claim to have acted from "necessity".'[69] Thus, on the one hand, the HCJ affirmed that the 'necessity defence' cannot serve as a legal authorization to use torture methods.[70] However, on the other, it deferred to the state's attorney general who stands at the head of the prosecution office, the authority to define the circumstances in which interrogators would not be prosecuted, when they claim to have used a prohibited method of torture due to 'necessity'. Allowing the head of the state prosecution (who is also the legal advisor to the government) to decide in advance on the circumstances in which the necessity defence would apply must surely lead to a more 'flexible' application of the defence. During a criminal procedure, it should be a judge who decides whether the defence applies in a given situation, and not the prosecution.[71] Second, and more importantly, only when examined *ex post* during a criminal trial is it possible to evaluate the circumstances and the facts. Giving an authorization in advance provides a wider margin of manoeuvre for abuses. If investigators know they bear the burden of proving that the necessity defence has to apply (to be exempt from criminal responsibility), they could be expected to be more careful with their use of interrogation methods. When they have an advance authorization it may have the opposite effect. By deferring to the state's attorney general, the court allowed the state to have the discretion to decide when investigators should not be

[68] HCJ 5100/94, *Public Committee Against Torture in Israel*, paragraph 34 (n 58). While the prohibition of torture is absolute according to human rights treaty law (state responsibility), the criminal defence of necessity is available for individuals by the 1998 International Criminal Court Statute in Article 31(1)(d). See Albin Eser, 'Grounds for Excluding Criminal Responsibility', in Otto Triffterer (ed.), *Commentary on the Rome Statute of the ICC: Observers' Notes, Article by Article* (Baden-Baden: Nomos Verlagsgesellschaft, 1999), 863–78. Albin Eser, 'Defences in War Crimes', *Israel Yearbook on Human Rights*, 24 (1994), 201–34. Yet, one must recognize that the conditions of the defence in practice seem hardly possible to be fulfilled. See, e.g., Paola Gaeta, 'May Necessity be Available as a Defense for Torture in the Interrogation of Suspected Terrorists?', *Journal of International Criminal Justice*, 2/3 (2004), 785, 789–90.

[69] HCJ 5100/94, *Public Committee Against Torture in Israel*, paragraph 38 (n 58).

[70] HCJ 5100/94, *Public Committee Against Torture in Israel*, paragraph 37 (n 58): 'The principle of "necessity cannot serve as a basis of authority."'

[71] Yet, Shany points at the 'unsatisfactory record of domestic courts [..] in protecting the basic human rights of enemy combatants in times of conflict'. Yuval Shany, 'The Prohibition Against Torture and Cruel, Inhuman and Degrading Treatment and Punishment: Can the Absolute be Relativized under Existing International Law?', *Catholic University Law Review*, 56/837 (2007), 847.

prosecuted. In effect, what the court explicitly ruled to be illegal was subsequently legitimized by the very same ruling.[72]

3.1.5 The follow-up: from deferring to legitimizing?

The *Torture* case provides an example of the possible shift of a court towards fulfilling an apologetic role. The deferral technique in the long term may allow for misuse of the discretion allocated to the state by the court. By allowing the executive to establish guidelines exempting criminal responsibility in case of necessity, the court paved the way for the use of physical methods of interrogation, torture and ill-treatment which continued over the next decade, despite being courageously declared illegal by the court.

On the basis of the HCJ's ruling, the attorney general in office in 1999, Mr Elyakim Rubinstein, who would become a Supreme Court judge, swiftly published guidelines effectively granting a priori permission to use physical force against detainees in so-called 'ticking bomb' cases.[73] The guidelines describe in detail the considerations to take into account when deciding whether or not the necessity defence applies to a particular case. They recommend that senior officials should be involved in this decision. The guidelines explicitly provide that where an interrogator has employed a means of interrogation in order to secure vital information the attorney general will consider refraining from initiating criminal proceedings. The vital information would be to prevent tangible danger of grave threat to state security or to human life, liberty, and integrity, and when, under the circumstances, no other reasonable means to prevent this injury exist. Although the attorney general mentioned that these guidelines 'shall not apply to means of interrogation the use of which constitutes "torture" as defined in 'Convention Against Torture',[74] following President Barak in the 1999 *Torture* ruling, the attorney general does not specify which acts amount to torture. Perhaps this explains why the guidelines have not prevented him—or his successors—from applying the necessity defence to what appear to be overt instances of torture.[75]

As a result, NGOs' reports and hundreds of victims' testimonies confirm the continuing practice of torture. This is even after the court's landmark decision, while the 'necessity defence' has continued to be a way of obtaining a priori authorization for using illegal interrogation methods.[76] Since the HCJ ruling in

[72] Consequently, Israel is using the court's decision to justify its use of torture in interrogations. See, for example, State of Israel, 'Fourth Periodic Report to Committee against Torture' (2 November 2006) UN Doc CAT/C/ISR/4, paragraphs 146–147.

[73] The attorney general's guidelines are reproduced in English in the Annex of the Report of the Public Committee against Torture in Israel: 'Accountability denied: the absence of investigation and punishment of torture in Israel', 2009, <http://www.stoptorture.org.il/files/Accountability_Denied_Eng.pdf>.

[74] 1999 Guidelines of the Attorney General, Section G(1).

[75] See e.g. Noam Hoffstadter, 'Ticking bombs—testimonies of torture victims in Israel', Public Committee against Torture, 2007.

[76] See Bana Shoughri-Badarneh, 'A Decade after the High Court of Justice "Torture" Ruling, What's Changed?', in Abeer Baker and Anat (eds) *Threat: Palestinian Political Prisoners in Israel*

1999, more than 700 allegations of torture in detailed affidavits have been submitted by human rights organizations.[77] Among the many allegations of torture and abuse, sleep deprivation and prolonged interrogations are commonplace. Similarly being bound to a chair in painful positions, beatings, slapping, kicking, threats, verbal abuse, and degradation are regularly carried out. Special methods of interrogation include bending the body into painful positions, manacling from behind for long periods of time, intentional tightening of handcuffs, exposure to extreme heat and cold, permanent exposure to artificial light, and detention in substandard conditions contrary to the basic standards set down by the UN. Various forms of psychological torture, such as threats and exploitation of family members, are also commonly used.[78] Allegations include being denied the right to contact attorneys and family members, often for extended periods of time. For example, the report Public Committee Against Torture in Israel (May 2007) provides a detailed description of nine cases of human 'ticking bombs'. These harsh testimonies, collected in 2004–2006, show how Palestinian detainees might find themselves tortured after being labelled as a 'ticking bomb' without having any effective legal review over this practice.[79]

Moreover, not only did the landmark HCJ decision fail to prevent illegal interrogations—it led to the *de facto* institutionalization of interrogators' immunity from prosecution under the auspices of the HCJ ruling.[80] Over the years, the

(London: Pluto Press, 2011), 114–23; Yuval Ginbar, '"Celebrating" a Decade of Legalised Torture in Israel'. Online at <http://projects.essex.ac.uk/ehrr/V6N1/Ginbar.pdf>. Public Committee Against Torture in Israel, 'Ticking Bombs—Testimonies of Torture Victims in Israel' (30 May 2007). Online at <http://www.stoptorture.org.il/en/node/69>. See also: 'The Committee is concerned that there are numerous, ongoing and consistent allegations of the use of methods by Israeli security officials that were prohibited by the September 1999 ruling of the Israeli Supreme Court, and that are alleged to take place before, during and after interrogations'. Concluding observations of the Committee against Torture, CAT/C/ISR/CO/4, 23 June 2009, paragraph 19.

[77] Türkel Commission, *The Public Commission to Examine the Maritime Incident of 31 May 2010. Second Report: Israel's Mechanisms for Examining and Investigating Complaints and Claims of Violations of the Laws of Armed Conflict According to International Law* (February 2013) 354. See <http://www.turkelcommittee.gov.il/files/newDoc3/The%20Turkel%20Report%20for%20website.pdf.>. The Türkel Commission is the Israeli state commission established in June 2010 in the aftermath of the Flotilla incident. It was mandated to examine 'whether the investigation and inquiry mechanism that is practised in Israel in general . . . is consistent with the duties of the State of Israel pursuant to the rules of international law'.

[78] Irit Ballas, 'Family matters', Public Committee against Torture, 2012; Maya Rosenfeld, 'When the exception becomes the rule', Public Committee against Torture, 2012; Elkhatib Samakh, 'Shackling as a form of torture and ill treatment', Public Committee against Torture, 2009.

[79] Public Committee Against Torture in Israel, 'Ticking Bombs', 12–90.

[80] For instance, in the case of Medhat Tareq Muhammad, the HCJ held that: '[. . .] the Attorney General and State Attorney decided that the forms of interrogation which were applied fall under the "defence of necessity," and therefore the interrogators bear no criminal liability in this case for the forms of interrogation applied by them.' Crim App 4705/02, *Anon* v. *State of Israel* (Decision of 30 December 2002), paragraph 1. An analysis of correspondence between complainants and the Attorney General's office shows that the grounds given for shelving complaints of torture and ill-treatment fall into one of two main categories: justification under the necessity defence, or denial. See Sharon Weill and Irit Ballas, 'Investigation of Torture Claims in Israel: Analysis of the 2012 High Court of Justice Ruling and the Türkel Commission Report', in Stuart Casey-Maslen, *The War Report*, (forthcoming Oxford: Oxford University Press, 2013) 426.

authorities have rejected more than 700 requests to open criminal investigations for allegations of torture and cruel, inhuman and degrading treatment during interrogations of Palestinians.[81] Complaints submitted to the authorities are reviewed by a GSS agent whose recommendations not to open a criminal investigation are always accepted by the high-ranking attorney in charge of the cases at the Ministry of Justice and by the state attorney general.[82] In 2009, three major human rights organizations filed a contempt of court motion to the HCJ. The motion was against the Israeli government and the GSS, for their responsibility for the policy that grants a priori permission to use torture in interrogations, in violation of the 1999 judgment. It was claimed that the pattern of shielding alleged torturers—as demonstrated by the systematic rejections of hundreds of complaints—demands the intervention of the HCJ. The motion provides evidence for the routine granting of *a priori* authorization by the interrogator's supervisors, and even by the head of the GSS himself, to use physical interrogation methods in accordance with established procedures known to interrogators, prosecutors and judges as 'the necessity interrogation procedure'. However, this petition was rejected on the grounds that the court does not address general policies in contempt procedures and recommended the submission of individual cases.[83]

In order to address the flawed mechanism of investigation, which effectively grants impunity to GSS interrogators, a specific petition was submitted to the High Court of Justice in February 2011 by the Public Committee Against Torture along with other NGOs. The petitioners argued that it was inconceivable that in hundreds of complaints of torture or ill-treatment that had been filed during 2001–10, not one had ever led to even a criminal investigation. The decision rendered in August 2012 was delivered by Justice Rubinstein, who was the State Attorney General in 1999 in charge of the drafting of the immunity guidelines. Justice Rubinstein ruled that the GSS examination practice of torture complaints in force since 1992, conducted in secrecy, was legitimized. The reason given was as a result of the need to strike a balance between the demands of impartiality and the demands dictated by the nature of GSS work. The HCJ ruled that there was no obligation automatically to open a criminal investigation for each complaint, only in cases in which the examination phase led to the disclosure of sufficient evidence. In so ruling, the

[81] Türkel Commission Report, 354. *The Public Commission to Examine the Maritime Incident of 31 May 2010* (n 77).

[82] Public Committee Against Torture in Israel, 'Accountability Denied: The Absence of Investigation and Punishment of Torture in Israel' (December, 2009), 93. Online at <http://www.stoptorture.org.il/files/Accountability_Denied_Eng.pdf>. For more details on the investigation process see: Türkel Commission Report, *The Public Commission to Examine the Maritime Incident of 31 May 2010*, 415 (n 77).

[83] HCJ, *Public Committee Against Torture in Israel* v. *Government of Israel*, Case No. 5100/94 (Contempt of Court, 2009). See: Public Committee Against Torture in Israel, 'High Court of Justice Rejected the Contempt of Court Petition Filed by PCATI and Other Organizations' (6 July 2009). Online at <http://www.stoptorture.org.il/en/node/1460>. Since then, the Public Committee Against Torture has submitted a dozen of such individual cases, none of which has resulted, until now, in a substantive ruling.

HCJ allowed the narrative of lack of evidence to prevail, a lack which it identified as being the result of false complaints, and not as a result of a structure that precluded the possession of such evidence, in order to justify the preliminary examination system (as well as the fact that no complaint had ever generated a criminal investigation). With this portrayal of the *facts* (or absence of facts), the HCJ was more concerned with false complaints—mentioned a few times in the ruling—and less with the possibility of true allegations, an option that was never cited.[84]

3.2 The Israeli *Targeted Killing* case (2006)

The *Targeted Killing* case provides another example of how deference may lead to the *de facto* legitimization of a state's illegal acts. As discussed in Chapter 2, the Israeli HCJ was willing to exercise its competence in the *Targeted Killing* case, though. The case dealt with an issue related to conduct of hostilities and questioned the legality of a general policy.[85] On the merits, the HCJ ruled that the targeted killings policy could not be categorically defined as legal or illegal. The legality of the tactic should be determined on a case by case basis, with one of the questions to be examined being whether it complied with the principle of proportionality. HCJ President, Justice Barak, emphasized that the question of proportionality was a difficult one and spans a spectrum of cases ranging between the two extremes—namely cases that are obviously legal and those that are obviously illegal. It is necessary to strike a balance:

> Achieving that balance is difficult. Here as well, one must proceed case by case, while narrowing the area of disagreement. Take the usual case of a combatant, or of a terrorist sniper shooting at soldiers or civilians from his porch. Shooting at him is proportionate even if as a result, an innocent civilian neighbour or passerby is harmed. That is not the case if the building is bombed from the air and scores of its residents and passersby are harmed.[86]

The court provided two further instructions. First, that civilians directly participating in hostilities could not be attacked if a less harmful means could be employed. Secondly, the HCJ deferred the responsibility of conducting independent investigations of a targeted killing operation to the state, in order to examine the

[84] HCJ 1265/11, *PCATI et al.* v. *Attorney General*, (2012). The Türkel Commission rendered its report in February 2013, a few months after the HCJ decision. It found that the current mechanism does not comply with the requirement of an effective investigation and that 'there are serious failures in the effectiveness and thoroughness and also in the promptness of the investigation process'. The Commission also recommended to videotape GSS investigations.
See the Türkel Commission Report, *The Public Commission to Examine the Maritime Incident of 31 May 2010*, 416 (n 77). For further analysis see Sharon Weill and Irit Ballas, 'Investigation of Torture Claims in Israel: Analysis of the 2012 High Court of Justice Ruling and the Türkel Commission Report', in Stuart Casey-Maslen, *The War Report* (n 80).

[85] On the rejection of the non-justiciability claims in that case, which challenge a general policy related to the conduct of hostilities, see Chapter 2.

[86] HCJ 769/02, *The Public Committee against Torture in Israel* v. *The Government of Israel et al.*, (2006), paragraph 46 (in English at <http://elyon1.court.gov.il/files_eng/02/690/007/a34/02007690.a34.pdf>).

legality of the action, and to pay compensation to innocent victims in appropriate cases.[87]

3.2.1 The follow-up: legitimizing state illegal practice?

The example of the obviously disproportionate *Targeted Killing* case, cited by President Barak bore an amazing resemblance to another case that was pending before the court—the targeted killing of Shehadeh.[88] In that case, on 22 July 2002, at around midnight, an Israeli Air Force plane dropped a one-ton bomb on a residential neighbourhood in Gaza City of the al-Daraj' neighbourhood, one of the most densely populated residential areas in the world. The military objective of this operation was to kill Hamas' military leader in the Gaza Strip, Salah Shehadeh, who at that time was in his house with his family. As a result of the operation, Shehadeh and fourteen civilians were killed, most of them children and infants, and 150 people were injured, about half of them severely. The houses in the vicinity were either destroyed or damaged. Seven members of the Matar family, whose neighbouring house was totally destroyed, were among the casualties. A few months after the targeted killing of Salah Shehadeh, 'Yesh Gvul' (an Israeli non-governmental organization) submitted a request to open a criminal investigation against the planners and executors of the operation to the Israeli military advocate general. After receiving a negative answer, a request was submitted to the state advocate general, who had the authority to review that decision. After being denied again, on 30 September 2003 Yesh Gvul and five well-known Israeli authors petitioned the Israeli HCJ demanding that the court review both authorities' decision not to open a criminal investigation into the matter of Salah Shehadeh.[89] The petition questioning the legality of the army's policy of targeted killings had been pending before the same court as the decision in the Shehadeh petition. As the Shehadeh decision depended on the outcome of a ruling on the legality of this policy, the court decided to suspend the Shehadeh petition until it had given a decision on the *Targeted Killings* petition—which it gave in December 2006. On 17 June 2007, the court held a hearing on Shehadeh. The court did not decide whether the aerial bombing

[87] HCJ 769/02, *The Public Committee against Torture in Israel*, paragraph 40 (n 86): 'after an attack on a civilian suspected of taking an active part, at such time, in hostilities, a thorough investigation regarding the precision of the identification of the target and the circumstances of the attack upon him is to be performed (retroactively)'. For more details see Antonio Cassese, 'On Some Merits of the Israeli Judgment on Targeted Killings', *Journal of International Criminal Justice*, 5/2 (2007), 339.

[88] Orna Ben-Naftali, 'A Judgment in the Shadow of International Criminal Law', *Journal of International Criminal Justice*, 5/2 (2007), 330.

[89] HCJ 8794/03, *Yoav Hess and others* v. *The Judge Advocate General*, (2008). Online at <http://www.adh-geneva.ch/RULAC/pdf_state/HCJ-decision-8794-03-1-.pdf>. The state's position was that a debriefing carried out by the defence authorities found that the collateral damage was caused because of an intelligence failure and therefore was not anticipated by the decision-makers. The attorney general adopted this position, and decided that there was no reason to order the opening of a criminal investigation regarding these facts. For more details, see Adalah—Briefing Paper, 'Israeli Military Probes and Investigations Fail to Meet International Standards or Ensure Accountability for Victims of the War on Gaza' (January, 2010); Sharon Weill, 'The Targeted Killing of Salah Shehadeh: from Gaza to Madrid', *Journal of International Criminal Justice*, 7/3 (2009), 617–31.

of a building such as that of Shehadeh could constitute prima facie evidence of a violation of the laws of armed conflict. If such a violation were found, those responsible could be criminally liable, thus the opening of a criminal investigation was needed. In fact the court did not review the merits of the decisions of the authorities (either military or civil) not to open an investigation.

Instead, the court deferred the decision to the state, instructing it to establish an objective and independent body 'in the spirit of the guidelines set down by the Court in the principled ruling on the Targeted Killings case'.[90] The state-established committee consisted primarily of former military and security officials, thus lacking the elementary powers needed to conduct a criminal investigation.[91] Its mandate was to function in accordance with the law that applies to the conduct of a military debriefing, meaning that all the testimonies and evidence are classified.[92] The legal saga, which lasted for more than eight years, ended with the State Commission decision not to open an investigation, while the evidentiary basis for their decision remains essentially unknown.[93] In its report the Commission recognized that: 'The principle of proportionality must be carefully adhered to.... In this context, maximum caution must be exercised in the selection of the method of striking the target and the type of weapon to be used in the operation.'[94] It affirmed that other 'possible courses of action were explored, as well as various methods of operation and the type of weapons that could be used to ensure a successful outcome', but these were found not to be suitable. It did not, however, offer any further explanation as to why a one-ton bomb could lawfully be chosen and how that choice would possibly accord with IHL customary rules of distinction, proportionality, and precautions in attacks.

Thus, the state was shielded from judicial scrutiny thanks to the *Targeted Killings* case. Instead of reviewing the military commander's decision in a specific targeted killings case, the court deferred that review to another body, the structure, nature, and mandate of which were entirely determined by the state; the very entity whose actions were to be investigated. This deferral was legitimized by the landmark ruling of the HCJ on the targeted killings case, in which the court ruled that the state has to investigate targeted killing actions. Since the *Shehadeh* case the HCJ has never reviewed the legality of any other specific targeted killing case.

[90] HCJ 8794/03, *Yoav Hess and others* v. *The Judge Advocate General*, paragraph 8.

[91] On 23 January 2008, the commission was appointed by the Prime Minister. It was composed of three members, two of them former military generals and another a former official from the security services Brigadier General (Res.) Zvi Inbar, formerly the military advocate general and the Knesset Legal Counsel was appointed head of the commission; with him were appointed as members of the commission Major General (Res.) Iztchak Eitan, formerly the head of the IDF Central Command and Mr Iztchak Dar, who formerly held a large number of operative positions in the GSS, amongst others as the Head of the Service's Israeli and Foreign Interests Section.

[92] Announcement from the State Attorney's Office to the HCJ (4 February 2008), paragraph 8 (file with the author).

[93] The Commission's report was published in February 2011. Prime Minister's Office, 'Salah Shehadeh—Special Investigatory Commission' (27 February 2011). Online at <http://mfa.gov.il/MFA/AboutIsrael/statestate/Law/Pages/Salah_Shehadeh-Special_Investigatory_Commission_27-Feb-2011.aspx>.

[94] Prime Minister's Office, 'Salah Shehadeh', paragraph 17.

4. The normative role of courts: limiting the political branches

After examining in previous sections the deferral role of courts and its inherent risk of becoming an apologetic tool, this section examines the limiting role of courts—that is the ultimate role of national courts from the rule of law perspective. That role is examined in the context of conduct of hostilities. The first part analyses the shift from avoiding towards exercising competence, and the second part focuses on the limiting role of court—and its own limits.

4.1 Judicial review of conduct of hostilities (Israeli HCJ)

Since 2000, the beginning of the second intifada, Israel has been engaged in an armed conflict against Palestinian armed groups. This is in addition to the ongoing situation of occupation. President Barak qualified the conflict as international armed conflict.[95] This led to a new situation in which petitions were filed at the court in an unprecedented manner during hostilities, challenging the legality of the conduct of the armed forces.[96] In addressing these petitions, the Israeli HCJ could have chosen the prudent path of holding that the actions of the armed forces during fighting were not justiciable. But, on the contrary, the Israeli HCJ developed a very active view of its role. It did not balk at exercising jurisdiction over issues related to the conduct of hostilities, even when the hostilities were actually taking place. Justice Barak made it clear that hostilities must be fought within the rule of law and not outside of it:

> The military operations of the army are not conducted in a legal vacuum. There are legal norms—some originating in customary international law, some originating in international law enshrined in treaties to which Israel is a party, and some originating in the basic principles of Israeli law—which provide rules as to how military operations should be conducted.[97]
>
> This combat is not taking place in a normative void. It is being carried out according to the rules of international law, which provide principles and rules for combat activity. The saying, "when the cannons roar, the muses are silent," is incorrect. Cicero's aphorism that laws are silent during war does not reflect modern reality.[98]

Moreover, the court maintained that its role in a democracy was to guarantee the upholding of the rule of law—it had to enforce the law against the other branches of the state, whether legislative or executive:

> [E]ven when the cannons speak, the military must uphold the law. The power of society to stand against its enemies is based on its recognition that it is fighting for values that deserve protection. The rule of law is one of these values.... [T]he position of the State of Israel is a

[95] HCJ 769/02, *The Public Committee against Torture in Israel*, paragraph 18 (n 86).

[96] For an analysis see David Kretzmer, 'The Supreme Court of Israel: Judicial Review during Armed Conflict', *German Yearbook of International Law*, 47/392 (2005), 425–35; Galit Raguan, 'Adjudicating Armed Conflict in Domestic Courts: The Experience of Israel's Supreme Court', *Yearbook of IHL*, 13 (2010), 61–95. Examples of cases are, HCJ 3451/02, *Almandi* v. *The Minister of Defense*, (2002) 56(3) PD 30; HCJ 3114/02, *Barake* v. *The Minister of Defense*, (2002) 56(3) PD 11.

[97] HCJ 4764/04, *Physicians for Human Rights* v. *The Commander of IDF Forces in Gaza*, (2004) 58 (5) PD 385, paragraph 7.

[98] HCJ 3451/02, *Almandi* v. *The Minister of Defense*, paragraph 9.

difficult one. Our role as judges is also not easy. . . . This is the price of democracy. It is expensive, but worthwhile. It strengthens the state. It provides a reason for its struggle. Our work, as judges, is hard. But we cannot escape this difficulty, nor do we wish to do so.[99]

In sum, there is no activity conducted by the executive that is precluded from the court's scrutiny at all times, including during war. As the court sees itself as an 'essential part' of the 'democratic triangle' (legislature-executive-judiciary), and understanding its role as the 'main guardian of the rule of law',[100] the court almost totally waives the requirements of standing, non-justiciability doctrine, or any other avoidance doctrine. By doing so, the Israeli HCJ can serve as an example of a judiciary that perceives IHL as a normative and binding law. It does not treat IHL as a foreign policy matter, and IHL should therefore be enforced by the court as part of its mandate for ensuring the rule of law.

Having said that, many cases delivered during real time combat corresponded to the first level of the 'judicial review ladder', 'Even in a time of combat, the laws of war must be upheld. Even in a time of combat, everything must be done in order to protect the civilian population'.[101]

Not only was the Israeli HCJ ready to confront legal issues related to conduct of hostilities, which are typically avoided by other jurisdictions as being under the discretion of the executive—it was even willing to do so during ongoing combat. In *Physicians for Human Rights* v. *The Commander of the IDF Forces in the West Bank* the petition was submitted during 'Operation Defensive Wall', which took place in Jenin in 2002. As the court states in the beginning of its decision:

The petitions before us were filed yesterday and today, during the height of IDF combat activities in the areas of the Palestinian Authority, in the context of "Operation Defensive Wall."[102]

Petitioners claimed that the Israeli Defence Forces violated IHL by firing upon medical teams, preventing the evacuation of the wounded and the sick to hospitals, preventing the removal of bodies for the purposes of burial, and preventing the supply of medical equipment to hospitals. The state explained that, in light of the brief period at its disposal to prepare a response, and especially in light of the fact that combat continued even as the petitions were being heard, it was not possible to investigate the petitioner's claims regarding these specific events. Although the court was 'unable to express a position regarding the specific events mentioned in the petition' the judges 'see fit to emphasize' that combat forces must fulfil the rules of IHL pertaining to the care of the wounded, the sick, and the removal and burial of bodies. It ordered the army to instruct the combat forces, 'down to the level of the lone soldier in the field' to prevent, as far as possible, and even in severe situations, incidents which are inconsistent with the rules of IHL.

99 HCJ 7015/02, *Ajuri* v. *The Commander of IDF Forces in the West Bank*, (2002), 56(6) PD 352, paragraph 41.

100 Yigal Mersel, 'Judicial Review of Counter-Terrorism Measures: the Israeli Model for the Role of the Judiciary during the Terror Era', *New York University Journal of International Law and Politics*, 38/12 (2006), 96.

101 HCJ 3114/02, *Barake* v. *The Minister of Defense*, 16.

102 HCJ 2936/02, *Physicians for Human Rights* v. *The Commander of the IDF Forces in the West*, (2002), 56(3) PD 3, paragraph 1.

A remarkable case, which further illustrates the readiness of the court to review the acts of the army in real time, is *Rafah* (2004)—the petition was filed and heard in the course of ongoing hostilities.[103] In that case, petitioners requested the court to examine whether the army was complying with various humanitarian obligations to which it is subject under IHL, including the protection of medical teams, evacuation of the wounded, the obligation of burying the dead, etc.[104] The petition was filed on the evening of 20 May 2004, two days after active combat had started in the area of Rafah in the Gaza Strip. The duty judge scheduled the hearing for the next morning, ordering the government to submit its position.[105] In the hearing, the state counsel was accompanied by the officer responsible for humanitarian affairs in the battle zones. While combat was ongoing, the officer was in telephone contact with the ground forces and provided the court with details of ongoing attempts to resolve the humanitarian concerns. The state asked that the petition be denied on justiciability grounds, emphasizing that 'extensive military operations are continuing in the area.... In this situation, great caution is required when the court exercises judicial review of the activities of the security forces. The activity lies on the border of the sphere of institutional justiciability.'[106] This position was clearly rejected by Justice Barak, who found no institutional obstacle in reviewing the legality of the conduct of the Israeli military: the conduct of hostilities, regulated by IHL, entitles the court to review whether the army complies with that law. The fact that there were ongoing operations did not exempt it from review:

> Indeed, all the military operations of every army are subject to the rules of international law governing these operations. [...] The purpose of the petition is to direct the immediate conduct of the army. Our judicial review is prospective. It is exercised while the military activity is continuing. [...] [The merits] have been resolved without endangering the lives of soldiers or the military operations. Subject to this restriction, this case is no different from other cases where this court examines the legality of military operations. [...] Indeed, we do not substitute our discretion for that of the military commander's, as far as it concerns military considerations. That is his expertise. We examine the results on the plane of the humanitarian law. That is our expertise.[107]

With the court pressure and guidance to the authorities, many of the claims were solved or mitigated and the important issues were resolved during the hearing. The ruling was given after the end of combat so it was somewhat irrelevant to the facts. Having succeeded in mediating between the sides, the court could have refrained from

[103] HCJ 4764/04, *Physicians for Human Rights* v. *The Commander of IDF Forces in Gaza*.

[104] For example, see paragraph 4 where the petitioners argued that the army should allow medical teams and ambulances to reach the wounded in Rafah in order to evacuate them; that the evacuation should take place without prior coordination with the humanitarian centre; that the transport of medical equipment between Rafah and the hospitals outside it should be allowed; that medical teams or civilians involved in the evacuation of the dead or wounded should not be harmed or threatened and that the electricity and water supply to the neighbourhood of A-Sultan should be renewed. The court in its ruling addressed Articles 27, 55, 56 and 59 of the Fourth Geneva Convention of 1949.

[105] Kretzmer, 'The Supreme Court of Israel', 430 (n 96).

[106] HCJ 4764/04, *Physicians for Human Rights* v. *The Commander of IDF Forces in Gaza*, paragraph 5.

[107] HCJ 4764/04, *Physicians for Human Rights* v. *The Commander of IDF Forces in Gaza*, paragraphs 7–9.

delivering a judgment. But it did not. The HCJ delivered a very detailed decision in which it described how the dispute was resolved. Recalling that the state has to comply with the law and declaring that the court is supervising the state's acts also during combat, its decision provides legal guidance to be considered in future cases.

The importance of the case is manifested by the fact the court does not avoid the case. It assumes its role as the guardian of the rule of law—even during combat.[108] That said, the court's review is still located at the bottom of the judicial ladder. The court defers the entire responsibility of finding a decision to the state—albeit within the framework of the law as defined by the court. Professor Kretzmer defines the court's role as a mediating role between the civilians and the army during the conduct of hostilities, which results in a restraining influence on the authorities, concluding that courts probably cannot do much more under these circumstances.[109] Although it is not interfering in the operation itself, it nonetheless reminds the state that its acts are subject to judicial scrutiny, and that the state must observe the law, and that the state must provide solutions that comply with the rules of IHL.

4.2 Limiting state act: the *Human Shield* case, 2005

The *Human Shield* case was an important one in that the court put a limit on state practice without any deference to the state.[110] In this case, the petitioners claimed that the army's use of Palestinian civilians as human shields and/or as hostages was illegal according to IHL. The army's actions, the petitioners alleged, constituted a grave breach of the Geneva Conventions.[111] The HCJ was requested to set an urgent hearing on this petition, since 'the army is still inside some of the Palestinian cities or their vicinity, and is operating in the West Bank' and its 'policy of using human beings during its activities in the West Bank has not yet ceased'.[112] The petitioners sought a temporary injunction ordering the state to stop using

[108] Similarly, more recently, a case was submitted during intense hostilities during Operation Cast Lead in the Gaza Strip. The case concerned the delay in evacuating Palestinian casualties and claims that medical personnel and ambulances were being attacked by the Israeli armed forces: HCJ 201/09, *Physicians for Human Rights* v. *Prime Minister of Israel*, (2009). The HCJ rejected the non-justiciability claim. The HCJ found that the army had taken the necessary steps according to the humanitarian obligations applicable, and the ruling was delivered while the operation was still ongoing.

[109] 'The presence of the Court "at the front" certainly facilitates amelioration of humanitarian concerns that the military might ignore if not forced to confront them.' Kretzmer, 'The Supreme Court of Israel', 434 (n 96).

[110] HCJ 3799/02, *Adalah—The Legal Center for Arab Minority Rights in Israel* v. *The Military Commander of Central Command*, (2005). Online at <http://elyon1.court.gov.il/files_eng/02/990/037/a32/02037990.a32.HTM>. Roland Otto, 'Neighbours as Human Shields? The Israel Defense Forces' "Early Warning Procedure" and IHL', *International Review of the Red Cross*, 86/856 (2004), 771–87.

[111] HCJ 3799/02, *Adalah—The Legal Center for Arab Minority Rights in Israel* v. *The Military Commander of Central Command*, paragraphs 64–80 (Petition). English translation of the petition is available online at <http://www.adalah.org/eng/features/humshields/3799petition-eng.pdf>. Other mentioned Articles of the Fourth Geneva Convention of 1949, which prohibit the use of human shields were 3, 8, 27, 28, 47 and 51, and Article 51(7) of the Additional Protocol I of 1977.

[112] HCJ 3799/02, *Adalah—The Legal Center for Arab Minority Rights in Israel* v. *The Military Commander of Central Command*, paragraph 2 (n 110).

individuals as 'human shields' or as hostages during the military actions in the West Bank until a final decision was given on the petition. The hearing was set two weeks later. In response to the request for a temporary injunction, the state declared that the army immediately issued an order to the forces in the field, in accordance with which it was absolutely forbidden for the armed forces to (1) use civilians as a means of 'living shield' to protect soldiers from attack; or (2) to hold Palestinian civilians as 'hostages' (to hold civilians as a means to pressure others); or (3) to use civilians in situations where they might be exposed to danger to life or limb.[113] The question under review before the court was then reduced to situations in which, as formulated by the state, Palestinian residents *assist* Israeli armed forces. More specifically, the question remaining for review was the 'early warning' procedure. The procedure meant that during the arrest of wanted persons, Israeli soldiers could seek assistance from Palestinian civilians. Civilians could give prior warning to the suspect in order to avoid a possible injury to him, or to those with him during the arrest as long as two conditions were met: (1) the civilian gave his consent to assist; and (2) the commander determined that the act posed no danger to the civilian. On 18 August 2002, following the death of a Palestinian civilian in the course of a similar action, a temporary interlocutory injunction was issued. The Respondents were ordered to refrain from using Palestinian civilians for any military acts. However, after the state issued specific rules for the early warning procedure,[114] in January 2003, the court limited the injunction and permitted the Israeli army's use of the 'early warning' order.

While the court and the parties agreed that the use of a human shield is prohibited, the question before the court was whether this procedure was still illegal if the local civilian gives his consent, and no damage to him is foreseen. The HCJ ruled that the 'early warning' procedure contradicted IHL.[115] Citing Regulation 23(b) of The Hague Regulations and Article 51 of the Fourth Geneva Convention, the court ruled that the civilian population cannot be used for the military needs of the occupying army. Then, based on the principles of distinction and the duty to distance innocent local residents from the zone of hostilities, the court concluded that a civilian could not be brought, even with his consent, into a zone in which combat activity is taking place. Also, the court stated that according to Article 8 of the Fourth Geneva Convention, protected persons cannot renounce their rights pursuant to IHL, whether in part or in their entirety. In any case, it was difficult to judge when the consent is given freely, and when it was the result of

[113] HCJ 3799/02, *Adalah—The Legal Center for Arab Minority Rights in Israel* v. *The Military Commander of Central Command*, paragraph 3 and 'Response on behalf of the Respondents to the Request for a Temporary Injunction', paragraph 2, unofficial translation available online at <http://www.adalah.org/eng/features/humshields/3799response2-eng.pdf>.

[114] In December 2002, the Israeli army introduced 'Operational Order—Prior Warning,' which allowed the army to seek 'assistance' from civilians provided that two conditions were met: (1) the civilian did not 'refuse to assist' and (2) the commander in the field determined that the act posed no danger to the civilian. This order was approved by the then attorney general and current Supreme Court Justice Elyakim Rubenstein.

[115] HCJ 3799/02, *Adalah—The Legal Center for Arab Minority Rights in Israel* v. *The Military Commander of Central Command*, paragraph 25 (n 110).

pressure. It ended by recalling that the damage potential of the act did not lend itself to accurate prediction and that in this context the court adopted a broader approach to the notion of 'danger' than just that of immediate physical gunfire danger. It allowed itself to also consider 'the danger which a local resident who "collaborates" with the occupying army can expect.'[116]

4.2.1 Follow-up to the Human Shield case

A month after the ruling was delivered, the state asked the HCJ to grant a second hearing to reconsider its decision, claiming, inter alia, that this new precedent would have a harmful impact on the army's functioning.[117] The state's application was rejected. The HCJ found that there was no legal basis to conduct another hearing before an expanded panel of the HCJ stating that:

> It is the duty of the army which holds a territory in a belligerent occupation to protect the life and dignity of a local resident. To place this resident, who is caught in the middle of a battlefield, in a position where he has to choose whether or not to acquiesce to the army's request to pass a warning to a wanted gunman is to place him in an impossible position. The choice itself is immoral and impairs the dignity of man.

Following the HCJ's decision, the army proceeded to modify its orders.[118] Yet, despite these official proclamations and the HCJ's decisions, Israeli and international experts and organisations, have affirmed that the use of 'human shields' continues unabated:

> The Israeli military is consistently violating these prohibitions by continuing its use of Palestinian citizens as human shields. In fact, these practices have become systematic: routinely, the soldiers force protected civilians to perform military tasks for them. Despite Adalah's numerous letters to the Military Advocate General, which contain detailed information on the victims who were used as such, there has not been any independent investigation or prosecution against those responsible for committing such crimes.[119]

In 2007, B'Tselem documented twelve such cases. In the aftermath of Operation Cast Lead in the Gaza Strip during December 2008 to January 2009, several allegations of use of Palestinians as human shields were raised in the Goldstone

[116] HCJ 3799/02, *Adalah—The Legal Center for Arab Minority Rights in Israel* v. *The Military Commander of Central Command*, paragraph 24 (n 110). For more details on the judgment, see Michael N. Schmitt, 'Human Shields in IHL', *Columbia Journal of Transitional law*, 47/292 (2009), 311–22.

[117] HCJ 10739/05, *Minister of Defense, et. al.* v. *Adalah, et. al* (2006). See also Adalah, 'News Update: Supreme Court Rejects State's Motion to Rehear Human Shields Case' (8 March 2006). Online at <http://www.adalah.org/eng/humanshields.php>.

[118] Israeli Ministry of Foreign Affairs, 'The Operation in Gaza—Factual and Legal Aspects' (29 July 2009), paragraphs 227–228. Online at <http://www.mfa.gov.il/MFA/Terrorism-+Obstacle+to+Peace/Hamas+war+against+Israel/Operation_in_Gaza-Factual_and_Legal_Aspects.htm>.

[119] Adalah, 'Update Report: On the Israeli Military's Continued Use of Palestinian Civilians, including Minors, as Human Shields' (July 2009). Online at <http://www.adalah.org/newsletter/eng/jul09/Rana_Human_Shields_update_report_Englsih_july_2009.pdf>. In 2007, B'Tselem documented twelve such cases. B'Tselem, 'Human Shields'. Online at <http://www.btselem.org/english/human_shields/timeline_of_events.asp>.

report.[120] The State of Israel published several reports in reaction, one of which noted that:

> IDF's rules of engagement strictly prohibit the use of civilians as human shields. Moreover, the Israel Supreme Court has ruled that use of civilians in any capacity for the purpose of military operations is unlawful, including the use of civilians to call terrorists hiding in buildings. Following this judgment, this latter practice has also been proscribed by IDF orders. The IDF is committed to enforcing this prohibition. The IDF took a variety of measures to teach and instil awareness of these rules of engagement in commanders and soldiers.[121]

Though several allegations of use of Palestinians as 'human shields' were raised by the Goldstone report, only one case was brought before an Israeli court.[122] In that 'human shield' case two soldiers were convicted of acting in 'excess of authority' and 'unbecoming conduct' for forcing a nine-year old Palestinian boy to open bags suspected of being booby-trapped.[123] Despite the gravity of the use of children as human shields, both soldiers, who were convicted of these charges, were sentenced to only a three-month probation period and a demotion of their rank. It is worth noting that this sentence is particularly astonishing compared to the prison sentence imposed in another looting case, in which the convict may have indeed 'harmed the "combat moral code" of the IDF', yet did not endanger the life of a nine-year old child. In an attempt to justify this lenient ruling, the Deputy Military Advocate for Operational Affairs stated that the court gave weight to 'the personal circumstances of the defendants and their contribution to Israel's national security', and that by using a child as a human shield 'the defendants did not seek to humiliate or degrade the boy.'[124] It was affirmed by the authorities that sufficient evidence was found in another case which involved a senior army commander.[125] Yet, whilst Israel recognizes that the use of 'human shields' amounts to a war crime,[126] and

[120] See Human Rights Council, 'Human Rights in Palestine and Other Occupied Arab Territories—Report of the United Nations Fact-Finding Mission on the Gaza Conflict' (25 September 2009) UN Doc A/HRC/12/48, 218–27. For allegations related to human shields see pages 218–29 of the 'Report of the United Nations Fact-Finding Mission on the Gaza Conflict'.

[121] Israeli Ministry of Foreign Affairs, 'The Operation in Gaza', paragraphs 227–8 (n 118).

[122] See Sharon Weill, 'The follow up to the Goldstone report in Israel and beyond' in Chantal Meloni and G. Tognoni (eds), *Is There A Court for Gaza?– A Test Bench for International Justice* (Asser/Springer, The Hague, 2012), pp. 105–120. For the allegations raised see, Human Rights Council, 'Human Rights in Palestine and Other Occupied Arab Territories—Report of the United Nations Fact-Finding Mission on the Gaza Conflict', 218–29; Public Committee Against Torture in Israel and Adalah, 'Exposed: The Treatment of Palestinian Detainees During Operation Cast Lead' (June 2010), 10–13.

[123] IDF MAG CORPS, 'Indictment Filed in Connection with "Cast Lead"—Military Advocate for Operational Affairs' (11 March 2011). Online at <http://www.mag.idf.il/163-3952-en/Patzar.aspx?pos=11>.

[124] IDF MAG CORPS, 'Investigating the Gaza Operation—an Interview with Deputy Military Advocate for Operational Affairs' (9 March 2011). Online at <http://www.law.idf.il/163-4544-en/Patzar.aspx?pos=1>.

[125] The State of Israel, 'Gaza Operation Investigations: Second Update' (July 2010), paragraph 37. Online at <http://www.mfa.gov.il/MFA_Graphics/MFA%20Gallery/Documents/GazaUpdateJuly2010.pdf>.

[126] IDF MAG CORPS, 'Human Shields—Legal Framework'. Online at <http://www.law.idf.il/592-1521-en/Patzar.aspx>.

insists that 'disciplinary proceedings are reserved for less serious offenses',[127] the senior army commander in this case was only subjected to disciplinary proceedings instead of a criminal trial, for reasons that remain unknown.[128] Similarly, in October 2007, the Military Advocate General decided not to prosecute the military commander of the West Bank, Brigadier-General Yair Golan, who ordered the use of the 'early warning' procedure in five cases. Instead, he was subjected to a soft disciplinary sanction.[129]

5. Concluding observations

5.1 The duration of the conflict and the timing of the review

The duration of the conflict and the timing of the review are two important factors for courts in determining the court's willingness to exercise its authority. Benvenisti identifies two types of wars: 'full scale military conflicts', such as the 1939–1945 war, and prolonged and low-intensity struggles, such as against terrorist threats. He argues that the respective needs of the executive to rely on courts as an agent of legitimacy and the institutional need of the judiciary to be independent from government, must both take a 'back seat' during short and intense crises. In contrast, when the conflict is prolonged, including a situation of enduring occupation, these factors become relevant again. On the one hand, the state needs to rely on the courts as a legitimating agency in their exercise of judicial review. On the other hand, courts will be more willing to review a state's act and to safeguard their institutional independency and reputation.[130]

The initial stages of armed conflicts are typically characterized by a strong sense of patriotism and unity of the state in support of the executive. As courts are state institutions, and judges are state citizens, they are an integral part of that position. This may partially explain the fact that 'State interests are attributed particular weight during wars.'[131] However, this is not necessarily the case when the review is carried out months or years after the facts (which frequently happens when a case is heard before a second or third instance). The time interval and public opinion that has since crystallized (perhaps because of media influence, or NGO reports concerning IHL violations), may impact on the court's willingness to exercise its authority. Once the conflict becomes protracted, it becomes easier for a court to exercise its

[127] The State of Israel, 'Gaza Operation Investigations', 6, fn 13 (n 125).

[128] Israel Defence Forces, 'IDF Military Advocate General Takes Disciplinary Action, 6 July 2010 Indicts Soldiers Following Investigations into Incidents during Operation Cast Lead' (6 July 2010). Online at <http://www.idfblog.com/2010/07/06/idf-military-advocate-general-takes-disciplinary-action-6-jul-2010-indicts-soldiers-following-investigations-into-incidents-during-operation-cast-lead/>.

[129] See, for further information, B'Tselem, 'Human Shields' (n 119).

[130] Benvenisti, 'National Courts and the "War on Terrorism"' in A. Bianchi (ed.), *Enforcing International Law Norms against Terrorism* (Oxford: Hart Publishing, 2004), 309–18.

[131] See more generally the critic of American Legal Realism, Brian Leiter, 'American Legal Realism', in Dennis M. Patterson (ed.), *A Companion to Philosophy of Law and Legal Theory* (2nd edn, Oxford: Blackwell, 2010) 249.

authority. It may make it more likely, institutionally, to rule against the state, a situation that is barely imaginable during the initial stages of an intense conflict. Indeed the willingness of the US highest court not only to exercise its competence but also to rule against the state's position in *Hamdan*, was highly related to the fact that the prisoner had been held more than four years in detention without legal procedure. The situation was highly criticized by the international community, the ICRC, and local NGOs. Obviously for the Canadian court the task was even easier, as it referred directly to US cases to rule on the illegality of acts six and eight years after the facts. Similarly, *Abbasi*, which was decided relatively close to the event, although it had to allow complete deference, was probably the farthest that a court could go, politically and legally, at that stage.

The Israeli HCJ is among the few national courts that has been willing to exercise its power of judicial review during actual fighting, as shown by the post-second intifada jurisprudence. Indeed, the Israeli-Palestinian conflict is a prolonged conflict, a fact that has certainly led to flexible procedural requirements for standing and justiciability.

5.2 Types of violations: individual rights v. conduct of hostilities cases

The growing trend of exercising judicial review is especially discernible in cases dealing with the protection of individual rights. The individuals are usually their own nationals whose rights need protection during protracted conflicts. Violations relating to individual rights in specific cases are more readily adjudicated. Courts are less willing to intervene in issues relating to the actual conduct of hostilities. Courts usually refrain from pronouncing on warfare means and methods, which may have an impact on future armed conflict. The methods of warfare are seen as not only being under the exclusive discretion of the state, but completely outside the realm of judicial review and law enforcement. One factor that explains this tendency is the endorsement of international human rights law within domestic law, facilitating the access to court and the development of local political culture in support of its legal enforcement. The human rights law movement of the last fifty years has made its mark by influencing domestic law and international jurisprudence. National courts have developed their own important jurisprudence relating to human rights, and have thus become its guardian.[132] This allows judicial intervention from both a practical and a policy standpoint. Courts thereby have an established domestic position in which they are empowered to limit the state in human rights violations. Human rights jurisprudence has also become gradually applicable in situations of armed conflict, as is evidenced by the Guantanamo Bay-related cases. Thus courts in addition to or instead of IHL, increasingly tend to apply international human rights law as applicable during armed conflicts. This is because human rights law is endorsed by national constitutional law and provides an easier access to court. However, the deficiency of this trend is that courts do not always address both

[132] Benvenisti, 'United We Stand', fn 52 and accompanying text (n 4).

branches of law (even if they are applicable) and the correct application for international law would require them both. In most of the cases, courts apply only human rights law, as endorsed by their own constitutional system.

It is submitted that although the courts are still reluctant to rule on the merits, they are increasingly willing to address cases in which individual rights are involved, instead of avoiding them. It is hoped that this trend will be extended in the future to include other kinds of IHL violations, as contraventions relating to the conduct of hostilities. This is a direction that has, remarkably, been led by the Israeli HCJ. As petitioners address courts more and more during actual combat situations, it can reasonably be expected that this emerging trend of reviewing how warfare is carried out, will also grow.[133] Other Western courts have been requested to exercise their jurisdiction during 'real time' in a context of prolonged hostilities. For example, a Canadian court was requested to rule on the application of the Canadian Charter over the Canadian forces' operations in Afghanistan as part of the International Security Assistance Force (ISAF) concerning transfer of detainees to local authorities suspected of committing torture. The court did not avoid the case, as requested by the state.[134] Seemingly, merely the willingness of the court to exercise review had an influence on the state's policy: in parallel with the November 2007 decision, which rejected the motion to dismiss, the Canadian government halted the transfer of detainees to Afghan custody.[135]

Reasons for emergence of this trend are because of growing domestic legislation that grants access to the courts, the superior training of specialized lawyers, journalists, diplomats and academics, the public's demand for scrutiny bolstered by the work of NGOs, and the development of a less cautious jurisprudence of a number of leading courts, which is cited across jurisdictions. Interestingly, human rights jurisprudence may influence that process, as the decision of the European Court of Human Rights in the *Al-Skeini* case suggests.[136] According to the UK

[133] For an analysis on the special features of the Israeli system's jurisdiction and the possibility of it influencing other jurisdictions, see Raguan, 'Adjudicating Armed Conflict', 86–90 (n 96). For example: 'The Israeli Court's jurisprudence is intrinsically linked to Israel's long-term military occupation in the West Bank and Gaza Strip [..]. The great distances between the battlefield and the courtroom, such as the one between American, British or Canadian courts and Iraq or Afghanistan, affects the perception of justiciability.' (87).

[134] Canadian forces have been serving in Afghanistan, first as part of Operation Enduring Freedom in 2001, and subsequently also as part of Canada's contribution to the NATO-led International Security Assistance Force (ISAF). In February 2007, Amnesty International, through a judicial review claim sought to prevent the Canadian part of ISAF from transferring Afghan detainees to the custody of the Afghan National Directorate of Security following allegations of torture. In November 2007, the Federal Court of Canada rejected the non-justiciability claim given that the application for judicial review was framed entirely in terms of the Charter. See, *Amnesty International Canada* v. *Canada (Minister of National Defence)*, paragraph 91 (n 47). On the merits, the court ruled a month later that protection under the Canadian Charter of Rights and Freedoms does not extend to Afghan detainees and did not apply to the conduct of Canadian forces in Afghanistan, thus rejecting the case. An appeal to the Supreme Court was rejected.

[135] *Amnesty International Canada* v. *Canada (Minister of National Defence)*. Stuart Hendin, 'Extraterritorial Application of Human Rights: the Differing Decisions of Canadian and UK Courts', *Windsor Review of Legal and Social Issues*, 28/57 (2010), 67.

[136] *Al-Skeini and others* v. *The United Kingdom*, (Judgment) ECtHR No. 55721/07 (7 July 2011).

act of state doctrine, English courts are prevented from considering a claim of an alien regarding the acts of the UK on foreign soil on behalf of the Crown.[137] Yet, the European Court of Human Rights in *Al-Skeini* ruled that the European Convention on Human Rights applied extraterritorially and bound the UK forces in Iraq (from the moment armed forces exercised effective control). The result was access to UK courts through the UK domestic Human Rights Act.[138] The claim in *Al-Skeini* was that the UK failed to comply with its procedural obligation to investigate killings of civilians by the armed forces. Interestingly, because of the special circumstances of the armed conflict, the European Court of Human Rights ruled that that obligation should be interpreted in a flexible manner.[139] As noted by a commentator:

> it is only if flexibility is added to the substantive application of human rights treaties extraterritorially that the preliminary question of applicability will cease being a vehicle for judicial avoidance.[140]

Naturally, not only flexibility but also IHL should be taken into account while observing the obligations of UK forces in Iraq during its occupation. While the European Court of Human Rights ruled on the extraterritorial application of the European Convention (and the UK Human Rights Act), similarly, IHL cases relating to conduct of hostilities should not be barred by the British act of state doctrine, or any other avoidance doctrine either in the UK or Europe.

5.3 The positive and negative role of deferral techniques from the rule of law perspective

The deferral techniques allowed an important transition from the tendency to apply avoidance doctrines toward judicial review. This transition is opening the gate towards the exercise of the most significant role of courts from the rule of law perspective: enforcer of IHL through its normative application. As has been shown, judicial review does not always mature into judicial responses beyond deferring the matter to the state's discretion. In some cases, the court may only send signals that it does not approve of the state's policy. Yet, this disapproval serves a very important purpose: it rejects the non-justiciability claims, which were traditionally accepted in situations of armed conflict, and it affirms that the review is within the courts'

[137] F.A. Mann, *Foreign Affairs in English Courts* (Oxford: Oxford University Press, 1986), 184–90.

[138] *Al-Skeini and others* v. *The United Kingdom*, paragraph 148 (n 136): '[...] the use of force by a State's agents operating outside its territory may bring the individual thereby brought under the control of the State's authorities into the State's Article 1 jurisdiction.' '[...] the United Kingdom assumed authority and responsibility for the maintenance of security in South East Iraq. In these exceptional circumstances, the Court considers that the United Kingdom, through its soldiers engaged in security operations in Basrah during the period in question, exercised authority and control over individuals killed in the course of such security operations, so as to establish a jurisdictional link between the deceased and the United Kingdom for the purposes of Article 1 of the Convention.'

[139] *Al-Skeini and others* v. *The United Kingdom*, paragraphs 168–77 (n 136).

[140] Marko Milanovic, 'Al-Skeini and Al-Jedda in Strasbourg', *European Journal of International Law*, 23/1 (2012), 12.

competence. Sometimes, the mere fact that the court exercises a review has influenced state policies, even when entire deference to the state had been given. Such an example is *Abbasi* and its influence on UK policy, (perhaps it even influenced the US Supreme Court decision in *Rasul*). Another example is from the HCJ expedited review cases during 'real time', which demonstrated the restraining influence on the armed forces, despite the fact that on the merits, a complete deference was given to the state. The state was more assiduous in applying the humanitarian obligations as requested by the law, than it would have been if these cases had been avoided. While deferring, the ground is prepared for future litigation in which the court will 'climb up' the rungs of the judicial ladder. Thus, deference is a halfway step, allowing the state to act according to legal standards, which, if violated again in the future, the court could more legitimately intervene. This was illustrated in *Hamdan* and the follow-up *Baumediene* case. It may be one of the reasons that torture legislation was not introduced in Israel, because of the strong signals sent by the HCJ that this legislation would be unconstitutional. The positive aspect of deference is that it reinforces courts' positions in their ability to exercise jurisdiction over IHL issues which have traditionally been avoided as 'political matters'. The ladder of judicial review may be climbed higher in the future as a result.

At the same time, there is a hidden danger with the deferral technique. If the state misuses the discretion allowed by the judiciary, the courts instead of using their role to limit abuses of the law, may facilitate a state's illegal policy. In the long run, deference could make the court an apologist to the state. This was clearly shown in the follow-up decisions in the *Torture* and *Targeted Killing* landmark cases. Although deference may be required at first judicial review to establish the courts' position and legitimacy in reviewing such cases, once the position is established, a court should refrain from using the deferral technique. This is not an easy task, as these cases involve sensitive and complex issues. The non-compliance of the State of Israel with the *Human Shield* ruling—a case in which no deference was allocated, is a clear red light. It is obviously beyond the scope of this research to analyse the effect on the state's regime in light of the state's non-compliance with the judiciary's decision. Yet, the effect on the state's policies may give an indication of the court's institutional limits within the state in which it operates. A state's non-compliance with a court ruling will affect the judiciary's willingness to render similar decisions in the future given the need for a court to maintain its authority and reputation.

4

The Twilight Zone of Utopia: Judges as Law Developers

Domestic judges are not called upon to amend and change international law. Their true mandate is to apply the law conscientiously and objectively. Private, subjective preferences and wishes should not determine the substance of a decision which the judge is entrusted with giving.[1]

That stance is supported by at least one leading national court. The following was stated by Lord Hoffmann:

> [T]he ordering of competing principles according to the importance of the values which they embody is a basic technique of adjudication. But the same approach cannot be adopted in international law, which is based upon the common consent of nations. It is not for a national court to 'develop' international law by unilaterally adopting a version of that law which, however desirable, forward-looking and reflective of values it may be, is simply not accepted by other states.[2]

Where national judges function as law developers in the name of ethical values, they perform a utopian role. The Vienna Convention on the Law of Treaties acknowledges in Article 31(1) that a treaty shall be interpreted in good faith in accordance with the ordinary meaning to be given to the terms of the treaty in their context and in the light of its object and purpose. According to Article 31(3)(b), state practice, which establishes the agreement of the parties regarding its interpretation, is a factor to be taken into account. When national judges interpret an international treaty rule beyond these directives in the name of ethical values they operate as agents of natural law. Similarly, if courts identify a new customary rule for the first time, which does not correspond to a general practice, such identification may be a utopian one.[3]

[1] Public sitting held on Monday 12 September 2011, at 10 a.m., at the Peace Palace, President Owada presiding, in the case concerning Jurisdictional Immunities of the State (*Germany* v. *Italy*: Greece intervening) CR 2011/17 (Prof. Christian Tomuschat, Oral Submission before the International Court of Justice for Germany), 21. Online at <http://www.icj-cij.org/docket/files/143/16677.pdf>.

[2] *Jones* v. *Ministry of Interior Al-Mamlaka Al-Arabiya AS Saudiya (the Kingdom of Saudi Arabia) and others*, (2006) UKHL 26; ILDC 521 (UK 2006), paragraph 76.

[3] According to Article 38(1)(b) of the ICJ Statute the court shall apply international custom, *as evidence of a general practice accepted as law.*

Rulings that are utopian are usually in conflict with the position of the executive. A decision that appears to be utopian, if it reflects the wishes of its government, would probably be apologetic. A utopian decision distinguishes itself from a decision, which, although being in favour of a commendable cause, is no more than a normative application of national law, as for example the *Filártiga* case. Universal civil jurisdiction for international crimes may be characterized as a utopian stand, yet in the US, when courts recognize such jurisdiction and award compensation, they merely apply domestic law—the Alien Tort Statute (ATS). Arguably, in their normative application of the law, some courts would tend to favour the rights of individuals (by, for instance, attributing responsibility to private corporations), while others would prefer to represent a more restrictive attitude in line with the state's position. However, as long as there is no distortion and misuse of the law, these are decisions within the framework of normative application. Each court has a certain margin of interpretation as described in the previous chapters.

From the rule of law perspective, utopian decisions of national courts pose a problem that is particular to the international legal order and the way international rules are established. Domestically, in common law legal traditions, courts are entrusted with developing the law, and the jurisprudence of higher courts is binding upon lower courts. The checks and balances of the branches of government function according to that system. The authority to develop laws is a result of an overall constitutional structure that determines the governmental organization of a state, it is a structure which includes granting the courts the power to develop laws. When dealing with international rules, however, the situation is quite different. When adjudicating between two parties, if the court chooses to develop the law rather than just applying the law appropriate to that particular case, unforeseen consequences may result. It is questionable whether a national court has the ability, or the willingness, to take into consideration the global consequences of its ruling, which may go far beyond the particular interests of the litigating parties. Benvenisti and Downs noted that national courts regard themselves as national agents responsible 'to protect primarily, if not exclusively', their own domestic rule of law, and not serve as a global agent of international law.[4] Indeed, courts are national institutions operating within their respective societies, which favour their own interest and which cannot be expected to act otherwise.[5]

1. The judicial activism role: the *Garzón* case

Courts may also perform an activist role. For the purpose of this study, an activist role is defined as the role performed when courts develop national law in order to harmonize it with international law, even though their national legislation does not

[4] Benvenisti and Downs, 'National Courts, Domestic Democracy, and the Evolution of International Law' *European Journal of International Law* 1/20 (2009), 61.

[5] Nollkaemper, *National Courts and The International Rule of Law* (Oxford: Oxford University Press, 2011), 56–7.

provide for such competence. Unlike utopian decisions, in activist rulings courts merely apply international law. They are not engaged in developing the law on an international level, but are harmonizing their national law with the norms of international law. In this way they are developing their own domestic law. Both activist judicial decisions and utopian decisions (which conflict with the state's position), typically trigger a significant political or legal response.

The case of Judge Baltasar Garzón in Spain is an example of an activist decision which had far-reaching consequences. A petition was filed in the *Audiencia Nacional*, by family members and associations representing victims of the Franco regime. On 14 December 2006, Judge Garzón opened a criminal investigation into allegations of crimes against humanity committed during the Spanish civil war and the subsequent Franco regime. He ordered exhumations and other preliminary steps in order to ascertain the facts. On 16 October 2008, he delivered a decision assuming jurisdiction over the case. While the jurisdiction was over specific crimes such as 'illegal detentions', given that they also constituted crimes against humanity, the judge found that they were not subject to prescription. The Spanish 1977 Amnesty Law of 15 October 1977, which affords amnesty for Franco-era crimes, was deemed not applicable.[6] The judge interpreted the Spanish Amnesty Law as not applying to serious crimes, such as crimes against humanity. The non-applicability of the Amnesty Law to crimes against humanity was based, inter alia, on the obligation to investigate crimes under international law in accordance with international jurisprudence. The decision was also supported by the Spanish Constitution and jurisprudence of the Spanish Supreme Court, which ruled that international law provided the interpretation of statutes concerning crimes against humanity. It was this interpretation which was required for the enforcement of domestic law. In that case, Judge Garzón performed a judicial activist role, because he attempted to harmonize international law with Spanish domestic law, in the context of accountability for crimes against humanity. From a national perspective, the judge's function can be seen as that of a law developer. At an international level, however, he was merely applying well established international rules.

This decision did not pass unnoticed: not only was the jurisdiction denied on appeal,[7] Judge Garzón was indicted under Spain's prevarication law which allows judges to be prosecuted for unjust judgments.[8] He was also suspended from his

[6] *Audiencia Nacional, Juzgado Central de Instrucción No. 5*, Diligencias Previas Proc. Abreviado 399/2006 V (Judgment of 16 October 2008). Jurisdiction was assumed, inter alia, over crimes committed by Franco and his high command during the war and the post-war period in respect of 'crimes against the state,' which under Articles 23.2, 23.4 and 65.1 of the Ley Organica Judicial corresponds to the jurisdiction of the *Audiencia Nacional*, carried out in the context of and connected to crimes against humanity.

[7] *Audiencia Nacional*, Sala de lo Penal, *Juzgado Central de Instruccion No. 5*, Pleno, Diligencias Previas Proc. Abreviado 399/2006 V, Auto (2 December 2008).

[8] The complaint was filed by 'Manos Limpias,' a right wing political organization on 26 January 2009 before the Criminal Chamber of the Supreme Court of Spain. Judge Garzón was indicted in April 2010 for the crime of *prevaricación*, alleging the abuse of his judicial authority by opening the inquiry into Franco-era crimes. The crime of *prevaricación* is defined in Article 446 of the Spanish Criminal Code: 'The judge or magistrate who, knowingly, dictates an unjust sentence or resolution'. On 24 March 2011 Judge Garzón brought a case to the European Court of Human Rights challenging the lawfulness of his criminal prosecution, alleging violation of Articles 6, 7, 8 10 and 18 of the

judicial functions.[9] On 27 February 2012 the Spanish Supreme Court acquitted Judge Baltasar Garzón, holding that the investigations into crimes committed during the Spanish civil war by General Francisco Franco's regime were contrary to the Amnesty Law, but did not amount to the crime of malfeasance.[10] On 24 March 2011, Judge Garzón filed a case against Spain before the European Court of Human Rights. Garzón claimed that the fact that he was subjected to criminal proceedings for his investigations into the crimes committed by the Franco regime violated his rights under the European Convention on Human Rights and infringed the principle of judicial independence. On 29 June 2012, a supplemental submission was filed stressing that the violation of the European Convention on Human Rights resulted from the prosecution itself, irrespective of conviction or acquittal.

While Garzón's interpretation clearly went beyond the purpose of the Spanish Amnesty Law, it is nonetheless difficult to justify that far-reaching reaction. It is probably even difficult to justify the Amnesty Law itself, in light of the fact that Spanish courts have consistently affirmed, while adjudicating cases based on universal jurisdiction, that amnesties granted by third states in order to prevent accountability of international crimes are not binding upon Spanish courts.[11] Ironically, Spain's jurisprudence suggests that Franco's crimes can only be prosecuted in third states based on universal jurisdiction.

2. The utopian role of courts: the *Ferrini* case

Utopian decisions which are contrary to the position of the state in IHL issues are extremely rare. Accordingly, the following section focuses on a single case: the Italian *Ferrini* case (2004).[12] This case is probably one of the best examples of a

European Convention on Human Rights. Online at <http://www.interights.org/userfiles/Garzon_ECHR_Application_final_full.pdf>.

[9] Unanimous Decision of the Spanish General Council of the Judiciary, 14 May 2010. See Daniel Makosky, 'Spain Judicial Panel Suspends Judge Garzón over Franco Probe' *Jurist.org* (14 May 2010) <http://jurist.org/paperchase/2010/05/spain-judicial-panel-suspends-judge-garzon-over-franco-probe.php>.

[10] The Supreme Court of Spain, Sentence No. 101/2012 (27 February 2012). Yet, on 9 February 2012 the Supreme Court of Spain convicted him in another case of *prevaricación*. In this case he was found responsible for illegally ordering wiretapping conversations between suspects and their lawyers in jail in an important corruption case. He was sentenced to eleven years' disqualification from judicial activity. See 'Prominent Rights Judge Is Convicted in Spain', *New York Times*, 9 February 2012, available at <http://www.nytimes.com/2012/02/10/world/europe/baltasar-garzon-prominent-rights-judge-convicted-in-spain.html?_r=0>.

[11] See the decision of the Central Investigative Court No. 5 of the *Audiencia Nacional* of 1 September 2000 (indictment of Miguel Angel Cavallo); decision of 20 September 1998 of the Central Investigative Court No. 6 (*Pinochet* case).

[12] *Ferrini* v. *Germany*, (Appeal Decision), Italian Court of Cassation, Civil section unit, No. 5044/4 of 6 November 2003 registered 11 March 2004 in 87 Rivista Diritto Internazionale, 539 (2004). Among many other comments on this ruling, see Andrea Bianchi, 'Italian Court of Cassation Ruling on Immunity from Suit for Damages for Deportation and Forced Labor during World War II (Comment to Decision)', *American Journal of International Law*, 99/1 (2005), 242–8; Pasquale De Sena and Francesca De Vittor, 'State Immunity and Human Rights: The Italian Supreme Court Decision on the Ferrini Case', *European Journal of International Law*, 16/1 (2005), 89–112; Carlo Focarelli, 'Denying Foreign State Immunity for

utopian decision related to armed conflicts that a national court has given. In *Ferrini* the Italian *Corte di Cassazione* allowed Italian victims of Nazi international crimes to claim reparations from Germany. This was done by abrogating Germany's state immunity and holding that Italian courts had jurisdiction to hear a claim directed against Germany for *acta iure imperii*. The nature of the crimes amounted to a violation of *jus cogens* rules.

Ferrini was deported during the Second World War from Italy to Germany where he was compelled to work for Germany. On 23 September 1998, Mr Ferrini brought a civil claim for reparations against Germany at the Arezzo Tribunal in Italy. Based on state immunity, this claim was rejected in the Arezzo tribunal as was a subsequent appeal in Florence. Appearing before the Italian *Corte di Cassazione*, Ferrini claimed that a foreign state cannot be granted immunity from jurisdiction when it allegedly violated *jus cogens* rules relating to the protection of fundamental human rights. The Italian *Corte di Cassazione* reversed the ruling of the lower courts. It decided that Germany could not enjoy state immunity before Italian tribunals for reparation claims which arose from international crimes recognized as *jus cogens*.

This ruling was innovative in a number of aspects relating to the Italian court's exercise of its jurisdiction. First, it rejected the non-justiciability claim, which was applied by the same court in a similar case just two years earlier. Second, the court did not refrain from exercising its jurisdiction based on Germany's state immunity, and it thereby created a new exception to the rule of state immunity for a civil suit arising from *jus cogens* violations. Lastly, by allowing the claim of reparation to be pursued, it implicitly granted individuals the right of reparation for IHL violations before domestic courts. In doing so it adopted a clear position on an issue that is controversial both in academic literature and state practice.[13] What characterizes *Ferrini* as a utopian decision is the fact that the decision contradicted settled practice regarding these issues, and the ruling conflicted with the stance of the Italian government. The following section critically analyses each of these issues—justiciability, immunity, and the right to a remedy for IHL violations. Each issue is examined independently in order to highlight the utopian character of the decision, and also its less pleasant aspect underneath its fascinating facade.

2.1 Justiciability

The *Marković* case was decided by the same court two years before *Ferrini*.[14] *Marković* concerned a civil claim against Italian officials for their responsibility

Commission of International Crimes: The Ferrini Decision', *International Comparative Law Quarterly*, 54 (2005), 951–8; Andrea Gattini, 'War Crimes and State Immunity in the Ferrini Decision', *Journal of International Criminal Justice*, 3/1 (2005), 224–42.

[13] *Case Concerning Jurisdictional Immunities of the State* (*Germany* v. *Italy*) (Counter-Memorial of Italy) (22 December 2009), paragraph 2.45; Roland Bank and Elke Schwager, 'Is there a Substantive Right to Compensation for Individual Victims of Armed Conflict against a State under International Law?', *German Yearbook of International Law*, 49/367 (2006), 380.

[14] *Presidency of the Council of Ministers* v. *Marković and ors*, Italian Court of Cassation, Application for preliminary order on jurisdiction, No. 8157, (2002).

for NATO's aerial bombing operation, in which a Belgrade radio station was targeted. The bombing of the radio station on 23 April 1999 during the armed conflict between NATO and the Federal Republic of Yugoslavia was arguably a non-military objective and resulted in the death of a number of civilians. Under these circumstances, the Italian *Corte di Cassazione* ruled that the methods chosen in the conduct of war operations was an 'act of government', i.e., a political, non-justiciable question.[15]

In order to reconcile that case with the bold willingness of the court to exercise jurisdiction in *Ferrini*, the Italian *Corte di Cassazione* stated that establishing civil or criminal responsibilities in war crimes allegations—perpetrated during military operations—were not excluded from review. The protection of fundamental rights was part of Italian law pursuant to Article 10 of the Constitution. While *Marković* similarly dealt with a civil war crime allegation (though against Italian officials) the court in *Ferrini* concluded, quite oddly, that 'it is evident that the principles contained in that decision [i.e. *Marković*] cannot be taken into consideration in the present case'. Although the court noted that the cases differed, it is hard to see on what basis it could sustain this affirmation. How did the question of justiciability lead to two opposite conclusions? As noted by Germany, 'these "explanations" do not explain anything';[16] instead the court's tendency to apply a double standard is clearly apparent.

The apparent double standard exercised by the Italian *Corte di Cassazione* became the schizophrenic position of the Italian government in subsequent procedures before international fora—the European Court of Human Rights (ECtHR) and ICJ. After being rejected in Italy, Marković argued before the ECtHR that there had been a violation of his right of access to a court to determine his civil rights, as provided by Article 6(1) of the 1950 Convention for the Protection of Human Rights and Fundamental Freedoms. In the proceedings before the ECtHR, Italy argued that the judge was entitled to apply the non-justiciability doctrine of 'political acts of state', even if it conflicted with the right to access the court.[17] In a parallel proceeding before the ICJ with regard to *Ferrini*, where the victim was Italian and the responsible state was Germany, Italy argued that 'access to justice is a fundamental guarantee of respect for the rule of law in

[15] Critics of this ruling argued that the court should have distinguished between the political decision of the government and the *jus in bellum* choice of methods of warfare. Political decisions such as the decision to engage in military operations are non-justiciable. By contrast methods of warfare in the course of military operations should be justiciable. How hostilities are conducted are not 'political' decisions and IHL provides judicial standards to assess their legality. See Micaela Frulli, 'When Are States Liable Towards Individuals for Serious Violations of Humanitarian Law? The *Marković* Case', *Journal of International Criminal Justice*, 1/2 (2003), 411–12.

[16] *Case Concerning Jurisdictional Immunities of the State* (*Germany* v. *Italy*) (Memorial of the Federal Republic of Germany), (12 June 2009), paragraph 58. Online at <http://www.icj-cij.org/docket/files/143/16644.pdf>. See also Andrea Gattini: 'It is hard to see why, in the minds of the supreme judges, the plaintiffs in Marković could not in any case have made an even tenuously plausible argument that the conduct of the Italian government amounted to a crime.' Gattini, 'War Crimes and State Immunity', 229 (n 12); Bianchi, 'Italian Court of Cassation', 245 (n 12).

[17] *Marković et al.* v. *Italy*, (Judgment on Merits), European Court of Human Rights No.1398/03 (14 December 2006). The ECtHR accepted Italy's position and ruled accordingly.

modern democracies' and that 'international rules on State immunity from jurisdiction cannot but be balanced against respect for this principle.'[18] Indeed, the differing arguments offered by the Italian government and its highest court in these two cases reflect a double standard. It demonstrates their willingness to render justice selectively, only to certain victims of war. Ironically, applying the jurisprudence of *Ferrini* to *Marković* would mean that Mr Marković should sue Italy before a Serbian court; Italy's immunity could be abrogated relying on Italy's own precedent set in *Ferrini.*

2.2 State immunity

State immunity vis-à-vis the exercise of jurisdiction by judicial bodies of other countries, derives from the principle of sovereign equality echoed in Article 2(1) of the UN Charter.[19] International criminal law has clearly established that functional immunity shall not eliminate the individual criminal responsibility of officials who commit international crimes. In contrast, the corresponding rule for civil liability of states has not yet been set. Therefore, the decision of the Italian *Corte di Cassazione* to abrogate the immunity of Germany was innovative. In fact, *Ferrini* (along with a single Greek case from 1997, which was overruled) is the only case that demonstrates the practice of waiving state immunity in civil claims before national courts. Not only is other national practice lacking, but subsequent case law has developed in the opposite direction specifically referring to, and expressing its reservation regarding the *Ferrini* ruling. The House of Lords went as far as to formulate *Ferrini* as: 'one swallow does not make a rule of international law'.[20] Professor Tomuschat, mentioned the 'splendid isolation' of the Italian Court of Cassation seven years after *Ferrini.*[21]

The Italian court essentially based its decision on two arguments: the hierarchy of norms and the coherency of international norms. While addressing the former, the Italian court attempted to define the relation between a procedural rule on immunity, and the extent of its application in a case of a violation of a substantive, peremptory norm of international law. According to the court, states responsible for violations of *jus cogens* norms are not entitled to sovereign immunity. This is because of the hierarchical supremacy of the former norm. Non-derogable norms stand at the peak of the international legal system and take precedence over all other

[18] *Case Concerning Jurisdictional Immunities of the State* (*Germany* v. *Italy*) (Counter-Memorial of Italy), paragraph 4.101 (n 13).

[19] On immunity as 'the subjection of an independent State to proceedings in another country relating to a dispute about its exercise of governmental power,' see Hazel Fox, *The Law of State Immunity* (New York: Oxford University Press, 2002), 11; Bianchi, 'Serious Violations of Human Rights and Foreign States' Accountability Before Municipal Courts' in L. Vohrar (ed), *Man's Inhumanity to Man. Essays in Honour of Judge Antonio Cassese* (The Hague/London/Boston: Kluwer Law International, 2003), 164.

[20] *Jones* v. *Ministry of Interior Al-Mamlaka Al-Arabiya AS Saudiya (the Kingdom of Saudi Arabia) and others*, paragraph 22 (n 2).

[21] *Case Concerning Jurisdictional Immunities of the State* (*Germany* v. *Italy*) (Memorial of the Federal Republic of Germany), paragraph 67 (n 16).

norms. They therefore create an exception to the applicability of immunity norms that are not non-derogable. A counter argument has been raised by academic literature: *jus cogens* norms are norms of substance while rules on immunity are procedural norms. On the theoretical level, there cannot be a conflict between them and therefore the hierarchy theory is irrelevant. Both norms are independently applicable and do not influence each other.[22] Moreover, according to Germany, there is no special and comprehensive legal regime that applies to cases of violations of *jus cogens* norms, and an exception to state immunity due to the breach of a *jus cogens* rule cannot be inferred.[23]

The Italian *Corte di Cassazione* then proceeded to its second argument, based on the need for a consistent international legal order that has consideration for contemporary developments of international criminal law. To that end, the court first established that the Germans' acts of deportation and forced labour constituted international crimes according to Article 6(b) of the 'Charter of the International Military Tribunal in Nuremberg'. The Charter defined war crimes as including 'deportation to slave labour', and consequent treaty and customary development of international criminal law.[24] The court mentioned inter alia the UN Convention of the Non-Applicability of Statutory Limitations to War Crimes and Crimes Against Humanity, and the principle of universal jurisdiction codified by the Geneva Conventions. As observed by Gattini, the court employed the concept of international crime 'not less than nine times',[25] before concluding that the lack of functional immunity of the state organ for criminal responsibility must also lead to the abrogation of state immunity. The court's oscillation between criminal, civil, individual, and state responsibilities has led several authors to criticize the failure of the court to distinguish between different concepts of responsibilities and their corresponding rules.[26]

[22] Bianchi, 'Italian Court of Cassation', 247 (n 12).

[23] *Case concerning Jurisdictional Immunities of the State* (*Germany* v. *Italy*: Greece intervening) (Prof. Robert Kolb), 50 (n 1). See also *Case Concerning Jurisdictional Immunities of the State* (*Germany* v. *Italy*) (Memorial of the Federal Republic of Germany), paragraph 87 (n 16).

[24] The court noted that deportation and forced labour were defined later as an 'international crime' by Article 2 of the Statute of the International Criminal Tribunal for the Former Yugoslavia and by Article 3 of the Statute of the International Criminal Tribunal for Rwanda.

[25] Gattini, 'War Crimes and State Immunity', 229 (n 12).

[26] Gattini, 'War Crimes and State Immunity', 230 (n 12); Bianchi, 'Italian Court of Cassation', 245–6 (n 12). However, Professor Dupuy firmly refuted these critics in the oral proceedings before the ICJ for Italy in the following terms: 'Nous y voilà, le droit international pénal, non pas du tout parce que le juge italien confondrait crimes individuels et crimes d'Etat, comme certains l'ont dit trop vite, mais parce que le droit international pénal atteste l'importance éminente pour la communauté internationale des valeurs bafouées par de telles actions.'[Translation: 'Here we have it— international criminal law—not at all because the Italian court would confuse individual crimes with crimes of the State, as some have been too quick to claim, but because international criminal law recognizes the cardinal importance that the international community attaches to the values which are flouted by such actions.'] *Public sitting held on Tuesday 13 September 2011, at 10 a.m., at the Peace Palace, President Owada presiding, in the case concerning Jurisdictional Immunities of the State (Germany* v. *Italy: Greece intervening) (Professor Dupuy, Oral Submission before the International Court of Justice for Italy)*, 60. Available at: <http://www.icj-cij.org/docket/files/143/16693.pdf>.

According to the Italian court, customary rules on immunity must be interpreted in light of other contemporary international criminal rules. All norms belonging to one legal system should be coherent and consistent.[27] Customary international law can only be correctly understood in relation to and in the context of other norms that form an integral part of the same legal system.[28] The norm that has been clearly established by the international community is that in the repression of international crimes (which violate *jus cogens* norms), functional immunity may no longer be invoked by a state's officials. Therefore, the coherency of the legal order as a whole dictates, by the same token, that immunity shall not apply to states that abrogate their civil responsibility. Moreover, Article 41 of the Draft Articles on International Responsibility of States, requires states not to provide assistance for the maintenance of situations that originated from *jus cogens* violations. The Article imposes the obligation of employing lawful means for terminating the end of the illicit acts. If this provision has significance, there must be an abrogation of immunity. Thus, the court ruled that jurisdictional immunity of foreign states is not an absolute rule of international law—it is subject to limitations and must be interpreted taking into account developments in contemporary international law. One of these exceptions is for violations of *jus cogens.*

2.2.1 Other examples of state practice

As far as state practice of other national courts is concerned, the Italian court stands alone in its reasoning. While international criminal law has clearly established that functional immunity will not be applicable in cases where state officials have committed international crimes, a corresponding rule for civil liability of states has not been established. In fact, *Ferrini* along with a single 1997 Greek case, which was later overruled, are the only cases exemplifying the practice of waiving state immunity in civil claims before national courts. For example, in the *Shimoda* case of 1963, victims of the nuclear bombing of Hiroshima and Nagasaki claimed reparation. While the judgment of the Tokyo District Court clearly stated that the use of the atomic bomb had violated IHL,[29] the court ruled, inter alia, that sovereign immunity precluded proceedings against the US before Japanese courts. Similarly, Asian victims of sexual slavery during the Second World War, the so called 'comfort women', filed claims against Japan in the United States based on the ATS. The case was rejected on grounds of state immunity.[30]

[27] *Ferrini* v. *Germany*, paragraph 9 (n 12).

[28] See also the position of the Italian government on this point: *Case Concerning Jurisdictional Immunities of the State* (*Germany* v. *Italy*) (Counter-Memorial of Italy), paragraph 9.2 (n 13).

[29] Citing a number of treaties such as: the Convention (II) with Respect to the Laws and Customs of War on Land and its Annex: Regulations concerning the Laws and Customs of War on Land (adopted 29 July 1899, entered into force 4 September 1900); and Protocol for the Prohibition of the Use of Asphyxiating, Poisonous or Other Gases, and of Bacteriological Methods of Warfare (adopted 17 June 1925, entered into force 8 February 1928).

[30] *Hwang Geum Joo* v. *Japan*, 172 F.Supp. 2d 52 (D.D.C. 2001). After the Supreme Court had granted a writ of certiorari, the case was again dismissed on the basis of the political question doctrine, 413 F.3d 45 (2005). See also the ruling of the House of Lords: *Jones* v. *Ministry of Interior Al-Mamlaka*

The Italian *Corte di Cassazione* directed itself mainly on the Greek *Distomo* case (1997). This case was a rare example of compensation being granted by a national court to individual claimants for injury suffered during the Second World War; however, that case was ultimately overruled. In that litigation the victims of the Distomo killings brought their compensation claim against Germany directly before a Greek court. The court ruled that sovereign immunity could not be invoked in connection with violations of a *jus cogens* rule. In its ruling, which was upheld by the Greek Supreme Court in May 2000, the trial court held that a Greek court could assume jurisdiction over civil claims related to Second World War crimes on the grounds that a country that committed war crimes must be deemed to have waived its sovereign immunity.[31] The Greek Ministry of Justice refused to enforce the judgment against German state property in Greece. Then, in a parallel case, the Greek Special Supreme Court, empowered to decide cases involving the interpretation of international law, ultimately ruled that the law had been wrongly interpreted.[32] The case went to the ECtHR in Strasbourg on the grounds that the claimants were being deprived of a remedy, in contravention of Article 6(1) of the Convention. In Strasbourg, applying *Al-Adsani*, the ECtHR held, that international law did not allow an exception to state immunity for civil claims resulting from international crimes. The ECtHR did, however, recognize the possibility that customary international law might develop in this direction in the future.[33] Surprisingly, the legal saga did not end there. After *Ferrini*, on 2 May 2005, the Court of Appeal of Florence declared the Greek *Distomo* decision as being enforceable in Italy. This decision was confirmed by the Italian *Corte di Cassazione* in May 2008.

Al-Arabiya AS Saudiya (the Kingdom of Saudi Arabia) and others, paragraphs 45–64 (n 2); the French decision in *Bucheron* (16 December 2003), 108 RGDIP 259 (2004); *Bouzari* v. *Iran*, Court of Appeal of Ontario (30 June 2004), 128 ILR 586—all upholding state immunity for civil responsibility of international crimes.

31 Greece's Court of First Instance of Leivadia in the *Prefecture of Voiotia case* in 1997. *Prefecture of Voiotia* v. *Federal Republic of Germany*, (Judgment), Hellenic Supreme Court No. 11/2000 (4 May 2000), published in *Nomiko Vima*, 49/212 (2001), 212–29.

32 *Federal Republic of Germany* v. *Miltiadis Margellos*, (Judgment), Supreme Special Court No. 6/2002 (17 September 2002). For a discussion see, Andrea Gattini, 'To What Extent are State Immunity and Non-Justiciability Major Hurdles to Individuals' Claim for War Damages?', *Journal of International Criminal Justice*, 1/2 (2003), 356–62.

33 *Kalogeropoulou* v. *Greece and Germany*, European Court of Human Rights No. 59021/00 (12 December 2002), 10: 'la Cour ne juge pas établi qu'il soit déjà admis en droit international que les Etats ne peuvent prétendre à l'immunité en cas d'actions civiles en dommages intérêts pour crimes contre l'humanité qui sont introduites sur le sol d'un autre Etat. [...] ce qui n'exclut pas un développement du droit international coutumier dans le futur.' [Translation: 'The Court does not find it established, however, that there is yet acceptance in international law of the proposition that States are not entitled to immunity in respect of civil claims for damages brought against them in another State for crimes against humanity... but does not preclude a development in customary international law in the future'.] See also, *Al-Adsani* v. *United Kingdom*, (Judgment), European Court of Human Rights No. 35763/97 (21 November 2001), paragraph 66. More then a decade later the ECtHR affirmed the same position. However the court ended the judgment by noting that 'in light of the developments currently underway in this area of public international law, this is a matter which needs to be kept under review by Contracting States'. *Jones and Others* v. *the United Kingdom* (application nos. 34356/06 and 40528/06), 14 January 2014, para. 215.

2.2.2 Denying immunity: from foreign state towards own state responsibility?

As suing a foreign government for law violations in national courts would normally be barred by state immunity, bringing a case before the courts of the responsible government may be a more feasible option. Yet, here too a claimant is liable to encounter all kinds of obstacles relating to immunity introduced by domestic legislation or judge made doctrines. These exempt the state's responsibility for any damage that was caused in armed conflict.[34] In the UK, for example, the act of state doctrine prevents courts from reviewing acts of the Crown beyond the sovereign territory of the UK. The principle of 'combat immunity' prevents courts from adjudicating disputes that arise during actual fighting.[35] In the United States, the 1948 Federal Tort Claims Act (FTCA) establishes that no claim may be brought that arises 'out of the combatant activities of the military or naval forces'.[36] Also, the act bans 'Any claim arising in a foreign country'.[37] Claims based on the violation of constitutional rights may be brought directly against the responsible officials under the Bivens rule.[38] Yet, in such a suit the plaintiff must prove that the alleged misconduct violated 'clearly established rights . . . of which a reasonable person would have known'.[39] Moreover, by virtue of the Westfall Act (1988) (28 U.S.C. § 2679), the US state itself—which is generally immune[40]—may be substituted as the defendant in any action where one of its employees is sued for damages. Thus, claims regarding armed conflicts reparation have almost no chance of success in the US. In Israel, the Civil Wrongs Act extended the definition of 'acts of war'. The Act grants immunity to the state against civil claims brought by subjects of a state which is an enemy of Israel and persons active in or members of a terrorist organization. Moreover, it sets serious procedural limitations on Palestinians' ability to bring claims against Israel.[41]

Introducing exceptions to a foreign state's immunity, is a utopian task for a national court in the name of justice. Decisions, like *Ferrini*, which touch on a nerve of the international legal order may present problems from the rule of law perspective, as far as dealing with the international legislative process goes. Instead, as a step

[34] See for example the rule in Germany where war damages are not covered by the ordinary regime of state responsibility, '[a]ccording to the understanding and the overall system of the German law in force at the time the act was committed (1944) the military acts during war in a foreign State, which are attributable under international law to the German Reich, did not fall within the scope of state liability for official act as enshrined [in the legislation at that time in force]'—the German *Distomo* case, BGHZ 155, 279 (English translation at 42 ILM 1030 (2003)).

[35] See *Bici* v. *Ministry of Defence*, (2004) EWHC 786 (QB), paragraphs 84–93.

[36] 28 U.S.C. § 2680 (j). [37] 28 U.S.C. § 2680 (k).

[38] *Bivens* v. *Six Unknown Federal Narcotics Agents*, 403 U.S. 388, 397 (1971).

[39] On the different US official immunity in the US see Chapter 3.

[40] *United States* v. *Lee*, 106 U.S. 196 (1882); *United States* v. *Mitchell*, 463 U.S. 206, 212 (1983) ('It is axiomatic that the United States may not be sued without its consent and that the existence of consent is a prerequisite for jurisdiction').

[41] In 2005, Amendment 7 to the Law exempted the state from liability for damages caused to particular categories of people, encompassing a broad group of persons. These persons are defined as: (1) a citizen of an 'Enemy State', unless he or she is legally in Israel; (2) an activist or member of a terrorist organization; and (3) anyone who incurred damage while acting as an agent for or on behalf of a citizen of an enemy state, or an activist or member of a terrorist organization. For the procedural obstacles see Sharon Weill and Valentina Azarov, 'Israel's Unwillingness to Prosecute International Crimes' (FIDH, September 2011), Annex 4.

towards effectively developing the right of remedy for damages resulting from armed conflicts, national courts should be more assertive in ascribing responsibility to their own state. Such responsibility can be achieved by refraining from applying self-developed immunity doctrines like 'the king can do no wrong' or by not interpreting strictly legislation on immunity which exempts the state from responsibility.

2.3 Right to remedy for IHL violations

While the obligation of the state to provide remedies for IHL law violations is well established, the question as to who are the beneficiaries of that right—and whether they include individuals—has been at the centre of a legal debate since the late 1990s.

National case law, mainly from Japanese and German courts, dealing with claims for reparations of war crimes in the aftermath of the Second World War were almost all rejected. The rejections were based on the claim that Article 3 of Hague Convention IV does not confer an individual right to reparation, the right to reparation being limited to the injured state.[42] This was confirmed by Japanese and German courts in a number of cases. In the Shimoda case, the plaintiffs were survivors of the atomic bombs in Hiroshima and Nagasaki. The plaintiffs claimed that Japan, by signing the 1951 Peace Treaty with the US—in which the Japanese government had waived their right to seek compensation from the US— obliged the Japanese government itself to pay them the wrongfully waived compensation. While the judgment clearly stated that the use of the atomic bomb was a clear violation of IHL,[43] the court nevertheless supported the argument of the Japanese government and ruled that individuals had no right to remedy under international law.[44] More recently, in 1998, the Tokyo district court stated in the *Filipino 'Comfort Women'* case:

[42] Article 3 of Hague Convention IV Concerning the Laws and Customs of War of 1907 states: 'A belligerent party which violates the provisions of the said Regulations shall, if the case demands, be liable to pay compensation. It shall be responsible for all acts committed by persons forming part of its armed forces'. Article 91 of the Additional Protocol I of 1977 reproduces the same obligation. See also The International Committee of the Red Cross customary law study identified in rule 150 that *'A State responsible for violations of IHL is required to make full reparation for the loss or injury caused'.* Henckaerts and Doswald-Beck, *Customary International Humanitarian Law—Volume I: Rules* (Cambridge University Press, Cambridge, 2005), 540. Alwyn V. Freeman, 'Responsibility of States for Unlawful Acts of their Armed Forces', in Académie de Droit International de La Haye, *Recueil des Cours*, Vol. 88 (Leiden: Martinus Nijhoff Publishers, 1955), 333; Nollkaemper, *National Courts*, 781 (n 5); Marco Sassòli, 'Reparation', in Vincent Chetail (ed.), *Post-Conflict Peacebuilding: A Lexicon* (Oxford: Oxford University Press, 2009), 284; Rudolf Dolzer, 'The Settlement of War-Related Claims: Does International Law Recognize a Victim's Private Right of Action? Lessons after 1945', *Berkeley Journal of International Law*, 20 (2002), 296; Christian Tomuschat, 'Reparation in Favour of Individual Victims of Gross Violations of International Human Rights and Humanitarian Law', in Marcelo G. Kohen and Luius Caflisch (eds), *Promoting Justice, Human Rights and Conflict Resolution through International Law* (Geneva, Graduate Institute of International Studies, 2007), 576–7; Frulli, 'When Are States Liable', 421 (claiming that while IHL treaty law has been recognized as conferring rights only upon states, a customary rule conferring that right also upon individuals is emerging) (n 15).

[43] The court relied on a number of treaties: the Convention Respecting the Laws and Customs of War and Land of 1899; Declaration prohibiting aerial bombardment of 1907; the Hague Draft Rules of Air Warfare of 1922–1923; and Protocol prohibiting the use in war of asphyxiating, deleterious or other gases and bacteriological methods of warfare.

[44] *Shimoda et al.* v. *The State,* Tokyo District Court (7 December 1963) (translated in *The Japanese Annual of International Law*, 8 (1964), 231). On the case see Richard Falk, 'The Shimoda Case: A Legal Appraisal of the Atomic Attacks on Hiroshima and Nagasaki', *American Journal of*

[t]hroughout its close examination of texts and the drafting process of Article 3 of the Hague Convention, the Court has been unable to recognize the alleged rule of customary international law that provides individual residents in an occupied territory the right to claim compensation directly against the occupying State for damages resulting from a violation of the Hague Regulations committed by members of the occupying forces.[45]

In Germany, a case similar to *Ferrini* concerning forced labour during the Second World War was brought before the German Federal Constitutional Court. In June 2004 the court held that an individual right to reparation did not exist at the time of the Second World War under either domestic or international law and it therefore dismissed the complaint. Although the court was not ready to confer an individual right deriving from Article 3 of the Hague Convention, it was ready to recognize such a right based on domestic legislation. Nonetheless, it ruled that even if the inter-state regime of state responsibility for wrongful acts did not preclude the possibility of a domestic system allowing individuals to claim remedies, this, however, 'does not allow the inference of a rule or assumption according to which a state violating international law must recognize a right of claim for injured persons on the basis of its domestic law.'[46]

In November 2006, the German Federal High Court of Justice examined in *35 citizens of the Former Federal Republic of Yugoslavia* v. *Germany* the question of whether individuals directly have the right to claim compensation before a national court for violations of IHL.[47] The facts of the case dealt with the incident involving NATO's bombing of a bridge at Varvarin, Serbia, on 30 May 1999, in which ten people were killed and 30 others injured, all civilians. Thirty-five victims of this bombing and their relatives, all citizens of the former Federal Republic of Yugoslavia, claimed compensation from Germany in a German court. The claimants

International Law, 59/4 (1965), 759–93; Yuki Tanaka and Richard Falk, 'The Atomic Bombing, The Tokyo War Crimes Tribunal and the Shimoda Case: Lessons for Anti-Nuclear Legal Movements', *The Asia-Pacific Journal*, 44/3 (2009).

[45] *Filipino 'Comfort Women'* case, Tokyo District Court (9 October 1998). The comfort women cases refer to several claims of compensation of women who during the Japanese occupation of China, Korea, and the Philippines during the Second World War, were forced to perform sexual slavery. All the claims based on Article 3 of the Hague Convention IV of 1907 were rejected. Only one decision in 1998 attributed damages to Korean women, on the basis of a constitutional obligation to apologize and compensate for the harm done under Japanese occupation. However, this ruling was reversed on appeal in March 2001 by the Hiroshima High Court. Fifteen Asian women brought a suit against Japan under the ATS before US courts. It was rejected on grounds of state immunity: *Hwang Geum Joo* v. *Japan*, 172 F.Supp. 2d 52 (D.D.C. 2001). On appeal it was dismissed on the basis of the political question doctrine: 413 F.3d 45 (2005).

[46] *Associazione Nazionale Reduci dalla Prigionia dall'Internamento e dalla Guerra di Liberazione and Others* v. *Germany*, (Joint Constitutional Complaint) BVerfG, 2 BvR 1379/01 (28 June 2004), paragraphs 38, 39. Similarly, see also the same case before the ECtHR: *Associazione Nazionale Reduci dalla Prigionia dall'Internamento e dalla Guerra di Liberazione and Others* v. *Germany*, (Decision as to the Admissibility), European Court of Human Rights No. 45563/04 (4 September 2007), in which Germany was not attributed responsibility for the damage caused by the German Reich. The ECtHR unanimously stated that, according to the Hague Convention of 1907 or the Additional Protocol I of 1977, there is no individual right for compensation for war crimes.

[47] *35 citizens of the Former Federal Republic of Yugoslavia* v. *Germany*, (Appeal Judgment) BGHZ 166, 384; III ZR 190/05 (2 November 2006).

based their right for direct remedies arising from violations of IHL, on Article 3 of Hague Convention IV and Article 91 of Additional Protocol I. The court held that under these provisions individuals have no right to compensation against a foreign state for violations of IHL; rather it is a state that needs to bring a claim for violations. Although the court mentioned the developments in international law since the Second World War according to which the individual constitutes 'at least . . . a partial subject of international law', this does not confer rights from all treaties. In particular, the court stated that 'the rule still applies that, irrespective of a primary claim by the affected people for the observance of international law, the country of nationality is still basically only entitled to a secondary claim for compensation for the unlawful acts of a foreign State against its citizens.' The court went on to say that this was undoubtedly the state of the law when the Hague Convention IV was adopted in 1907 and has remained unchanged by Additional Protocol I. Furthermore, the court ruled that under customary international law, no other rule has evolved as supported by Draft Articles on the Responsibility of States for Internationally Wrongful Acts. The Draft Articles explicitly discuss the right of states to invoke the responsibility of other states for international wrongful acts. The court recognized that there was a trend 'that has been developing since 1945, i.e., towards recognition in international law literature' of the exercise of rights by individual people. The court also observed however, that at this stage, the position was 'no more than the statement of an *ideal* in the area of IHL, to be achieved in the future but not yet incorporated in the practice of international law.'[48] It further mentioned that 'only futuristic goals' could be derived from the standpoint of the Basic Principles and Guidelines on the Right to a Remedy and Reparation for Victims of Gross Violations of International Human Rights Law and Serious Violations of International Humanitarian Law (Adopted and proclaimed by General Assembly resolution 60/147 of 16 December 2005) and that these principles are too general to provide a 'dynamic' interpretation of Article 91 of Additional Protocol I.

Other jurisdictions have ruled in a similar way.[49] The only jurisdiction that explicitly applied Article 3 as conferring an individual right upon individuals was Greece.[50] Having rejected Germany's claim of immunity, the Greek court determined that the claim could be based on Article 3 of 1907 Hague Convention IV and Article 46 of the 1907 Hague Regulations. It found that in the absence of a rule of international law prohibiting this, the claims could be made by individuals and not necessarily by their state. In addition, the Israeli HCJ in the *Targeted Killing*

[48] See also: 'There was a tendency in international law towards the recognition that individuals may *enforce* individual rights. For the field of IHL, this was however not more than the articulation of an idealized expectation as to the development of international law. There was also no evidence for such a development in international or foreign court decisions.'

[49] *Goldstar (Panama) S.A.* v. *United States*, 967 F. 2d. 965, 968–9 (4th Cir. 1992) (the US Court of Appeals of the 4th Circuit found that Article 3 of 1907 Hague Convention did not provide a private right of action in relation to the intervention by the US in Panama); *Presidency of the Council of Ministers* v. *Marković and ors*, paragraph 106 (n 14).

[50] Greek Court of First Instance of Leivadia, Prefecture of Voiotia (30 October 1997). However, as already discussed the litigation was prevented from being enforced due to state immunity.

case (2006) stated, based on Article 3, that in appropriate cases in which civilians are hurt during a targeted killing operation, they should be compensated.[51]

2.3.1 Peace agreement

Peace settlements negotiated at the end of a war have to consider the material ability of the sides to carry them out. At the same time, peace settlements are seen in a more global, historical context of recognition of responsibility and apology which are no less important in a post-war society. However, a national judge adjudicating between two litigating parties would not take into account this complexity of post-war recovery and the global perspective of historical events.[52] Indeed, sometimes the right to reparation for individual victims must be balanced against and perhaps even diluted by considerations pertaining to the difficulty of post-conflict recovery. After a conflict the responsible state is often in economic straits, and the financial burden will also be imposed on innocent civilians.[53] Conventional agreements permit injured nations to seek reparation, and enable the responsible nation to survive. By its existence, the responsible nation can thus be a place to bring a complaint to and (perhaps eventually) be a source of reparation payment. Granting every individual a separate right of claim before a judicial body against the responsible state would preclude such a course. It would therefore seem preferable to establish ad hoc mechanisms and special conventional regimes for the individual victims. These mechanisms would be based on the concrete possibility of reparation for individual victims in the future.

Clearly, the peace agreements in the aftermath of the Second World War did not point to a recognition of an individual right to a remedy for an IHL violation. They instead decided that war reparations should be made according to the classical inter-state model. Thus, the entire process of reparation was based on the understanding that compensation would be effected within the framework of inter-state relationships. Indeed,

> approximately 95 per cent of all claims were regulated by lump-sum agreements with the respective home state of the victims, which received money and distributed it under own discretion without there being any intent to provide full coverage for every individual damage.[54]

[51] HCJ 769/02, *The Public Committee against Torture in Israel*, paragraph 40: 'In appropriate cases it is appropriate to pay compensation as a result of harm caused to an innocent civilian (*see [..]* §3 of *The Hague Regulations*; §91 of *The First Protocol*).'

[52] Pablo de Greiff, 'Justice and Reparations', in Pablo de Greiff (ed.), *The Handbook of Reparations* (Oxford: Oxford University Press, 2006), 454–66.

[53] Sassòli mentions two cases: 'After World War I, Germany's situation revealed the negative consequences that reparations can have, not only on the country's economy, but also on the international financial system and the resurgence of armed conflicts more generally. In a similar way, reparations by Iraq through the UN Compensation Commission, financed through the "oil-for-food" programme, have shown that reparations may have catastrophic humanitarian consequences for innocent people.' Sassòli, 'Reparation', 289 (n 42).

[54] Rainer Hofmann and Frank Riemann, 'Compensation for Victims of War: Background Report' (International Law Association, 17 March 2004), 1–49.

Similarly, the San Francisco Peace Treaty of 1951 recognized Japan's obligation to pay reparations to the states it invaded during the war. The determination of the exact reparation was left to bilateral agreements which did not allow claims by individuals.[55]

According to the mechanism of diplomatic protection, states may waive the rights of their nationals in bilateral agreements.[56] As for the significance of the peace agreements in the case of *Ferrini*: by virtue of Article 77 (4) of the Peace Treaty of 10 February 1947, Italy waived, on behalf of its nationals, any right to request compensation from Germany and German nationals in relation to damages occurred during World War II.[57] In this context, Germany before the ICJ argued that,

> By claiming that individual suits can be entertained by Italian courts, the *Corte di Cassazione* now seeks to topple the fundamental determinations made in Potsdam. Its intention is to open up a second level of reparation, reparation in each and every individual case, alongside the collective mode of settlement agreed upon by the Victorious Powers which, in 1945, acted as trustees of the entire group of States that had declared war on Germany, among them also Italy.[58]

It is hard to see how more than fifty years after the agreements, national courts can today re-examine their validity.[59] As stated by Gattini, in the context of settlement with Japan, 'At this point, this complex settlement cannot be put in jeopardy because of change in overall political conditions.'[60] Allowing national courts to review settlements would destroy the entire architecture of the peace process which had received definite approval, and would amount to 'the overthrow of a legally consolidated situation under international law.'[61] Post-war settlements need to stabilize the relations of former belligerent states, re-establish friendly relations, and recover internal societies, which often suffer from economic destruction.

[55] 'Even if we assume, however, as the appellants contend, that the 1951 Treaty (1951 Treaty of Peace between Japan and the Allied Powers, 3 U.S.T. 3169) does not of its own force deprive the courts of the United States of jurisdiction over their claims, it is pellucidly clear the Allied Powers intended that all war-related claims against Japan be resolved through government-to-government negotiations rather than through private tort suits. Indeed, Article 26 of the Treaty obligated Japan to enter "bilateral" peace treaties with non-Allied states "on the same or substantially the same terms as are provided for in the present treaty," which indicates the Allied Powers expected Japan to resolve other states' claims, like their own, through government-to-government agreement.' *The Hwang Geum Joo et al.* v. *Japan*, 367 U.S. App. D.C. 45 (D.C. Cir. 2005).

[56] Sassòli, 'Reparation', 284 (n 42).

[57] The agreement was valid with relation to the Federal Republic of Germany (FRG), even if it was not a party to the peace treaty, by virtue of the Bonn Agreement of 2 June 1961 between Italy and the FRG.

[58] Public sitting held on Monday 12 September 2011, at 10 a.m., at the Peace Palace, President Owada presiding, in the case concerning Jurisdictional Immunities of the State (*Germany* v. *Italy*: Greece intervening), 35 (n 1).

[59] But see the interpretation given by the Italian Court of Cassation in the *Civitella* case (October 2008), in which the court dismissed the argument that the action of Italian nationals was foreclosed by the 1947 Treaty or the Bonn Agreement. See Annalisa Ciampi, 'The Italian Court of Cassation Asserts Civil Jurisdiction over Germany in a Criminal Case Relating to the Second World War: The *Civitella* case', *Journal of International Criminal Justice*, 7/3 (2009), 612.

[60] Gattini, 'To What Extent are State Immunity and Non-Justiciability Major Hurdles', 364–5 (n 32).

[61] Gattini, 'To What Extent are State Immunity and Non-Justiciability Major Hurdles', 366 (n 32).

A variety of conflicting interests are negotiated and finally, a balance is struck between them, which finds expression in the agreement. By reviewing the very validity of the peace agreements themselves, these cornerstones of conflict resolution would be jeopardized. It is proposed that political pressure for including reparations should be exercised during the settlement negotiations, and not decades later through the courts. If post-war peace settlements were to be reviewed by the courts, it could lead to contradictory rulings, and to a large number of individual suits that would exceed the working capacity of the national courts.

2.3.2 Ad hoc mechanisms and other practices since the 1990s

The awarding of individual reparations for violations of IHL, a trend significantly led by academics, is a recent practice in international law.[62]

The 2005 International Committee of the Red Cross customary study identifies:

> [A]n increasing trend in favour of enabling individual victims of violations of IHL to seek reparation directly from the responsible State... Reparation has been provided directly to individuals via different procedures, in particular via mechanisms set up by inter-State agreements, via unilateral State acts such as national legislation or reparation sought by individuals directly before national courts.[63]

For the most part, the mechanisms allowing victims of breaches of IHL to claim remedies were ad hoc mechanisms established by specific agreements. Such agreements include the Eritrea-Ethiopia Claims Commission and the special mechanisms set in Bosnia-Herzegovina and Kosovo,[64] or, exceptionally, by a resolution of the UN Security Council. The United Nations Compensation Commission (UNCC) established in 1991 by UN Security Council Resolution 687, is concerned with claims for compensation for damage as a result of the Iraq invasion of Kuwait.[65] This was the first time that the UN empowered individuals to assert

[62] As observed, 'despite the expansion and development of international law, and in more recent times, of international criminal law, victims of serious violations of IHL are still not considered to be entitled to reparation under international law'. Paola Gaeta, 'Are Victims of Serious Violations of IHL Entitled to Compensation?', in Orna Ben-Naftali (ed.), *International Human Rights and Humanitarian Law* (Oxford: Oxford University Press, 2011), 307.

[63] Henckaerts and Doswald-Beck, *Customary IHL*, 541 (n 42). See also, 'Report on the Protection of War Victims' (Geneva, June 1993), Section 4.3 in *International Review of the Red Cross*, 296 (1993), 391–445, in which the International Committee of the Red Cross recommended that a procedure shall be set to provide reparation for damage inflicted on the victims of violations of IHL 'so as to enable them to receive the benefits to which they are entitled.'

[64] 'General Framework Agreement for Peace in Bosnia and Herzegovina' (Paris, 14 December 1995), Annex 7: Agreement on Refugees and Displaced Persons (reproduced in 35 ILM 136 (1996)). 'Regulation No. 1999/23 of 15 November 1999 on the Establishment of the Housing and Property Directorate and the Housing and Property Claims Commission'.

[65] Norbert Wühler, 'The United Nations Compensation Commission', in Albrecht Randelzhofer and Christian Tomuschat (eds), *State Responsibility and the Individual—Reparation in Instances of Grave Violations of Human Rights* (The Hague: Martinus Nijhoff Publishers, 1999), 213–29; Andrea Gattini, 'The UN Compensation Commission: Old Rules, New Procedures on War Reparations', *European Journal of International Law*, 13/1 (2002), 161–81. Veijo Heiskanen, 'The United Nations Compensation Commission', *Recueil des Cours*, 296 (2002), 390.

claims through the reparation regime established in the aftermath of an armed conflict. As has been observed,

The UNCC has processed over 2.6 million claims seeking a total of nearly $350 billion in compensation, almost all of which were claims of individual claimants. Given the limited resources of the Commission it was clear that it could in the end only provide... "rough" justice for the claimants as a whole, rather than "precise" justice for each individual.[66]

Another example is the Eritrea-Ethiopia Claims Commission (EECC) established pursuant to the Agreement between the Government of the Federal Democratic Republic of Ethiopia and the Government of the State of Eritrea of 12 December 2000. This Commission is competent to decide claims stemming from violations of IHL. It has reviewed approximately 400,000 claims submitted by individuals of the two states.[67]

Nonetheless, these are not perfect solutions. As pointed out by Sassòli:

Mass compensation programmes inevitably reopen past wounds, including those of the victims. When either those who are supposed to be its beneficiaries, or those who must finance it, perceive reparation as being unfair it may even contribute to creating new tensions and conflicts. For the sake of those who are to finance reparation, the process should go hand in hand with an educational account of historical facts.[68]

As far as individual criminal responsibility for war crimes is concerned, the mechanism evolved from ad-hoc mechanisms to a permanent court—the ICC. According to the Rome Statute, victims have the direct possibility of receiving a remedy from the perpetrator as set out by Article 75(2) of the Rome Statute stating that: 'The Court may make an order directly against a convicted person specifying appropriate reparations to, or in respect of, victims, including restitution, compensation and rehabilitation.' Such an order can be requested by the victim who is entitled to apply to the court. Article 79 provides for the establishment of a trust fund for the benefit of the victims of crimes and their families within the jurisdiction of the court. Nonetheless this mechanism is available only to victims of crimes prosecuted by the ICC.[69] Reports of the International Commission of Inquiries seem to adopt the position that individuals do have a right for remedy. In the Darfur report it was stated that gross breaches of human rights impose an obligation on the states of

[66] Hofmann and Riemann, 'Compensation for Victims of War', 18 (n 54).

[67] Liesbeth Zegveld, 'Remedies for Victims of Violations of IHL', *International Review of the Red Cross*, 85/851 (2003), 522. See also Natalie Klein 'State Responsibility for IHL Violations and the Work of the Eritrea Ethiopia Claims Commission So Far', *German Yearbook of International Law*, 47 (2005), 261–4.

[68] M. Sassòli, 283 (n 42). See also Report of the Secretary-General, 'The Rule of Law and Transitional Justice in Conflict and Post-Conflict Societies' (23 August 2004) UN Doc S/2004/616, paragraph 54: 'Material forms of reparation present perhaps the greatest challenges [..]. Difficult questions include who is included among the victims to compensate, how much compensation is to be rewarded, what kinds of harm are to be covered, how harm is to be quantified, how different kinds of harm are to be compared and compensated and how compensation is to be distributed.'

[69] Liesbeth Zegveld, 'Victims' Reparation Claims and International Criminal Courts—Incompatible Values?', *Journal International Criminal Justice*, 8/1 (2010), 86–92.

which the perpetrators are nationals to make reparation.[70] The UN Fact Finding Mission to Gaza recommended that: 'The international community needs to provide an additional or alternative mechanism of compensation by Israel for damage or loss incurred by Palestinian civilians during the military operations.'[71] Similarly, the ICJ, in its Advisory Opinion, affirmed that Israel has the obligation to make reparation for the damage caused to all natural and legal persons concerned.[72]

2.3.3 Back in time to Ferrini*: the question of intertemporal law*[73]

While no position is taken on whether an individual right for IHL violations which can be enforced by a national court exists today,[74] during the Second World War, when the facts of *Ferrini* occurred, no such right existed.[75]

The International Law Association Committee on Compensation for Victims of War, which was charged with examining whether a right to remedy has emerged, recognized such a right in its 2010 resolution, according to which: 'Victims of armed conflict have a right to reparation from the responsible parties.'[76] However, in its commentary to the resolution it explicitly mentioned that a right to remedy

[70] 'Report of the International Commission of Inquiry on Darfur to the United Nations Secretary-General, pursuant to Security Council resolution 1564 of 18 September 2004' (Geneva, 25 January 2005), paragraphs 598, 601.

[71] Human Rights Council, 'Human Rights in Palestine and Other Occupied Arab Territories—Report of the United Nations Fact-Finding Mission on the Gaza Conflict', 403.

[72] *Legal Consequences on the Construction of a Wall in the Occupied Palestinian Territory* (Advisory Opinion) ICJ Rep 2004, paragraph 152. The rules of military occupation were specifically recognized as conferring individual rights by the German Constitutional Court in *Associazione Nazionale Reduci dalla Prigionia dall'Internamento e dalla Guerra di Liberazione and Others* v. *Germany*.

[73] The doctrine of intertemporal law (= non retroactivity) has its origin in the *Island of Palmas* case: 'A juridical fact must be appreciated in the light of the law contemporary with it, and not of the law in force at the time when a dispute in regard to it arises or falls to be settled.' *United States* v. *The Netherlands*, 2 R.I.A.A. 829 (4 April 1928).

[74] A number of authors suggest that it does exist in light of recent state practice and the development of remedy rights in human rights law and international criminal law. Luke T. Lee, 'The Right of Victims of War to Compensation', in Ronald St. John Macdonald (ed.), *Essays in Honour of Wang Tieya* (Dordrecht: Martinus Nijhoff Publishers, 1993), 489; Emanuela C. Gillard, 'Reparation for Violations of IHL', *International Review of the Red Cross*, 85/851 (2003), 536; Frits Kalshoven, 'State Responsibility for Warlike Acts of the Armed Forces: From Article 3 of the Hague Convention IV of 1907 to Article 91 of Additional Protocol I and Beyond', *International and Comparative Quarterly*, 40/4 (1991), 827; Zegveld, 'Remedies for Victims', 506; Riccardo Pisillo-Mazzeschi, 'Reparation Claims by Individuals for State Breaches of Humanitarian Law and Human Rights: An Overview', *Journal of International Criminal Justice*, 1/2 (2003), 342; Rainer Hofmann, 'Victims of Violations of IHL: Do They Have an Individual Right to Reparation against States under International Law?', in Pierre-Marie Dupuy, Bardo Fassbender, Malcolm N. Shaw and Karl-Peter Sommermann (eds), *Common Values in International Law—Essays in Honour of Christian Tomuschat*, (Kehl: N.P. Engel Verlag, 2006), 357.

[75] Gillard, 'Reparation for Violations', 537 (n 74). As Tomuschat has noted 'the notion that an individual might derive direct claims from a violation of IHL is a child of our time and in any event does not go back beyond the emergence of the human rights movement'. Tomuschat, 'Reparation in Favour of Individual Victims', 576 (n 42).

[76] Article 6 of International Law Association Resolution 2/2010, 'Reparation for Victims of Armed Conflict' adopted at the 74th Conference of the International Law Association (The Hague: The Netherlands, 15–20 August 2010).

only emerged in the 1990s. There is no doubt that during the Second World War, an individual right to reparation was not recognized.[77]

This position was reaffirmed in 2007 by the ECtHR: 'there was no legal provision, whether of an international or of a domestic character, supporting the applicants' claims against the Federal Republic of Germany.... neither international public law nor domestic law recognised claims for compensation for forced labour at the time.'[78]

3. When utopia appears in court: the role of national judges

As a result of the innovative findings of *Ferrini*, Germany initiated proceedings before the ICJ, challenging the Italian courts' violation of the customary rule of sovereign immunity.[79] The Italian position before the ICJ showed that utopian policy considerations were an explicit factor in the ruling of the Italian *Corte di Cassazione* in *Ferrini:*

> Italian judges, facing such a blatant and long-lasting denial of reparation in violation of all relevant rules of international law, could not simply turn down victims' claims by recognizing the principle of State immunity. Clearly, the judges had the feeling that by applying a purely procedural principle in the face of the gravity of crimes for which no reparation has yet been made, they would create a typical situation of denial of justice. Had Italian courts granted immunity they would have put a full stop to the entire question of reparation to thousands of victims. They would have effectively denied any possibility for these claims to achieve any objective. On the contrary, they had *very serious justifications* for setting aside the immunity of Germany and verifying whether the claims were substantiated on the merits. [emphasis added][80]

Judges who apply the law to the facts of the case before them do not need *good reasons*[81] or *very serious justifications* to legitimize their ruling. The Italian court was not being detached from recent developments in international law that favour the interest of persons over that of states in situations of gross violations of human

[77] International Law Association, Report of the International Committee on Compensation for Victims of Armed Conflict, 'Draft Declaration of International Law Principles on Compensation for Victims of War (Substantive issues)' (Rio De Janeiro, 2008), 13. See also International Law Association, Report of the International Committee on Compensation for Victims of Armed Conflict, 'Draft Declaration of International Law Principles on Compensation for Victims of War Armed Conflict (Substantive issues)' (The Hague, 2010), 14.

[78] *Associazione Nazionale Reduci dalla Prigionia dall'Internamento e dalla Guerra di Liberazione and Others* v. *Germany*, (Decision as to the Admissibility), paragraph 4.

[79] Jurisdictional Immunities of the State (*Germany* v. *Italy*: Greece intervening) (Judgment) (International Court of Justice, 3 February 2012).

[80] *Case Concerning Jurisdictional Immunities of the State* (*Germany* v. *Italy*) (Counter-Memorial of Italy), paragraph 6.16 (n 13).

[81] 'Italian judges had good reasons to deny immunity to Germany on account of the extremely serious nature of the violations of IHL for which reparation had been requested . . . '. *Case Concerning Jurisdictional Immunities of the State* (*Germany* v. *Italy*) (Counter-Memorial of Italy), paragraph 6.17 (n 13).

rights. Yet, it introduced a new practice, in order to render justice and to make international rules meaningful. As argued by Germany:

> The judges slipped into the role of legislators, wishing to remedy the structural weakness of international law, to wit, that it lacks a complete set of remedies. It may indeed be desirable to improve the effectiveness of international law by complementing the enforcement mechanisms. Yet, this is what international law is still about at the present stage of its development.[82]

In the proceeding before the ICJ, the role of national judges was to be reviewed by the international judges of the ICJ. The ICJ was called upon to decide whether national judges are required to apply existing international law or, in relevant circumstances and as required by justice, they can also function as active contributors to the development of international law. The ICJ needed to decide not only the fate of state immunity in civil law cases arising from *jus cogens* violations. It also had to decide more generally on whether national courts can perform a utopian function.[83] Was the national utopian ruling as the one of the Italian *Corte di Cassazione* legitimate? Or as Germany claimed, national judges are not entrusted with the task of amending and changing international law.[84]

Judge Rosalyn Higgins opened her general lecture at The Hague Academy by stating that 'the judge does not "find rules" but he makes choices ... between claims which have varying degrees of legal merits.'[85] Indeed, as long as the judge 'makes choices between claims which have varying degrees of legal merits', the judge performs his or her normative function, which allows a certain amount of discretion. Yet, when a judge chooses a stance that goes beyond that, and enters the twilight zone of utopia, that choice is no longer an implementation of a legal rule, but the execution of a moral value.

[82] *Case Concerning Jurisdictional Immunities of the State* (*Germany* v. *Italy*) (Memorial of the Federal Republic of Germany), paragraph 13 (n 16). See also Gattini: 'changing or developing the content of the rule, judicial activism alone is not sufficient and, to date, the position of the governments on our issue has been quite inflexible.' Gattini, 'War Crimes and State Immunity', 241–2 (n 12).

[83] See also Bianchi in 2005: 'This terrain [State immunity] is one where the strain between conservatism and innovation-which marks the contemporary epoch of international law-is most evident [..]. To argue in favour or against the immunity of foreign states and their organs before municipal courts for alleged egregious violations of international human rights and humanitarian law is tantamount to taking a stance on a variety of issues that remain controversial, including ... What role should domestic courts play in adjudicating claims involving issues of international law.' Bianchi, 'Italian Court of Cassation', 247–8 (n 12).

[84] 'the Corte di Cassazione wishes to revolutionize the system of operation and enforcement of international law, decreeing that, where there appears to be a lacuna in the available array of remedies, domestic judges should simply fill in that gap—and this is wrong.' Public sitting held on Monday 12 September 2011, at 10 a.m., at the Peace Palace, President Owada presiding, in the case concerning Jurisdictional Immunities of the State (*Germany* v. *Italy*: Greece intervening) (Prof. C. Tomuschat), 21, 25–26 (n 1). See also *Case Concerning Jurisdictional Immunities of the State (Germany* v. *Italy)* (Memorial of the Federal Republic of Germany), paragraph 62: 'judges are not legitimated to place themselves at the forefront of processes of change.'

[85] Cited in Public sitting held on Tuesday 13 September 2011, at 10 a.m., at the Peace Palace, President Owada presiding, in the case concerning Jurisdictional Immunities of the State (*Germany* v. *Italy*: Greece intervening), 62 (n 26).

While decisions based on utopian ideals are usually quite captivating, one must not forget that the same Italian court was ready to deny exactly the same justice and access to reparation for victims of international crimes in *Marković*. The *Marković* decision indicates that utopian discourses of judges are not applied equally in all circumstances, thereby opening the door to political preference. Arguably, before developing the law and rendering decisions in the style of *Ferrini*, courts should first be ready to provide remedies in cases like *Marković*. Only then will their position be coherent. In light of the poor practice of the Italian *Corte di Cassazione* itself, it is hardly possible to commend the court's performance in *Ferrini*.

5

Conclusion

The critical analysis of case law made in this book has disclosed a spectrum of functional roles of national courts. The roles identified were: (1) the *apologist* role of courts, in which they serve as a legitimating agency for the state's actions. For this purpose courts misuse (and even distort) the law; (2) the *avoiding* role of courts, in which the courts, motivated by extra legal considerations, avoid exercising jurisdiction over a case; (3) the *deferral role* of courts, in which, while maintaining a dialogue with the other political branches of the government, courts defer to the state's discretion; (4) the *limiting* or *normative application* role of the courts, in which courts apply the law independently even if they are required to impose limits on the executive or the legislator; (5) the *judicial activist* role of the courts, in which they promote the application of international law where it contradicts their national law, without having been explicitly authorized to do so; and (6) the *utopian* role of courts, in which courts develop international law introducing moral judgments in favour of the protection of the individual, beyond the requirements of the law.

While the spectrum serves as a useful framework to describe the varying possible roles of national courts when applying IHL, the study also assumes an external, political, 'good' outside this spectrum, which is the principles of the rule of law—to which courts should aspire through the exercise of the *normative application* function. It then becomes possible to legitimize or criticize the different roles (or functions) of national courts in the light of these fundamental requirements. Thus, after having identified the different roles of national courts, this conclusion evaluates the extent to which each of the functions are harmonized with the principles set by the rule of law. The first section starts by outlining the fundamental principles of the rule of law i.e. their structural and functional aspects. The second section examines more specifically how the different roles identified in the previous chapters comply with the rule of law requirements. Lastly, the third section provides some hypotheses on the factors that lead courts to choose any of the categories, and especially the necessary conditions for the optimal fulfilment of their role from the standpoint of the international rule of law.

1. The rule of law and national courts: structural and functional aspects

Today it seems that there is a remarkable consensus on what the rule of law requires.[1] More specifically, regarding the judiciary—it means that the judiciary have to be independent, impartial, accessible, and to provide an effective and equal enforcement of the law. Whether national courts possess these features depends on the national legal system in which they operate. In assessing these features, two aspects need to be examined—the national legal framework that empowers national courts to apply international law (the structural aspect) and the court's *de facto* application of the international law (the functional aspect—which was under review in this book). The structural aspect relates to the domestic governmental and legal frameworks that empower domestic courts to enforce international law and to establish their independent position vis-à-vis the other political branches. These *structural* aspects are the preliminary requirements necessary for national courts to be able to apply international law in domestic systems. The functional aspect relates to the court's *de facto* application of international law. While national systems may comply with the structural requirements to a varying degree, as in most Western democratic states, this does not guarantee the rule of law. Even if, structurally, independency, impartiality, and the other elements are guaranteed by procedural rules and the principle of separation of powers, it may well be that the *de facto* function of the court will not correspond to these principles. Interestingly, the division between the *structural* and *functional* roles of the judiciary is echoed in the International Criminal Court complementarity principle set out in Article 17 of the Rome Statute: while the term 'unable' indicates structural deficiencies of national courts, 'unwilling' refers to functional deficiencies. In the following section, the rule of law principles are examined in light of their structural and functional aspects.

[1] Marmor, A.,'The Ideal of the Rule of Law', in D. Patterson (ed.), *A Companion to Philosophy of Law and Legal Theory* (2nd edn, Oxford: Wiley-Blackwell, 2010), 666–74, 666. One of the most inclusive definitions is probably the one formulated by Raz, who identified eight fundamental elements, common to all legal systems: (1) all law should be prospective, open, and clear; (2) the law should be relatively stable; (3) the making of particular laws (particular legal orders) should be guided by open, stable, clear, and general rules; (4) the independence of the judiciary must be guaranteed; (5) the principles of natural justice must be observed; (6) the courts should have review powers over the implementation of the other principles; (7) the courts should be easily accessible; and (8) the discretion of the crime-prevention bodies should not be allowed to pervert the law. In addition, many of the principles which can be derived from the basic idea of the formal rule of law depend for their validity 'on the particular circumstances of different society' Joseph Raz, 'The Rule of Law and Its Virtue', The Law Quarterly Review, 93/2 (1977), reproduced in Keith C. Culver (ed.), *Readings in the Philosophy of Law* (2nd edn, Ontario: Broadview Press, 2008), 16.

1.1 Independency and impartiality

1.1.1 Structural aspects

The independence of the judiciary is a general principle of law which requires that the courts be independent from the parties to the dispute. When two sides fall into a conflict that they cannot resolve between themselves, it is natural for them to resort to a third party conflict resolver. This is the prototype *triadic structure* of courts (i.e. two disputing parties and a third-party decision-maker).[2] This structure finds legitimacy in the fact that the conflict resolver is perceived as being independent and impartial vis-à-vis the two parties in conflict. Courts, in order to achieve their institutional legitimacy, must therefore be perceived as being neutral, independent, and capable of resolving a conflict between two sides without imposing their own interest.[3]

According to Nollkaemper a threat to independency may be understood in two ways:

i. Direct pressure from the political branches

The independent position of courts vis-à-vis political powers is guaranteed by several requirements prescribed by human rights law. These include formal procedural requirements relating to the appointment of judges and their working conditions, the demand that judicial proceedings be conducted openly, fairly, and that the rights of the parties be respected.[4] More specifically, the Institut de Droit International recommended in its 1993 resolution on the *Activities of National Judges and the International Relations of the States* that national courts should decide cases involving international claims independently from the state.[5]

[2] M. Shapiro, *Courts: A Comparative and Political Analysis* (Chicago: The University of Chicago Press, 1981), 8.

[3] Indeed, courts invest enormous rhetorical effort in maintaining their reputations for neutrality and independence. Shapiro and Stone Sweet, *On Law, Politics and Judicialization* (Oxford: Oxford University Press, 2002), 6. Martin Shapiro, 'Political Jurisprudence', *Kentucky Law Journal*, 52/294 (1964), 295–6. For a contrasting position, which reflects the liberal position on courts, objectivity and neutrality, see for example Shabtai Rosenne, who states that while the 'function of the *existence* of the judicial function is political, the performance of that function is not'. Cited in Koskenniemi, *From Apology to Utopia—The Structure of International Legal Argument'* (New York: Cambridge University Press, 2005), 29–30.

[4] Article 14 of the International Covenant on Civil and Political Rights; Article 6(1) of the European Convention on Human Rights (adopted 4 November 1950, entered into force 3 September 1953), 213 U.N.T.S 222; UN Basic Principles on the Independence of the Judiciary Adopted by the Seventh United Nations Congress on the Prevention of Crime and the Treatment of Offenders held at Milan from 26 August to 6 September 1985 and endorsed by UN General Assembly Resolution 40/32 (29 November 1985) and UN General Assembly Resolution 40/146 (13 December 1985). Principle 2 provides that the judiciary 'shall decide matters before them impartially, on the basis of facts and in accordance with the law, without any restrictions, improper influences, inducements, pressures, threats or interferences, direct or indirect, from any quarter or for any reason'. Principle 11 of the UN Basic Principles on the Independence of the Judiciary provides that 'securing that the term of office of judges, the independence, security, adequate remuneration, conditions of service, pensions and the age of retirement shall be adequately secured by law.'

[5] 'National courts should be empowered by their domestic legal order to interpret and apply international law with full independence'—Article 1(1) of the Resolution on the Activities of National Judges and the International Relations of the States, Institut de Droit International (Milan 1993).

Structurally, the independence of the judiciary is realized mainly through the separation of powers principle. In the context of IHL, it acquires a special dimension. Hence, the principle of separation of powers has been used by states as the justification for granting power in foreign affairs exclusively to the executive. This is illustrated, for example, in the justification for the use of avoidance doctrines in the US.[6] The requirement of independency, on the other hand, should 'reshape'[7] the relations between the political and judicial branches in a way that would require the political branches to refrain from guiding the juridical branch. It would demand that the judiciary would also supervise the legality of its actions in the domain of foreign affairs.

ii. Limitation on the courts' competence imposed by the political branches
Denying a court the possibility of applying international law is limiting its independence. It would 'amount to just as much interference by the political branches as direct political pressure'.[8] Thus, national legislation relating to immunity of the state, amnesty laws, rules that confer the executive with the exclusive binding interpretation of treaty law, and which restrict the application of IHL, actually limit the independency of the court.

1.1.2 Functional aspects

i. The independent position of the court vis-à-vis the political branches
When the structural requirements related to independency are fulfilled, the extent of the application of IHL by national courts is dependent on a number of factors. The domestic judicial tradition and the level of independency and strength of the courts vis-à-vis the political branches all play a part. Here, the analogy to the court's authority for judicial review of administrative acts of the state under domestic law is useful.[9] The more a legal system is used to limiting the state, through far-reaching constitutional powers of review, the more it can be expected that the judiciary will enforce IHL, even to the extent of imposing limits on state acts or legislation. Another factor that may enhance a court's standing as being more independent, is whether the conflict, or the legal question, was reviewed by an international court.

Online at <http://www.idi-iil.org/idiE/resolutionsE/1993_mil_01_en.PDF>. For a comment see Benvenisti, 'Judges and Foreign Affairs: A Comment on the Institute de Droit International's Resolution on "The Activities of National Courts and the International Relations of their State"' *European Journal of International Law* 1/5 (1994), 423–39.

6 See Chapter 2 for the justification of the act of state and the political question doctrines.

7 Nollkaemper, *National Courts and The International Rule of Law* (Oxford: Oxford University Press, 2011), 54.

8 Nollkaemper, *National Courts*, 53 (n 7).

9 'If national constitutional courts are willing to strike down laws passed by the national legislature, then they should have the institutional clout to do the same thing when enforcing international law.' Mattias Kumm, 'International Law in National Courts: The International Rule of Law and the Limits of the Internationalist Model', *Virginia Journal of International Law*, 44/19 (2003), 24. See also Benvenisti who proposes on the basis of that analogy to adjust the requirement of standing: Benvenisti, 'Judges and Foreign Affairs', 438 (n 5).

Politically, it may be easier for national courts to apply the law independently where their decisions are handed down in the wake of international courts' decisions.

Courts are a national institution operating within a defined role in the governmental structure of the state. They have to be mindful of the effect of their ruling to maintain their legitimacy in their societies.[10] Courts also have to be aware of the implicit accord with which the political branches granted them the competence to exercise judicial review and to apply IHL. As the state needs to rely on the judiciary as a legitimizing agency, the judiciary needs to be conferred the necessary independence as a mainstay of their legitimacy in the eyes of the public.[11] A court which exceeds the implicit limits of this pact risks a legislative counter-response that may impose limitations on the court's authority for judicial review. Thus, courts must consider the consequences of their ruling, i.e. that it may result in follow-up legislation that would invalidate the ruling or, more generally, their jurisdiction. The non-compliance of the state with a court ruling may jeopardize the position of the courts and of the governmental system as a whole along with the entire system of checks and balances. This observation also applies in the context of IHL. IHL is a branch of law that regulates the most extreme situations of violence in which a state can be involved—armed conflict. Naturally, in times of war it seems reasonable that 'courts cannot and should not neglect entirely the international political consequence of a limitation of government power in foreign affair'.[12]

In their pursuit of the appropriate balance, courts have developed different avoidance doctrines, discussed in Chapter 2. The doctrines are an attempt to define whether the question before them is or should be within the realm of the law or should be resolved by political actors. While avoidance doctrines completely deny access to courts, and leave the issue entirely outside the realm of the law, there are preferable solutions that could be chosen by courts in the process of defining and affirming the legitimate boundaries of their independent institutional position. For example, the use of the deferral technique offers courts a gradation of options for applying the law while at the same time maintaining dialogue with other branches of the government. As shown in Chapter 3, there are more and more cases in which the judiciary have moved away from the traditional tendency to avoid jurisdiction in armed conflict-related issues. Progressively, with the use of deference techniques, courts have begun to exercise their judicial authority as an IHL enforcer. Here, the independence of the courts plays a predominant role and once their independent position is established, courts may impose limits on the executive and offer

10 Paradoxically too much independence can limit the effectiveness of international law, as the judiciary may lose its ability to compel the executive to act. Nollkaemper argues that the political dimension of international law not only *de facto* limits the possibility of full independence of national courts but also questions the very desirability of such independence. Nollkaemper, *National Courts*, 59 (n 7).

11 Benvenisti, 'Judges and Foreign Affairs', 425–7 (n 5). In 1994, when the article was written Benvenisti held the view that this pact did not include judicial review in foreign affairs, because of the absence of the state's interest in having legal legitimization for its acts abroad and because of little public demand to have scrutiny over them.

12 Nollkaemper, *National Courts*, 58 (n 7).

protection against governmental abuse of power in accordance with the rule of law principles. When human rights issues are at stake, in a context of a conflict, courts have proved to be more assertive. One of the reasons for their ability to impose limits on their government, even in the context of an armed conflict, is the expanded role played by national courts in safeguarding human rights on a constitutional level over the past few decades, during which they established and legitimized their position as rights' guardians.

ii. National courts' impartiality

As the judge is a state agent, in cases in which the state is a party to the proceedings, the question arises as to whether the court can truly be as independent and impartial as it is when adjudicating a dispute between two private parties. Seemingly, in such cases, the triadic structure is necessarily weakened as one of the parties may perceive the third as an ally of its adversary.[13] In this respect, when the state is a party to IHL proceedings, and evidentiary or normative presumptions are made in its favour—as shown in Chapter 1 through the deconstruction of the fact-finding and legal tests made by the Israeli High Court of Justice (HCJ)—the bias in favour of the state is only reinforced. This is valid for the interpretation of the law and establishing the facts. As for the latter, because of the complexity of establishing the facts in IHL cases, in which the state is usually in possession of exclusive information, it is already in a better position than its adversary. Granting additional judge-made presumptions in its favour seems to impair the neutrality of the judiciary which is already fragile because of the inherent impartiality that exists when dealing with IHL.[14]

Koskenniemi observes a *structural bias* within the international legal order: 'Out of any number of equally "possible" choices, some choices—typically conservative or *status quo* oriented choices—are *methodologically privileged* in the relevant institutions.'[15] This observation also seems to be valid for national courts which apply IHL. The inherent impartiality of national judges is related to the combination of a number of factors that influence national judges to be willing to serve their state's national interest while applying IHL. First, the subjective default orientation of the judge himself tends to defend and favour his own national interest. This is especially true in times of armed conflicts. The reason for this is that courts are themselves state institutions. They consist of judges who are citizens of the state, and who therefore share the same

[13] Shapiro, *Courts: A Comparative*, 27 (n 2).

[14] Therefore, along with the common law principle of 'equality of arms', the state's position should not be binding nor attributed a greater weight than the adverse party. This equality of arms principle is a part of the guarantees for having a fair trial in criminal adversary procedures. The IDI resolution: Article 1.3: 3. 'Nothing should prevent national courts from requesting the opinion of the Executive, provided that such consultation has no binding effect.' On this point see Benvenisti, 'Judges and Foreign Affairs', 431–2 (n 5).

[15] Koskenniemi, *From Apology to Utopia*, 607 (n 3). See also D. Kennedy, *A Critique of Adjudication (fin du siècle)* (Mass: Harvard University Press, Cambridge, 1997), 59–60.

sociological and psychological mindset.[16] Second, as opposed to other fields of private civil and penal law, the state does not have the same interest in the law of armed conflict being independently and impartially applied.[17] Similarly, in cases of this kind public opinion prevails over state national interest and does not demand the same level of scrutiny as with regard to compliance with the law in other fields. Courts cannot be expected to stand alone against the state and/or public opinion in the name of law, particularly in relation to sensitive issues such as armed conflicts.

As shown in the case studies, the link between the national court with the nationality of the victim and the responsible party may be determinative of the role played by the court. In *Ferrini*, where the victim was Italian and the responsible state was Germany, the Italian court was ready to deliver a utopian decision to render justice. This was contrary to the position adopted by its own government in the *Marković* case. In that case, delivered only two years before *Ferrini*, the responsible state was the Italian government, and the victim was a Serb—the court chose on that occasion to avoid justice. Similarly, the analysis of the US ATS cases in Chapter 2 demonstrates a very similar practice, in which courts, render different judgments for similar acts, in accordance with the nationality of the victims and/or the responsible party. This was especially pertinent in cases related to allegations of torture committed by US officials, in which the court backed up the government and provided State officials immunity. At the same time when dealing with other (non ally) states, the court condemns acts of torture in an affirmative way. The result is judicial practice based on double standards, bias and impartiality. The national bias of judges was clearly present also with the Israeli HCJ and the Serbian judiciary discussed in Chapter 1.

It would appear that courts of democratic states should, at the first stage, engage in applying the law against their own nationals and government. Thus before rendering cases like *Ferrini*, courts should not avoid cases like *Marković;* before imposing responsibility upon aliens through the ATS, US courts should first provide remedies in cases like *Rasul*. Only then, judging a third state's act, would a court appear to be impartial.

[16] See generally the critique of American Legal Realism, an intellectual movement in the US during the 1930s: 'How a judge responds to the facts of a particular case is determined by various psychological and sociological factors, both conscious and unconscious. The final decision, then, is the product not so much of "law" (which generally permits more than one outcome to be justified) but of these various psychological factors, ranging from the political ideology to the institutional role to the personality of the judge.' Brian Leiter, 'American Legal Realism', in Dennis M. Patterson (ed.), *A Companion to Philosophy of Law and Legal Theory* (2nd edn, Oxford: Blackwell, 2010), 249.

[17] 'While in the domestic sphere all branches of government stand to gain from judicial independence and judicial review, the situation is different with respect to foreign affairs. In this sphere, the political branches of government do not have the same interest in impartial judicial scrutiny of their policies.... Their only interest is the judicial vindication of their action abroad.' Benvenisti, 'Judges and Foreign Affairs', 426 (n 5).

iii. The temporal dimension

The initial stages of an armed conflict are typically characterized by a strong sense of national unity and support for the executive. Therefore, during such periods the court is likely to accord particular weight to state interest. However, once the conflict becomes protracted and the review is conducted later during (or after) an armed conflict, the situation changes. The period of time that has elapsed since the occurrence of the facts, the public opinion and/or historical narrative that has been formed during this time, the demand for scrutiny having been reinforced by media and NGOs' reports as well as testimonies of soldiers and victims, would have an impact on a court's willingness to exercise judicial review over the acts of the government. These factors would influence a court, along with its institutional ability to deliver a ruling that would limit the executive or attribute to the state responsibility for its violation of the law. This was well illustrated by the Guantanamo cases discussed in Chapter 3. The ability and willingness of the US Supreme Court, demonstrating its independence and impartiality, to rule against the state's position in *Hamdan*, was most certainly related to the fact that Hamdan had been detained for years without any legal procedure. The state's position was highly criticized during that time by the international community, the International Committee of the Red Cross (ICRC), local and international NGOs, and even other national courts. Similarly, Israel's judicial activism is due to the fact that the state is involved in a protracted military occupation.

There is another temporal aspect that is particular to grave violations of IHL and criminal cases. War crimes are not subject to statutory limitations, as provided by the 1968 *UN Convention on the Non-Applicability of Statutory Limitations to War Crimes and Crimes against Humanity*. This principle was identified by Rule 106 of the *2005 ICRC Customary Study*. Therefore, war crimes trials (as well as civil suits based on grave IHL violations, in places where national legislation provides for such reparations) can be held a long time after the facts of the case occurred. When war crime cases are dealt with by the courts of the responsible state during its post-conflict era sufficient time after the facts, the court will have an easier time in ruling against one of their own nationals. The historical narrative has established the responsibility of committing war crimes, and enough time has passed to ensure that the people directly involved in the violations no longer belong to the circle of decision-makers/administration/bureaucracy. In contrast, during an ongoing armed conflict, when responsible individuals still hold key positions of the government and the army, it is hardly conceivable for such trials to take place. In this context, the war crimes trials carried out in Serbia are among the rare examples of prosecution of war crimes just a few years after they were committed. As shown in Chapter 1 until the national historical narrative, recognizing the nation's own responsibility in the conflict, has not crystallized, there is an impact on judicial independence and impartiality (or on its ability and willingness) to apply IHL.

1.2 Effectiveness

1.2.1 Structural aspects

i. Validity, applicability, and enforceability of international norms within domestic systems

National courts will only be competent to apply IHL (and international law more generally) if the international rules are: (1) valid, applicable, and enforceable norms within their own national legal system, and (2) sufficiently clear and detailed so the rules can be enforced by a court. In a number of states the validity and applicability of the international rules within the national legal order is automatic (for example, in France, the Netherlands, Russia, Switzerland, Turkey, and the US). In other places an explicit act of endorsement by the national legislator is required (UK, Israel, India, Germany, and Italy). In the latter cases, states must adjust their own domestic legal system to be able to enforce international rules. They are required to incorporate them into domestic legislation or to empower courts constitutionally to directly apply international law. Even in cases where courts may directly apply international law, in view of the fact that international law treaties are not always sufficiently detailed to be enforced by a court, states should enact adapting legislation. Treaties are usually drafted in general terms as a result of their negotiation process. To become prescriptive law that can be enforced *ratione materiae* by domestic courts, treaties need to be detailed and clear. Therefore, all systems have to adjust their own domestic laws to be able to enforce those IHL rules which are not self-executing.[18]

ii. Skills

Access to a court is only meaningful if the court can provide an effective remedy for violations. Since the courts' judgments establish the law in the case before them, the litigants can only be guided by law if the judge applies the law correctly.[19] Watts adds that an 'open and fair hearing, absence of bias, are obviously essential for the correct application of the law.'[20] In this regard, the structural aspect assuring that the judges are equipped with the necessary skills in order to apply international law finds expression in a number of factors such as: legal education provided to judges; the curriculum at law faculties and special workshops provided by the Ministries of Justice, which can be in collaboration with international bodies such as UN, ICRC or regional agencies; other expertise required in the process of the qualification of judges; the creation of special international law benches, such as the one created in

[18] Sassòli, Bouvier and Quintin, *How Does Law Protect in War?* (3rd edn, Geneva: ICRC, 2011), 360–1. When the doctrine of self-execution is understood in this sense, it is related to structural requirements in conjunction with the validity of the rules. Other understandings of this doctrine have been developed by US courts, including the right of action and the intent of the government to recognize the treaty as enforceable before domestic courts. These two versions are related to the functional requirement of standing and are discussed in this chapter at 1.3.2.i .

[19] Raz, 'The Rule of Law and Its Virtue', 18 (n 1); Arthur Watts, 'The International Rule of Law', *German Yearbook of International Law*, 36/15 (1993), 39.

[20] Watts, 'The International Rule of Law', 39 (n 19).

Serbia; legislation allowing judges adjudicating international law cases to cite and rely upon international case law, international law academic writings, and other expert reports such as the UN and the ICRC.

1.2.2 Functional aspects

Judges have developed different doctrines and ways of interpretation, guided by policy considerations, for preventing the effective and equal application of the law upon all its subjects.

i. Validity and applicability of the international norms in domestic systems

Whether IHL rules represent applicable norms in the domestic legal system is not merely a normative decision but may be also a policy choice of the courts. While national constitutions may explicitly allow the importing of international law into their respective domestic legal systems, the courts still have the ability to decide, by using their interpretative tools, whether IHL is applicable or not. For example, if the constitution allows the direct application of one source of international law—treaty law or customary law, the constitutional reference to one source could be interpreted as implicitly incorporating the other source as well.[21] Other examples are the weight that should be given to those international norms where there is a conflict between an applicable international obligation and a domestic norm. The determination that a rule is of a customary nature is a finding of major importance for the direct applicability of IHL in dualist systems.

ii. Enforceability of international norms by national courts

Even when a norm is applicable in a given domestic legal system according to the constitution or any other endorsing legislation, there is no guarantee that the norm will be enforced by a national court. The US self-executing doctrine relating to the direct application of IHL is probably the best example of this. The US Constitution establishes that international treaties are part of the supreme law of the land.[22] At the same time, their enforcement has been restricted by judges through the development of self-executing doctrines.[23] One version of this judge-made doctrine

[21] Benvenisti, 'Judicial Misgivings Regarding the Application of International Norms: An Analysis of Attitudes of National Courts', *European Journal of International Law* 4/2 (1993), 162–4.

[22] The Supremacy Clause, United States Constitution. Article VI, clause 2, provides as follows: 'This Constitution, and the Laws of the United States which shall be made in Pursuance thereof; and all Treaties made, or which shall be made, under the Authority of the United States, shall be the supreme Law of the Land; and the Judges in every State shall be bound thereby, any Thing in the Constitution or Laws of any State to the Contrary notwithstanding'. Vazquez notes that: 'The history of the Supremacy Clause thus shows that its purpose was to avert violations of treaties attributable to the United States, and that the Founders sought to accomplish this goal by making treaties enforceable in the courts at the behest of affected individuals without the need for additional legislative action, either state or federal.' Carlos M. Vazquez, 'The Four Doctrines of Self-Executing Treaties', *American Journal of International Law*, 89/4 (1995) 699.

[23] The distinction between self-executing and non-self-executing treaties was introduced into United States jurisprudence by the Supreme Court for the first time in *Foster* v. *Neilson*, 27 U.S. (2 Pet.) 253 (1829).

is directly linked to policy reasons. Under this version, the possibility of invoking a treaty before a domestic court, is defined by the explicit deference to the state's position on the issue. Accordingly, a treaty is enforceable in US courts only if the state recognized such a competence while ratifying the treaty.[24] Hence, scholars such as John Yoo, who served as part of the legal team of the Bush administration during the war in Afghanistan, held the view that the Geneva Conventions cannot be enforced by a domestic court, but only by political or military channels.[25] This position was reflected in the famous footnote in *Johnson* v. *Eisentrager*, where the Supreme Court stated that it would not consider the merits of the Geneva Conventions.[26] A different position was introduced in *Hamdan*. The Supreme Court in *Hamdan* labelled the aforementioned passage in *Johnson* v. *Eisentrager* as a 'curious statement' and noted that it was 'buried in a footnote'. Although it ruled that the case before it did not require a decision on whether the Geneva Conventions could be directly enforced by a US court—because the domestic Article under review endorsed the international obligation—it applied the common Article 3 of the Geneva Conventions.[27] Indeed, *Hamdan* dealt with a domestic act that endorsed the Geneva Conventions. Yet the court could potentially have held the same position as in *Johnson* v. *Eisentrager*. Accordingly the Geneva Conventions are binding but cannot be enforceable by US courts, as in *Eisentrager* the question dealt similarly with the enforceability of the Geneva Conventions through a domestic act.[28] As astutely noted by Koh, who later became the legal advisor of the Obama administration, the 'majority of the Court denied the government's claim that enemy aliens could never enforce the Geneva Conventions in U.S. courts.'[29] Thus, the fact that the same court gave different rulings on that point would seem to indicate that the varying judgments are more the product of a policy choice than of a unified legal position.

iii. Skills

Seeking a remedy in court means that not only will judgments be given effect, but that the judgment will effectively apply the law by a competent court. In this regard, judges must apply the law correctly. Functionally, in their interpretation and application of IHL, judges may rely (to the extent made possible by their own legal system with international case law) on domestic cases from other jurisdictions

[24] Vazquez, 'The Four Doctrines of Self-Executing Treaties', 702–7 (n 22).

[25] J.G. Ku and J.C. Yoo, 'Hamdan V. Rumsfeld: The Functional Case for Foreign Affairs Deference to the Executive Branch' *Constitutional Commentary*, 23 (2006), 179, 190. See also, J.C. Yoo, 'Treaties and Public Lawmaking: A Textual and Structural Defense of Non-Self-Execution' *Columbia Law Review* 99/8 (1999), 2218.

[26] *Johnson* v. *Eisentrager*, 339 U. S. 763 (1950), at 789, n. 14.

[27] *Salim Ahmed Hamdan* v. *Donald H. Rumsfeld* et al., 548 U.S. 557 (2006) 63–5. Article 21 of the Uniform Code of Military Justice states that: 'The provisions of this chapter conferring jurisdiction upon courts-martial do not deprive military commissions, provost courts, or other military tribunals of concurrent jurisdiction with respect to offenders or offenses that *by statute or by the law of war may be tried* by military commissions, provost courts, or other military tribunals'.

[28] See discussion in Chapter 3.

[29] Harold Hongju Koh, 'Setting the World Right', *The Yale Law Journal*, 115/2350 (2006), 2350, 2363.

dealing with similar legal questions, academic writings, and other expert reports such as the ICRC or the UN. To a large extent, this is not what happened in the Serbian cases discussed in the first chapter.

The first step in the correct application of IHL is to qualify the conflict. An accurate qualification of the conflict is of major importance as the applicable IHL treaty and customary law depends on this preliminary determination. Nonetheless, this task is not always carried out by national courts, or at the very least—it is not always done accurately. The most striking example is probably the adjudication of cases related to the 'war on terror'. A vast academic literature has attempted to define the scope of this 'war', its qualification and hence the applicable law.[30] Different western jurisdictions, such as Australia, Canada or the UK,[31] (involved in reviewing legal questions related to detainees in Guantanamo) have completely ignored the applicability of IHL and the question of the qualification of the conflict.[32] National courts, contrary to academic writers, international courts and UN bodies (which have been examining at length the relations between IHL and international human rights law during armed conflict)[33] have been less attentive to the distinction between these two branches of international law. Indeed, courts do not always address both branches of law, even if they are applicable. In most cases, courts only look at human rights law. The reason for this is because access to the court is guaranteed more effectively through domestic human rights acts and constitutions. Moreover, politically and institutionally, human rights issues are less

[30] To mention only a few: Marco Sassòli, 'La Guerre contre le Terrorisme, le Droit International Humanitaire et le Statut de Prisonnier de Guerre', *Canadian Yearbook of International Law*, 39/211 (2001), 211–52; Marco Sassòli, 'Use and Abuse of the Laws of War in the "War Against Terrorism"', *Law and Inequality: A Journal of Theory and Practice*, 22 (2004), 195–221; Luigi Condorelli and Yasmin Naqvi, 'The War against Terrorism and *Jus in Bello*: Are the Geneva Conventions Out of Date?', in Andrea Bianchi (ed.), *Enforcing International Law Norms against Terrorism* (Oxford: Hart Publishing, 2004), 25–37; Christopher Greenwood, 'International Law and the "War against Terrorism"', *International Affairs*, 78/2 (2002), 301–17. For a resources list see Sassòli, Bouvier and Quintin, *How Does Law Protect in War?*, 129, 131–2 (n 18).

[31] *Hicks* v. *Ruddock et al.* discussed in Chapter 2; *Canada (Prime Minister)* v. *Khadr*, (2010); and *R (Abbasi)* v. *Secretary of State for Foreign and Commonwealth Affairs* discussed in Chapter 3.

[32] One of the rare cases which explicitly attempted to qualify the 'war on terror' was the *Hamdan* case of the US Supreme Court (*Salim Ahmed Hamdan* v. *Donald H. Rumsfeld et al.* (n 27)), whose outcome remains highly questionable: 'The United States Supreme Court found in *Hamdan* v. *Rumsfeld* that the military commissions set up in Guantanamo violated precisely those judicial guarantees prescribed by common Article 3 to the Four Geneva Conventions of 1949. Yet the court left open the question whether Hamdan, arrested in Afghanistan when the country was still occupied by the United States and its allies, should rather be covered, as I would submit by the law of international armed conflicts.' Marco Sassòli, 'Transnational Armed Groups and IHL' (Program on Humanitarian Policy and Conflict Research at Harvard University—Occasional Paper Series, Winter 2006), 20.

[33] See, for example, Cordula Droege, 'The Interplay between IHL and International Human Rights Law in Situation of Armed Conflict', *Israel Law Review*, 40/2 (2007), 310–55; Françoise J. Hampson, 'The Relationship between IHL and Human Rights Law from the Perspective of a Human Rights Body', *International Review of the Red Cross*, 90/871 (2008), 549–72. *Legal Consequences on the Construction of a Wall in the Occupied Palestinian Territory* (Advisory Opinion) ICJ Rep 9 July 2004, 43 ILM (2004) 1009, paragraph 106.

controversial in terms of judicial enforcement. This was the case in most of the Guantanamo cases that have been discussed in this book.[34] Yet, for a correct application of international law, there are situations in which it is necessary to rely on both branches i.e. IHL and international human rights law. Useful examples include the rules on detention during international armed conflict and the right to life and liberty in armed conflicts of a non-international character.[35] The Israeli HCJ is among one of those rare national courts that explicitly discuss the application of IHL and human rights law and their relationship.[36] The doctrinal framework was articulated in 2006 in the *Targeted Killing* case where the HCJ declared that IHL is the *lex specialis* law applicable during armed conflict. When there is a lacuna in that law, it can be supplemented by human rights law.[37]

1.3 Accessibility

1.3.1 Structural aspects

By denying the individual the right to invoke international law before the courts, the political branches of the state interfere with the possibility of having an accessible judiciary. Given the central position of the courts in ensuring the rule of international law, their accessibility is of paramount importance. For that purpose, it is not enough that a state endorses international law rules in its domestic legislation to make them enforceable. In order to make these laws enforceable, access to the courts must likewise be guaranteed by legislation.

[34] *Salim Ahmed Hamdan* v. *Donald H. Rumsfeld et al.* is in fact a remarkable exception in the context of American jurisprudence and application of IHL. See D. Weissbrodt and N.H. Nesbitt, 'The Role of the United States Supreme Court in Interpreting and Developing Humanitarian Law' Minnesota Law Review, 95/4 (2011), 1411–23.

[35] For the Guantanamo cases, for instance, if the detainees were to be defined as prisoners of war, they could have been held in detention without any criminal procedure until the end of hostilities. For other relevant situations in non-international armed conflict see Marco Sassòli and Laura M. Olson, 'The Legal Relationship between IHL and Human Rights Law where It Matters: Admissible Killing and Internment of Fighters in Non International Armed Conflict', *International Review of the Red Cross*, 90/871 (2008), 599.

[36] The official position of the State of Israel is that human rights treaties do not apply in the Occupied Palestinian Territories (OPT). See, State of Israel, 'International Covenant on Civil and Political Rights—Second Periodic Report' (20 November 2001), UN Doc CCPR/C/ISR/2001/2 (2001), paragraph 8. At first, when the question of the applicability of international human rights law in the OPT arose before the HCJ it was left open, and the Court was 'willing without deciding the matter, to rely upon the international conventions.' HCJ 7957/04, *Mara'abe et al.* v. *Israel Prime Minister et al.*, paragraph 27.

[37] HCJ 769/02, *The Public Committee against Torture in Israel et al.* v. *The Government of Israel et al.*, paragraph 18. This position has since been cited as a matter of evidence. See, for example, 'where there is a lacuna in the laws of armed conflict [..] it is possible to fill it by resorting to international human rights law.' HCJ 6659/06, *A and B* v. *The State of Israel*, (2008), paragraph 9.

1.3.2 Functional aspects

i. Standing

When courts rule that an international norm is valid and applicable in a given domestic system, access to the court can still be denied by the court itself. Rules on standing have been developed by courts, through which they define their role in applying IHL. For example, one of these rules is the demand for a 'private cause of action'. Under this doctrine (which in the US is another version of the self-executing doctrine) private parties may only enforce a treaty provision if they possess a private right of action conferred by the treaty. A treaty that does not confer upon the individual a private right is not self-executing. This approach has been criticized by various American scholars who claim that a private right of action is unnecessary, at least in cases in which the treaty is invoked defensively.[38] Nonetheless, it still represents the accepted understanding of the doctrine in US federal courts, and American jurisprudence increasingly refers to this requirement as the condition for a treaty to be self-executing.[39]

ii. Non-justiciability

The rule of law requires not only access to a court but an equal access to all its subjects. Providing access to court on a 'double standards' mode is obviously evidence of a practice contradicting this requirement. The issue of standing may well be regulated by national legislation and allow individuals or NGOs to access the court. However, avoidance doctrines developed by judges may impose *de facto* limitations upon the access to the court. These include doctrines of non-justiciability such as the political question or the act of state doctrine and questions of the convenient fora and subsidiarity rules—all doctrines developed by courts. One of the most pertinent case studies in this context is probably the one discussed in Chapter 2 concerning the legality of Israeli settlement. The access to a court for

[38] Vazquez, 'The Four Doctrines of Self-Executing Treaties', 719–22 (n 22). Henkin claims that courts should not require a private right of action both for defensive and offensive claims: 'lower courts, however, have suggested that treaties may be enforced in court only when they create a private right of action. This suggestion is untenable. Throughout our history, this Court has enforced treaties at the behest of the right holder, both defensively and offensively, even when the treaties have been no more explicit with respect to judicial enforcement than the GPW, and in many cases far less so.' Louis Henkin et al., 'Amicus Brief of Law Professors in Support of the Petitioner in the Hamdan case (Geneva—Enforceability)' (6 January 2006), 11 available at <http://www.hamdanvrumsfeld.com/HamdanvRumsfeldAmicusBriefofLawProfessorsLouisHenkinetal.pdf>. Hamdan was a case in which the obligations of the Geneva Conventions were raised defensibly—the claim was that Hamdan's rights were violated because the state violated the obligations set out in the Geneva Conventions. See *Salim Ahmed Hamdan* v. *Donald H. Rumsfeld et al.* (n 27). See also Benvenisti: 'if a judicial enforcement of international law is the goal, the doctrine of standing must be applied to admit individual suits that invoke international law, even when they fail to show an infringed personal right'. Benvenisti, 'Judges and Foreign Affairs', 440 (n 5).

[39] *Tel Oren* v. *Libyan Arab Republic*, 726 F.2d 774, (D.C. Cir. 1984) (J. Bork, concurring); *Argentine Republic* v. *Amerada Hess Shipping Corp.*, 488 U.S. 428, 440–2 (1989). Other cases are listed in Vazquez, 'The Four Doctrines of Self-Executing Treaties', 719, fn 114 (n 22).

reviewing this legal question has been denied not only by Israeli courts, but also by Canadian courts. Canada has ruled that the best forum for reviewing the legality of the settlements in the OPT are Israeli courts—the very same forum which systematically denies access on that issue, and which is unlikely to change its position because of strong institutional concerns. In ruling so, the victims were denied justice at national level.

1.4 Equal enforcement

The principle of the rule of law requires that the law be equitable and even-handed. This rule has two implications and it dictates that: (1) all of the law's subjects must be equal before the law, meaning that no state, organization or individual is above IHL (the structural aspect); (2) the law should be equally enforced upon all its subjects (the functional aspect).

Indeed IHL applies equally to all its subjects that are party to an armed conflict. No state or any other organ enjoys a normatively privileged status that implies a different treatment. IHL is a unique branch of law in the sense that it regulates the behaviour of its subjects during situations of armed conflict.[40] Based on the clear distinction between *jus ad bellum* and *jus in bellum* all belligerents are equally bound and protected by IHL, irrespective of the reasons that triggered the original conflict and which side is deemed responsible for it (although the applicable rules may differ according to the subject, whether it is a state, a non-state actor or an individual).[41] If, in practice, powerful states or other actors violate the law, even if intentionally, it does not mean that the law is not applicable to them.

The legislation itself, i.e., the structural aspect, is usually not an obstacle for the equal application of international law. The law's provisions are usually of equal application by definition and it is very rare that the law itself explicitly provides for its uneven application. Yet courts are frequently responsible for a selective enforcement of the law (the functional aspect). A 'double standards' application of the law through, for example, the application of the avoidance doctrines, is a practice contradicting this requirement. Indeed, the application of these avoidance doctrines is closely related to the question of the equal application of the law. In politically sensitive cases courts will choose to follow their government's stance and won't exercise their competence, while in politically 'easy cases' they will decide to do so.

[40] One side would necessarily breach the law as the use of force between states is prohibited by Article 2(4) of the United Nations Charter. As for non-international armed conflict—it is illegal to use force against state agents according to domestic criminal law.

[41] This principle was recognized in the preamble of 1977 Additional Protocol I. See also Sassòli, Bouvier and Quintin, *How Does Law Protect in War?*, 114–15 (n 18).

2. Back to the spectrum: assessing the roles of national courts in light of the rule of law principles

I will now proceed to examine how each of the functional roles of courts, as previously identified, are harmonized with the principles of the rule of law. The extent of compliance with the principles of independence, impartiality, effectiveness, accessibility, and equality while performing a given role will be discussed.

The *apologist* role of states, as Chapter 1 shows, is manifested through the court legitimating states' illegal acts and policies even if this involves a misuse or a distortion of the law. The Israeli case study looks at a court which seriously addresses IHL and is characterized by holding a high level of knowledge of the law of military occupation, which it has been applying for more than forty years. Nonetheless in order to facilitate Israel's illegal settlement policy, the court misinterpreted Article 43 of the Hague Regulations in a manner which clearly violates the purpose of the law. The Serbian case study on the other hand, shows how the same role of legitimating the state has been achieved by a far less sophisticated court, whose professional competences are new.

It is submitted that the apologist application of IHL must remain outside the legitimate choices available under the rule of law. The apologist application of IHL violates the founding principles of the rule of law as they relate to the judiciary's function. First, it completely defies the fundamental requirement that the judiciary be independent and impartial. A court that serves as a legitimating agency for the state's illegal actions, does not maintain its neutral position. The neutral position is the basis of a court's legitimacy, based on a 'triadic structure', i.e. two litigating parties and a third neutral body serving as a conflict resolver. In the apologist function, this fundamental structure is dissolved and the court becomes no more than the executive's long arm. In times of conflict this may be as dangerous as lethal arms. In addition, the right to access a court cannot be realized in a meaningful manner, as the rule of law requires access to a court in which justice is done. Similarly the demand that the law should be effectively applied is not fulfilled. The law must guide the behaviour of its subjects upon which all subjects shall rely. For this reason, the rule of law's founding principle is that the law will comply with certain procedural rules, such as decisions being published, not being retroactive, but being sufficiently clear and settled. If judges provide a distorted interpretation of the law to justify the state's act, whether that may be related to their lack of skills or not, the law is not effective. It does not provide for a reliable source upon which subjects can base their choices of action and legitimate expectation of how the society shall be governed. Misuse of international law by national jurisdictions may have far-reaching negative consequences beyond the specific facts of the case over the long term as this promotes development of a bad law, which runs the risk of being cited and adopted by other national jurisdictions.

The law imposes on courts a margin of interpretation allowing only limited political manoeuvre. Given that further political objectives may be in certain situations irresistible (especially during ongoing hostilities, in which total independence of courts is not always feasible), the study identifies other functional ways for courts to address these political constraints which may be more acceptable from the rule of law perspective. The second chapter discussed the avoiding role of courts, developed by courts to deal exactly with this kind of situation. Policy considerations, mainly related to their own institutional position within their domestic governmental system and concerns of non-compliance with their decisions, may lead courts to choose the avoiding function, allowing the legal issue to be dealt with by political actors. Courts avoid or adjudicate cases in a way that correspond to their relationship with the government and their degree of independency vis-à-vis the political branches. The willingness to exercise competence is not related to the legal question itself because, as is shown in the case studies, while in one jurisdiction the issue is not justiciable, in another it is. This was well illustrated by the US and Israeli *Targeted Killing* cases.

Is the use of avoidance doctrines a deficiency or a legitimated self-restraint policy within the rule of law framework? From the rule of law perspective the avoiding role of courts remains highly problematic as it violates several of its basic concepts. The most notable concept is the right of access to court and the requirement of a legal system to enforce the law in an equal and effective manner. Through the use of avoidance doctrine developed by judges, the court denies a party access to court. Consequently the law is not enforced and alleged violations remain unaccounted for and no remedy is provided. While courts have established factors for the application of avoidance doctrines, it has not always been possible to predict when courts would render a judgment on its merits, as extra-legal considerations are often involved. This means that the law and the avoidance doctrines are often applied in a double standards mode, in breach of the equality principle, which most often corresponds to the state position. Such application was clearly demonstrated through the ATS case studies. When the state directs a court as to when to exercise its competence and when not to, the principles of independence and impartiality of the court are also diminished.

Having said that, the positive aspect of the avoiding role of courts is that, unlike while exercising an apologist role, courts do not produce distorted jurisprudence, which risks being cited by other jurisdictions. Thus, in cases in which the court is not sufficiently independent and does not possess a strong enough position to apply the laws governing armed conflicts, it may be preferable to avoid exercising its competence. By doing so it prevents a situation in which it would distort the law, and confer a rubber stamp legitimizing abuse and misuse of international law. In both situations, whether performing an apologetic or avoidance function, the political branches would be able to pursue its acts, even if these are in violation of IHL. In the latter case, however, the political branch would not enjoy the legal aura provided by a court in a democratic society. Thus, for example, it may be preferable that Israeli courts avoid ruling on whether Article 49(6) of the Fourth Geneva Convention has been violated through the Israeli settlement policy, than to issue a decision that will, in a complete distortion of the law, rule that the law was respected. While avoiding exercising competence on this question, Israeli courts do not provide a legal justification for the illegal act. The issue is left to be decided in the political sphere. NGOs could then advance the argument that the law has been violated and maybe gain public support, which is more difficult to achieve if a court with a good reputation, like the Israeli HCJ, had approved the illegal policy. Therefore, it seems that recourse to such avoidance doctrines shall be justified during a transition phase. Once courts establish a firm institutional position that enables them to apply IHL, whether it is in support or against the position of the state, the recourse to avoidance doctrines should be denied. This is because for an international society to be governed by the rule of law, the role of the courts should be directed toward the *normative application* mode. This is the mode which seems to be the favourite option from the rule of law perspective.

The normative application mode prevails over the ideal of the international community to be ruled by a law that is enforced by courts, and that courts exercise their competence as an independent and impartial body. Of course within the normative application role, legal choices are also motivated by political preference. Indeed, IHL was drafted by states to govern the use of force during armed conflicts. An important degree of discretion was left to accommodate the needs of the military, and therefore positive law itself provides a margin of discretion. Yet this is not to be confused with a position that all interpretations can be endorsed due to the indeterminacy of the law.

In order to deal with the inherent political complexity of international law, the normative application role has been applied in varying degrees, from complete deference to the state all the way up to imposing limits on the political branches. During the process of a court forming its authority to apply the law of armed conflict upon the executive, courts have developed a nuanced and gradual way to do it. This takes the form of an open dialogue with the other legislative and executive branches, through use of the deference technique.

The deferral technique paves the way for an important transition toward the exercise of judicial review. Cases relating to armed conflicts issues, previously seen as touching forbidden area and therefore avoided, have entered the sphere of judicial review, opening the gate for the exercise of the most significant role of courts from the rule of law perspective. At first glance, it may appear that deferring to the state and avoiding a case amount to the same thing; both situations let the state pursue its acts. But despite the similarity, the difference is significant. When the court exercises its power of judicial review over a case, as opposed to avoidance, even when it culminates in a decision of complete deference, it sends an important signal to the political branches. The messages is that this time the court deferred, but next time, the court may well decide to climb up the 'judicial review ladder', and increase its level of interference. Having opened the gate of judicial review, a reversion to the doctrine of avoidance is less likely. Thus, deference is a mid-way position. It allows the state to act according to legal standards, while at the same time signalling that if the law is violated again in the future, the court may decide to affirm its position and intervene more explicitly. Courts are still novices in applying this relatively new mode, which is mainly applicable for human rights violations and less for conduct of hostilities, as demonstrated in Chapter 3.

Yet the follow-up to the Israeli HCJ *Torture* and *Targeted Killing* cases well illustrates the deficiency of the deferral technique. Instead of promoting the normative application of the law, it may lead to an apologist transformation of the court's ruling by the misuse of the discretion allocated to the state. In the long run, deference may lead the court in effect to being apologist to the state. Thus, ideally, courts should slowly abandon this technique. Instead, courts need to instruct the state explicitly and unequivocally as to what the law says and the legal consequences of wrongdoing as required by the rule of law. Yet, this is not an easy task. IHL cases involve sensitive and complex issues, as indicated by the *Human Shield* ruling and the non-compliance of the State of Israel. This provides an indication of the court's institutional limits and its willingness to impose future limits on the state while at the same time balancing the need to maintain its own authority and respect.

Courts exercise a *judicial activist* role when they impose international law on domestic law, without being explicitly entrusted to do so by their national system. The disparity between national and international law may occur for diverse reasons. One such reason may be for example when the domestic legal process results in legislation that corresponds to the state's self-interest and not with the international requirement. This has been apparent with universal jurisdiction legislation.[42] Other impediments caused by national legislation may be justifications and defences that exclude criminal responsibility for IHL violations, statutes of limitation, and immunity or amnesty laws (as shown by the *Garzón* case). A theoretical solution for this disparity may be found in Kelsen's observation that 'even when national courts apply a domestic rule they apply international law.'[43] Thus, it may be argued that as in certain national legal systems laws that are unconstitutional may be repealed by the court, domestic laws contradicting international law shall be repealed.[44] As seen by the *Garzón* case though, this may trigger a significant political objection.

As stated by Judge Higgins, a judge makes choices between claims which have varying degrees of legal merits. Yet, as Chapter 4 shows, a judge may choose a stance that goes beyond that legitimate 'normative application' scale, rendering a utopian decision. This is when a national court interprets a rule beyond its purpose

[42] For example, universal jurisdiction, if enacted, has in most cases been either replaced or restricted by other jurisdictional conditions. See Antonio Cassese, *International Criminal Law* (Oxford: Oxford University Press, 2003), 309.

[43] Hans Kelsen, 'Law as a Coercive Order' in Hans Kelsen, *General Theory of Law and State* (Cambridge, Mass: Harvard University Press, 1949), 347.

[44] See Common Article 1 of the Four Geneva Conventions which states that 'The High Contracting Parties undertake to respect and to ensure respect for the present Convention in all circumstances'. Apparently the Israeli HCJ has followed this approach, and so has the Israeli military courts in the occupied territories. For example domestic Israeli law on illegal combatants, which enables the state to detain enemy 'unlawful combatants' until the end of hostilities without penal prosecution, was brought to review before the HCJ also in light of IHL. The Ofer military court ruled in *Swartz* that a military court is competent to cancel an order of the military commander if it contradicts IHL, MC 06/5, *Swartz* v. *The Military Commander* (2005). That competence was affirmed by the Ofer military court of appeals (MCA) in the case of *Hassin*; MCA 1779/08, *Hassin* v. *The Military Prosecutor* (2010) (on file with the author). However, the final ruling of a court may well be in contradiction of IHL. This is less a structural problem of the rule of law, and related more to a functional assessment.

and the intention of the drafters in the name of ethical values. Both extremes of the spectrum, utopian and apology, reflect in fact a policy approach, a political function of the court. They only differ in the content of the social values and political goals pursued. Both modes of function do not correspond to the rule of law principles (as far as it concerns the issue of effective application of the law) for very similar reasons.

One of the main problems faced by the international legal order is the legislative process and the possibilities of elaborating international law. As the international legislative processes are mainly in the hands of national (and sometimes international) executives, we often reach an impasse. Therefore, we tend to be willing, in order to improve the existing structure, to empower leading national courts with legislative authority. Yet, in light of their current practice—their support of the executive and the double standards application mode, in which the ruling may vary depending on the nationality of the victims or the responsible state—it becomes questionable whether it is desirable to delegate to courts an additional competence, namely that of law developer. It seems that at this stage national courts should first reinforce their reputation as institutions that enforce international law in a legitimated mode.

Certainly further reflection on the relations between legislative bodies at national level and international level is needed. After all, 'A court is [only] a court.'

3. Looking forward

As this study has shown, the functional role of the courts is a combination of contradictions and of mixed attitudes—sometimes they hold an apologist role, in other cases a normative, activist, utopian or an avoiding one. Seemingly, national courts are in the process of defining their own role as enforcing organs of international law.

Some hypotheses which influence courts in their choice of functional role consist of legal and extra-legal factors, including:

(1) National courts will not be able to derive jurisdiction from international law beyond the competence accorded to them by their own national constitutional framework. Therefore the validity of IHL within domestic systems and the authority of courts to apply it must be guaranteed at national level. Most importantly, can IHL be directly applied; what is the normative status of international law where it conflicts with a domestic rule? May courts repeal domestic legislation contradicting international law as being unconstitutional?

(2) The traditional independence and activism of courts in a given country. How successful have courts been in limiting the state with regard to other branches of law? As observed by scholars, because of the special nature of international law, and more specifically the law applicable during armed conflict, too much independence is not necessarily a guarantee of a better

enforcement of the IHL; courts have to take into account political concerns and consequences of their ruling.

(3) Is there an active and independent civil society and media presence which could influence public opinion and demand judicial scrutiny over IHL issues?

(4) The importance of the interests of their country that may be jeopardized; seemingly it would be easier for courts to deliver a ruling against the state for past violations, such as human rights violations, which do not have an impact on future policies.

(5) The national courts' contribution to the global legal system—have international tribunals and institutions already reviewed the same issue/context? For example, the exercise of universal jurisdiction over crimes that originated in the Balkans or Rwanda has already been established. These crimes were more easily prosecuted after the establishment of the international ad hoc tribunals which provided authoritative legal analysis on the subject. This served as a legal guidance for national courts. Moreover, politically too, it was easier for national courts to function where their decisions are subsequent to international courts' decisions.

(6) What is the level of the court and the objective capacities and skills of the judges with regard to IHL? Beyond treaty law, are judges also familiar with IHL jurisprudence, customary law, and academic writings?

(7) The existence of a national IHL legal expertise: do private and military lawyers, state prosecution attorneys, NGO legal advisors, rely upon IHL in their claims? Are they sufficiently familiar with IHL rules, and do they have the procedural tools and know-how required for the purposes of applying them in the particularity of each domestic system? Is IHL education available in universities, through professionals' training courses, International Committee of the Red Cross teaching projects, and the like?

It is hoped that this study will serve as a tool for future reflection—reflection on the factors which lead courts to choose any of the functional roles identified and the conditions for optimal fulfilment of the international rule of law.

Bibliography

BOOKS AND ARTICLES

Allott, P., *Towards the International Rule of Law: Essays in Integrated Constitutional Theory* (Cameron May, London, 2007).

Arieli, S. and Sfard, M., *The Wall of Folly* (Yediot Sfarim, Tel Aviv, 2008).

Balkin, J.M., 'Deconstructive Practice and Legal Theory' (1987) 96 Yale Law Journal 743, pp. 743–86.

Balkin, J.M., 'Deconstruction' in D. Patterson (ed.), *A Companion to Philosophy of Law and Legal Theory* (Blackwell Publishing, Oxford, 1999), pp. 367–74.

Barak, A., 'Foreword: A Judge on Judging: The Role of a Supreme Court in a Democracy' (2002–2003) 116 Harvard Law Review 19, pp. 19–162.

Barak, A., *The Judge in a Democracy,* (Princeton University Press, New Jersey, 2006).

Batros B. and Webb P., 'Accountability for Torture Abroad and the Limits of the Act of State Doctrine Comments on Habib v. Commonwealth of Australia', (2010) Journal of International Criminal Justice 8, pp. 1153–74.

Bazyler, M., 'Abolishing the Act of State Doctrine' (1986) 134 University of Pennsylvania Law Review 325, pp. 325–98.

Beaulac, S., 'The Rule of Law in International Law Today' in G. Palombella and N. Walker (eds), *Relocating the Rule of Law* (Hart Publishing, Oxford, 2009), pp. 197–223.

Ben-Naftali, O., 'A Judgment in the Shadow of International Criminal Law' (2007) 5 Journal of International Criminal Justice 2, pp. 322–31.

Ben-Naftali, O., Gross, A. and Michaeli, K., 'Illegal Occupation: the Framing of the Occupied Palestinian Territory', 24 Berkeley J. Int'l L. (2005) 551, 584–7.

Ben-Naftali, O. and Michaeli, K., 'We Must Not Make a Scarecrow of the Law: A Legal Analysis of the Israeli Policy of Targeted Killings' (2003) 36 Cornell International Law Journal, pp. 233–92.

Benvenisti, E., 'Judges and Foreign Affairs: A Comment on the Institute de Droit International's Resolution on "The Activities of National Courts and the International Relations of their State"' (1994) 5 European Journal of International Law 1, pp. 423–39.

Benvenisti, E., 'Judicial Misgivings Regarding the Application of International Norms: An Analysis of Attitudes of National Courts' (1993) 4 European Journal of International Law 2, pp. 159–83.

Benvenisti, E., 'National Courts and the "War on Terrorism"' in A. Bianchi (ed.), *Enforcing International Law Norms against Terrorism* (Hart Publishing, Oxford, 2004), pp. 308–25.

Benvenisti, E., 'Reclaiming Democracy: The Strategic Uses of Foreign and International Law by National Courts' (2008) 102 American Journal of International Law 2, pp. 241–74.

Benvenisti, E., *The International Law of Occupation* (2nd edn, Princeton University Press, Princeton, 2004).

Benvenisti, E., 'United We Stand: National Courts Reviewing Counterterrorism Measures' in A. Bianchi and A. Keller (eds), *Counterterrorism: Democracy's Challenge* (Hart Publishing, Oxford, 2008). Available at: <http://papers.ssrn.com/sol3/papers.cfm?abstract_id=965638>, pp. 1–33.

Benvenisti, E. and Downs, G.W., 'National Courts, Domestic Democracy, and the Evolution of International Law' (2009) 20 European Journal of International Law 1, pp. 59–72.

Bhuta, N., 'The Antinomies of Transformative Occupation' (2005) 16 European Journal of International Law 4, pp. 721–40.
Bianchi, A., 'Italian Court of Cassation Ruling on Immunity from Suit for Damages for Deportation and Forced Labor during World War II (Comment to Decision)' (2005) 99 American Journal of International Law 1, pp. 242–8.
Bianchi, A., 'Serious Violations of Human Rights and Foreign States' Accountability Before Municipal Courts' in L. Vohrar (ed.), *Man's Inhumanity to Man. Essays in Honour of Judge Antonio Cassese* (Kluwer Law International, The Hague/London/Boston, 2003), pp. 149–82.
Bickel, A.M., *The Least Dangerous Branch—The Supreme Court at the Bar of Politics* (Yale University Press, New Haven/London, 1962).
Bickel, A.M., 'The Supreme Court, 1960—Term Foreword: The Passive Virtues' (1961) 75 Harvard Law Review 40, pp. 40–244.
Bothe, M., 'Occupation, Belligerent' in R. Bernhardt (ed.), *Encyclopedia of Public International Law* (1997), iii, pp. 763–5.
Boyd, K. Lee, 'Universal Jurisdiction and Structural Reasonableness' (2004) 40 Texas International Law Journal 1, pp. 1–58.
Bradley, C., *International Law in the U.S. Legal System*, OUP, 2013.
Bradly Wendel, W., 'Legal Advising and the Rule of Law' in K. Tranter et al. (eds), *Reaffirming Legal Ethics—Taking Stock and New Ideas* (Routledge, Abingdon, 2010), pp. 45–56.
Brown, R.L., 'When Political Questions Affect Individual Rights: The Other Nixon v United States' (1993) Supreme Court Review 125, pp. 125–55.
Brownlie, I., *Principles of Public International Law* (7th edn, Oxford University Press, New York, 2008).
Brownlie, I., *The Rule of Law in International Affairs: International Law at the Fiftieth Anniversary of the United Nations* (Martinus Nijhoff Publishers, The Hague, 1998).
Caron, D., 'Towards A Political Theory of International Courts and Tribunals' (2007) 24 Berkeley Journal of International Law, pp. 401–22.
Carruthers, J.M. and Crawford, E.B., 'Kuwait Airways Corporation v. Iraqi Airways Company' (2003) 52 International and Comparative Law Quarterly 3, pp. 761–74.
Carty, A., 'The Continuing Influence of Kelsen on the General Perception of the Discipline of International Law' (1998) 9 European Journal of International Law 2, pp. 344–54.
Casper, J.D., 'The Supreme Court and National Policy Making' (1976) 70 American Political Science Review 1, pp. 50–63.
Cassese, A., 'Implementation of International Rules within National Systems'—Chapter 12—in *International Law* (2nd edn Oxford University Press, New York, 2005), pp. 220–32.
Cassese, A., *International Criminal Law* (Oxford University Press, Oxford, 2003).
Cassese, A., *International Law* (2nd edn, Oxford University Press, New York, 2005).
Cassese, A., 'On Some Merits of the Israeli Judgment on Targeted Killings' (2007) 5 Journal of International Criminal Justice 2, pp. 339–45.
Cassese, A., 'On the Use of Criminal Law Notions in Determining State Responsibility for Genocide' (2007) 5 Journal of International Criminal Justice 4, pp. 875–87.
Cassese, A., 'Remarks on Scelle's Theory of "Role Splitting" (*dédoublement fonctionnel*) in International Law' (1990) 1 European Journal of International Law, pp. 210–231.
Cassese, A., *Violence and Law in the Modern Age* (Princeton University Press, Princeton, 1988).
Charlesworth, H., 'Comment' (2003) 24 Adelaide Law Review 13, pp. 13–14.
Charney, J.I., 'International Criminal Law and the Role of Domestic Courts' (2001) 95 American Journal of International Law 1, pp. 120–4.
Charney, J.I., 'Judicial Deference in Foreign Relations' (1989) 83 American Journal of International Law 4, pp. 805–13.

Chesney, R.M., 'Unravelling Deference: *Hamdan*, the Judicial Power, and Executive Treaty Interpretations' (2006) 92 Iowa Law Review, pp. 1723–82.

Chesney, R., 'Who May Be Killed? Anwar al-Awlaki as a Case Study in the International Legal Regulation of Lethal Force' (2011) 13 Yearbook of International Humanitarian Law, pp. 3–60 (forthcoming).

Chesterman, S., 'An International Rule of Law?' (2008) 56 American Journal of Comparative Law, pp. 331–61.

Chesterman, S., 'The Rule of Law', in Max Planck Encyclopedia of Public International Law, online at <http://www.mpepil.com>.

Chetail, V., 'The Contribution of the International Court of Justice to International Humanitarian Law' (2003) 85 International Review of the Red Cross, pp. 235–69.

Chinkin, C., 'International Humanitarian Law, Human Rights and the UK courts' in Boisson de Chazournes, L. and Kohen, Marcelo G., (eds) *International law and the quest for its implementation*: liber amicorum (Vera Gowlland-Debbas, Martinus Nijhoff, Leiden, The Netherlands, 2010).

Chinkin C., 'U.N. Human Rights Council fact-finding missions: lessons from Gaza' in Arsanjani, M., Cogan, J., Sloane, R. and Wiessner, S., (eds) *Looking to the future: essays on international law in honor of W. Michael Reisman* (Martinus Nijhoff, Leiden, 2010).

Chinkin, C. and Charlesworth, H., *The boundaries of international law: a feminist analysis* Melland Schill studies in international law (Manchester University Press, Manchester, UK, 2000).

Ciampi, A., 'The Italian Court of Cassation Asserts Civil Jurisdiction over Germany in a Criminal Case Relating to the Second World War: The *Civitella* case' (2009) 7 Journal of International Criminal Justice 3, pp. 597–615.

Clapham, A., 'Extending International Criminal Law beyond the Individual to Corporations and Armed Opposition Groups' (2008) 6 Journal of International Criminal Justice 2, pp. 899–926.

Cole, D., 'Challenging Covert War: The Politics of the Political Question Doctrine' (1985) 26 Harvard International Law Journal 1, pp. 115–88.

Collins, L., 'Foreign Relations and the Judiciary' (2002) 51 International and Comparative Law Quarterly 3, pp. 485–510.

Condorelli, L. and Naqvi, Y., 'The War against Terrorism and *Jus in Bello*: Are the Geneva Conventions Out of Date?' in A. Bianchi (ed.), *Enforcing International Law Norms against Terrorism* (Hart Publishing, Oxford, 2004), pp. 25–37.

Cornell, D., 'Violence of the Masquerade: Law dressed up as Justice' (1990) 11 Cardozo Law Review, pp. 1047–64.

Cotterrell, R., *The Sociology of Law* (Butterworths, London, 1984).

Crawford, J., 'International Law and the Rule of Law' (2003) 24 Adelaide Law Review 3, pp. 3–12.

Cryer, R., Friman, H., Robinson, D., Wilmshurst, E., *An Introduction to International Criminal Law and Procedure* (Cambridge University Press, Cambridge, 2007).

D'Amato, A., 'Is International Law Coercive?' (2008) Northwestern University School of Law Paper Series, pp. 1–36.

D'Argent, P., *Les Réparations de Guerre en Droit International Public* (Bruylant, Brussels, 2003).

Dahl, R., 'Decision-Making in a Democracy: The Supreme Court as a National Policy-Maker' (1957) Journal of Public Law 6, pp. 279–95.

Daillier, P. and Pellet, A., *Droit International Public* (7ème éd., L.G.D.J., Paris, 2002).

Davies, M., 'Kuwait Airways Corp v Iraqi Airways Co.—The Effect in Private International Law of Breach of Public International Law by a State Actor' (2001) 2 Melbourne Journal of International Law 2, pp. 523–34.

Davis, J., *Justice across Borders: The Struggle for Human Rights in U.S. Courts* (Cambridge University Press, Cambridge, 2008).

De Greiff, P., 'Justice and Reparations' in P. De Greiff (ed.), *The Handbook of Reparations* (Oxford University Press, Oxford, 2006), pp. 451–77.

De Sena, P. and De Vittor, F., 'State Immunity and Human Rights: The Italian Supreme Court Decision on the Ferrini Case' (2005) 16 European Journal of International Law 1, pp. 89–112.

Del Ponte, C. and Sudetic, C., *Madame Prosecutor: Confrontations With Humanity's Worst Criminals and the Culture of Impunity* (Other Press, New York, 2009).

Denza, E., 'The Relationship between International and National Law' in M.D. Evans (ed.), *International Law* (2nd edn, Oxford University Press, New York, 2006), pp. 423–46.

Department of Justice, 'Department of Justice Position in "Unocal"' (2003) 97 American Journal of International Law 3, pp. 703–6.

Derrida, J., 'The Force of Law: The Mystical Foundation of Authority' (1990) 11 Cardozo Law Review 920, pp. 920–1046.

Dicey, A.V., *Introduction to the Study of the Law of the Constitution* (10th edn, Macmillan, London, 1959).

Dicey, A.V., *Introduction to the Study of the Law of the Constitution* (Macmillan, London, 1885).

Dinstein, Y., 'Legislation Under Article 43 of the Hague Regulations: Belligerent Occupation and Peace building' (Program on Humanitarian Policy and Conflict Research at Harvard University—Occasional Paper Series, Fall 2004), pp. 1–18.

Dinstein, Y., *The International Law of Belligerent Occupation* (Cambridge University Press, Cambridge, 2009).

Dinstein, Y., 'The Israeli Supreme Court and the Law of Belligerent Occupation: Article 43 of the Hague Regulations' (1995) 25 Israeli Yearbook on Human Rights 1, pp. 1–20.

Dinstein, Y., 'The Legislative Power in Administered Territories' (1972) 2 Tel Aviv University Law Review, pp. 505–11 (in Hebrew).

Dinstein, Y., 'The Maintenance of Public Order and Life in the Administered Territories' (1984) 10 Tel Aviv Law Review, pp. 405–12 (in Hebrew).

Dolzer, R., 'The Settlement of War-Related Claims: Does International Law Recognize a Victim's Private Right of Action? Lessons after 1945' (2002) 20 Berkeley Journal of International Law, pp. 296–341.

Dörmann, K. and Geiβ, R., 'The Implementation of Grave Breaches into Domestic Legal Orders' (2009) 7 Journal of International Criminal Justice 4, pp. 703–21.

Droege, C., 'The Interplay between International Humanitarian Law and International Human Rights Law in Situation of Armed Conflict' (2007) 40 Israel Law Review 2, pp. 310–55.

Dugard, J. and Reynolds, J., 'Apartheid, International Law, and the Occupied Palestinian Territory' (2013) European Journal of International Law 24/3, p. 1–47.

Dupuy, P.-M., 'The Unity of Application of International Law at the Global Level and the Responsibility of Judges' (2007) 1 European Journal of Legal Studies 2, p. 1–23.

Dutli, M.T., 'The ICRC Advisory Service on International Humanitarian Law' in M. Bothe (ed.), *Towards a Better Implementation of International Humanitarian Law* (Arno Spitz, Berlin, 2001), pp. 223.

Dworkin, R., *A Matter of Principle* (Mass: Harvard University Press, Cambridge, 1985).

Ellis, M.S., 'Coming to Terms with Its Past—Serbia's New Court for the Prosecution of War Crimes' (2004) 22 Berkeley Journal of International Law, pp. 165–94.

Eser, A., 'Defences in War Crimes' (1994) 24 Israel Yearbook on Human Rights, pp. 201–34.

Eser, A., 'Grounds for Excluding Criminal Responsibility' in O. Triffterer (ed.), *Commentary on the Rome Statute of the ICC: Observers' Notes, Article by Article* (Nomos Verlagsgesellschaft, Baden-Baden, 1999), Article 31 pp. 863–78.

Evans, M., 'International Wrongs and National Jurisdiction' in M. Evans (ed.), *Remedies in International Law: the Institutional Dilemma* (Hart Publishing, Oxford, 1998), pp. 173–90.

Falk, R., 'Casting the Spell: The New Haven School of International Law' (1995) 104. The Yale Law Journal 7, pp. 1991–2008.

Falk, R., *Human Rights Horizons: The Pursuit of Justice in a Globalizing World* (Routledge, New York, 2000).

Falk, R., *The Role of Domestic Courts in the International Legal Order* (Syracuse University Press, Syracuse, 1964).

Falk, R., 'The Shimoda Case: A Legal Appraisal of the Atomic Attacks on Hiroshima and Nagasaki' (1965) 59 American Journal of International Law 4, pp. 759–93.

Fassbender, B., 'Can Victims Sue State Officials for Torture? Reflections on Rasul v. Myers from the Perspective of International Law' (2008) 6 Journal of International Criminal Justice 2, pp. 347–69.

Ferdinandusse, W., *Direct Application of International Criminal Law by National Courts* (Cambridge University Press, Cambridge, 2006).

Finnis, J., *Natural Law and Natural Rights* (Oxford University Press, New York, 1980).

Fletcher, G., 'Citizenship and Personhood in the Jurisprudence of War: Hamdi, Padilla and the Detainees in Guantánamo Bay' (2004) 2 Journal of International Criminal Justice 4, pp. 953–66.

Focarelli, C., 'Denying Foreign State Immunity for Commission of International Crimes: The Ferrini Decision' (2005) 54 International Comparative Law Quarterly, pp. 951–8.

Fox, G., 'Re-examining the Act of State Doctrine: An Integrated Conflicts Analysis' (1992) 33 Harvard International Law Journal 2, pp. 521–70.

Fox, H., *The Law of State Immunity* (Oxford University Press, New York, 2002).

Franck, T.M., *Fairness in International Law and Institutions* (Oxford University Press, New York, 1995).

Franck, T.M., *Political Questions/Judicial Answers: Does the Rule of Law Apply to Foreign Affairs?* (Princeton University Press, Princeton, 1992).

Frulli, M., 'When Are States Liable Towards Individuals for Serious Violations of Humanitarian Law? The *Marković* Case' (2003) 1 Journal of International Criminal Justice 2, pp. 406–27.

Fuller, L., *The Morality of Law* (Yale University Press, New Haven, 1964).

Gaeta, P., 'Are Victims of Serious Violations of International Humanitarian Law Entitled to Compensation?' in O. Ben-Naftali (ed.), *International Human Rights and Humanitarian Law* (Oxford University Press, Oxford, 2011), pp. 305–27.

Gaeta, P., 'May Necessity be Available as a Defense for Torture in the Interrogation of Suspected Terrorists?' (2004) 2 Journal of International Criminal Justice 3, pp. 785–94.

Gallagher, K., 'Civil Litigation and Transitional Business—An Alien Tort Statute Primer' (2010) 8 Journal of International Criminal Justice 3, pp. 745–67.

Gallagher, K., 'Universal Jurisdiction in Practice: Efforts to Hold Donald Rumsfeld and Other High-Level United States Officials Accountable for Torture' (2009) 7 Journal of International Criminal Justice 5, pp. 1087–116.

Gasser, H.P., 'International Committee of the Red Cross (ICRC)' in Max Planck Encyclopedia of International Law, online at <http://www.mpepil.com>.

Gattini, A., 'The UN Compensation Commission: Old Rules, New Procedures on War Reparations' (2002) 13 European Journal of International Law 1, pp. 161–81.

Gattini, A., 'To What Extent are State Immunity and Non-Justiciability Major Hurdles to Individuals' Claim for War Damages?' (2003) 1 Journal of International Criminal Justice 2, pp. 348–67.

Gattini, A., 'War Crimes and State Immunity in the Ferrini Decision' (2005) 3 Journal of International Criminal Justice 1, pp. 224–42.

Gillard, E.C., 'Reparation for Violations of International Humanitarian Law' (2003) 85 International Review of the Red Cross 851, pp. 529–53.

Ginbar, Y., 'Celebrating' a Decade of Legalised Torture in Israel', pp. 169–87. Available at: <http://projects.essex.ac.uk/ehrr/V6N1/Ginbar.pdf>.

Graig, P.P., 'Formal and Substantive Conceptions of the Rule of law: An Analytical Framework' in *Public Law* (1997), pp. 467–87.

Greenspan, M., *The Modern Law of Land Warfare* (University of California Press, Berkley, 1959).

Greenwood, C., 'International Law and the "War against Terrorism"' (2002) 78 International Affairs 2, pp. 301–17.

Greenwood, C., 'The Administration of Occupied Territories' in E. Playfair (ed.), *International Law and the Administration of Occupied Territories* (Clarendon Press, Oxford, 1992), pp. 241–66.

Gross, A., 'Human Proportions: Are Human Rights the Emperor's New Clothes of the International Law of Occupation?' (2007) 18 European Journal of International Law 1, pp. 1–35.

Halberstam, M., 'Sabbatino Resurrected: The Act of State Doctrine in the Revised Restatement of U.S. Foreign Relations Law' (1985) 79 American Journal of International Law 1, pp. 68–91.

Hampson, F., 'The Relationship between International Humanitarian Law and Human Rights Law from the Perspective of a Human Rights Body' (2008) 90 International Review of the Red Cross 871, pp. 549–72.

Harel, A., 'Despite Court Ruling, Palestinian Use of Route 443 Likely to be Limited' *Haaretz* (10 May 2010). Available at: <http://www.haaretz.com/print-edition/news/despite-court-ruling-palestinian-use-of-route-443-likely-to-be-limited-1.289321>.

Hartmann, F., *Paix et Châtiment. Les Guerres Secrètes de la Politique et de la Justice Internationales* (Flammarion, Paris, 2007).

Hayek, F.A., *The Political Idea of the Rule of Law* (National Bank of Egypt, Cairo, 1955).

Hazan, P., *La Justice Face a la Guerre* (Stock, Paris, 2000).

Henckaerts, J.M. and Doswald-Beck, L., *Customary International Humanitarian Law—Volume I: Rules* (Cambridge University Press, Cambridge, 2005).

Hendin, S., 'Extraterritorial Application of Human Rights: the Differing Decisions of Canadian and UK Courts' (2010) 28 Windsor Review of Legal and Social Issues, pp. 57–86.

Henkin, L., *How Nations Behave: Law and Foreign Policy* (Columbia University Press, New York, 1979).

Henkin, L., 'Is There a "Political Question" Doctrine?' (1976) 85 Yale Law Journal 5, pp. 597–625.

Higgins R., 'The Changing Position of Domestic Courts in the International Legal Order'—Speech at the First International Law in Domestic Courts Colloquium, The Hague, 17 March 2008, pp. 1–12.

Higgins, R., 'The ICJ and the Rule of Law'—Speech to the United Nations University (11 April 2007). Available at: <http://www.unu.edu/events/files/2007/20070411_Higgins_speech.pdf>.

Hofmann, R., 'Victims of Violations of International Humanitarian Law: Do They Have an Individual Right to Reparation against States under International Law?' in P.M. Dupuy, B. Fassbender, M.N. Shaw and K.P. Sommermann (eds), *Common Values in International Law—Essays in Honour of Christian Tomuschat*, (N.P. Engel Verlag, Kehl, 2006), pp. 341–59.

Imesis, A., '"Moderate" Torture on Trial: Critical Reflections on the Israeli Supreme Court Judgment Concerning the Legality of the General Security Service Interrogation Methods' (2001) 5 International Journal of Human Rights 3, pp. 71–96.

International Committee of the Red Cross—Advisory Service on International Humanitarian Law, 'The Model Law—Geneva Conventions (Consolidation) Act Legislation for Common Law States on the 1949 Geneva Conventions and their 1977 and 2005 Additional Protocols' (31 August 2008). Available at: <http://www.icrc.org/web/eng/siteeng0.nsf/htmlall/geneva-conventions-protocols-model-law-310808>.

International Committee of the Red Cross—Advisory Service on International Humanitarian Law, 'What is International Humanitarian Law?' (July 2004). Available at: <http://www.icrc.org/eng/assets/files/other/what_is_ihl.pdf>.

International Committee of the Red Cross, 'National Implementation of International Humanitarian Law—Biannual Update, January—July 2009' (2009) 91 International Review of the Red Cross 875, pp. 627–42.

International Committee of the Red Cross, 'The International Committee of the Red Cross (ICRC): Its Mission and Work (Adopted by the Assembly of the ICRC on 19 June 2008)' (2009) 91 International Review of the Red Cross 874, pp. 399–413.

Israeli Ministry of Foreign Affairs, 'Judgments of the Israel Supreme Court: Fighting Terrorism within the Law' (2 January 2005), pp. 1–106.

Jennings, R., 'The Judiciary, International and National, and the Development of International Law' (1996) 45 International Comparative Law Quarterly, pp. 1–12.

'Judicial Decisions: International Military Tribunal (Nuremberg) Judgment and Sentences' (1947) 41 American Journal of International Law 1, pp. 172–333.

'Judicial Enforcement of International Law Against the Federal and State Governments' (1991) 104 Harvard Law Review 6, pp. 1269–88.

Kaldor, M., *Old Wars and Organized Violence in a Global Era* (Policy Press, Cambridge, 2nd edition, 2006).

Kalshoven, F., 'State Responsibility for Warlike Acts of the Armed Forces: From Article 3 of the Hague Convention IV of 1907 to Article 91 of Additional Protocol I and Beyond' (1991) 40 International and Comparative Quarterly 4, pp. 827–58.

Kalshoven, F., Greenwood, C. and David, E. in the *Prisoner-of-War Cases* submitted to the Tokyo High Court (1997), published in H. Fujita/I. Suzuki/K. Nagano (eds), *War and the Rights of Individuals: Renaissance of Individual Compensation* (Nippon Hyoron-sha Co. Ltd Publishers, Tokyo, 1999).

Karayanni, M., 'Choice of Law under Occupation: How Israeli Law Came to Serve Palestinian Plaintiffs' (2009) 5 Journal of Private International Law 1, pp. 1–48.

Kelsen, H., *General Theory of Law and State*, trans A. Wedberg (Harvard University Press, Cambridge, Mass. 1949).

Kelsen, H., *Law and Peace in International Relations* (Harvard University Press, Cambridge, Mass. 1942).

Kelsen, H., *Principles of International Law* (Rinehart & Company, New York, 1952).

Kennedy, D., *A Critique of Adjudication (fin du siècle)* (Harvard University Press, Cambridge, Mass. 1997).

Kennedy, D., 'The Turn to Interpretation' (1985) 58 Southern California Law Review 251, pp. 251–76.

Kleffner, J.K., *Complementarity in the Rome Statute and National Criminal Jurisdictions* (Oxford University Press, Oxford, 2008).

Knop, K., 'Here and There: International Law in Domestic Courts' (2000) 32 New York University Journal of International Law and Politics, p. 501.

Koh, H., 'Bringing International Law Home' (1998) 35 Houston Law Review, p. 623.

Koh, H. Hongju, 'International Law as Part of Our Law' (2004) 98 American Journal of International Law 1, pp. 43–57.

Koh, H. Hongju, 'Setting the World Right' (2006) 115 The Yale Law Journal, pp. 2350–79.

Koh, H. Hongju, *The National Security Constitution: Sharing Power After the Iran-Contra Affair* (Yale University Press, New Haven, 1990).

Koh, H. Hongju, 'Transnational Public Law Litigation' (1991) 100 The Yale Law Journal 8, pp. 2347–402.

Koh, H. Hongju, 'Why Do Nations Obey International Law?' (1997) 106 The Yale Law Journal 8, pp. 2599–659.

Koh, H. Hongju, 'Why Transnational Law Matters' (2006) 24 Penn State International Law Review 4, pp. 745–54.

Kolb, R., *Ius in Bello—Précis de Droit International des Conflits Armés* (2e éd., Helbing & Lichtenhahn/Bruylant, Bâle/Bruxelles, 2009).

Koskenniemi, M., *From Apology to Utopia—The Structure of International Legal Argument'* (Cambridge University Press, New York, 2005).

Koskenniemi, M., 'International Legal Theory and Doctrine', in Max Planck Encyclopaedia of International Law (2008), available at <http://www.mpepil.com>.

Koskenniemi, M., 'The Politics of International Law', (1990) 1 European Journal of International Law, pp. 4–32.

Koskenniemi, M., 'The Politics of International Law—20 Years Later', (2009) 20 European Journal of International Law 1, pp. 7–19.

Koskenniemi, M., *The Politics of International Law* (Hart Publishing, Oxford, 2011).

Koskenniemi, M., 'What is International Law For?' in Evans, M. (ed.), *International Law* (Oxford University Press, Oxford, 3rd edition, 2010), pp. 32–53.

Kreicker, H., 'National Prosecution of Genocide from a Comparative Perspective' (2005) 5 International Criminal Law Review 313, pp. 313–28.

Kretzmer, D., 'The Advisory Opinion: The Light Treatment of International Humanitarian Law' (2005) 99 American Journal of International Law 1, pp. 88–102.

Kretzmer, D., *The Occupation of Justice: The Supreme Court of Israel and the Occupied Territories* (State University of New York Press, Albany, 2002).

Kretzmer, D., 'The Supreme Court of Israel: Judicial Review during Armed Conflict' (2005) 47 German Yearbook of International Law, pp. 392–455.

Ku, J.G. and Yoo, J.C., 'Hamdan V. Rumsfeld: The Functional Case for Foreign Affairs Deference to the Executive Branch' (2006) 23 *Constitutional Commentary*, pp. 179–226.

Kumm, M., 'International Law in National Courts: The International Rule of Law and the Limits of the Internationalist Model' (2003) 44 Virginia Journal of International Law, pp. 19–32.

Lee, L.T., 'The Right of Victims of War to Compensation' in R. St. J. Macdonald (ed.), *Essays in Honour of Wang Tieya* (Martinus Nijhoff, Dordrecht, 1993), pp. 489–96.

Leiter, B., 'American Legal Realism' in D.M. Patterson (ed.), *A Companion to Philosophy of Law and Legal Theory* (2nd edn, Blackwell, Oxford, 2010), pp. 249–66.

Mann, F.A., *Foreign Affairs in English Courts* (Oxford University Press, Oxford, 1986).

Marmor, A., 'The Ideal of the Rule of Law' in D. Patterson (ed.), *A Companion to Philosophy of Law and Legal Theory* (2nd edn, Wiley-Blackwell, Oxford, 2010), pp. 666–74.

McDougal, M.S. & Reisman, W.M., 'International Law in Policy-Oriented Perspective' in R. St. J. MacDonald & J. Douglas (eds), *The Structure and Process of International Law: Essays in Legal Philosophy, Doctrine and Theory* (Martinus Nijhoff, Boston, 1983), pp. 103–29.

Meloni C. and Tognoni G.(eds), *Is There a Court for Gaza? A Test Bench for International Justice* (T.M.C. Asser Press, The Hague, 2012).

Melzer, N., *Interpretative Guidance on the Notion of Direct Participation in Hostilities Under International Humanitarian Law* (ICRC, Geneva, 2009).

Menon, J.A., 'Guantanamo Torture Litigation' (2008) 6 Journal of International Criminal Justice 2, pp. 323–45.

Meron, T., 'Classification of Armed Conflict in the Former Yugoslavia, Nicaragua's Fallout' (1998) 93 American Journal of International Law 2, pp. 236–42.

Mersel, Y., 'Judicial Review of Counter-Terrorism Measures: the Israeli Model for the Role of the Judiciary during the Terror Era' (2006) 38 New York University Journal of International Law and Politics 12, pp. 67–120.

Milanovic, M., 'Al-Skeini and Al-Jedda in Strasbourg' (2012) 23 European Journal of International Law, (forthcoming). Available at: <http://papers.ssrn.com/sol3/papers.cfm?abstract_id=1917395>.

Murray, C.R.G., 'The Ripple Effect: Guantanamo Bay in the United Kingdom's Courts' (2010) 1 Pace International Law Review Online Companion 9, pp. 15–40.

Negbi, M., *Justice under Occupation: the Israeli Supreme Court versus the Military Occupation in the Occupied Territories* (Cana Publishing House, Jerusalem, 1981) (in Hebrew).

Nollkaemper, P.A., 'Internationally Wrongful Acts in Domestic Courts' (2007) 101 American Journal of International Law 760, pp. 760–99.

Nollkaemper, P.A., *National Courts and The International Rule of Law* (Oxford University Press, Oxford, 2011).

Norberg, N., 'The US Supreme Court Affirms the Filartiga Paradigm' (2006) 4 Journal of International Criminal Justice 2, pp. 387–400.

O'Keefe, R., 'The Grave Breaches Regime and Universal Jurisdiction' (2009) 7 Journal of International Criminal Justice 4, pp. 811–31.

Onuf, N., *International Legal Theory: Essays and Engagements, 1966–2006* (Routledge, New York, 2008).

Oppenheim, L., 'The Legal Relations between an Occupying Power and the Inhabitants' (1917) 33 Law Quarterly Review 363, pp. 363–70.

Otto, R., 'Neighbours as Human Shields? The Israel Defense Forces' "Early Warning Procedure" and International Humanitarian Law' (2004) 86 International Review of the Red Cross 856, pp. 771–87.

Pictet, J. (ed.), *Commentary: Fourth Geneva Convention Relative to the Protection of Civilian Persons in Time of War* (ICRC, Geneva, 1958).

Pisillo-Mazzeschi, R., 'International Obligations to Provide for Reparations' Claims?' in A. Randelzhofer, C. Tomuschat (eds), *State Responsibility and the Individual, Reparation in Instances of Grave Violations of Human Rights* (Martin Nijhoff Publishers, The Hague, 1999), pp. 149–72.

Pisillo-Mazzeschi, R., 'Reparation Claims by Individuals for State Breaches of Humanitarian Law and Human Rights: An Overview' (2003) 1 Journal of International Criminal Justice 2, pp. 339–47.

Playfair, E., 'Playing on Principles? Israel's Justification for its Administrative Acts in the Occupied West Bank' in E. Playfair (ed.), *International Law and the Administration of Occupied Territories* (Clarendon Press, Oxford, 1992), pp. 205–38.

Posner, T.R., 'Kadic v. Karadzic, 70 F. 3d 232 (June 18, 1996)' (1996) 90 American Journal of International Law 4, pp. 658–63.

Raguan, G., 'Adjudicating Armed Conflict in Domestic Courts: The Experience of Israel's Supreme Court' (2010) 13 Yearbook of International Humanitarian Law, pp. 61–95.

Raz, J., *The Authority of Law* (Oxford University Press, Oxford, 1979).

Raz, J., 'The Politics of the Rule of Law' (1990) 3 Ratio Juris, pp. 331–9.

Raz, J., 'The Rule of Law and Its Virtue' (1977) 93 The Law Quarterly Review 2, p. 195.

Reisman, W.M., *Nullity and Revision: The Review and Enforcement of International Judgments and Awards* (Yale University Press, Yale, 1971).

Reisman, W.M., 'The View from the New Haven School of International Law' (1992) 86 American Society of International Law Proceedings, pp. 118–25.

Richards, 'The International Dimension of Judicial Review', *The 2006 Gray's Inn Reading* (7 June 2006).

Rigaux, F., 'Hans Kelsen on International Law' (1998) 9 European Journal of International Law 2, pp. 325–43.

Roberts, A., 'Comparative International Law? The Role of National Courts in Creating and Enforcing International Law' (2011) 60 International and Comparative Law Quarterly, pp. 57–92.

Roberts, A., 'Prolonged Military Occupation: The Israeli-Occupied Territories Since 1967' (1990) 84 American Journal of International Law 1, pp. 44–103.

Roberts, A., 'Righting Wrongs or Wronging Rights? The United States and Human Rights Post-September 11' (2004) 15 European Journal of International Law, pp. 721, 735–737.

Roberts, A., 'Transformative Military Occupation: Applying the Laws of the War and Human Rights' in M.N. Schmitt and J. Pejic (eds), *International Law and Armed Conflict: Exploring the Fault Lines: Essays in Honour of Yoram Dinstein* (Martinus Nijhoff Publishers, Leiden, 2007), pp. 439–95.

Roberts, A., 'What is a Military Occupation?' (1984) 55 The British Yearbook of International Law 1, pp. 249–305.

Rosenne, S., *The Law and Practice of the International Court, 1920–2005*, Vol. II Jurisdiction (4th edn, Martinus Nijhoff, Leiden, 2006).

Rubinstein, A., 'The Changing Status of the "Territories": From Escrow to Legal Mongel' (1988) 8 Tel Aviv University Studies in Law, pp. 59–79.

Ryngaert, C., 'Universal Tort Jurisdiction over Gross Human Rights Violations' (2007) 38 Netherlands Yearbook of International Law 3, pp. 32–41.

Sampford, C., 'Legal Ethics in a Post-Westphalian World: Building the International Rule of Law and other Tasks' in K. Tranter et al. (eds), *Reaffirming Legal Ethics—Taking Stock and New Ideas* (Routledge, Abingdon, 2010), pp. 73–95.

Sampford, C., 'Reconceiving the Rule of Law for a Globalizing World' in S. Zifcak (ed.), *Globalisation and The Rule of Law* (Routledge, London, 2005), pp. 9–31.

Sandoz, Y., *The International Committee of the Red Cross as Guardian of International Humanitarian Law* (ICRC, Geneva, 1998), available at: <http://www.icrc.org/eng/resources/documents/misc/about-the-icrc-311298.htm>.

Sands, P., 'The "Political" and the "Legal": Comments of Professor Tushnet's Paper' (2007) 3 International Journal of Law in Context 4, pp. 319–22.

Sassòli, M., 'Article 43 of the Hague Regulations and Peace Operations in the Twenty-First Century' (Program on Humanitarian Policy and Conflict Research at Harvard University, June 2004), pp. 1–26.

Sassòli, M., 'La Guerre contre le Terrorisme, le Droit International Humanitaire et le Statut de Prisonnier de Guerre' (2001) 39 Canadian Yearbook of International Law 211, pp. 211–52.

Sassòli, M., 'Legislation and Maintenance of Public Order and Civil Life by Occupying Powers' (2005) 16 European Journal of International Law 4, pp. 661–94.

Sassòli, M., 'Reparation' in V. Chetail (ed.), *Post-Conflict Peacebuilding: A Lexicon* (Oxford University Press, Oxford, 2009), pp. 279–90.

Sassòli, M., 'State Responsibility for Violations of International Humanitarian Law' (2002) 84 International Review of the Red Cross 846, pp. 401–34.

Sassòli, M., 'The Legal Qualification of the Conflicts in the Former Yugoslavia: Double Standards or New Horizons for International Humanitarian Law?' in W. Tieya and S. Yee (eds), *International Law in the Post-Cold War World: Essays in Memory of Li Haopei* (Routledge, London, 2001), p. 307.

Sassòli, M., 'Transnational Armed Groups and International Humanitarian Law' (Program on Humanitarian Policy and Conflict Research at Harvard University—Occasional Paper Series, Winter 2006), pp. 1–50.

Sassòli, M., 'Use and Abuse of the Laws of War in the "War Against Terrorism"' (2004) 22 Law and Inequality: A Journal of Theory and Practice, pp. 195–221.

Sassòli, M., Bouvier, A. and Quintin, A., *How Does Law Protect in War?* (3rd ed., Geneva, ICRC, 2011).

Sassòli, M. and Olson, L.M., 'Prosecutor v. Tadic (Judgment), Case No. IT-94-a-A. 38 ILM 1518 (1999)' (2000) 94 American Journal of International Law 3, pp. 571–8.

Sassòli, M. and Olson, L.M., 'The Judgment of the ICTY Appeals Chamber on the Merits in the Tadic Case' (2000) 82 International Review of the Red Cross 839, pp. 733–69.

Sassòli, M. and Olson, L.M., 'The Legal Relationship between International Humanitarian Law and Human Rights Law where It Matters: Admissible Killing and Internment of Fighters in Non International Armed Conflict' (2008) 90 International Review of the Red Cross 871, pp. 599–627.

Schabas, W., 'The Contribution of the Eichmann Trial to International Law' (2013) 26 Leiden Journal of International Law 3, pp. 667–699.

Scharpf, F.W., 'Judicial Review and the Political Question: A Functional Analysis' (1966) 75 Yale Law Journal 517, pp. 517–98.

Scheiber, H.N., 'Taking Responsibility: Moral and Historical Perspectives on the Japanese War-Reparations Issues' (2002) 20 Berkeley Journal of International Law 233, pp. 233–49.

Schlag, P., 'A Brief Survey of Deconstruction' (2005) 27 Cardozo Law Review 741, pp. 741–52.

Schmitt, M.N., 'Human Shields in International Humanitarian Law' (2009) 47 Columbia Journal of Transitional Law 2, pp. 292–338.

Schupack, A.N., 'The Arab-Israeli Conflict and Civil Litigation against Terrorism' (2010) 60 Duke Law Journal, pp. 207–48.

Schwenk, E.H., 'Legislative Power of the Military Occupant under Article 43, Hague Regulations' (1944–1945) 54 Yale Law Journal 2, pp. 393–416.

Sfard, M., 'The Price of Internal Legal Opposition to Human Rights Abuses' (2009) 1 Journal of Human Rights Practice 1, pp. 37–50.

Shamgar, M., 'Legal Concepts and Problems of the Israeli Military Government—The Initial Stage' in M. Shamgar (ed.), *Military Government in the Territories Administrated by Israel 1967–1980, The Legal Aspect,* (The Harry Sacher Institute for Legislative Research and Comparative Law, The Hebrew University, Jerusalem, 1982), p. 13.

Shamir, R., 'Landmark Cases and the Reproduction of Legitimacy: The Case of Israel's High Court of Justice' (1990) 24 Law & Society Review 3, pp. 781–806.

Shany, Y., 'Capacities and Inadequacies: a Look at the Two Separation Barrier Cases' (2005) 38 Israel Law Review, pp. 230–46.

Shany, Y., 'National Courts as International Actors: Jurisdictional Implications' (2008) Hebrew University International Law Forum, Research Paper No. 22–08, available at http://papers.ssrn.com/sol3/papers.cfm?abstract_id=1292056.

Shany, Y., 'The Prohibition Against Torture and Cruel, Inhuman and Degrading Treatment and Punishment: Can the Absolute be Relativized under Existing International Law?' (2007) 56 Catholic University Law Review, pp. 837–49.

Shapiro, M., *Courts: A Comparative and Political Analysis* (The University of Chicago Press, Chicago, 1981).

Shapiro, M., 'Political Jurisprudence' (1964) 52 Kentucky Law Journal, pp. 294–345.

Shapiro, M. and Stone Sweet, A., *On Law, Politics and Judicialization* (Oxford University Press, Oxford, 2002).

Shaw, M.N., *International Law* (5th edn, Cambridge University Press, Cambridge, 2003).

Shehadeh, R., *Occupier's Law—Israel and the West Bank* (Institute for Palestine Studies, Washington DC, 1985).

Shelah, O. and Drucker, R., *Boomerang—the Failure of Leadership in the Second Intifada* (Keter Publishers, Tel Aviv, 2005).

Shelton, D., 'Righting Wrongs: Reparations in the Articles on State Responsibility' (2002) 96 American Journal of International Law, pp. 833–56.

Shklar, J.N., 'Political Theory and the Rule of Law' in A.C. Hutchinson & P. Monahan (eds), *The Rule of Law: Ideal or Ideology* (Carswell, Toronto, 1987), pp. 1–16.

Shoughri-Badarneh, B., 'A Decade after the High Court of Justice "Torture" Ruling, What's Changed?' in A. Baker and A. Matar (eds), *Threat: Palestinian Political Prisoners in Israel* (Pluto Press, London, 2011), pp. 114–23.

Simma, B., 'Universality of International Law from the Perspective of a Practitioner' (2009) 20 European Journal of International Law, p. 265.

Singer, M., 'The Act of State Doctrine of the United Kingdom: An Analysis, with Comparisons to United States Practice' (1981) 75 American Journal of International Law 2, pp. 283–323.

Slaughter, A.M., 'A Global Community of Courts' (2003) 44 Harvard International Law Journal, pp. 191–219.

Sloss, D. (ed.), *The Role of Domestic Courts in Treaty Enforcement: A Comparative Study* (Cambridge University Press, Cambridge, 2009).

Sloss, D., 'When Do Treaties Create Individually Enforceable Rights? The Supreme Court Ducks the Issue in *Hamdan* and *Sanchez-Llamas*' (2006–2007) 45 Columbia Journal of Transnational Law, pp. 20–113.

Spiro, P.J., 'Hamdan v. Rumsfeld. 126 S.Ct.2749' (2006) 100 American Journal of International Law 4, pp. 888–95.

Stahn, C., *The Law and Practice of International Territorial Administration: Versailles to Iraq and Beyond* (Cambridge University Press, Cambridge, 2008).

Stephens, B., 'Upsetting Checks and Balances: the Bush Administration's Efforts to Limit Human Rights Litigation' (2004) 17 Harvard Human Rights Journal, pp. 169–206.

Steyn, J., 'Guantanamo Bay: The Legal Black Hole' Twenty-seventh FA Mann Lecture, British Institute of International and Comparative Law (25 November 2003), pp. 1–14.

Tamanaha, B.Z., *On the Rule of Law: History, Politics, Theory* (Cambridge University Press, Cambridge, 2004).

Tomuschat, C., 'Individual Reparation Claims in Instances of Grave Human Rights Violations: The Position under General International Law' in A. Randelzhofer/ C. Tomuschat (eds), *State Responsibility and the Individual* (Kluwer Law International, The Hague, 1999), pp. 1–25.

Tomuschat, C., 'Reparation for Victims of Grave Human Rights Violations' (2002) 10 Journal of International and Comparative Law, pp. 157–84.

Tomuschat, C., 'Reparation in Favour of Individual Victims of Gross Violations of International Human Rights and Humanitarian Law' in M. G. Kohen and L. Caflisch (eds), *Promoting Justice, Human Rights and Conflict Resolution through International Law* (Graduate Institute of International Studies, Geneva, 2007), pp. 569–90.

Tzanakopoulos, A., 'Domestic Courts in International Law: The International Judicial Function of National Courts' (2011) 34 Loyola of Los Angeles International & Comparative Law Review, p. 153.

Van Panhuys, H. F., 'In the Borderland between the Act of State Doctrine and Questions of Jurisdictional Immunities', (1964) 13 The International and Comparative Law Quarterly 4, pp. 1193–213.

Vazquez, C.M., 'The Four Doctrines of Self-Executing Treaties' (1995) 89 American Journal of International Law 4, pp. 695–723.

Vázquez, C.M., 'The Military Commissions Act, the Geneva Conventions, and the Courts: A Critical Guide' (2007) 101 American Journal of International Law 1, pp. 73–98.

Villiger, M.E., 'Domestic Courts and the International Rule of Law—the Perspective of the European Courts of Human Rights' paper presented at *The First International Law in Domestic Courts (ILDC) Colloquium*, Peace Palace, The Hague, 28 March 2008.

Villiger, M.E., 'Non-Retroactivity of the Convention' in *Commentary on the 1969 Vienna Convention on the Law of Treaties* (Martinus Nijhoff Publishers, Leiden-Boston, 2009).

Von Glahn, G., *Law among Nations: An Introduction to Public International Law* (5th edn, Macmillan, New York, 1986).

Warbrick C., 'International Law in English Courts: Recent Cases', (2003) 52 The International and Comparative Law Quarterly 3, pp. 815–24.

Watts, A., 'The Importance of International Law' in M. Byers (ed.), *The Role of Law in International Politics* (Oxford University Press, Oxford, 2000), pp. 5–16.

Watts, A., 'The International Rule of Law' (1993) 36 German Yearbook of International Law 15, pp. 15–45.

Wechsler, H., 'Toward Neutral Principles of Constitutional Law' (1959) 73 Harvard Law Review 1, pp. 1–35.

Weill, S., 'Reframing the Legality of the Israeli Military Courts –Military Occupation or Apartheid?' in A. Baker & A. Matar (eds), *Threat—Palestinian Political Prisoners in Israel* (Pluto Press, London, 2011), pp. 136–48.

Weill, S., 'The follow up to the Goldstone report in Israel and beyond' in C. Meloni and G. Tognoni (eds), *Is There A Court for Gaza?—A Test Bench for International Justice* (Asser/Springer, The Hague, 2012), pp. 105–120.

Weill, S., 'The Targeted Killing of Salah Shehadeh: from Gaza to Madrid' (2009) 7 Journal of International Criminal Justice 3, pp. 617–31.

Weill, S., and Ballas, I., 'Investigation of Torture Claims in Israel: Analysis of the 2012 High Court of Justice Ruling and the Türkel Commission Report', in Casey-Maslen, S. (ed.), *The War Report* (Oxford University Press, Oxford, 2013).

Weill, S. and Jovanovic, I., 'National War Crimes Prosecution in Post-Conflict Era and Pluralism of Jurisdictions: the Experience of the Belgrade War Crimes Chamber' in A. Nollkaemper, C. Ryngaert and E. Kristjánsdóttir (eds), *Importing International Law in Post-Conflict States: The Role of Domestic Courts* (Intersentia, Antwerp, 2012), pp. 241–68.

Weissbrodt, D. and Nesbitt, N.H., 'The Role of the United States Supreme Court in Interpreting and Developing Humanitarian Law' (2011) 95 Minnesota Law Review 4, pp. 1339–423.

Yap, J., 'Corporate Civil Liability for War Crimes in Canadian Courts: Lessons from *Bil'in (Village Council) v. Green Park International Ltd*' (2010) 8 Journal of International Criminal Justice 2, pp. 631–48.

Yates, J. and Whitford, A., 'Presidential Power and the US Supreme Court' (1998) 51 Political Research Quarterly 2, pp. 539–50.

Yoo, J.C., 'Treaties and Public Lawmaking: A Textual and Structural Defense of Non-Self-Execution' (1999) 99 Columbia Law Review 8, pp. 2218–58.

Zander, M., 'The Act of State Doctrine' (1959) 53 The American Journal of International Law 4, pp. 826–52.

Zegveld, L., 'Remedies for Victims of Violations of International Humanitarian Law' (2003) 85 International Review of the Red Cross 851, pp. 497–527.

Zegveld, L., 'Victims' Reparation Claims and International Criminal Courts—Incompatible Values?' (2010) 8 Journal International Criminal Justice 1, pp. 79–111.

Zolo, D., 'Hans Kelsen: International Peace through International Law' (1998) 9 European Journal of International Law 2, pp. 306–24.

REPORTS

ICRC

'Report on the Protection of War Victims' (Geneva, June 1993), in 33 International Review of the Red Cross, (1993) Special Issue n. 296, pp. 391–419.

'The Rule of Law at National and International Level,' United Nations, General Assembly, 65th Session, Sixth Committee, on Agenda Item 85, Statement by the ICRC (New York, 14 October 2010).

NGO Reports and Media Release

Adalah, 'Israeli Military Probes and Investigations Fail to Meet International Standards or Ensure Accountability for Victims of the War on Gaza'- Briefing Paper (January, 2010), pp. 1–17.

Adalah, 'Update Report: On the Israeli Military's Continued Use of Palestinian Civilians, including Minors, as Human Shields' (July 2009), pp. 1–5.

Al-Haq, *Legitimising the Illegitimate?* (Al-Haq Organisation, 2010).

Association for Civil Rights in Israel (ACRI), 'Ban on Palestinian Movement on Route 443: Background Information' (June 2009). Available at: <http://www.acri.org.il/pdf/Route443Aug09.pdf>.

B'Tselem, 'Forbidden Roads: The Discriminatory West Bank Road Regime' (B'Tselem, August 2004).

B'Tselem, 'Routine Torture: Interrogation Methods of the General Security Service' (B'Tselem, February 1998), pp. 1–50.

'Court Dismisses Targeted Killing Case On Procedural Grounds Without Addressing Merits' Center for Constitutional Rights (CCR) (7 December 2010). Available at:

<http://ccrjustice.org/newsroom/press-releases/court-dismisses-targeted-killing-case-procedural-grounds-without-addressing->.

Humanitarian Law Center, 'Regional Debate on the Judgment by the ICJ on Genocide' (Transcript) (29 June 2007).

Humanitarian Law Center, 'The Trial to Anton Lekaj was Fair Although Conducted Before a Non-Jurisdictional Court' (23 September 2006). Available at: <http://www.hlc-rdc.org/?p=12873&lang=de>.

Humanitarian Law Center, 'War Crimes Trials in Serbia' (December 2007), pp. 1–18.

Human Rights Watch, 'Unfinished Business Serbia's War Crimes Chamber' (HRW Report, 28 June 2007), pp. 1–33.

Ivanišević, B., *Against the Current—War Crimes Prosecutions in Serbia* (2007) International Center for Transitional Justice (2008), pp. 1–55.

Public Committee Against Torture in Israel, 'Accountability Denied: The Absence of Investigation and Punishment of Torture in Israel' (December, 2009), pp. 1–98.

Public Committee Against Torture in Israel and Adalah, 'Exposed: The Treatment of Palestinian Detainees During Operation Cast Lead' (June 2010), pp. 1–49.

Public Committee Against Torture in Israel, 'Israel—Briefing to the Human Rights Committee Jerusalem' (June, 2010), pp. 1–47.

Public Committee Against Torture in Israel, 'OMCT—World Organisation Against Torture Israel—Briefing to the UN Committee Against Torture' (Jerusalem & Geneva, April 2009), pp. 1–24.

Public Committee Against Torture in Israel, 'Ticking Bombs—Testimonies of Torture Victims in Israel' (30 May 2007), pp. 1–99.

Weill, S. and Azarov, V., 'Israel's Unwillingness to Prosecute International Crimes' (FIDH, September 2011), pp. 1–28.

Regional Organizations

Council of Europe, 'Secret Detentions and Illegal Transfers of Detainees Involving Council of Europe Member States' (2007) Rapporteur Mr Dick Marty, Doc. 11302 Rev.

OSCE Mission to Serbia and Montenegro, 'Report on War Crimes before Domestic Courts' (Belgrade, October 2003).

OSCE Mission to Serbia and Montenegro, 'Strategy on Support to the National Judiciary in Conducting War Crimes Trials' (Belgrade 11 April 2003).

State Reports and Statements

'Commission of Inquiry into the Methods of Investigation of the GSS Regarding Hostile Terrorist Activities' (October 1987).

IDF MAG CORPS, 'Indictment Filed in Connection with 'Cast Lead'—Military Advocate for Operational Affairs' (11 March 2011).

IDF MAG CORPS, 'Investigating the Gaza Operation—an interview with Deputy Military Advocate for Operational Affairs' (9 March 2011). Available at: <http://www.mag.idf.il/163-4544-en/patzar.aspx>.

Israel Defence Forces, 'IDF Military Advocate General Takes Disciplinary Action, 6 Jul. 2010 Indicts Soldiers Following Investigations into Incidents during Operation Cast Lead' (6 July 2010).

Israeli Ministry of Foreign Affairs, 'The Operation in Gaza—Factual and Legal Aspects' (29 July 2009). Available at: <http://www.mfa.gov.il/MFA/Terrorism-+Obstacle+to+Peace/Hamas+war+against+Israel/Operation_in_Gaza-Factual_and_Legal_Aspects.htm>.

'Press Briefing by Colonel Daniel Reisner, Head of the International Law Branch of the IDF Legal Division' (15 November 2000). Available at: <http://www.mfa.gov.il/MFA/MFAArchive/2000_2009/2000/11/Press%20Briefing%20by%20Colonel%20Daniel%20Reisner-%20Head%20of>.

Prime Minister's Office, 'Salah Shehadeh—Special Investigatory Commission' (27 February 2011). Available at: <http://www.pmo.gov.il/PMOEng/Communication/Spokesman/2011/02/spokeshchade270211.htm>.

State of Israel, 'Fourth Periodic Report to Committee against Torture' (2 November 2006) Un Doc CAT/C/ISR/4.

State of Israel, 'Gaza Operation Investigations: Second Update' (July 2010), pp. 1–40. Available at: <http://www.mfa.gov.il/NR/rdonlyres/1483B296-7439-4217-933C-653CD19CE859/0/GazaUpdateJuly2010.pdf>.

State of Israel, 'International Covenant on Civil and Political Rights—Second Periodic Report' (20 November 2001), UN Doc CCPR/C/ISR/2001/2 (2001).

Statement by Ms Carla del Ponte, ICTY Chief Prosecutor, to the OSCE Permanent Council (Vienna, 4 November 2003) PC.DEL/1278/03.

Türkel Commission, The Public Commission to Examine the Maritime Incident of 31 May 2010, Second Report: 'Israeli Mechanisms for Examining and Investigating Complaints and Claims of Violations of the Laws of Armed Conflict According to International Law' (February 2013).

United Nations

General Assembly

'The Rule of Law at the National and International Levels', UNGA Res. 62/70 (8 January 2008) UN Doc A/RES/62/70.

'The Rule of Law at the National and International Levels', UNGA Res. 63/128 (15 January 2009) UN Doc A/RES/63/128.

'The Rule of Law at the National and International Levels', UNGA Res. 64/116 (15 January 2010) UN Doc A/RES/64/116.

Human Rights Committee

Human Rights Committee, 'Concluding Observations of the Human Rights Committee: Israel 21/08/2003' UN doc CCPR/CO/78/ISR (21 August 2003).

Human Rights Council

Human Rights Council, 'Human Rights in Palestine and Other Occupied Arab Territories—Report of the United Nations Fact-Finding Mission on the Gaza Conflict' (25 September 2009) UN Doc A/HRC/12/48.

Report of the Special Rapporteur on Extrajudicial, Summary or Arbitrary Executions, Philip Alston, Addendum, 'Study on Targeted Killings', UN Doc A/HRC/14/24/Add.6 (28 May 2010).

'Report of the Special Rapporteur on the situation of Human Rights in the Palestinian Territories Occupied since 1967', UN Doc A/65/331 (30 August 2010).

'Report of the Independent International Fact-Finding Mission to Investigate the Implications of the Israeli Settlements on the Civil, Political, Economic, Social and Cultural Rights of the Palestinian People Throughout the Occupied Palestinian Territory, including East Jerusalem', UN Doc A/HRC/22/63 (7 February 2013).

Human Rights Treaty Bodies

'Concluding Observations of the Committee on the Elimination of Racial Discrimination Israel', UN Doc CERD/C/ISR/CO/14 -16 (9 March 2012). (42)

'Concluding Observations of the Committee Against Torture: Canada, 48th Session', UN Doc CAT/C/CAN/CO/6 (25 June 2012). (134)

Other

'Report of the International Commission of Inquiry on Darfur to the United Nations Secretary-General, pursuant to Security Council resolution 1564 of 18 September 2004' (Geneva, 25 January 2005).

'The Rule of Law Coordination and Resource Group—Joint Strategic Plan 2009–2011', United Nations Rule of Law (February 2009).

United Nations Office for the Coordination of Humanitarian Affairs in the occupied Palestinian territory, *Movement and Access in the West Bank* (September 2011).

United Nations Office for the Coordination of Humanitarian Affairs in the occupied Palestinian territory, *The Humanitarian Impact on Palestinians of Israeli Settlements and Other Infrastructure in the West Bank* (July 2007).

Secretary-General

Report of the Secretary-General pursuant to paragraph 2 of Security Council Resolution 808 (1993) (3 May 1993) UN Doc S/25704.

Report of the Secretary-General, 'The Rule of Law and Transitional Justice in Conflict and Post-Conflict Societies' (23 August 2004) UN Doc S/2004/616.

Report of the Secretary-General 'In Larger Freedom: Towards Development, Security and Human Rights for All' (21 March 2005) UN Doc A/59/2005.

Report of the Secretary-General 'Uniting Our Strengths: Enhancing United Nations Support for the Rule of Law' (14 December 2006) UN Doc A/61/636.

Report of the Secretary-General, 'Strengthening and Coordinating United Nations Rule of Law Activities' (6 August 2008) UN Doc A/63/226.

Report of the Secretary-General, 'Annual Report on Strengthening and Coordinating United Nations Rule of Law Activities' (17 August 2009) UN Doc A/64/298.

Report of the Secretary-General, 'Delivering Justice: Programme of Action to Strengthen the Rule of Law at the National and International Levels' (16 March 2012) UN Doc A/66/749.

OTHER DOCUMENTS

International Law Association, 'Report of the International Committee on Compensation for Victims of Armed Conflict, "Draft Declaration of International Law Principles on Compensation for Victims of War (Substantive issues)"' (Rio De Janeiro, 2008), pp. 1–31.

International Law Association, 'Report of the International Committee on Compensation for Victims of Armed Conflict, "Draft Declaration of International Law Principles on Compensation for Victims of War Armed Conflict (Substantive issues)"' (The Hague, 2010), pp. 1–30.

Lord Justice Richards, 'The International Dimension of Judicial Review' The 2006 Gray's Inn Reading (7 June 2006), pp. 1–10.

Oxford Reports on International Law in Domestic Courts, Analysis of O'Keefe (30 November 2006). Available at: <http://www.oxfordlawreports.com>.

Oxford Reports on International Law in Domestic Courts, Analysis of Erin Culbertson and Dinah Shelton (21 July 2008). Available at: <http://www.oxfordlawreports.com>.

OTHER PRIMARY SOURCES

Bush, G., 'Memorandum on Humane Treatment of al Qaeda and Taliban Detainees' (7 February 2002), pp. 1–2. Available at: <http://www.washingtonpost.com/wp-srv/nation/documents/020702bush.pdf>.

Henkin, L. et al., *Amicus Brief of Law Professors in Support of the Petitioner in the Hamdan case (Geneva—Enforceability)* (6 January 2006). Available at: <http://www.hamdanvrumsfeld.com/HamdanvRumsfeldAmicusBriefofLawProfessorsLouisHenkinetal.pdf>.

Index